A Twice-Told Tale

A Twice-Told Tale

Reinventing the Encounter in Iberian/Iberian American Literature and Film

Edited by
Santiago Juan-Navarro and
Theodore Robert Young

DELAWARE
Newark: University of Delaware Press
London: Associated University Presses

Associated University Presses
440 Forsgate Drive
Cranbury, NJ 08512

Associated University Presses
16 Barter Street
London WC1A 2AH, England

Associated University Presses
P.O. Box 338, Port Credit
Mississauga, Ontario
Canada L5G 4L8

The paper used in this publication meets the requirements of the American National Standard for Permanence of Paper for Printed Library Materials Z39.48-1984.

Library of Congress Cataloging-in-Publication Data

A twice-told tale : reinventing the encounter in Iberian / Iberian American literature and film / edited by Santiago Juan-Navarro and Theodore Robert Young.
p. cm.
Includes bibliographical references and index.
ISBN 0-87413-733-0 (alk. paper)
1. Spanish American literature—20th century—History and criticism.
2. Historical fiction, Spanish American—History and criticism. 3. Latin America—In literature. 4. Latin American—Discovery and exploration—Spanish. I Juan Nararro, Santiago, 1960– II. Young, Theodore Robert.

PQ7081.A1 T85 2001
860.9'358—dc21

00-040433

PRINTED IN THE UNITED STATES OF AMERICA

Contents

Acknowledgments

WE WOULD LIKE TO THANK ALL CONTRIBUTORS FOR THEIR INVOLVEMENT IN this project and the wonderful exchange of ideas it produced. Several of the articles bound into this volume are the fruit of extensive interactions between the editors and the authors via written means, both electronic and on paper, and in person at multiple conferences and meetings over the last few years. The drive for intellectual excellence of the writers here compiled and their patience with the editorial process are the underpinnings of this volume's success.

We would also like to thank our publishers at the University of Delaware Press, especially the Chair of their Board of Editors, Dr. Donald C. Mell, and his staff for their accessibility and professionalism in making this book a reality. Their suggestions as well as those of the outside readers enhanced the integrity of the final project.

Closer to home, we would also like to thank the Latin American and Caribbean Center at Florida International University for its generous support. We gratefully acknowledge the assistance of Dr. Peter Machonis and of Dr. James López with translations from French and Spanish, respectively. Moreover, we are indebted to Monica Ramallo-Young for graciously proofreading the entire completed manuscript. Most of all, we must acknowledge the support of our spouses in this and all of our intellectual endeavors, without which we could never realize true success in any of our projects.

Editors' Note on Translations

As is increasingly the case with studies addressing foreign-language texts, *A Twice-Told Tale* must deal with the issue of how to best introduce citations without limiting the readers' access to the text at hand. Pursuant to the editorial policy of the University of Delaware Press and the Associated University Presses, we have provided the entirety of the volume in English. In general, where published editions of a primary text exist in English, we chose to utilize these resources in acknowledgment of the literary and editorial achievement of those publishers, and in order to facilitate access to the primary texts as a whole. Both the original-language text and the English translation are indicated in each article's bibliography so that scholars may refer to the texts in their original. In most articles, either the authors or the editors have supplied the quotations from the published, English-language translations of all texts cited. However, in some cases the authors themselves have furnished translations; these are so indicated in the corresponding notes. All other unattributed translations are by the editors.

Introduction

1992 BELONGS TO HISTORY. THE QUINCENTENNIAL OF THE SO-CALLED "DIScovery" left in its wake an unprecedented amount of cultural production. Conferences, debates, exhibitions, monographs, special editions in professional journals, newspaper articles, and television programs multiplied at a dizzying pace in the years preceding the event. It is difficult to calculate the volume of bibliographic material left behind, and despite the titanic efforts of James Axtell (1992a, 1992b, 1995) and David Block (1994), a more comprehensive and profound interpretative endeavor is required. If it were necessary to summarize the nature of the debate regarding the quincentennial, there is one concept that adequately defines the spirit of the moment: revisionism. Compared with the noncritical celebration that invariably characterized the events surrounding the quatercentenary in 1892, 1992 witnessed a critical revisiting of the Old World–New World encounter. The far-reaching debate that took place on the margins of the extravagant spectacles sanctioned and orchestrated by the governments of Spain and the Americas challenged the most deeply rooted clichés and stereotypes regarding this most historic of events. The very term used to designate the event itself was placed under scrutiny. "Discovery" lost ground to other descriptions such as concealment, cover-up, encounter, reencounter, mishap, collision, link-up, contact, clash, conquest, colonization, invasion, occupation, domination, subjugation, annihilation, despoilment, enslavement, transculturization, contamination, contagion, extermination, genocide, ethnocide, ecocide (Olivier 1992, 92). The object of the debate was also subjected to revision. Whereas indigenous peoples were reduced to footnotes during the quatercentenary, they now not only control the debate, but have in fact begun to rewrite it, generating a shift in its perspective and focus (Barreiro 1990; Grim 1992; Bamonte and Della Marina 1992; Gentry and Grinde 1994). The past two decades have seen the rise of postcolonial criticism, cultural studies, and the New Historicism, allowing for a reconsideration of this subject matter from the point of view of the colonized subject, rather than from that of the colonizing metropolis. In contrast to the glorification of historic events in previous celebrations, we have witnessed a demythification of the histories and value systems that had underscored the dominant Eurocentric vision of this phenomenon.

This prodigious academic production was accompanied by a similar proliferation of popular historical narrative concerning the encounter. Novels, short stories, poems, and films inspired by this event have inundated the inter-American cultural marketplace. In cases such as the Latin American New Novel, some critics have suggested that historical narrative has become dominant precisely as a consequence of the quincentennial (Menton 1993). This creative production reflects the revisionist tendencies that have characterized the academic investigations produced in the shadow of the quincentennial. Hispanic filmmakers and writers on both sides of the Atlantic were also attempting to rethink the ways in which the colonial encounter has been portrayed. As a result of both their quality and quantity, these works form a corpus that deserves further attention; yet, increased interest in this subject has not resulted in any book-length project. *A Twice-Told Tale* aims to fill this gap by exploring contemporary reconstructions of the age of "discovery," exploration, and conquest vis-à-vis fifteenth- and sixteenth-century sources (histories, chronicles, and *relaciones*). The contributors discuss the problem of interpreting the encounter from historical periods that foster radically different perspectives (the "imperial eye" of European colonial discourse and the historical revisionism of contemporary culture).

The first three essays included in Part 1 of this collection attempt to contextualize contemporary visions of the encounter within recent trends in intellectual history: literary postmodernism and historical revisionism. Eduardo Subirats's "Three Visions of America" explores different worldviews that have influenced modern perceptions of America since the sixteenth century: the providential historical design of Christian imperial Spain; the antischolastic, techno-scientific, and economic discourse of American colonization by the empiricist philosophers; and the reflexive, marginal, and hybrid vision based on the hermeneutic restoration of historic indigenous languages and cultures represented by the Inca Garcilaso. Subirats argues that these three worldviews appear in unequal proportion throughout the history of Spanish consciousness and national identity, and continue to maintain their significance in the contemporary world.

Unlike those who link the boom of historical novels to official quincentennial celebrations, Viviana Plotnik and Victoria E. Campos see in this proliferation a sign of resistance against the institutional discourse on the encounter. In "Postmodernity, Orphanhood, and the Contemporary Spanish American Historical Novel," Viviana Plotnik focuses on how the Iberian discovery and conquest of the Americas is fictionalized in the current Spanish American historical novel. She argues that this kind of novel signals a shift in perspective regarding history and a lack of confidence in master narratives characteristic of the postmodern sensibility. Plotnik's paper explores that shift in the context of Spanish American literary history and international postmodernism. According to Plotnik, the current Spanish American novel can be understood in the light of what Linda Hutcheon defines as "historiographic metafiction." This concept implies the presence of a parodic and/or ironic dialogue with the historical and artistic past, as well as the problematization of historical knowledge and narrative representation. Other related aspects studied in the article include the presence of decentered perspectives, the subversion of traditional notions of the central and the marginal, the absence of paternal figures, and the predominant motif of orphanhood. Plotnik argues that the current Spanish American historical novel questions the historical and literary past and commits a symbolic parricide through the construction of multiple, marginal, ironic, and parodic voices.

Victoria E. Campos's "Toward a New History: Twentieth-Century Debates in Mexico on Narrating the National Past" examines contemporary debates among Mexican intellectuals on the nature and aims of historical discourse. Reconsidering existing representations of "reality," groups of artists and scholars in Mexico have sought to redirect the course of society by transforming the narrated past into a site for addressing the present. Convinced of the need to decolonize historical narratives, mid-twentieth-century historians challenged the control of cultural discourses in Mexican society. In her essay, Campos explores these national debates regarding history, and the changes they brought about in contemporary Mexican literature. After presenting a chronological consideration of these debates, Campos concludes by examining recent literary reconfigurations of the Mexican past that focus on the encounter vis-à-vis these theoretical and political concerns.

Part 2 addresses the way contemporary works on the encounter reveal the colonial Other as a cultural construct. In "Constructing Cultural Myths: Cabeza de Vaca in Contemporary Hispanic Criticism, Theater, and Film," Santiago Juan-Navarro explores the historical process of the glorification of Cabeza de Vaca, leading to his ultimate transformation into a cultural hero, and summarizes the literary and historiographic foundations of the Cabeza de Vaca myth. Two recent examples of filmic and dramatic reinventions of the encounter are then discussed in the light of the political implications of the quincentennial: Nicolás Echevarría's film *Cabeza de Vaca* (1990) and José Sanchis Sinisterra's play *Naufragios o la herida del Otro* (1990). These two works, which revolve around the mythical figure of the Spanish conquistador, are marked by the ideological attitudes that pervaded the Hispanic world in the early 1990s. Juan-Navarro's essay examines how these attitudes are reflected in these cinematic and dramatic texts and how they convey a revisionist interpretation of the conquest that seeks to legitimate dissimilar cultural and political agendas. Within this context, knowing how

Cabeza de Vaca was transformed into a cultural hero by both institutional and counterinstitutional agencies becomes essential to understanding some of the most blatant paradoxes of contemporary historical literature and film, and in particular, the paradox of simultaneously assuming an oppositional and revisionist attitude at a time when revisionism is no longer oppositional, but, on the contrary, part of the literary and historiographic mainstream.

Theodore Robert Young's "You Are What You Eat: *Tropicalismo* and *How Tasty Was My Little Frenchman*" analyzes the manner in which Brazilian filmmaker Nelson Pereira dos Santos utilizes the late 1960s artistic phenomenon of *tropicalismo* to question the record of Brazil's sixteenth-century colonial period in his film *How Tasty Was My Little Frenchman* (1971). The *tropicalista* aesthetic synthesized new meaning out of the juxtaposition of irreverent samplings: a postmodern cultural cannibalism. In essence, the filmmaker "cannibalizes" *tropicalismo*'s musical stylistics along the lines of modernism's anthropophagous manifesto, transposing it into a filmic idiom. Young's study concentrates on how dos Santos confronts "official" history with a polemic reinvention of Brazil's colonial period. Ultimately his article aims to reveal the political implications of *tropicalismo* as a reaction to Brazil's authoritarian military regime of the 1960s and 1970s.

The politics of gender constitute the focus of Part 3. Wa-kí Fraser de Zambrano's "Transhistorical and Transgeographical Seductions" relates Columbian and Cortesian sexual paradigms to the historical and textual hybridization of Spanish novelist Rosa Montero's *Te trataré como a una reina* (1983). Centering on the fifteenth, sixteenth, nineteenth and twentieth centuries, her essay integrates a nostalgia for Cuba, chronicles of the New World, Spanish *costumbrismo,* the age of the sex crime, Jack the Ripper, the comic strip and the graphic novel for adults, soap opera, and melodrama. The essay demonstrates that the novel's fictive and mythic sexual paradigms, explored in a marginalized, contemporary *barrio* of Madrid, show themselves to be rooted in gender difference and to have contributed to the construction of masculinity, femininity, subjectivity, desire, and a culture of violence over the last five hundred years, best witnessed in the colonial discursive dynamic of the couple. The essay makes clear that the novel presents and judges the effects of colonization with specific evaluative and anticolonial intentions.

"Marina: A Woman before the Mirror of Her Time in Carlos Fuentes's *Ceremonias del Alba*" by Gladys M. Ilarregui parallels and contrasts two major Mexican works: the *Florentine Codex, Book XII,* recorded by Bernardino de Sahagún in the first half of the post-contact period; and the creative work, four centuries later, of Carlos Fuentes in *Ceremonias.* Her intention is to uncover Marina as portrayed in both writings, and in this colonial/contemporary search find a voice and a new identity for a woman subjected to such a variety of interpretations (Baudot, Glantz, Gonzalvo, Cypess). Ilarregui points out that despite such critical attention, few have seen Marina from the viewpoint of her positionality in the writing of male recorders and male interpreters. Between the voiceless Marina (the interpreter whose words are not hers) and the Marina who talks, discusses, and interprets history, Ilarregui proposes an alternative Marina through a feminist appropriation of her role and her status as a woman in two particular and specific periods of time and space.

According to Abel Posse, the Spanish conquest was motivated as much by eroticism as by a search for wealth. In "*Daimón* and the Eroticism of the Conquest," Terry Seymour seeks to answer the following questions: How does Posse's treatment of eroticism differ from that of the chronicles? How does the imaginary sex life of the conquistador Lope de Aguirre help us to understand modern Latin American history (specifically, the political repression and guerrilla movements of the 1960s and 1970s)? And, finally, why does Posse "gender" historical discourse with the use of character types (conquistador, Amazon queen, mystical nun, etc.)? To what extent is this gendering something the author adopts from history or from earlier historical novels, and to what extent does he depart from these models or try to break with them? Seymour ends by arguing that in *Daimón* Posse presents sexual desire as a challenge to all forms of order, a subversive force that is locked in eternal battle with political and sexual repression.

Part 4 revisits the myths of *mestizaje* and transculturation in contemporary historical works. In "From Cult to Comics: The Representation of Gonzalo Guerrero as a Cultural Hero in Mexican Popular Culture," RoseAnna M. Mueller explores Guerrero's personage, considered by many to be the true father of Mexican *mestizaje,* in several literary and artistic manifestations. The study ranges from an analysis of comic books to institutional and literary representations of this Mexican historical figure. Mueller contends that Gonzalo Guerrero's role as a cultural icon has been shaped by the needs of the social context, and hence he has been transformed into a cultural hero in the collective imagination of modern Mexico.

A second contribution to the discussion of cultural exchange is provided by Kimberle S. López in "Naked in the Wilderness: The Transculturation of Cabeza de Vaca in Abel Posse's *El largo atardecer del caminante.*" In her study, López compares the figure of Álvar Núñez Cabeza de Vaca in his chronicle *Naufragios* (1542) to that of the fictional character of the same name in Posse's novel. López investigates how Cabeza de Vaca stands out as unique among conquistadors for his willingness to participate in the process of transculturation between the Old and New Worlds in the two works. Because of Cabeza de Vaca's extended involvement with the indigenous peoples whom he encountered in his wanderings, López concludes that, although a conquistador in theory, he was in practice a man more open to contact and exchange with other cultures than the other conquistadors who left written records. She argues that *El largo atardecer del caminante* explicity attributes Cabeza de Vaca's transculturation to an internal sense of nonconformity with the goals of the conquest due to a desire to shed the noble Spanish identity that burdened him. The character's nakedness thus becomes symbolic of his rejection of the ideological and cultural baggage of the conquistador, and simultaneously marks the birth of a *mestizo* culture.

Part 5 revolves around the reinvention of the past through apocryphal chronicles. Erik Camayd-Freixas's "Penetrating Texts: Testimonial Pseudo-Chronicle in *La noche oscura del Niño Avilés* by Edgardo Rodríguez Juliá Seen from Sigüenza y Góngora's *Infortunios de Alonso Ramírez*" explores the process of construction of textual authority as inscribed in the fictional reappropriation of testimonial chronicles. The pretense of historical verity suggested by the mimicry of nonfictional discursive forms, taken only half seriously in the interest of ludic plausibility, was already present in Sigüenza's protomodern 1690 account of Puerto Rican pauper Alonso Ramírez's toils around the world. The *Infortunios* is a fictional retelling of the chronicles of Indies, now from the perspective of a Creole boy, a reluctant discoverer and Puerto Rican Magellan. Camayd-Freixas argues that three hundred years later another Puerto Rican chronicler, Edgardo Rodríguez Juliá, recaptured the handshake between author and character in his search for the deformed and handless body of Child Avilés, founder of New Venice in 1797. Camayd-Freixas compares the two texts, demonstrating how *criollo* reconversions of European imperial discourse into testimonial pseudo-chronicles always produce new versions of history and inversions of ideology. The author analyzes how Sigüenza transforms heroic conquistadors into meek, plebian paupers, and Juliá's Child Avilés becomes a degraded Columbus.

Mary Ann Gosser-Esquilín deals with the value of apocryphal accounts as a supplement to the historical record. In "Ana Lydia Vega's *Falsas crónicas del Sur:* Reconstruction and Revision of Puerto Rico's Past," Gosser-Esquilín contends that most contemporary Latin American writers owe a debt to the original rhetorical experiments of the writers of colonial *crónicas* and *relaciones.* She discusses these techniques in detail in texts by the Inca Garcilaso de la Vega, Bernal Díaz del Castillo, and Bartolomé de Las Casas, while delineating twentieth-century critical perspective of these works. Referring to Enrique Pupo-Walker and Roberto González Echevarría, Gosser-Esquilín studies colonial writings as vehicles through which unrecorded history could be best presented. She then juxtaposes this analysis with a work by Ana Lydia Vega. Gosser-Esquilín agrues that Vega returns to the models of the chronicles, transforming her own work into "false chronicles" that heighten the elusive quality of today's so-called New World Order. She concludes that Vega's shifting literary paradigms illustrate a contemporary change in political paradigms.

The relationship of contemporary apocryphal fiction to the literary tradition is the focus of Luis Correa-Díaz in "Cervantes in America: Between New World Chronicle and Chivalric Romance." Correa-Díaz's article studies contemporary Columbian writer Pedro Gómez Valderrama's short story "En un lugar de las Indias" in relation to its literary and historical sources. Specifically, Correa-Díaz investigates the manner in which Valderrama inverts the figures of Cervantes and the character Don Alonso Quijano, and how this leads to an inversion of the historical and literary reality of author and fictional character, creating the concept of a *Quijote indiano/caribeño.* He further analyzes how this new figure amplifies the traditional concept of quixotism, and how this short story establishes a relation between the genres of the *novela de caballería* and the *crónica de Indias,* both precursors of Hispanic American literature.

The controversial figures of Christopher Columbus and Lope de Aguirre are scrutinized in two essays included in the sixth section of the anthology. Molly Swift explores the multifaceted representations of the admiral's literary adventures within the contemporary imagination. In "The Americanization of Christopher Columbus in the Works of William Carlos Williams and Alejo Carpentier," Molly Metherd argues that North American poet William Carlos Williams's *In the American Grain* and Cuban novelist Alejo Carpentier's *El arpa y la sombra* take advantage of the complex and malleable history of the conquest in order to reemplot the character of Christopher Columbus and the discovery of America. Swift demonstrates that while Williams and Carpentier utilize the same documents from Columbus's voyages, each author emplots them differently, thus attributing dissimilar characteristics to Columbus, to his motivations, and to the repercussions of his voyage. She concludes that these two contemporary writers seek to expose the limitations and exclusionary nature of authoritative literary histories.

Bart L. Lewis surveys contemporary reconstructions of Lope de Aguirre and the myth of El Dorado. In "'This Miraculous Lie': Lope de Aguirre and the Search for El Dorado in the Latin American Historical Novel," Lewis analyzes how contemporary novelists turn the search for El Dorado into art, and, particularly, into Latin American art grounded in politics and culture. His focus is on modern reinventions of Pedro de Ursúa's legendary expedition and on the controversial figure of Lope de Aguirre. Lewis attempts to arrive at a contrastive analysis between the historical archive of the expedition and its novelized accounts, with the intent of understanding how art transforms the historical theme and why these novelists have undertaken such a transformation. With techniques varying from traditional *criollista* narrative to postmodern historiographic metafiction, the Latin American novel of El Dorado, written by its artistic descendants, finds the voice of Lope de Aguirre himself, silenced by the historical record, and gives it discourse, reflection, and resonance.

The final section of this book deals with one of the most characteristic features of Latin American new historical fiction: the use of intertextuality, parody, and carnivalization to present an alternative vision of history. In "A Fool's Point of View: Parody, Laughter, and the History of the Discovery in *Maluco: La novela de los descubridores* by Napoleón Baccino Ponce de León," Magdalena Perkowska-Alvarez examines the role of humor— laughter, parody, and irony—in challenging the accepted historical versions of the discovery and revaluating the anonymous, although fictional, accounts of that period. Her study focuses on one of the most representative novels of this tendency, *Maluco* (1989) by the Uruguayan Napoleón Baccino Ponce de León, which rewrites Magellan's circumnavigation of the globe from the point of view of the fleet's buffoon. Perkowska argues that the irreverent gaze of the novel's narrator, socially displaced but also actively displacing himself among various spheres of the expedition, resignifies history. The buffoon's laughter and irony reorganize the accepted accounts of Magellan's voyage according to a dialogical principle that dissolves the dichotomy between the grandiose and the petty, the positive and the negative, the public and the private, the central and the peripheral, which underscored and determined the writing of history.

Finally, Susan P. Berardini's "*La isla amarilla:* (Re)vision and Subversion of the Discovery" examines historical subversion in Paloma Pedrero's *La isla amarilla,* and the use of (meta)theater as a means of communication, exploration, and discovery not only for the characters but also for the public. Berardini argues that Spanish playwright Pedrero proposes a humorous view of Western life and the supposed technological advances therein enjoyed. She demontrates how Pedrero's play is an inversion of the historical events of the conquest in that it allows the Pacific Islanders to "discover" and explore the "civilized" world, and she contends that the Spanish drama constitutes a comic (re)vision of Spain as a colonizing country in the modern era.

As is evident in this brief treatment, the essays compiled here focus on two clearly defined areas of study: colonial issues and twentieth-century literature and film. Some of the articles concentrate on texts from the sixteenth and seventeenth centuries; thus the documentation utilized belongs to the Latin American colonial period. Others direct the reader's attention to twentieth-century retrospective views of the period of "discovery" and conquest; in these cases, the object of analysis concentrates primarily on the discursive practices of our time. Even though at first glance this double focus might appear to imply a lack of uniformity, in actuality the oscillation between colonial past and postcolonial present constitutes the essence of this collection. Our objective has been precisely to explore the double interpretation (the "twice-told tale") of a key period in the configuration of Latin American identity. This obvious duality demands a transgression of the rigid barriers of disciplines that separate colonial studies from present-day analysis of contemporary fiction and film.[1]

The historical revisionism that emerges from the articles included in this work is part of a larger tendency in contemporary thought. Of special relevancy to this project's theme is the growing trend within the field of philosophy of history to question the basic assumptions of historicism as much with regards to its ends as with regards to its methodologies. As Keith Jenkins indicates, "[b]oth philosophy and literature, for example, have engaged very seriously with the question of what is the nature of their own nature" (Jenkins 1991, 1). This highly accentuated relativism in contemporary critical theory has strongly impacted the epistemological practices of the New Historians, for whom the search for the truth in the past increasingly constitutes an unattainable utopia.[2] It is now all but impossible to discuss an exclusive or definitive historical discourse; in its place there appear to be only positions, perspectives, models, and angles that fluctuate in accordance with various paradigms. The postmodern thinker calls upon multiple discursive forms while simultaneously reflecting on the use of such forms and their possible limitations. The pluralism and contingency of all historical narrative thus has a genuinely democratic effect, given that, as Jenkins indicates, "querying the notion of the historian's truth, pointing to the variable facticity of facts, insisting that historians write the past from ideological positions, stressing that history is a written discourse as liable to deconstruction as any other, arguing that the 'past' is as notional a concept as 'the real world' to which novelists allude in realist fictions—only ever existing in the present discourses that articulate it—all these things destabilize the past and fracture it, so that, in the cracks opened up, new histories can be made" (Jenkins 1991, 66).

As a consequence of their self-reflexive and deconstructionist tendencies, New Historical theory as well as the most recent historical narrative aspire to undermine traditional visions of the historian and of the historiographic enterprise. The concept of the historian as witness, proposed by classical historiography and exploited by the historians of the Indies for decades, has been overturned by contemporary epistemology (Lozano 1987, 12). While this concept was based upon the necessity for immediacy between the author of history and the event narrated, such a possibility has been rendered untenable by new paradigms of research. There are no entirely evident facts. Those of which we become aware (including those that appear to be empirical) are inevitably perceived in a particular manner and are not "natural," but rather theoretical. Equally, the positivist view of the historian as a scientist has been compromised. The philosophers and historians from the late nineteenth century (Taine, Compte, Ranke) maintained that the facts spoke for themselves and that governing laws inevitably would emerge from scientific analysis of the same. In revealing the process of mediation inherent in the writing of history, as well as its unavoidable ideological component, postmodern historiography dismantles the positivist assumptions. Following the track indicated by Nietzsche in *The Use and Abuse of History,* the new philosophers of history affirm that there exist no facts per se; for a fact to exist, first we must introduce meaning into it: "history is never itself, is never said or read (articulated, expressed, discoursed) innocently, but . . . it is always for someone" (Jenkins 1991, 71). All historians orientate the texts which they write in specific directions. As Paul Veyne indicates, the facts do not exist in isolation. The fabric of history is what may be termed a plot, an episode of real life that the historian weaves as he wishes, and in which the facts have their own correlations and relative importance. The mask of objectivity defended by historiographic empiricism and positivism loses all validity when we become conscious of the document's fetishism and its consequent methodology based on an ingenuous realism. Indeed, the personality most recently adopted by the historian, that of the reconstructor of a mysterious past manifest as a detective novel plot, is equally submitted to revision. This vision of history implies the clarification of a preexisting puzzle that can be resolved with the help of clues and evidence. The underlying notion is the need to reconstruct a precritical reality within an organic whole in which the facts acquire their only possible meaning. By making evident the multiplicity of discursive versions and by uncovering the ideological manipulation of the author as well as the impossibility of ultimate closure, the postmodern historical theorist demonstrates the artifice and limitations of this new "fiction of the historian."

The present-day view of history seeks foremost to problematize that which traditionally had been represented as a merely mechanical task that corresponded to a simplistic conception of representation. Two specific tendencies within postmodernism fulfill a crucial role in its epistemological revisionism and thus require a more detailed commentary: the substitution of a fragmentary notion of the past in place of the organic vision of history, and the reevaluation of the role of narrative in historical writing. The first of these traits finds one of its most radical expressions in the work of Michel Foucault, while Hayden White has taken the second to its utmost extreme in his formal analysis of history. Both cases are theoretical projects that seek to expose the process of mediation inherent in the textualization of the past. Foucault's work dismantles the attempts at a global theorization of the historical phenomenon by means of fragmentary narratives (microhistories) that focus on differences rather than concentrating on continuities. White's studies reveal the poetic (tropological) and cultural nature of all historical work. These two thinkers offer self-reflexive alternatives to the so-called crisis in historical thought.

The theoretical tendencies we have just outlined allow us to understand some of the most recurrent characteristics observed in contemporary reconstructions of the encounter between the Old and New Worlds. Among the new historico-narrative practices of Latin America, Fernando Aínsa has identified ten of these characteristics: (1) the rereading of history based on critical historicism; (2) the impeachment of the legitimacy of official versions of the past; (3) the multiplicity of perspectives that aspire to express multiple historical truths; (4) the abolition of epic distancing; (5) the parodistic and irreverent rewriting of history; (6) the fantastic and anachronistic superimposition of different historical periods; (7) the use of textual historicity or the completely mimetic invention of chronicles and *relaciones;* (8) the adoption of false chronicles disguised as historicism or the gloss of authentic texts in grotesque or exaggerated contexts; (9) the distanced, "nightmarish," or anachronistic rereading of history by means of carnivalesque writing; and (10) the preoccupation with language manifest in the glut of archaisms, pastiches, parodies, and an acute sense of humor. The oppositional character that can be deduced from the aforementioned traits is clear not only in the literary and filmic texts analyzed here, but also in the critical discourse used to analyze the works. Moreover, from both we can deduce a new broad and inclusive concept of the historical effort. New discursive forms that simultaneously claim both creative and epistemological value now join the archaeological impulse of traditional academic historiography. This favors an encounter between historiography per se and other forms of historical reflection that can include the novel, the theater, and film. In contrast to the traditional subordination of the discourse of creative fiction (which since the Renaissance has borne the stigma of "untruthful stories"), recent decades have seen the reclamation of fiction as a supplement to history. In the field of Iberian and Iberian American literature and film, this reclamation has manifest itself in a historical revisionism without precedent. In terms of the thematic repertory of these new modalities of historical fiction, the encounter—or clash—of the "Old World" with the "New" occupies a preferential position. As long as there has existed reflection about the origins of Latin American identity, the period of "discovery" and of conquest has stimulated and will continue to stimulate the imagination of the creators of the Iberian American construct. The essays compiled here will help the reader to understand this unique occurrence in the theoretic, historical, and literary fields in which this construct developed and in which it has recently been reinvented.

Notes

1. For many years, Latin American specialists have devoted themselves either to the colonial period prior to independence from Europe, or to the nineteenth- and twentieth-century periods. Only very recently have colonial texts begun to be read from a contemporary, postcolonial perspective. Regarding the question of the state of colonial studies, see Rolena Adorno's paradigmatic essay, "New Perspectives in Colonial Spanish American Literary Studies." Adorno is unquestionably one of the key figures in the new colonial literary criticism that aspires to a synthesis uniting sophisticated post-structuralist readings of the colonial past, and analysis of the foundational texts of Latin American literature in light of the historical context of their production. For other approaches to the reconsideration of the colonial past see the essays included in René Jara and Nicolás Spadaccini's anthology, *1492–1992: Re/Discovering Colonial Writing.*

2. This group of historians associated with the basic assumptions of postmodernism includes Hayden White, Dominick LaCapra, Hans Kellner, F. R. Ankersmit, and Keith Jenkins, among others. The point of departure for all of them is earlier research on the narrative in historiography, the deconstructionist school in literary theory, and the interdisciplinary work of Michel Foucault.

Bibliography

Adorno, Rolena. 1990. "New Perspectives in Colonial Spanish American Literary Studies." *Journal of the Southwest* 32 (summer): 173–91.

Aínsa, Fernando. 1991. "La nueva novela histórica latinoamericana." *Plural* 241 (September): 82–85.

Axtell, James. 1992a. *Beyond 1492: Encounters in Colonial North America.* New York: Oxford University Press.

———. 1992b. "Columbian Encounters: Beyond 1992." *William and Mary Quarterly* 49: 335–60.

———. 1995. "Columbian Encounters: 1992–95." *William and Mary Quarterly* 52: 649–96.

Bamonte, Gerardo, and Giulia Della Marina, eds. 1992. *La "Festa" degli indios: Il quinto centenario visto dagli indigeni dell'America Latina.* Chieti Scalo: Vecchio Faggio Editore.

Barreiro, José, ed. 1990. *View from the Shore: American Indian Perspectives on the Quincentenary.* Special issue of *Northeast Indian Quarterly* 7, no. 3.

Block, David. 1994. "Quincentennial Publishing: An Ocean of Print." *Latin American Research Review* 29, no. 3: 101–28.

Gentry, Carole M., and Donald A. Grinde, Jr., eds. 1994. *The Unheard Voices: American Indian Responses to the Columbian Quincentenary 1492–1992.* Los Angeles: University of California Press, American Indian Studies Center.

Grim, John A., ed. 1992. *Shaman and Preachers, Color Symbolism, and Commercial Evangelism: Reflections of Early Mid-Atlantic Religious Encounter in Light of the Columbian Quincentennial.* Special Issue of *American Indian Quarterly* 16, no. 4.

Jara, René, and Nicholás Spadaccini, eds. 1989. *1492–1992: Re/Discovering Colonial Writing.* Minneapolis: University of Minnesota Press.

Jenkins, Keith. 1991. *Re-thinking History.* New York: Routledge.

Lozano, Jorge. 1987. *El discurso histórico.* Madrid: Alianza Editorial.

Menton, Seymour. 1993. *Latin America's New Historical Novel.* Austin: University of Texas Press.

Olivier, Alfredo Matus. 1992. "España vista desde América en la lengua y la cultura (Introducción a una semántica del quinto centenario)." *Signos* 25: 91–109.

Veyne, Paul. 1972. *Como se escribe la historia.* Madrid: Fragua.

A Twice-Told Tale

Part One
Recontextualizing the Encounter

Three Visions of America

EDUARDO SUBIRATS

I. The Providential Design

I wish to concisely describe three worldviews that have fundamentally influenced modern perceptions of America from the sixteenth century until today. Three worldviews that appear in unequal proportion throughout the history of Spanish consciousness and national identity. Three philosophies that have firmly maintained their significance in the contemporary world.

The first is profoundly associated with Christian imperial Spain. It fueled the ethical values that took shape throughout the Spanish crusades against Islam, it bitterly underscored the expulsion of the Jews, and it inaugurated the Catholic Spanish state. It is the ideology of the conquest as it was formulated by the first chroniclers of America and, above all, as it was expressed by the Roman Catholic Church through its bulls and strategies for promulgating the faith.

At the heart of this understanding of American reality was the idea of a providential historical design whose center the Spanish crown occupied. The Catholic state assumed the role of Christendom's chosen people in order to forcibly impose its value system upon the entire globe. As early as 1493, Pope Alexander VI's bull *Intercoetera* alluded to this historical and theological dimension that the Catholic monarchs Ferdinand and Isabella had already adopted. Its ultimate meaning was directed toward the territorial possession of the New World and the exploitation of its immense wealth, but only as an instrument for the forced conversion of its native peoples, and the political construction of a Christian world, the first modern, internationalist utopia.

Such a providential link between Spain and America crystalized politically in the form of colonial domination, and spiritually as theological and linguistic subordination. America was defined, according to this principle, as vassal. The precise verb used in Alexander VI's bull to clarify this relationship was *deprimoere* (to push down, to belittle, repress, or suppress). American subjugation to the Spanish crown was elevated, in the light of the

Christian principles of vassalage and Western rationalism, to the status of a redemptive precept.

Ginés de Sepúlveda formulated this concept of liberty for the Indian through Christian slavery as the destruction of the demonic powers that dominated him; that is, the destruction of his memory and the physical remnants of his civilization. This constituted one of the motives behind the menacing language of the requisitions read by the Christian soldiery immediately prior to plundering and subjugating the Americans. It was precisely under these terms that the colonization of America was ecclesiastically legitimized as a holy war against indigenous people.

The spiritual significance of colonial dependency was expressed through the linguistic predominance of Castilian over the native languages of America. This predominance, formulated functionally and/or grammatically by Nebrija, was not based solely on a concrete relationship of domination, nor as a mere consequence of the prohibition and destruction of the original languages of the continent. Rather, it was conceived of as a metaphysical axiom. Fray José de Acosta stated it dramatically in his propaganda treatise, *De Procuranda Indorum Salute:* American languages, insofar as they were pagan languages, were not intrinsically capable of expressing the metaphysical categories of the fundamental dogmas of Christian theology. Only Castilian was capable of expressing the concept of a sole creator God—prime mover and absolute being.

This unidirectional relationship between the Christian master, heroic and virtuous, and the Indian, believed to occupy a state of nature (and therefore of sin) from which only his enslavement could free him, was severed in favor of a dialectical relationship. According to this dialectical revision, the American vassal was subjugated to the Christian Spaniard, recognizing in him the universal expression of absolute truth in a political and theological sense. Further, the vassal's very desire became his aspiration to feel like and become like his master. This was the theological and political position held by Las Casas. It was a point of view ahead of its time, and without a doubt somewhat revolutionary: a strictly modern principle because it implied a strategy of propagandistic seduction in place of the holy war of extermination and its concomitant practice of forced conversion. Las Casas's dialectical revision of American servitude was modern because it carried implicitly within it the ideal of abstract subjectivity, empty and infinite.

Spain's relationship to the Americas has been dominated by this political and theological principle of spiritual hegemony. I wish to emphasize that this same theological principle has not undergone any significant modifications throughout modern history. It seems particularly important to point out that the final collapse of the Spanish empire in 1898 most certainly denoted the self-consciousness of both political and moral defeat, as well as a crisis and even trauma for Spanish imperial identity, but by no means did it bring about a revision of those heroic and transcendental metaphysical categories under which American reality had been understood. Simply stated, within the postcolonial context, said theological and political hegemonic principle shed its administrative significance in order to conserve the meaning of a purely spiritual hegemony.

"If we have not been able to say 'Yes' to life, may we learn how to say it to death, and make it glorious, worthy of Spain," wrote Maetzu the morning after the destruction of the Spanish flotilla in Santiago. This vindication of death, profoundly rooted in the Christian concept of heroism, embodied what would eventually become the starting point for an entire philosophy and literature of Spanish identity. In the midst of the political and military bankruptcy of 1898, and the entering into crisis of the historical values that had defined the mythical grandeur of Christian Spain, intellectuals such as Gavinet, Unamuno, Azorín, and Maeztu extolled a national identity capable of overcoming the conflict with the ex-colonies in the name of a transcendental spirituality, of a heroic nihilism, of the quixotic myth. The lost grandeur of colonial Spain was reformulated by them in tragic existentialist terms.

Valera consoled himself regarding the tragedy: imperial power has been lost, he wrote, but the Spanish race is the most numerous of the century. Menéndez Pelayo refashioned the more or less chimeric value of the Spanish language as a politically cohesive principle for the vast territory encompassed by the ex-colonies, and attempted to do so with plans originally prepared for none other than Queen Isabella, "la Católica." Her authority, at one time considered inseparable from the providential might of the empire, was now sublimated into somewhat more discreet "principles of good taste," in whose name the Spanish intellectual nevertheless hoped to establish the aesthetic hierarchies of the Americas.

Although of itself not especially important, Angel Gavinet's novel *The Conquest of the Kingdom of Maya* is a curious and symptomatic example of this spiritual redefinition of Spanish imperial hegemony. In this novel, failed Spanish imperialism is recast epically among dazzling conquests in exotic, unknown African lands in the search for glory and honor, and in total heroic disdainment of any of the pragmatic and productive objectives of modern colonialism. The new meaning of Spanish empire is exalted ethically through virtuous sacrifices in the name of conjugal fidelity, or is celebrated aesthetically through the sheer beauty of sublime acts, the spirit of conquest as regenerative war and destruction, and an extended, insipid et cetera.

The hero, the horde, destruction, sacrifice, death, glory, and the other myths Gavinet extols do little more than anticipate in literature the Spanish fascist utopia. In fact, the descriptive process of the novel ends precisely with a program for "another, more perfect civilization," based on "the superiority of the blood" and the "betterment of the race by the means most recommended by anthropologists."

The fascist glorification of a heroic spiritual past, simultaneously universal and nationalistic, culminates a few decades later with the rebirth of Spanish thought in Ramiro de Maetzu's lengthy essay *Defense of Hispanism.* Here a firm hand outlines the solution: Restore the universalist Christian values of the Counter-Reformation as a starting point for the spiritual redefinition of the rejuvenated nation, or, in other words, the ideology of Hispanism.

II. The Techno-scientific Discourse

The second paradigm of colonial and postcolonial representations of America is neither theological nor metaphysical, but rather antischolastic, empiricist, rational, progressive, and techno-scientific. A clear example of this new conceptualization can be appreciated in a series of etchings published in 1576 by the Flemish painter Jan van der Straet on the theme of the discovery, which carries the telling title of *Nova Reperta.* One of the plates displays a collection of diverse objects: a printing press, compass, medicine, a canon . . . and, in the middle of them all, the American continent.

This new representation of America was no longer heroic, nor did it appeal to theological and metaphysical principles: it was empiric and democratic, it equated the continent with other inventions of the pragmatic sciences, and it was based on a productive model of knowledge and power. This new technological and economic discourse of American colonization was first formulated in modern conceptual terms by the philosopher Francis Bacon in his treatise of 1620, *Novum Organum.*

The frontispiece of this treatise displays the Columns of Hercules in the foreground. It is a symbol of a long-surpassed mythological limit, and, as such, of a distancing from the classical model of the universe. But it is also a symbol of heroic and virtuous potential, associated with the ancient foundational "work" of classical civilization. Beyond those mythical limits, two caravels navigate on open seas, their sails swollen by the wind. This Odyssean scene recalls the voluptuousness of adventure and the thirst for new experience and riches. The bow of one ship has already crossed the waters that separate the symbolic limit between the Old World and the infinite ocean. Below the etching a legend heralds: *Multi pertransibut & augebitur scientia.* The phrase is taken from the Book of Daniel in the Old Testament. "Many will pass, and science shall advance." Wisdom, or the science of the Book, to which Daniel's prophecy alludes, is here substituted for the enterprise of the discovery.

According to Francis Bacon, an inherent link and continuity existed between intercontinental exploration and the "light" of inductive knowledge as a principle of production and domination. In antiquity, the philosopher wrote, when philosophy could access only deductive knowledge, little was known of the earthly orb. Navigation barely reached the limits of a mundane, domestic world. Therefore, there existed no real possibility of knowledge based on experience, that is, on a confrontation with the new and the unknown.

Modern inductive reasoning, on the other hand, has according to this work "a universal reach." Its "method of interpretation . . . leads the spirit in such a manner so as to permit it to easily penetrate the essence of things." The scientific method thus becomes the new universal principle in the enterprise of techno-scientific conquest, a universal principle that in turn reformulated, within its categories of progressive human domination, that same redemptive principle that had underscored and characterized the Christian ideal of a completely converted universe.

In *Novum Organum,* this argument culminated in a significant commentary concerning the indigenous peoples of America. Once again, their nature or being was cast in a negative light. But no longer was the inferiority of the colonized subject a product of his abominable sins, nor of his paganism and idolatry, as was the case argued by Sepúlveda and de Acosta. What condemned these people to bondage was the imperfection of their knowledge, dependent upon that of their "idols." Their subservience was thus the result of the local or "sub-urban" nature of their forms of knowledge, which is to say their anticritical and antiempirical nature.

Obviously, neither modern Hapsburg Spain nor that of the Bourbons utilized this illustrated scientific paradigm when imposing their hegemonic interests upon America. This applies also to writers that within Spanish culture have earned the title of learned men, such as Father Feijoo. They maintained the strict limits placed upon the epistemological skepticism and the empiricism of modern scientific philosophy regarding those ultimate truths pertaining to the theological jurisdiction of the Inquisition or the metaphysical jurisdiction of Scholasticism. Spanish consciousness consistently felt its spiritual principles of domination threatened by the antimetaphysical trends of modern scientific epistemology, at least until the intellectual advent of Unamuno.

Furthermore, the techno-economic, philosophic, and social backwardness of Spain has historically been linked to the persistence, from Ginés de Sepúlveda to Ramiro de Maetzu, of a traditionalist metaphysical and ethical worldview that stands in stark contrast to that of modern empirical rationalism. This link has served to articulate a more extensive characterization that includes the so-called "black legend"—the Protestant and liberal version of the despotism and cruelty of the Catholic Spanish monarchy—and, later, the discourse of modern industrialized society regarding the underdevelopment of Hispanic cultures in general.

Spanish progressivism was finally able to break the historical continuity of traditionalist Catholic nationalism only within the mediating context of the numerous events surrounding the quincentennial of 1992. Solely in this context did it become possible to change the theological and heroic categorizations of the Christian conquest and colonization of America to those of the postmodern representation of a techno-scientific, media-centered, and ostentatious modernity. And solely in this context was Spanish predominance and exemplariness in relation to America able to overcome its anachronistic chauvinistic emblems and assume the modern conception of an ambiguous discovery, compatible with and assimilable to the scientific and technical discoveries of the Age of Discovery.

III. The Hermeneutic Reconstruction

There is a third vision of America—a reflexive one. It is based on the hermeneutic restoration of historic languages and cultures destroyed in the name of universal modernism. An original vision, needless to say. A marginal vision as well. It is the intellectual perspective of a philosopher and descendent of Inca aristocracy, a man exposed at an early age to the philosophical writings of a Hispanic Jew exiled to Italy, so that he came to know the Latin humanist tradition. His work, based on the critical tradition of European humanism and ancient Inca spirituality, outlines a complex dialogical utopia among plural and diverse cultures and religions, according to the pantheistic principle of the unity of "the world many and one." I am speaking of the Inca Garcilaso.

In his chronicle *Comentarios reales,* Garcilaso comments on a curious linguistic and dialogical situation. The matter at hand receives the philosophically pompous title: "Deduction of the name 'Perú.' " The chronicler recounts how the bearded ones first arrived to the coasts of the ancient kingdom of Tawantinsuyu—"the four parts of the universe," according to the word's etymology. These adventurers, according to the Inca Garcilaso, happened upon a simple fisherman on the banks of a river. They called out to him. The fisherman, frightened, pronounced first his name: "Berú." The Spaniards continued making inquiries. The fisherman then repeated the name of the river in which he was fishing: "Pelú." The discoverers took care of the rest. They fused Berú and Pelú and deduced that "Perú" must be the name of that immense territorial expanse whose inhabitants, language, history, and civilization was entirely unknown to them. As Inca Garcilaso says immediately following his "Deduction": "The Christians understood according to their desire."

The violent and arbitrary nature of this imposed name, which is simply a metaphor of the name imposed upon those we recognize only elliptically as "Indians," inaugurates the false dilemma of American identity. Faced with the false reality of an imposed identity, Garcilaso proposes the hermeneutic restoration of the destroyed community by recovering its proper names as well as those of its gods, and with them the reconstruction of memory.

Garcilaso's narrative in *Comentarios reales* responds to this challenge by means of an original melding of the epic, mythic, chronicle, and poetic genres—or, in his own words, "fact" and "fable," and the retelling of the "stories" of Inca civilization. For this reason, the narrator is simultaneously an intellectual "I" and a collective voice that portrays itself as a historic memory throughout the narrative chronicle.

This is, in turn, a memory of the "heart" and a memory of "lineage," according to Garcilaso. It is the recovery of a remote and profound voice. Its meaning escapes the logic of domination formulated under the theological principle of universal conversion, or under the empirical, inductive principles of the production-oriented sciences that were to replace it. It was and is a poetic voice. It has to do with the evocative power of this word and its secret connection to an experience that is both intimate and communal: As Garcilaso says, a voice "heard and preserved in the heart" (Vega 1976, 1:47).

Translated by James López

Bibliography

Acosta, José de. 1984–87. *De Procuranda Indorum Salute.* Madrid: Consejo Superior de Investigaciones Científicas.

Bacon, Francis. 1980. *Novum Organum.* Indianapolis: Bobbs-Merrill.

Gavinet, Angel. 1988. *La conquista del reino de Maya. Los trabajos del infatigable creador Pio Cid.* Barcelona: Editorial Planeta.

Maeztu, Ramiro de. 1998. *Defensa de la hispanidad.* Madrid: Rialp.

Vega, Garcilaso de la (the Inca). 1976. *Comentarios reales.* 2 vols. Caracas: Ayacucho, 1976.

Postmodernity, Orphanhood, and the Contemporary Spanish American Historical Novel

VIVIANA PLOTNIK

> *América es la hija de Europa, y necesita asesinarla para poder históricamente comenzar a vivir. Sólo practicando el parricidio histórico-cultural podrá. . . .*
>
> [America is the child of Europe, and it needs to kill her in order to begin historically to live. Only by practicing historico-cultural patricide will it be able to. . . .]
>
> —H. A. Murena, *El pecado original de América*

THE HISTORICAL NOVEL HAS BEEN PREDOMINANT IN SPANISH AMERICAN narrative for the last thirty years, particularly the novel focused on the Iberian travels of discovery and conquest in the Americas.[1] This is not just a matter of thematic proliferation; this type of novel signals a shift in perspective as well as a lack of belief in master narratives characteristic of the postmodern sensibility.[2]

The topic of the Iberian discovery and conquest of the Americas had also dominated the Spanish historical novel during the nineteenth century, but it was mainly inscribed within the parameters of romanticism.[3] Filled with heroic characters as well as villains, the nineteenth-century historical novel depicted a precolonial or colonial past in order to exalt the cultural roots of the new independent Spanish American nations and to help create the appropriate mentality for the consolidation of a national consciousness. Current literary criticism views those nineteenth-century texts as too faithful to historiography, and that faithfulness was privileged and emphasized under realism, naturalism, and positivism (Menton 1993, 17–19). The nineteenth-century historical novel followed historiographic narratives closely—a correlation between history and story was aspired to, and assumed.

In contrast, the contemporary Spanish American novel whose topic is the discovery and conquest of the Americas distorts official history through the use of hyperbole and anachronism, and revises the past from an ironic or parodic perspective, indicating a mistrust of historiography. It ultimately reduces history to a narrative discourse that is rewritten in a self-reflexive manner. History becomes an intertextual space where sources are revealed, contested, and parodied—a stage where theatrical and carnivalesque motifs predominate (Plotnik 1992, 47–48). Narrators are frequently involved in writing and reading activities; the novels indicate a self-reflexive aspect when commenting on the narrative process and its difficulties, and present themselves as an artifice by reminding the reader that what he/she is reading is manipulated by the narrator. One notices the textual mediation of historical knowledge as well as the self-reflexivity of the novels when, for instance, in Carpentier's *El arpa y la sombra,* Columbus reads his own travel journal and, centuries later, the Pope—who during his youth used to read picaresque Spanish novels—reads a biography about Columbus; or when in Baccino Ponce de León's *Maluco,* one of the members of the maritime expedition reads "an old novel of adventures at sea" (Baccino Ponce de León 1990, 159); and in Saer's *El entenado,* the protagonist writes an autobiographical theater play.

Also characteristic of the contemporary Spanish American historical novel is the presence of a decentered perspective and a predominance of marginality or eccentricity regarding events, class, race, religion, gender, or ethnicity. These novels subvert traditional notions of centrality and marginality regarding characters as well as historical facts. The protagonist is frequently a member of a Spanish travel expedition who occupies a low position in the social hierarchy.[4] Sometimes he/she is of Jewish origin, which means that he/she belongs to one of the most persecuted minorities of the times.[5] When Christopher Columbus is the protagonist, we do not have the heroic subject trumpeted by nineteenth-century biographies, but a demythified, lying, and duplicitous admiral, as in Carpentier's *El arpa y la sombra.* In Freilich's *Colombina descubierta,* Columbus is Jewish, poor, mentally ill, and an old woman.

In contrast to the discredit suffered by Columbus, another historical figure, Lope de Aguirre, is rescued as a rebel fighting against the imperial Spanish system in Posse's *Daimón,* Otero Silva's *Lope de Aguirre, príncipe de la libertad,* and Funes's *Una lanza por Lope de Aguirre.* It is not unusual to have in these novels the indigenous people's point of view.[6] The traditionally hegemonic historical agent—a European and powerful Christian male—is decentered and we find (hi)stories narrated from multiple perspectives and positions.

The contemporary Spanish American historical novel can be inscribed in what Linda Hutcheon defines as "historiographic metafiction." This concept implies the presence of a parodic or ironic dialogue with the historical and artistic past, and also the problematization of the possibility of historical knowledge and narrative representation. Historiographic metafiction views history as a human construction whose accessibility is conditioned by textuality: we can only know the past through texts. Therefore, the historical past is not denied, but our capacity to know it is questioned. Historiographic metafiction does not aim to reproduce or reflect the past—the past is constituted as a discourse and an artifice. History becomes an intertext that contributes to fiction as other texts do. The intertextual character of the past is emphasized and incorporated in the contemporary novel through irony and parody. As Umberto Eco states: "the past, since it cannot really be destroyed, because its destruction leads to silence, must be reinvented but with irony, not innocently" (Eco 1984, 67).

According to Lukács, the presence of secondary historical characters in the novel validates the fictional world. In contrast, the contemporary Spanish American historical novel does not attempt to legitimize the narrative nor give it a sense of verisimilitude; narrators offer evidence of its artificiality and question historical discourses as well as their own. They incorporate aspects and points of view present in chronicles and historiography related to the discovery and conquest of the Americas, but at the same time they deconstruct them and create new versions of history. Paratextual conventions used in historiographic writing such as footnotes are incorporated and parodied in the novel, questioning the authority and objectivity of historical sources. In Carpentier's *El arpa y la sombra,* Columbus reads his own travel diary and denies any truth to most of what he had written in it; Posse's *Los perros del paraíso* has elements of a history manual, but the narrated version of the Spanish conquest as well as the quotes from fictive historiographic sources are absurd, hyperbolic, and parodic; in Saer's *El entenado,* texts written by various characters in order to tell the story of a member of Cabot's expedition to South America are defined as distortions, and it is not clear whether the protagonist's own memoirs are the product of real or imagined experiences; and in *Maluco,* the protagonist—a jester who travels with Magellan around the world—contradicts official chronicles he considers false, and writes a new version of the voyage, which can not be confirmed as truthful either.

Lévi-Strauss defines a "bricolage" as a reelaboration based on heterogeneous but limited materials that are used and combined in new ways. We could propose that the contemporary Spanish American historical novel incorporates and combines as "bricolage" elements of travel literature, Menippean satire, and chronicles of discovery and conquest, as well as aspects of historiographic, picaresque, (auto)biographical, and epistolary narrative.[7]

The frequent presence of parodic elements and the combination of characters from different historical times resemble Menippean satire.[8] In it, "the subject moves with extreme and fantastic freedom; from heaven to earth, from earth to the nether world, from the present into the past, from the past into the future. In the comic afterlife visions of Menippean satire, the heroes of the absolute past, real-life figures from various eras of the historic past . . . and living contemporaries jostle one another in a most familiar way, to talk even to brawl; this confrontation of times from the point of view of the present is extremely characteristic" (Bakhtin 1981, 26).

As in Menippean satire and travel literature, an (auto)biographical focus predominates in the contemporary Spanish American historical novel. Frequently, it traces the personal consequences of the travels of discovery; the narrative emphasis is not on historical events, but on reflections triggered by the encounter with that Other world. Therefore, microhistory, with its stress on the private and personal aspects of events, is emphasized. Narrators describe their personal experiences of a historical event that has marked and influenced them very deeply in confessions, memoirs, autobiographies, and letters.[9]

Usually the protagonist of the contemporary Spanish American historical novel dealing with the topic of Iberian discovery and conquest is a *pícaro* who in his worldly adventures resorts to tricks and even assumes false identities in order to survive or accomplish his goals. For example, in Carpentier's *El arpa y la sombra,* Columbus constantly lies, and everything written in his travel diary is portrayed as an invention; the protagonist of Saer's *El entenado* assumes various roles and identities in order to survive; in Baccino Ponce de León's *Maluco,* the protagonist is a jester and a rogue; and the Spaniards in Posse's *Los perros del paraíso* are delinquents trying to achieve their objectives by any means. Frequently, as in traditional picaresque narrative, the protagonist is an orphan and a socially marginal character who neither rejects nor embraces society. A pseudo-(auto)biographical writing predominates; social conditions are observed critically, and there is a horizontal spatial movement as well as a vertical social one (Guillén 1971). A picaresque life implies the constant use of maskings in a world that is like a stage (Wicks 1989).

A common thread in many of these novels is the absence of paternal figures. The texts in which Columbus is the protagonist usually discredit his reputation as hero, "discoverer" or symbolic father. Orphanhood implies the absence of authority and a break with one's origins and ancestral determinism as well as a new beginning. The orphan represents a blank slate where history can begin to be written, or perhaps a pen that inscribes history in a blank space.

Traditionally, in the Spanish American cultural and historical self-narratives, the conquest of the Americas by the Spaniards constitutes *the* traumatic event that determined a historical rift as well as the origin of the problems accosting the Spanish American territories. That historical rift is usually described as a sudden state of orphanhood. For example, according to Octavio Paz: "The history of Mexico is the history of a man seeking his parentage, his origins. He has been influenced at one time or another by

France, Spain, the United States and the militant indigenists of his own country, and he crosses history like a jade comet, now and then giving off flashes of lighting. What is he pursuing in his eccentric course? He wants to go back beyond the catastrophe he suffered: he wants to be a sun again, to return to the center of that life from which he was separated one day. (Was that day the Conquest? Independence?)" (Paz 1961, 20).

And that separation is synonymous with orphanhood: "Our solitude has the same roots as religious feelings. It is a form of orphanhood, an obscure awareness that we have been torn from the All, and an ardent search: a flight and a return, an effort to re-establish the bonds that unite us with the universe" (Paz 1961, 20).

Similarly, H. A. Murena argues that with the Spanish conquest, "the people of the Americas have suffered an unprecedented historical rift, a rift after which history has never started again" (Murena 1965, 14). For Murena, it was not only the conquered natives who experienced a traumatic historical rift, but also the conquerors and the immigrants who arrived centuries later. He believes that all Latin Americans are, or feel, exiled from history and are constantly searching for answers to explain the causes of the guilt that resulted in their exile. According to Murena, they redeem their feelings of guilt through self-destruction and the necessary parricide regarding Europe and the past: "The Americas are constituted by exiles [*desterrados*] and are a place of exile, and everyone in exile deeply knows that in order to be able to live he has to shut off the past, he must erase the memories of that world to which he can not return; otherwise, he will be hanging from them and will not be able to live. In order to live in this world, one has to burn one's bridges, one has to disallow spiritually what one has left behind because this is the new world, and here one starts a new life and does not continue the previous one. To kill or to die: there is no other alternative" (Murena 1965, 32). For Murena, the feeling of being in exile and the need for parricide is universal because: "every child is . . . parricidal. Man is parricidal because he imagines himself immortal and can not tolerate the material proofs of his origin" (Murena 1965, 32–33). Therefore "the drama of the Americas is a repetition of the drama of man being a foreigner in the world" (Murena 1965, 51).

It is noteworthy how all these references to orphanhood and parricide vis-à-vis Europe present in the Spanish American essay return and can be found in the contemporary historical novel. They return now embodied in characters who leave Europe for the Americas and who are either orphaned or rebellious regarding their parents' wishes and expectations, and who also contradict official versions of historical events.

Filiation is a type of relationship characterized by sequence and chronological order. As Michel de Certeau states, Western historiography usually produces causality and coherence in order to create order among phenomena. Elements of filiation and order are combined in a concept of temporality: "History furnishes the empty frame of a linear succession which formally answers to questions on *beginnings* and to the need for *order.* It is thus less the result obtained from research than its condition: the web woven a priori by the two threads with which the historical loom moves forward in the single gesture of filling holes" (Certeau 1988, 12; original emphasis).

Although on the one hand the Spanish American novel creates a filiation by rewriting and integrating points of view present in the chronicles and diaries of discovery and conquest, on the other it questions those historical and literary "origins" and commits a symbolic parricide. By eliminating linearity and center, the Spanish American novel subverts historiography.

According to the conventional history of Spanish American literature, the chronicles and diaries of discovery and conquest are not only testimonies of a transcendental historical event, but also the foundational writing or the beginning of the Spanish American literary tradition. According to Roberto González Echevarría: "Due to their fictional character, the importance of the chronicles in the creation of the modern Latin American novel is a cliché generally accepted by both literary critics and novelists, The usual quote that serves as proof is from Bernal Díaz, referring to *Amadís* while contemplating Tenochtitlán, or from Columbus asserting that the manatees he saw were mermaids, although not as beautiful as classic tradition portrayed them" (González Echevarría 1988, 439).

Scholars usually remark upon the chronicles' and diaries' mythic and literary aspects as well as their role in creating heroic, picaresque, and tragic characters (Vidal 1985; Pupo-Walker 1982). Therefore, these texts are viewed as contributors to our literary heritage: "The rocks of the historical edifice the chroniclers wanted to build were joined by the magic mortar of imagination and fantasy. . . . [T]hese historians laid the foundations of what became the great Latin American narrative of today" (González Echevarría 1984, 10). Similarly, Pupo-Walker states that the origins of Spanish American literature are in the chronicles of discovery and conquest: "[I]n the chronicles of discovery there persists . . . a paradoxical reconstruction of the past; it is a kind of invention or mistake that, for me, should be understood as the seminal seed of Latin American narrative's imaginative creation. I think it is necessary to point out . . . in our cultural history this first act of invention that is present in the chronicles of discovery and conquest" (Pupo-Walker 1984, 91).

Therefore, the historiography related to the discovery and conquest of the Americas was contaminated with fiction: "Suddenly it was necessary to describe an unknown vastness that was, for the improvised chroniclers, simultaneously reality and fantasy. On many occasions, the news gathered in those books demanded from the narrator expressive recourses common in works of fiction. Therefore . . . American historiography . . . gave way to creative temptation" (Pupo-Walker 1982, 89–90).

Historiographic discourse is currently perceived as closer to literature than to science. This perception is shared by Michel de Certeau, Lionel Gossman, and Hayden White. According to Certeau: "Historiography (that is, 'history' and 'writing') bears within its own name the paradox—almost an oxymoron—of a relation established between two antinomic terms, between the real and discourse. Its task is one of connecting them and, at the point where this link cannot be imagined, of working *as if* the two were being joined" (Certeau 1988, xxvii). Certeau also states that in Western civilization, history replaces old myths and theology and allows society to tell its own story: "It functions as foreign civilizations used to, or still do, telling tales of cosmogonic struggles confronting a present time with an origin" (Certeau 1988, 45). He considers that fiction haunts historiography because literature is, for history, the repressed that must be recognized and legitimated (Certeau 1986, 219).

Lionel Gossman reminds us that for a long time the relationship between history and literature was not problematical because the first was considered part of the latter. History and literature were separated during the nineteenth century when a distinction between an empirical realm and an aesthetic one was established. At the time of a triumphal bourgeoisie and industrial capitalism, the product of art had to seem radically different from other products. If during the Enlightenment poets and historians shared aspirations and experiences, with positivism history had to become a science.

As Nietzsche did, the new historians question the possibility of reconstructing the past with objectivity. For Lionel Gossman, historiography constitutes its object through language, which is not a copy of events:

> Evidence—texts, documents, articles—is by definition a sign, and it signifies within a system of signs. The historian's narrative is constructed not upon reality itself or upon transparent images of it, but on signifiers which the historian's own action transforms into signs. It is not historical reality itself but the present signs of the historian that limit and order the historical narrative (just as, conversely, the historical narrative limits and orders them). Almost all historians acknowledge this implicitly in the act of placing their notes—sources, evidence—at the foot of the page. The division of the historiographical page is a testimony to the discontinuity between past "reality" and the historical narrative. (Gossman 1978, 32)

Hayden White argues that the supposed materiality and accessibility of historical contexts are a result of historians' skills in creating fictions. Historical documents are as opaque as literary texts, and the world to which those documents refer is not more accessible. White also emphasizes the fact that historiography uses techniques similar to those used by literary fiction:

> The events are made into a story by the suppression or subordination of certain of them and the highlighting of others, by characterization, motific repetition, variation of tone and point of view, alternative descriptive strategies, and the like—in short, all of the techniques that we would normally expect to find in the emplotment of a novel or a play. For example, no historical event is intrinsically tragic; it can only be conceived as such from a particular point of view or from within the context of a structured set of events of which it is an element enjoying a privileged place. For in history what is tragic from one perspective is comic from another. . . . Considered as potential elements of a story, historical events are value-neutral. Whether they find their place finally in a story that is tragic, comic, romantic or ironic . . . depends upon the historian's decision to configure them according to the imperatives of one plot-structure or mythos rather than another. (White 1978, 47)

According to White, "historians *constitute* their subjects as possible objects of narrative representation by the very language they use to *describe* them" (White 1978, 57, original emphasis). Consequently, he deflates the distinction between history and fiction: "Of course, it is a fiction of the historian that the various states of affairs that he constitutes as the beginning, the middle, and the end of a course of development are all 'actual' or 'real' and that he is merely recording 'what happened' in the transition from the inaugural to the terminal phase. But both the beginning state of affairs and the ending one are inevitable poetic constructions, and as such are dependent upon the modality of the figurative language used to give them the appearance of coherence" (White 1978, 60).

It is worth noting how literary theory, philosophy of history, and contemporary Spanish American fiction coincide in their view of historiography as narrative discourse. One could read historiographic texts and chronicles of discovery and conquest as "discourses of power" as defined by Michel Foucault; that is to say, as a productive network of knowledge regarding, in this case, the indigenous American space and Other (*Microfísica*). Therefore, contemporary Spanish American novels can be read as "strategies of resistance": "They are an opposition to the effects of power which are linked with knowledge, competence, and qualification: struggles against the privileges of knowledge. But they are also an opposition against secrecy, deformation, and mystifying representations imposed on people" (Foucault 1984, 420).

Functioning as "strategies of resistance," contemporary historical novels oppose discourses of power through the construction of multiple, marginal, ironic, and parodic voices. The novels contradict the (hi)stories narrated in diaries and chronicles—supposedly their own literary origins—and, at the same time, the characters contradict their parents or, when orphaned, ignore their origins.

Notes

1. Some of the Spanish American historical novels about the Iberian discovery and conquest of the Americas published in the last thirty years are: Miguel Angel Asturias's *Maladrón* (Guatemala, 1969); Carlos Fuentes's *Terra nostra* (Mexico, 1975); Abel Posse's *Daimón* (Argentina, 1978); Alejo Carpentier's *El arpa y la sombra* (Cuba, 1979); Antonio Benítez Rojo's *El mar de las lentejas* (Cuba, 1979); Miguel Otero Silva's *Lope de Aguirre, príncipe de la libertad* (Venezuela, 1979); Alejandro Paternain's *Crónica del descubrimiento* (Uruguay, 1980); Libertad Demitrópulos's *Río de las congojas* (Argentina, 1981); Juan José Saer's *El entenado* (Argentina, 1983); Abel Posse's *Los perros del paraíso* (Argentina, 1983); Jorge Ernesto Funes's *Una lanza por Lope de Aguirre* (Argentina, 1984); Homero Aridjis's *Memorias del Nuevo Mundo* (Mexico, 1988); Napoleón Baccino Ponce de León's *Maluco* (Uruguay, 1990); Alicia Freilich's *Colombina descubierta* (Venezuela, 1991); Augusto Roa Bastos's *Vigilia del Almirante* (Paraguay, 1992); and Abel Posse's *El largo atardecer del caminante* (Argentina, 1992).

2. I am adopting Jean-François Lyotard's conception of postmodernism as a crisis of the legitimation of knowledge that implies an "incredulity toward metanarratives" (Lyotard 1984, xxiv), as well as Stanley Aronowitz's definition: "the shift in sensibility Nietzsche announced about a century ago has finally arrived. Postmodernism, the name given to this shift, is marked by the renunciation of foundational thought; of rules governing art; and of the ideological 'master discourses' " (Aronowitz 1987/88, 99).

3. One of its main characteristics was the idealization of the indigenous people, which was a result of the influence of Rousseau's ideas as well as Voltaire's and Chateaubriand's novels—especially *Atala*—and the need to assert a non-Spanish past in the Americas (Melendez 1961).

4. Often the protagonists are simple soldiers or, for example, a deckhand in *El entenado,* a jester in *Maluco,* and a poor old woman in *Colombina descubierta.*

5. Regarding the overwhelming presence of Jewish characters in many of the novels, Fernando Reati points out, in an excellent article, the literary echo of Salvador Madariaga's theory—proposed in his *El muy magnífico Señor Don Cristobal Colón*—according to which Columbus descended from a Genoese Jewish family:

> For Madariaga, as well as for other historians and writers who pay attention to Jewish participation in the conquest of the Americas, 1492 constituted a phenomenon of complex consequences because, although it is true that on the one hand it resulted in the exploitation and slavery of native Americans, on the other, it made it possible for European marginal groups such as converted Moors and Jews to search for new opportunities in lands far away from persecution. [Although, as Reati admits later, it did not take the Inquisition too long to establish itself in the Americas, because it looked with suspicion at all those "new Christians" who had became part of the conquest]. That is why the Jewish presence in the Spanish enterprise becomes an important topic in several novels about the conquest such as Abel Posse's *Daimón* (1978), Antonio Benítez Rojo's *El mar de las lentejas* (1979) and Napoleón Baccino Ponce de León's *Maluco* (1990). Two other texts, Carpentier's *El arpa y la sombra* (1979) and Abel Posse's *Los perros del paraíso* (1983), agree with Salvador Madariaga when they portray Columbus as a descendant of converted Jews and, therefore, as belonging to one of the antihegemonic and marginal groups of the European society of the time. (Reati 1996, 82)

6. Although the novels are not narrated from an indigenous first-person point of view, the vision of the vanquished regarding the conquest, the Spaniards, and Christianity is present in most of the mentioned texts.

7. For Bakhtin, the novel is constituted as "heteroglossia" through the incorporation of different genres and languages: tales, songs, poems, dramas, confessions, diaries, travel journals, biographies, and letters, as well as rhetoric, colloquial, academic, and religious languages.

8. According to Bakhtin, carnivalesque and parodic elements are characteristic of Menippean satire.

9. For example, *El arpa y la sombra* and *Los perros del paraíso* fictionalize biographical aspects of historical figures such as Columbus, Pope Pious IX, King Ferdinand, and Queen Isabella. *El entenado* is a fictionalized memoir of a historical but marginal figure, whereas *Maluco* is an autobiographical account of a fictive character placed in an accurate historical context.

Bibliography

Aronowitz, Stanley. 1987/88. "Postmodernism and Politics." *Social Text: Theory, Culture, Ideology* 18 (winter): 99–115.

Baccino Ponce de León, Napoleón. 1990. *Maluco: La novela de los descubridores.* Barcelona: Seix Barral.

Bakhtin, M. M. 1981. *The Dialogic Imagination: Four Essays.* Edited by Michael Holquist. Translated by Caryl Emerson and Michael Holquist. Austin: Univiversity of Texas Press.

Carpentier, Alejo. 1985. *El arpa y la sombra.* 1979. La Habana: Letras cubanas.

Certeau, Michel de. 1986. *Heterologies: Discourse on the Other.* Translated by Brian Massumi. *Theory and History of Literature* 17. Minneapolis: University of Minnesota Press.

———. 1988. *The Writing of History.* Translated by Tom Conley. New York: Columbia University Press.

Durán, Manuel. 1984. "Notas sobre la imaginación histórica y la narrativa hispanoamericana." In *Historia y ficción,* edited by Roberto González Echevarría, 287–96.

Eco, Umberto. 1984. *Postscript to "The Name of the Rose."* Edited and translated by William Weaver. San Diego: Harcourt Brace Jovanovich.

Foucault, Michel. 1980. *Microfísica del poder.* Edited and translated by Julia Varela and Fernando Alvarez-Uría. Madrid: Ediciones de La Piqueta.

———. 1984. "The Subject and Power." In *Art after Modernism,* edited by Tucker and Wallis, 417–32. New York: Museum of Contemporary Art.

Freilich, Alicia. 1991. *Colombina descubierta.* Caracas: Planeta.

Funes, Jorge Ernesto. 1984. *Una lanza por Lope de Aguirre.* Buenos Aires: Funes.

González Echevarría, Roberto. 1984. "Prólogo." In *Historia y ficción en la narrativa hispanoamericana: Coloquio de Yale,* edited by Roberto González Echevarría, 9–13. Caracas: Monte Avila Editores.

———. 1988. "Colón, Carpentier y los orígenes de la ficción latinoamericana." *La torre* 2, no. 7 (July-September): 439–52.

———, ed. Prólogo. 1984. *Historia y ficción en la narrativa hispanoamericana. Coloquio de Yale.* Caracas: Monte Avila Editores. 9–13.

Gossman, Lionel. 1978. "History and Literary Reproduction or Signification." In *The Writing of History: Literary Form and Historical Understanding,* edited by R. Canary and H. Kozicki, 3–39. Madison: University of Wisconsin Press.

Guillén, Claudio. 1971. "Toward a Definition of the Picaresque." In *Literature as System: Essays toward the Theory of Literary History,* 71–106. Princeton: Princeton University Press.

Hutcheon, Linda. 1990. *A Poetics of Postmodernism: History, Theory, Fiction.* Cambridge: Routledge.

Lévi-Strauss, Claude. 1964. *El pensamiento salvaje.* Translated by Francisco González Aramburo. Mexico: Fondo de Cultura Económica.

Luckács, Georg. 1962. *The Historical Novel.* Translated by Hannah and Stanley Mitchell. London: Merlin.

Lyotard, Jean-François. 1984. *The Postmodern Condition: A Report on Knowledge.* Translated by Geoff Bennington and Brian Massumi. Minneapolis: University of Minneapolis Press.

Melendez, Concha. 1961. *La novela indianista en Hispanoamerica (1832–1889).* Puerto Rico: Ediciones de la Universidad de Puerto Rico.

Menton, Seymour. 1989. "La novela histórica en la última década." *El pez y la serpiente* 28 (winter): 203–06.

———. 1993. *Latin America's New Hisotrical Novel.* Austin: University of Texas Press.

Murena, H. A. 1965. *El pecado original de América.* Buenos Aires: Sudamericana.

Nietzsche, Friedrich. 1986. *The Use and Abuse of History.* Translated by Adrian Collins. New York: Macmillan.

Otero Silva, Miguel. 1979. *Lope de Aguirre, príncipe de la libertad.* Barcelona: Seix Barral.

Paz, Octavio. 1961. *The Labyrinth of Solitude.* Translated by Lysander Kemp. New York: Grove Press.

Plotnik, Viviana. 1992. *La reescritura del descubrimiento de América en cuatro novelas hispanoamericanas contemporáneas: Intertextualidad, carnaval y espectáculo.* Ann Arbor: UMI Dissertation Services.

Posse, Abel. 1981. *Daimón.* Barcelona: Argos Vergara.

———. 1983. *Los perros del paraíso.* Barcelona: Argos Vergara.

Pupo-Walker, Enrique. 1982. *La vocación literaria del pensamiento histórico en América.* Madrid: Gredos.

———. 1984. "Primeras imágenes de América: notas para una lectura más fiel de nuestra historia." In *Historia y ficción,* edited by Roberto González Echevarría, 85–103.

———, Reati, Fernando. 1996. "Cristóbal Colón y el descentramiento del sujeto histórico: *Colombina descubierta,* de Alicia Freilich." *Escritura y desafío. Narradoras venezolanas del siglo XX.* Ed. Edith Dimo and A. Hidalgo de Jesús. Caracas: Monte Avila. 81–93.

Saer, Juan José. 1983. *El entenado.* Mexico: Folios Ediciones.

Vidal, Hernán. 1985. *Socio-historia de la literatura colonial hispanoamericana: Tres lecturas orgánicas.* Minneapolis: Institute for the Study of Ideologies and Literatures.

White, Hayden. 1978. "The Historical Text as Literary Artifact." In *The Writing of History: Literary Form and Historical Understanding,* edited by R. Canary and H. Kozicki, 41–62. Madison: University of Wisconsin Press.

Wicks, Ulrich. 1989. *Picaresque Narrative, Picaresque Fictions: A Theory and Research Guide.* Westport, CT: Greenwood Press.

Toward a New History: Twentieth-Century Debates in Mexico on Narrating the National Past

VICTORIA E. CAMPOS

I. A Return to the Chronicle in Late-Twentieth-Century Mexico

Since the 1960s, Latin American novels dealing with the period of Columbian exploration and conquest have proliferated to such an extent[1] that their numbers might lead us to suspect that they are the result of the 1992 quincentenary commemorating what was, until recently, referred to as the "discovery."[2] Yet violently disbanded student demonstrations in 1968 and a series of debates that took place in Mexico in the mid- and late-twentieth century lead us to a different hypothesis vis-à-vis the Mexican context.

On 2 October 1968, 200,000 university students, professors, members of leftist organizations, and sympathetic citizens assembled at the Plaza de las Tres Culturas in Mexico City to demand that the government ease restrictions on freedom of speech and open up the political process. The government of President Gustavo Díaz Ordaz (1964–1970) responded by sending troops into Tlatelolco Plaza, whereupon 3,500 protesters were jailed and over 300 participants shot (Poniatowska 1980, 62). Although Mexicans appeared to quickly forget the events,[3] Mempo Giardinelli argues that Mexican literature in the 1970s and 1980s bears a seal, "an ethical-aesthetic mark" (Borsó 1991, 67–68), particular to the generation that emerged from the events of 1968. Politically charged, the individuals who demonstrated and witnessed the government's brutal repression began to define their difference (both at the narrative and ideological levels) from those Mexicans whom many had long revered as the nation's cultural elite or, just simply, "the untouchables" (Navarro 1968, 140). A significant change—a "watershed in Mexican history" (Borsó 1991, 66)—appeared to have taken place. While it is debatable whether the new cultural vanguard's efforts to distance itself from more conservative Mexicans has altered the tenor of

Mexican politics, its efforts to use history to address and reconfigure the present has indelibly transformed Mexican cultural production.

One of the most notable changes evident in post-1968 Mexican narrative is a return to the national past. Most historical novels recently published in Mexico have fictionalized the country's immediate past (Molina 1993, 58). The rationale for doing so, argues the Mexican novelist Silvia Molina, has been to create "a contemporary chronicle of Mexico." Although the historical context and protagonists vary among these works, many of these writers of historical fiction coincide in their assessment of the story they want to chronicle: the deceit they suspect has been "systematically" (Paso 1982, 319) perpetuated in official histories.

Mexican novelists like Fernando del Paso, Carmen Boullosa, and Homero Aridjis, who take the remote past as their point of reference, do not differ so much in their own narrative approach. They, too, make their immediate present and the contemporary Mexican social and political reality central in defining their assessment of and mode of representing a more distant historical time. Whereas David Martín del Campo, for example, chooses to dramatize social reforms initiated at the beginning of the twentieth century and Aridjis deals with the early-sixteenth-century Hispanic foundation of Mexico, both express a fundamental dissatisfaction with existing historical representations and the institutions that have sponsored them.[4] These writers' concerns parallel the late-twentieth-century Mexican ethos typified in both Del Paso's now-famous invocation to assault "the official version of the past" (Paso 1982, 319) and Héctor Aguilar Camín's earlier arguments in favor of "rethinking a past whose former versions appear altogether insufficient" (Pereyra et al 1980, 158).

Two imperatives guide late-twentieth-century Mexican historical fiction: the critical revision of former representations of the Mexican past and a presentist sensibility. When writers such as Homero Aridjis return to historical documents, it is so that they may "reorder" those narratives and readers' understanding of Mexico and the present. The literary end product of this historical and creative revision is what we have referred to here as the "historical novel" and what Seymour Menton has called the "new historical novel." These terms, however, make some Mexican writers feel uneasy (Lara Zavala 1995, 180). Instead, literary critics and Mexican novelists have preferred to compare writers' recent narrative production in Mexico to the chronicle. Ursula Kuhlmann writes that what has given these texts a closer formalistic resemblance to the chronicle has been Mexican contemporary writers' decision to move their work away from the novelistic genre in order to bring it closer to the testimonial one (Kuhlmann 1989, 204).

Late-twentieth-century historical novels in Mexico have been called by many terms, such as "chronicles," "literature-testimony," "testimonial novels," and "*crononovelas*."[5] These expressions are not incompatible. Both in the contemporary and Spanish American colonial contexts, the chronicle as well as the testimonial recount the past from the point of view of the narrator's direct experience or contact with eyewitnesses, thus lending the narratives a privileged perspective vis-à-vis the credibility or "truthfulness" of the account given. Moreover, these narrators—again, both contemporary and colonial—engage in dialogue with other perspectives of authority both to imitate the "master text's" discursive form and to "correct the record, giving a truer *relación*."[6] Contemporary writers' and critics' predisposition to call the new narrative style in Mexico the "chronicle" immediately puts the new novels in relationship to the Spanish American chronicles of the Indies.

Using a discourse that follows the Renaissance dialectical form of legal writing (González Echevarría 1987a, 108), early Spanish American chronicles imitated the *relación*,[7] whose function, writes Roberto González Echevarría, was to serve "as a textual link with the source of power," that is, with the Spanish state or, more to the point, the Spanish crown (González Echevarría 1987a, 110–11). According to Walter Mignolo, it was not "the divine word nor . . . the words of the wise man" that in the sixteenth and seventeenth centuries guaranteed the validity of the chronicler's or historiographer's epistemological claims; rather, it was those individuals and institutions collectively protecting the dominance of social ideas regarding ethics, or "*el bien vivir*," that ratified the truth of an account. A text's authoritative claims, in other words, rested on "the word of power" (Mignolo 1981, 370).

The same year (1980) that the Mexican cultural critic Carlos Monsiváis helped launch a debate in Mexico about the social uses of history, he also published a study about the chronicle in Mexico, *A ustedes les consta: Antología de la crónica en México*. In his introduction, Monsiváis recounts the history of this narrative genre, highlighting in each of the genre's phases both the chronicle's custodian and the aims of the chronicler's discourse. In the case of the Spanish *crónicas de Indias*, for example, Monsiváis notes that this historiographic tool allowed the conqueror to voice his perspective, and the missionary to interpret public deeds.[8] Even though the writing of the chronicle changed hands in the nineteenth century from the conqueror and missionary to the man of letters, Monsiváis notes that the interpretative role still mostly fell to those individuals who represented the interests of the state, which, in its turn, safeguarded the interests of cultural and economic elites. Contemporary writers' adoption of the chronicle, therefore, appears paradoxical vis-à-vis their desire for narrative experimentation and sociopolitical reform. This late-twentieth-century return to the discursive forms of the colonial past and, in some cases, to the topic of the *novo-hispano* past itself lies in writers' frustrations with the unchanging, neocolonial state of Mexican society and politics.

Jorge Ruffinelli has argued that the contemporary chronicle genre in Mexico has mostly served to reveal society in the "historical process of constituting itself" (Ruffinelli 1987, 69). Novelists like Homero Aridjis and Carmen Boullosa have chosen to dramatize the process of narrative and political exclusion. Returning to Spanish American colonial documents, Aridjis, Boullosa, and others[9] collect historical material with which to retrospectively fictionalize the colonial past, but they also restructure the narrative by demonstrating how chroniclers used historiographic discourse to configure a present and a set of social relations convenient to themselves and the imperialist ambitions of the Spanish kings.[10] In their letters, chronicles, and *relaciones,* fifteenth-, sixteenth-, and seventeenth-century writers promised the king seamless, true, and therefore apparently complete accounts. Contemporary novelists magnify these seams, and from the edges of the grafted documentary fragments, late-twentieth-century writers animate figures both omitted from colonial writings and marginalized from the new Hispanic society.

According to Monsiváis, the point of the new narrative style in Mexico was to bring out the "demagoguery and paternalism" of such previously mysterious and powerful individuals as the conquistador, missionary, viceroy, Hispanic governing council (the *Cabildo*), and the inquisitor. The goal after 1968 was to liberate the writer from institutional obligations and pressures from public officials and their archive (Monsiváis 1980a, 68). Rejecting its use as a corroborator of elite perspectives and nationalist goals, writers including Monsiváis and Elena Poniatowska thus helped redefine the chronicle as a forum for criticism and others' historical recovery (Monsiváis 1980a, 28). In their critical rewriting of historical documents pertaining both to the public record and the populace's collective memory, Mexican writers of historical fiction have sought to decolonialize a genre that helped colonialize Mexican society.

The contemporary historical novel in Mexico is self-reflexive about its own mode of production. Its writers demythicize national heroes and nationalist representations and criticize structures of power, elite institutions, and authoritarian discourses. In a return to traditional strategies of storytelling,[11] these novelists seek to confront the present and reconfigure the future (Garramuño n.d.). Mexican writers' post-Tlatelolco return to former historical representations and their presentist revision of same strongly echo polemical changes that had taken place in Mexican historiography in the mid- and late-twentieth century. It is to these debates and the changes they provoked in historical narratives that we now turn.

II. The Debate of 1945: From Documentation to Interpretation

In 1945 and 1980, several groups of Mexican intellectuals engaged in public debates on the nature and aims of historical discourse. In both instances, scholars reconsidered existing representations of "reality," and instead of asking how a historian or artist might best mirror the nation and its past, these intellectuals sought to reveal who held the mirror and to what end. Directly linking social realities with cultural representations, these mid- and late-twentieth-century writers pointed to the tangible abuses wrought by former historical documents. These two generations argued that there was a clear cause-and-effect relationship between Mexicans' relative absence from historical writings and the sociopolitically marginalized condition of the nation vis-à-vis Europe, and of the majority of Mexicans vis-à-vis the elites. This "coincidence" provoked these intellectuals to conclude that histories had been written with those very political ends in mind: "to put aside," to keep out, to disempower. Revealing the political abuses that they argued were present in canonical histories (or the archive), these mid- to late-twentieth-century writers of history redefined their goals as scholars and public intellectuals: they sought to study the historical processes that on a social and narrative level had created cultural boundaries and political exclusions. Because they believed that they themselves had also been marginalized, these intellectuals sought to different degrees to produce versions of the national past that would legitimize alternative cultural and political routes in the present.

Discussions that began as an inquiry about the nature of history thus turned into a consideration of the abuses and uses of historical narration. For Edmundo O'Gorman in 1945, as well as for José Joaquín Blanco in 1980, the question about the social function of history turned on the conviction that Mexican historical memory and twentieth-century Mexican society itself were structures that were still fundamentally colonialized.

Starting in the mid-1930s, Mexican academic institutions made some fundamental changes in the way they organized the study of history.[12] Turning to the writings of Oswald Spengler, Ortega y Gasset, Max Scheler, William Dilthey, Martin Heidegger, Karl Marx, and others, historians in Mexico began to define history in relation to their immediate circumstances. Historiography, argued the Mexican historian Edmundo O'Gorman, involved a sustained reference to the present, "or what is the same, reference to our life, which is for us the radical truth" (Matute 1974, 36). Along with his colleagues and teachers who had newly arrived from Civil War and post-Civil War Spain, O'Gorman represented a new generation of intellectuals in Mexico whose new approach to history was meant to confront Europe's anti-New World bias.

This new group of scholars argued that Europeans and Spanish American *criollos* had de-centered New Spain (colonial Mexico) through their historical representations and allegations about the Indies' "newness," or historical vacuum. To many mid-century intellectuals in Mexico, the continent's identity appeared to be inextricably entangled in Europe's traditions, aspirations, and ideas about history, historicity, and cultural unity. America, said O'Gorman, was animated from without; in using colonialism as its means of passage to universal authority, Europe had led the Amerindian territories from historical specificity to historical and historiographical dependency. And now, argued the Mexican philosopher Leopoldo Zea (1988), it was time for Mexican intellectuals to assume responsibility for their past by narrating it themselves (Villegas 1960, 142).

Intellectuals during this time spoke about history as a social instrument; allegedly deployed to realize political ends, history, they argued, had been used as a tool of colonialism. But just as this new generation of historians in Mexico argued that restricted access to historical representation had helped dominate Spanish America, it also held that by democratizing representation, history could become a tool of decolonialization. In essence, the changes these historians sought to enact in historical representation extended to themselves, as opposed to Europeans; theirs, in other words, was a democratization that made a bid for redistributing cultural authority from Europe to Mexico. Many now believed that the success of Mexico's future lay in "reclaiming" its past. The challenge facing these intellectuals, therefore, was how to reconfigure existing historical accounts and how to reassign meaning to the Mexican nation and culture.

Zea suggested that the solution lay in assuming control over the colonizer's language: "Uncivilized is not . . . the one who poorly speaks another language that is not his own," he wrote, "but rather the one who poorly utilizes his own language" (Zea 1988, 43). Zea, O'Gorman, Luis Villoro, the Spanish Civil War exiles Ramón Iglesia and José Gaos, and others addressed how intellectuals in Mexico approached representation. In particular, they examined the perspective that they claimed a traditionally trained historian identified as a professional ideal: objective analysis. Directly putting this goal into question, these new scholars challenged the belief that the past could be scientifically assessed and reported. Instead, they argued that historical representation was essentially subjective. Their claim was significant not so much because it augured a new direction in historical analysis, but because this proposition enabled this new generation of intellectuals to reject the notion that former (i.e., colonialist) representations of Mexico contained objective and hence irrefutable historical "truths."

Challenging the credibility of the historiographic techniques others had used to support their documentary claims, these new intellectuals in Mexico set about defining a methodology that they themselves saw as more akin to literature than "history." This group began blurring the distinctions between the two genres by asserting that just as a scholar interpreted a work of fiction, so too did a historian interpret the past.[13] It was, they asserted, a historian's preferences and not any intrinsic or natural characteristic that magnified the importance of an event; it was a historian, finally, who glossed some moment in the past as significant, "historical," and "true."[14] O'Gorman argued that historical knowledge was the product of subjective discrimination, and that as such, history could not be seen as the "accumulation" (Matute 1974, 38) of discovered facts, but rather as a "narrative method" involving selection, exclusion, reordering, and recasting of the diverse parts into a whole. Historical "truth," therefore, was as multiple as the authors who historicized—that is, narrated—the past.

The relativist philosophy that sustained many of this generation's ideas about history provoked the debate of 1945. At a conference dedicated to discussions about the techniques for teaching history, Edmundo O'Gorman and Silvio Zavala deliberated about the nature of their discipline and their role within it. Representing the positivist school of thought, Zavala defended positivist historians' belief in truth and textual authority, maintaining that historical studies were important in and of themselves. A document, Zavala stated, could lead a student and historian to ascertain universal truths about the past; a document, in other words, had a value in itself. But in practical terms, Zavala argued that historical documents were irrelevant; that is to say, historical representations were incapable of influencing social change. O'Gorman refuted these claims.

Reflecting his relativist orientation, O'Gorman argued that truth only existed in the historian who endowed a document with significance; information documented as "truth," therefore, was a construct of the historian's interpretative skills and narrative tactics. And far from reposing in a museum, historical representations, argued O'Gorman, determined society to the extent that they functioned as a mechanism of political control.

The questions raised by these two historians led to a second debate a month later. This time, the topic more specifically targeted the question of objectivity, or "historical truth." Zavala's colleague Rafael Altamira (1866–1952), expressed a concern about the effects of the new relativist tendencies in Mexican historiography; he proposed that the new representational approach threatened to displace the emphasis from the historical subject to the historians themselves (Matute 1974, 41). Yet undeniably, and in spite of the new generation's interests in debunking colonialist representations of Mexico, the relativist philosophy offered these intellectuals the opportunity to lend themselves greater authority as the new interpreters and narrators of the national past and national identity.

Determined to make Mexicans as much the producers of cultural icons as Europeans themselves, these new scholars sought to lead readers back into the nation, and colonial Mexico became one of the most active sites of intellectual interest.[15] Seeking to extricate themselves from Europe's colonial and colonialist portrayals of Mexico's past, intellectuals in the 1940s and '50s thus began to produce new narratives about that past. Their aim was to return to former documents in order to rewrite narrative structures whose writers' (and patrons') power had hinged on presuming an absolute authority as much over historical analysis as over political governance.

In 1945, relativistically oriented historians such as Edmundo O'Gorman and Leopoldo Zea broke with the idea that Mexico was a primitive, or "precultural" society, and that as such, it depended on Europe for its historical content. In 1968, a new generation of intellectuals in Mexico initiated their own polemical reorientation of historical narrative. Transforming the narrated past into a site for addressing the present, these writers sought to redefine history for a specific political end: as a means of redistributing social and political power to the margins of Mexican society.

III. The Events of 1968: Defining a New Historical Beginning

In Mexico, several events in 1968 mobilized as many as 600,000 Mexicans.[16] From June to November, the government restricted and sometimes completely obstructed protests that students organized. With regard to the demonstrators' petitions for the release of political and student prisoners, the abolition of the "crime of social disruption" (*delito de disolución social)*, and so on, President Díaz Ordaz expressed indifference and later an impassive amnesia about the effects of the soldier patrols' homicidal brutality at Tlatelolco Plaza on 2 October: "Which dead, which October 2, which night of Tlatelolco?"[17]

These troubling phenomena precipitated some "transformations" in Mexican society: solidarity among the working and middle classes, the public airing of grievances despite a penal code regarding "offense of principals" (*delito de opinión*), and the emerging visibility of the underprivileged of Mexico. Frustrated by the absence of many democratic liberties and the desperate and stagnant condition of the country's poor, some demonstrators and sympathizers also began to scrutinize the institutions, structures, middle-class morality, class divisions, and repressive biases that regulated Mexican society (Klahn 1989, 926; Aguilar et al. 1985, 134). In particular, intellectuals examined concepts that had come to seem fundamental to Mexicans' identity.

Carlos Monsiváis, Guillermo Bonfil Batalla, Enrique Florescano, and others assessed such notions as "high culture," "national unity," "national progress," and "national identity" as strategic concepts that appeared to have conserved a nationalistic representation of one Mexico in gross contrast to what they perceived to be the country's fragmented and pluralistic reality. Rather than viewing the country as an entity held together by common values, Monsiváis, for example, described Mexico as a nation "walled in" by hegemonic ideals that reflected the elite minority's assessment of its unique economic and political circumstances but that completely failed to comprehend or address the disenfranchised majority of the Mexican population (Monsiváis 1980b, 35). Along with Octavio Paz, these critics argued that Mexico's privileged minorities had not only deployed all of their resources to disseminate the positive value and patriotic good of these "national" ideals, but that simultaneously they had also represented themselves as the defenders of those ideals. After 1968, many in Mexico's intelligentsia considered these carefully structured images to have served only one purpose: to pacify the populace's discontent.

Many writers after 1968 viewed the production of historical narratives as a reflection of the way Mexican society itself had been constructed. Thus, in their own historical narratives, they explored the parallels between historiographic omissions and the creation of socially marginalized groups. These intellectuals, in other words, saw a similarity between the imperceptibility of narrative gaps (i.e., the historically forgotten) and the cultural preeminence of national elites vis-à-vis the exotic strangeness of those on the cultural and political margins. Resolved to do more than dismantle traditional narrative structures as their older contemporaries had done, these "post-Tlatelolco" writers sought to use the writing of history as a mode of critique capable of both demythifying propagandistic images and dismantling Mexico's restrictive social structures.

José Joaquín Blanco and his 1968 contemporaries argued that criticism of the status quo and a critical history could potentially provide an "escape route" from the kind of colonialist oppression they observed in late-twentieth-century Mexico (Pereyra et al. 1980, 80). Quite clearly, this generation's reference to "colonialism" had a different meaning from its predecessor's usage in 1945. Whereas intellectuals in mid-twentieth-century Mexico claimed that their cultural antagonist was Europe, the generation that coalesced after events in 1968 identified as its nemesis Mexican national elites and the nationalist government. In order to define their critical narrative style, writers after 1968 examined national histories and national "myths" written after the 1910 Revolution. The triumphant representations of postrevolution Mexico that they examined appeared to subsume the reality of Mexico's divisions and diversity within a nationalistic portrait of Mexican unity. For Monsiváis, the Mexico described by the country's official chroniclers was a "fictional nation imposed from above by a few" (Monsiváis 1980c, 12). Challenging these deliberate misrepresentations, these newly oriented intellectuals introduced a "tone of denunciation" into their narrative reconfigurations of the national past.[18]

Considered by some critics to be "neorealist" writers (Klahn 1989, 927), this new generation produced "hybrid texts" (Duncan 1986, 9) that mixed traditionally distinct narrative categories such as history and fiction. This heterogeneous approach to representation not only underscored the narrative texture of "reality," it also made the work's—and by analogy, the nation's—interpretative "unity" impossible.[19] With regard to former representations of Mexican reality that seemed to transform all of Mexico into "an infinite fiction,"[20] writers sought to produce multigeneric works that would reflect the process that allegedly had guided the construction of disingenuous nationalistic ideals and images—works, in other words, that would be both "history and novel" (Paso 1982, 321).

Pledging history to serve the present, writers such as Blanco, José Emilio Pacheco, Héctor Aguilar Camín, and others sought to break the country's nationalistic ties to the revolution in order to facilitate a new politics and a new history. Carlos Monsiváis suggested that the notion intellectuals needed to challenge was one that held that a national history was grounded in one foundational origin or event, as, for example, the 1910 Revolution in Mexico. Monsiváis proposed substituting instead a Foucauldian concept that placed the legitimacy of a nation on one whose history reflected new foundations, and thus new historical beginnings.[21]

The 1968 student protest movement gave participants the sense that they could influence two jealously guarded arenas: Mexican culture and politics. On the one hand, protesters challenged the present relevance of the 1910 Revolution and of the PRI (Institutional Revolutionary Party), which based its political legitimacy on that era and its social ideals. This new generation, moreover, examined the process of historical production; seeking to do more than learn from the past, these individuals focused attention on the writing of history itself.

Writers like Elena Poniatowska sought to inaugurate actual social change through their reconfigured narratives of Mexican society. It is possibly too early to determine the political success that these literary works may have had in Mexican society, but what is clear is that the events of 1968 greatly influenced the nature of Mexican historical narrative: "there was in Mexico, because of 1968, a sort of cultural revolution because more than a political revolution, '68 was . . . a change in the form . . . of making history. . . . The true cultural significance is carried out in the historical reconstruction of the past and of the present in Mexico" (Poniatowska 1986, 204). Echoing their older contemporaries, these writers turned to documents to explain the origins of the nation in which they lived. What these younger Mexicans claimed to see daily was a Mexico divided. They spoke, on the one hand, about a country that was visible and whose constituents were enfranchised, and yet they also referred to the "other Mexico" (Paz 1987, 108),[22] one containing the "poor and miserable," who had been suppressed and hidden.

Those writers who identified themselves with the ethos sparked by the 1968 student movement sought to reconfigure dominant discourse to make the absent present. The Marxist Mexican historian Adolfo Sánchez Vázquez had earlier argued that a writer could use history "intentionally" (333) to transform the disenfranchised into "cultural beings." Octavio Paz and others argued that Mexican elites had denied the country's marginalized sectors any historicity; consequently, reasoned this "new" generation, access to historical representation signified access to the nation.

After 1968, some Mexican intellectuals like Monsiváis, Pacheco, Poniatowska, and Blanco sought to make political elites responsible for the effect of their policies and their indifference. One of the ways they believed it was possible to make the upper classes accountable was to make the repressed, subterranean Mexico discernible in Mexican life and legible in their rewritings of Mexican history. In the new narratives that emerged, the focus thus moved from the known and visible (or touristic) to those sectors of Mexican society for which officials had neither historiographically nor politically accounted.[23] The goal of writing, therefore, became more explicit: post-1968 writers committed themselves to documenting traces of the absent and elucidating the very process of erasure; by doing so, they hoped to recover figures exiled from other pages in others' histories of the Mexican past.

The events of 1968 had politicized a mostly middle-class sector of Mexico's population, which, in turn, sought to reconstitute the margins by politicizing the periphery and its diverse constituents. This generation's activism did not give rise to the debate of 1980; instead, the cause of the polemic involved these Mexicans' politicization of historical inquiry and historical narration.

IV. The Debate of 1980: Polemicizing the Ends of History

The Mexican publisher Siglo XXI[24] compiled an anthology of essays in 1980 by a group of Mexican scholars and critics considering "the purpose of historical scholarship" (Pereyra et al. 1980, 11). In the collection *Historia, ¿Para qué?,* the fundamental issue at hand was defining the value and social utility of history. With the exception of Luis González, the other nine contributors revealed a striking consensus, arguing that history served a pragmatic purpose. All of them (Carlos Pereyra, Luis Villoro, Héctor Aguilar Camín, Arnaldo Córdova, José Joaquín Blanco, Enrique Florescano, Adolfo Gilly, Guillermo Bonfil Batalla, and Carlos Monsiváis) claimed that history was relevant insofar as it corresponded to present interests, and some (Pereyra, Villoro, Blanco, Florescano, Gilly, and Bonfil Batalla) asserted that the genre had the power—and the historian, the obligation—to enhance an individual's sense of political efficacy, "of social dominion" (Pereyra et al. 1980, 26; Florescano in Pereyra et al. 1980, 115). The other uses these intellectuals specified underscored their conviction that contemporary historiography (and contemporary historical narrative) carried out important political ends: it put into question "ritualized versions of the past" (Pereyra et al. 1980, 24, 28), and it was a means of transforming society, participating in politics, defending social causes, and denouncing oppressive falsehoods, such as those found in "egregious myths" and "sacred texts distributed by the system" (Blanco in Pereyra et al. 1980, 78, 83). History, these writers argued, was a genre that, after 1968, had to provide a detailed understanding of oppression and the oppressed, give an explanation of myths and the reality these veiled, describe the emergence of the mentality that had resulted from exploitation and repression, and define the "margins of liberty" in which people lived (Monsiváis in Pereyra et al. 1980, 188).

Three years after the events of 1968, Carlos Fuentes wrote that it was up to the left to "seize" from the dominant classes the course of the development of civil society.[25] In this anthology, many of the essayists identified history as a means of activating social and historical change, and thus as a way of influencing society's development. Fundamentally, the transformations they prescribed for Mexico aimed at using history as a primary tool for interested historical recovery.

Also involved with the anthology, Luis González criticized the kind of revisionist historical methods his colleagues advocated in their essays. González suggested that his contemporaries' critical study of the past was motivated more by a pleasure in discovering the vile motives that allegedly underpinned capitalist institutions than by an interest in simply recording events (Pereyra et al. 1980, 62). Echoing some of the very same issues that had sparked the debate between Silvio Zavala and Edmundo O'Gorman in 1945, Enrique Krauze took González's criticisms further.

Krauze's critical review of the 1980 anthology appeared in *Uno más uno,* a newspaper whose assistant general director, Héctor Aguilar Camín, was one of the contributors whose essay Krauze particularly criticized. Krauze argued that by relativizing the objective historical truths to be had from historical texts, writers like Florescano, Córdova, Gilly, and Camín had confused "political militancy" with "the scientific vocation" of history (Krauze 1981a, 3–4). Like González, Krauze rejected the notion that history should have any pragmatic utility. Indeed, Krauze's adamant defense of traditional historiographic structures seemed to confirm the arguments that both mid- and late-twentieth-century relativist and politically oriented intellectuals made about the abuses achievable through such discourses of authority as history. In language reminiscent of reactionary nationalist rhetoric, Krauze presented himself as a "defender of *laws* of the past" (Krauze 1981a, my emphasis). Against historians who were arguing that history was not linear but fragmented, and not a reservoir of monolithic origins but multiple beginnings, Krauze sought to characterize and criticize these critical historians as little different from their apparent antagonists, the ruling national elites. To

Krauze, 1968 intellectuals were "statists" and also hierarchical and moralistic "like all people of authority" (Krauze 1981a, 4).

Hopeful about the Mexican left but hostile to the "generation of 1968," Krauze faulted this group of intellectuals for their dogmatism, intolerance, and reductionism (Krauze 1981b, 38). Yet Krauze's greatest discomfort with this group of writers went far beyond their structural and antagonistic approach to the national past. Of the four twentieth-century generations Krauze described—the generations of 1915, 1929, 1950, and 1968, only the last group, he claimed, lacked the trace of the Mexican Revolution. It was not, Krauze suggested, an absence occasioned by some historical event, but rather the result of the 1968 "elite's" decision to erase this historical legacy, to "kill" it.

For Krauze and other Mexican writers like Octavio Paz and Carlos Fuentes, Mexico was synonymous with the revolution. In this regard, Krauze initiated a polemic that not only dealt with the potential uses of history, but that also centered on the role of the revolution as a point of departure for contemporary Mexican history.

Daniel Cosío Villegas writes that the revolution "created" intellectuals and then asked them to serve as artistic publicity agents for the country's revolutionary institutions (Monsiváis 1976, 332). If, as Monsiváis argues, the true utility of the Mexican intellectual after 1910 was to fulfil the function of "legitimizing the regime" (Monsiváis 1976, 307), then those writers who decided to define a new role for the intellectual and representation after the events of 1968 chose the opposite tactic—that of critique.

The student protests and the Tlatelolco massacre, argues Karl Kohut, were simply "the manifestation of the crisis of the Mexican Revolution" (Kohut 1991, 15). In the field of history, post-1968 innovations in historical interpretation and historiographic techniques announced the revolution's decline, or end. Whereas Krauze yearned to return to Mexico's liberal political legacy, these new intellectuals sought change. To that end, they replaced criticism for the kind of "tolerance" Krauze encouraged and the fatalistic and ambivalent attitudes about the revolution present in novelists like Mariano Azuela, Martín Luis Guzmán, Agustín Yáñez, Carlos Fuentes, and Fernando del Paso.[26] By so redefining their approach to representation, this new generation of Mexican writers sought to lay the ground for the beginning of another historical period in Mexican society.

V. Narrative Reconfigurations: From the Cyclical to the Linear

The historic events of 1968 in Mexico coincided with the decline of the boom that took place in Latin American literature as a result of the mass distribution of works by Julio Cortázar, Gabriel García Márquez, Guillermo Cabrera Infante, Alejo Carpentier, Mario Vargas Llosa, etc. (Sommer and Yúdice 1986, 205). Like their post-Boom contemporaries, the creative methods that Mexican writers began to define for their craft during these political events, intellectual debates, and shifts in literary influence, included a return to history and realism. Preferring to make the story the central element of their texts (rather than experimental structures or language) (González Echevarría 1987b, 249), writers moved their narratives toward the model of the "declaratory novel" (Shaw 1989, 93). Straightforward and lineal, these works sharply contrasted with the circular narratives that typified much of post-1910 Mexican literary production.

Carlos Fuentes described the "new Hispanic American novel" in 1969 as one whose circularity "doubts the relationship between history and progress" (Sommer and Yúdice 1986, 194). This structural characteristic parallels the determinism, passivity, or resignation that thematically dominates many of Mexico's twentieth-century literary classics, like Azuela's *Los de abajo* (1916), Guzmán's *La sombra del caudillo* (1929), Juan Rulfo's *Pedro Páramo* (1955), Fuentes's *La muerte de Artemio Cruz* (1962), and Elena Garro's *Los recuerdos del porvenir* (1963).[27] In these cynical works, the ideals of the past engage in battle with the gross reality of the author's time; it is the past, in other words, that controls the present. In post-1968 Mexican narrative, however, the "revindication of the historical order" (Lara Zavala 1995, 179) signals an attempt to reverse this pattern.

Just as relativist historians in 1945 sought to assume cultural control from Europeans, and post-1968 intellectuals sought to shift political control to the margins where they felt themselves to be, so, too, did postboom Mexican writers decide to take charge of the past. Mexican novelists' re-adoption of a linear development expresses a renewed faith in progress—in a history that moves forward, rather than repeating the disappointments and betrayals of the post-1910 revolutionary past.

González Echevarría has suggested that the major difference distinguishing boom and postboom literature is the construction of the argument; "it is a question," he writes, "of a difference in narrative discourse" (González Echevarría 1987a, 249–50). The two debates on history and the evolution of the contemporary Mexican historical novel, or chronicle, have both redefined the language writers use to describe and interpret national reality and the historical past. Analytical about their own process of narration and selectivity, these new texts show us the multilayered nature of Mexican society's historical foundations. No matter how remote or how "strange" a historical time or people may retrospectively appear to be, no foundation is impermeable and no death incapable of being literarily resuscitated. Writers in late-twentieth-century Mexico disrupt the mythical with its circular time and structure in favor of a linear narration that returns to the past in order to set it "straight," in order to emancipate the revolution-laden present onto a new historical trajectory.

NOTES

1. Some of the novels belonging to this genre include Carlos Fuentes's *Terra nostra* (1975), Miguel Otero Silva's *Lope de Aguirre, Príncipe de la libertad* (1975), Alejo Carpentier's *El arpa y la sombra* (1979), Antonio Benítez Rojo's *El mar de las lentejas* (1979), Eugenio Aguirre's *Gonzalo Guerrero* (1980), Alejandro Paternain's *Crónica del descubrimiento* (1980), Abel Posse's *Los perros del paraíso* (1983) and *El largo atardecer del caminante* (1992), Aridjis's *Memorias del Nuevo Mundo* (1988), Juan José Saer's *El entenado* (1988), Herminio Martínez's *Las puertas del mundo* (1992), and Augusto Roa Bastos's *Vigilia del Almirante* (1992).

2. Menton suggests that this designation changed in 1984 when the historian Miguel León-Portilla coined the term "*Encuentro de Dos Mundos*" (Menton 1993, 28).

3. Poniatowska writes that immediately after the massacre, many in Mexico continued their lives without protest as if nothing had taken place (Poniatowska 1980, 62).

4. The examples I am citing refer to David Martín del Campo's *Alas de ángel* and Homero Aridjis's *Memorias del Nuevo Mundo* (1988).

5. These terms appear, respectively, in Monsiváis 1980a; Poniatowska 1992, 116; and Lara Zavala 1995, 179. According to Lanin A. Gyurko, María Luisa Mendoza uses the term "*crononovela*" or "docunovel" to describe the "combination of chronicle and fiction" that makes up her 1968—inspired work, *Con él, conmigo, con nosotros tres* (Gyurko 1994, 270).

6. Roberto González Echevarría also refers to the seignorial and bureaucratic authority of legal and historiographic discourses as "the authority of the Archive" (González Echevarría 1987a, 129).

7. Walter Mignolo points out that in the sixteenth and seventeenth centuries, the chronicle, annal, and "even *relación*," were considered synonyms when referring to historiographic texts (Mignolo 1981, 380), although he does note that when individuals spoke of the chronicle at that time, they did so as a synonym of "history" (Mignolo 1982, 59).

8. Monsiváis discusses the missionaries' use of the chronicle in more detail (Monsiváis 1987, 756).

9. Other writers inlcude Armando Ayala Anguiano, *Hernán Cortés: Cómo conquisté a los aztecas,* Eugenio Aguirre, *Gonzalo Guerrero* (1980), and Herminio Martínez, *Diario maldito de Nuño de Guzmán* (1990).

10. We see this reconfiguration in Aridjis's *Memorias del Nuevo Mundo* and Carmen Boullosa's *Son vacas, somos puercos, filibusteros del mar Caribe* (1991).

11. I am indebted to Garramuño's meticulous bibliographic references regarding this trend in Latin American contemporary historical novels.

12. These changes were the direct result of the many Spanish Civil War exiles, who were repatriated to Mexico on the specific condition that they teach in Mexican educational centers. See Clara E. Lida 1988.

13. This idea comes directly from the German intellectual William Dilthey, whose works Mexican historians were avidly reading during this time. For a discussion of Dilthey's historiographic approach; see H. P. Rickman 1976.

14. "Las preferencias del historiador son las que comunican sentido pleno y significatividad a ciertos hechos que, por eso mismo, son efectivamente los más

importantes, los más históricos, y en definitiva los más verdaderos" (Edmundo O'Gorman, quoted in Matute 1974, 43).

15. Enrique Florescano notes that the most varied and numerous studies of the colonial period were carried out from 1940 to 1965 (Florescano 1967, 544).

16. Poniatowska writes that this number makes this march the largest in Mexico's history of political demonstrations (Poniatowska 1971, 16).

17. Gustavo Díaz Ordaz gave a press conference in 1977 on the occasion of being named Mexico's ambassador to Spain by President José López Portillo (Poniatowska 1980, 73).

18. John Brushwood points out that this critical tone characterizes much of post-1968 literary production in Mexico (Brushwood 1983, 95).

19. Sara Sefchovich writes that the idea was to "render literal and palpable the impossibility of reducing the literary work to one interpretation or judgment" (Sefchovich 1987, 212).

20. Christopher Domínguez Michael uses this term to describe Monisváis's perception of the nationalist descriptions Mexican elites disseminated among foreigners and the populace (Domínguez Michael 1991, 69).

21. For this, Monsiváis ("Pasión" 192) cited Michel Foucault who, in *The Archaeology of Knowledge,* argued that a new history no longer involved "tradition nor the tracing of a line" but rather "transformations that served like new foundations."

22. Although not belonging to this generation, Octavio Paz empathized with the student movement and contributed his influential voice to this generation's strong criticism of the government's actions during the 1968 Tlatelolco Plaza demonstration.

23. Poniatowska's work provides us ready examples of this new kind of literature: *Hasta no verte, Jesús mío* (1969), *La noche de Tlatelolco* (1971), and *Fuerte es el silencio* (1980).

24. It is interesting to note that the publishing house Siglo XXI was founded as a direct result of the Mexican government's restrictions on the freedom of the press in the 1960s and 1970s.

25. "[C]orresponde a las fuerzas políticas de izquierda . . . arrebatar a la clase dirigente el movimiento de la sociedad civil" (Fuentes 1971, 191).

26. Lanin A. Gyurko 1994 provides an excellent analysis of these writers' works.

27. I am indebted here to Gyurko's close study of these very elements in twentieth-century Mexican narrative.

Bibliography

Aguilar, Alonso, et al. 1985. *Cultura, historia y luchas del pueblo mexicano.* Mexico: Editorial Nuestro Tiempo.

Borsó, Vittoria. 1991. "El nuevo problema del realismo en la novela 'postlatelolco.'" In *Literatura mexicana hoy: Del 68 al ocaso de la revolución,* edited by Karl Kohut, 66–82. Frankfurt am Main: Vervuert Verlag.

Brushwood, John. 1983. "La novela mexicana (1967–1982): Los que siguieron narrando." *Symposium* 37, no. 2:91–105.

Domínguez Michael, Christopher. 1991. Introduction to *Antología de la narrativa mexicana del siglo XX.* Vol. 2. Mexico City: Fondo de Cultura Económica.

Duncan, J. Ann. 1986. *Voices, Visions, and a New Reality: Mexican Fiction Since 1970.* Pittsburgh: University of Pittsburgh Press.

Florescano, Enrique. 1967. "Notas sobre la producción histórica en México." *La Palabra y el Hombre* 43 (July-September): 525–47.

Fuentes, Carlos. 1971. *Tiempo mexicano.* Mexico City: Joaquín Mortiz.

Garramuño, Florencia. n.d. *Genealogías culturales: La reescritura en la novela contemporánea.* Buenos Aires. Forthcoming.

González Echevarría, Roberto. 1987a. "The Law of the Letter: Garcilaso's *Commentaries* and the Origins of the Latin American Narrative." *Yale Journal of Criticism* 1, no. 1: 107–31.

———. 1987b. *La ruta de Severo Sarduy.* Hanover, N.H.: Ediciones del Norte.

Gyurko, Lanin A. 1994. "Twentieth-Century Fiction." In *Mexican Literature: A History,* edited by David William Foster, 243–303. Austin: University of Texas Press.

Klahn, Norma. 1989. "Un nuevo verismo: Apuntes sobre la última novela mexicana." *Revista Iberoamericana* 55, no. 148–49: 925–35.

Kohut, Karl, ed. 1991. *Literatura mexicana hoy: Del 68 al ocaso de la revolución.* Frankfurt am Main: Vervuert Verlag.

Krauze, Enrique. 1981a. "Las caras de la historia." *Uno más uno,* 21 February, 2–5.

———. 1981b. "Cuatro estaciones de la cultura mexicana." *Vuelta* 60, no. 5: 27–42.

Kuhlmann, Ursula. 1989. "La crónica contempóranea en México: Apuntes para su análisis como praxis social." *Revista de crítica literaria latinoamericana* 15, no. 30: 199–208.

Lara Zavala, Hernán. 1995. "Algunas opciones de la novela en México." *Inti* 42:179–83.

Lida, Clara E. 1988. *La Casa de España en México.* Mexico City: El Colegio de México.

Matute, Alvaro. 1974. *La teoría de la historia en México (1940–1973).* Mexico City: Secretaría de Educación Pública.

Menton, Seymour. 1993. *Latin America's New Historical Novel.* Austin: University of Texas Press.

Mignolo, Walter. 1981. "El metatexto historiográfico y la historiografía indiana." *Modern Language Notes* 96: 358–402.

———. 1982. "Cartas, crónicas y relaciones del descubrimiento y la conquista." In *Historia de la literatura hispanoamericana: Época colonial,* edited by Iñigo Madrigal, 57–116. Vol. 1. Madrid: Cátedra.

Molina, Silvia. 1993. "Literatura e historia en México." In *Literatura mexicana hoy II: Los de fin de siglo,* edited by Karl Kohut, 53–58. Frankfurt am Main: Vervuert Verlag.

Monsiváis, Carlos. 1980. "La pasión de la historia." In *Hisotria ipara qué?,* edited by Carlos Pereyra, et. al. Mexico: Siglo XXI, 1980.

———. 1976. "Notas sobre la cultura mexicana en el siglo XX." In *Historia general de México.* Vol. 4. Mexico City: El Colegio de México.

———. 1980a. *A ustedes les consta: Antología de la crónica en México.* Mexico: Ediciones Era.

———. 1980b. "Los de atrás se quedarán." *Nexos* 26 (February): 35–43.

———. 1980c. "Los de atrás se quedarán." *Nexos* 28 (April): 11–23.

———. 1987. "De la santa doctrina al espíritu público (sobre las funciones de la crónica en México)." *Nueva revista de filolgía hispánica* 35, no. 2: 753–71.

Navarro, Raúl Béjar. 1968. *El mito del mexicano.* Mexico: UNAM.

Paso, Fernando del. 1982. "La novela que no olvidé." In *Los novelistas* edited by Norma Klahn, Mexico: Fondo de Cultura Económica, 1991. 318–22.

Paz, Octavio. *Posdata.* 1987. Mexico City: Siglo XXI.

Pereyra, Carlos, et al. 1980. *Historia ¿Para qué?* Mexico City: Siglo XXI.

Poniatowska, Elena. 1971. *La noche de Tlatelolco.* Mexico: Ediciones Era.

———. 1980. *Fuerte es el silencio.* Mexico: Ediciones Era.

———. 1986. *¡Ay, vida, no me mereces!: Carlos Fuentes, Rosario Castellanos, Juan Rulfo: La literatura de la Onda.* Mexico City: Joaquín Mortiz.

———. 1992. "Entrevista con Elena Poniatowska." *Confluencia* 7, no. 2 (spring): 115–22.

Rickman, H. P. 1976. Introduction to *Selected Writings,* by W. Dilthey. Cambridge: Cambridge University Press.

Ruffinelli, Jorge. 1987. "La crónica como práctica narrativa en México." *Hispanic Journal* 8, no. 2 (spring): 67–77.

Sánchez Vázquez, Adolfo. 1977. *The Philosophy of Praxis.* Atlantic Highlands, N.J.: Humanities Press.

Sefchovich, Sara. 1987. *México: País de ideas, país de novelas.* Mexico: Editorial Grijalbo.

Shaw, Donald. 1989. "Towards a Description of the Post-Boom." *Bulletin of Hispanic Studies* 66, no. 1: 87–94.

Sommer, Doris, and Geroge Yúdice. 1986. "Latin American Literature from the 'Boom' On." In *Postmodern Fiction: A Bio-Bibliographical Guide,* edited by Larry McCaffery, 189–214. New York: Greenwood Press.

Villegas, Abelardo. 1960. *La filosofía de lo mexicano.* Mexico: Fondo de Cultura Económica.

Zea, Leopoldo. 1988. *¿Por qué América Latina?* Mexico City: UNAM.

Part Two
The Colonial Other as a Cultural Construct

Constructing Cultural Myths: Cabeza de Vaca in Contemporary Hispanic Criticism, Theater, and Film

SANTIAGO JUAN-NAVARRO

ÁLVAR NÚÑEZ CABEZA DE VACA WAS SECOND IN COMMAND, UNDER CAPTAIN Pánfilo de Narváez, of an ill-fated expedition of six hundred men that set sail from Spain in 1527 to survey and to conquer the eastern seaboard area of North America. Shipwrecked first in northwestern Florida and then near the area of what is now Galveston, Texas, only Cabeza de Vaca and three shipmates (Dorantes, Castillo, and the African slave Esteban) survived. Over a period of eight years, the four men made their way across the continent through what would eventually become the borderland between northern Mexico and the southern United States. According to Cabeza de Vaca's published *relación de méritos,* known as *Naufragios* (*Shipwrecks*), he lived with a number of different indigenous communities, earning his keep as an itinerant peddler and gaining the respect of the local people for his supposedly miraculous healing powers. When he finally arrived in what was then known as Nueva Galicia, he was persuaded by the Spanish authorities to take an active role in the pacification of the area. In 1540 he returned to Spain, where the king appointed him governor of the provinces of Río de la Plata.

Since the publication of the first two editions in 1542 and 1555, Cabeza de Vaca's *Naufragios* has not ceased to arouse the interest of readers and critics. Charles V's granting of an important post to Cabeza de Vaca illustrates the original persuasiveness of the conquistador's successful literary re-creation of events. The exaggeration of the so-called miraculous cures helped to evolve a providentialist view of the conquest. Some sixteenth-century historians, such as Bartolomé de Las Casas, saw in *Naufragios* a twofold use: scientific, in as much as it offered invaluable information concerning the indigenous people who inhabited the Gulf coast of what is nowadays the southwestern United States, and moral, because of Cabeza de Vaca's belief in a pacific evangelization. During the nineteenth century, and with the annexation of all of Mexican territory north of Rio Grande, the U.S. public developed an interest in Cabeza de Vaca and his work, considering both as landmarks in the history and culture of their own country. This foundational character of *Naufragios* has also been appropriated by Chicano studies to the extent that critics such as Bruce-Novoa have wanted to see in Álvar Núñez's account a precursor to twentieth-century Chicano literature. More recently, *Naufragios* has solicited the attention of filmmakers and playwrights alike, who have used Álvar Núñez's work to legitimate their own cultural and political views. This study focuses on significant contemporary reinventions of this mythical figure in Hispanic literary criticism, film, and drama.

I. Cabeza de Vaca in Contemporary Literary Criticism

Formal Aspects

Critics have focused primarily on *Naufragios*'s textual hybridity, especially concerning the continual interaction between fictional and historiographic discourses. A pioneering work in this regard is David Lagmanovich's "Los *Naufragios* de Álvar Núñez como construcción narrativa" (1978), which focuses on the "narrative quality" of the text. For Lagmanovich, *Naufragios* is organized around a network of "conflicts and tensions" that functions on different levels. On a generic plane, Cabeza de Vaca's work exposes a tension between its historical and literary elements. On a structural level, the conflict is between lineal chronology and a subjectivity that adopts an episodic form (Lagmanovich 1978, 35). Both elements are closely related to the literary tradition. Its lineal narrative conforms to the literary model of the travelogue and is articulated according to the literary notions of omen and recognition. The episodic aspect results from interpolated stories in which the real and the marvelous, the fantastic and the testimonial coexist, framed by a final episode that contains and controls all the others: the prophecy of the "Mora de Hornachos" (Lagmanovich 1978, 35).

Because *Naufragios* anticipates the features and techniques of the modern novel, Lagmanovich confers an inaugural value upon it. To the model of the chronicle or *relación* (Lagmanovich does not establish a distinction between the two), Cabeza de Vaca's *Naufragios* adds the following innovations: a "modern realism" that anticipates the picaresque, a moral discourse on Amerindians that antecedes that of Las Casas, and the presence of the marvelous that prefigures twentieth-century Latin American narrative (Lagmanovich 1978, 36).

The principal value of Lagmanovich's essay resides in filling an important void in Cabeza de Vaca studies: the analysis of the fictional aspect of the *relación*. Nevertheless, his essay does succumb to at least three misconceptions. Firstly, the sharp distinction between historical discourse and narrative construction has been widely undermined by recent historiographical theory. As contemporary philosophers of history have recurrently pointed out (Jenkins 1991; LaCapra 1985; White 1973, 1978, 1987), historical narratives are "verbal fictions, the contents of which are as much *invented* as *found*" (White 1978, 82). From this point of view, any historical work is susceptible to literary analysis, without necessarily concluding that the nature of the work is purely fictional. Secondly, Lagmanovich's decision to examine *Naufragios* from a literary point of view is taken on the grounds that its historiographic value has "abundantly" and "conveniently" been elucidated by numerous essays, among which he mentions those of Hallenbeck and Covey. Thirdly, Lagmanovich's perspective shows an evident confusion regarding the concept of "historical" work. He refers to essays that discuss Cabeza de Vaca's itinerary from the Florida peninsula to Nueva Galicia. However, most of these "historical" works elude the formal aspect of sixteenth-century historiography; that is, in which sense Cabeza de Vaca's text is or is not what it purports to be: namely, a *relación de méritos* that follows the dictates of the historical discourse of the time. Even the details regarding the itinerary are highly controversial, and therefore we can never truly conclude that the subject matter has been exhausted, as Lagmanovich suggests.

A step forward in the analysis of the history vs. fiction dichotomy in relation to Cabeza de Vaca's work is offered by Robert E. Lewis (1982), Antonio Carreño (1987), and Enrique Pupo-Walker (1982, 1987, 1989, 1990a, 1990b, 1996). Lewis focuses his analysis on the preface (*prohemio*) to *Naufragios* as a historiographic metatext that provides crucial information on the origin and purpose of the work. Three problems of intentionality are superimposed in this initial segment and coexist in tension throughout the work: the autobiographical personal narrative, the *relación de servicios,* and the *noticia verdadera* (Lewis 1982, 686). According to Lewis, the first of these aspects is manifested in the problem of organizing Cabeza de Vaca's chaotic memories in a coherent artistic manner. The second problem refers to the attempt to present a favorable image of the author as a loyal servant to the crown. The *noticia verdadera,* in turn, refers to the problem of representing as credible events that border on unbelievable. From Lewis's point of view, the appropriate treatment of these three problems may not have been circumscribed by the historiographic practices of the era, and might have forced Cabeza de Vaca to introduce elements characteristic of the literary tradition in his discourse. Among these elements, Lewis underscores the characterization of the author as a heroic protagonist in whom the intrepid explorer, the humane conquistador, the Quixote-like personage, and the miraculous holy man are intertwined (Lewis 1982, 693). Lewis's pragmatic theses point to Cabeza de Vaca's use of novelistic rhetoric to make his message even more persuasive. From this perspective, *Naufragios*'s final success was due to the effect it had on its audience. It could be pointed out that later readers assumed the truthfulness of even the most incredible events narrated, and that Charles V, its most immediate addressee, offered the governorship of La Plata to the author.

Similarly, Antonio Carreño seeks to resolve this tension between the rhetoric of historiography and the rhetoric of the novel that characterizes *Naufragios.* Carreño sees in this tension one of the foundational elements of the novel as a genre. The "suspension of disbelief" between the "experienced reality" (history) and the "imagined reality" (literature) is only one of the elements that convert the first accounts of the conquest into an antecedent of the picaresque novel (Carreño 1987, 515). As in the picaresque, Cabeza de Vaca's account is an antinovel inasmuch as it violates the epic norms of the time. For Carreño, the inversion of the chronicle's patterns through the emphasis on Cabeza de Vaca's submission, starvation, and captivity makes him into the antihero par excellence of the chronicle. Both *Naufragios,* and the picaresque novels are presented as reliable documents opposed to fictional stories (*fábulas*). Likewise, the journey metaphor resembles that of the picaresque novel. As in this genre, *Naufragios,* too, is presented as the story of an initiation and a conversion materialized through a process of adjustments, in which the act of imposture acquires a dominant role. Both the picaresque and Cabeza de Vaca's account respond to a deterministic worldview, albeit the latter is of a supernatural type (the Mora de Hornachos prophecy), whereas the picaresque favors the sociocultural. Finally, as in the picaresque, the narrator is the protagonist (both the narrated object and subject of the narrative), an element that accounts for his parallel evolution in response to the lived events (Carreño 1987, 515).

As expressed by the title of one of his essays *(La vocación literaria del pensamiento histórico en América)*, Pupo-Walker's work is also devoted to the imaginative component underlying the chronicles of the conquest. From the sixteenth century on, the chronicles are characterized by a successful intersection of autobiographical projection, forensic documentation, and the philological reflections of Renaissance humanism. In the case of *Naufragios* a conflictive articulation of rhetorical mechanisms takes place (Pupo-Walker 1987, 537). These mechanisms originate in various intertextual models, depending on the different narrative stages upon which the narrative framework of *Naufragios* is constructed. The first seven chapters, for example, are presented as forensic documents conforming to the rhetorical principles of the *relaciones de servicios.* In chapters 8 to 20, however, the narrative shifts to an autobiographical account in which the testimonial form of the diary is dominant. In its final chapters, *Naufragios* becomes a chronicle of Cabeza de Vaca's pilgrimages, healing, and evangelism. In this last stage the intertextual model is given, according to Pupo-Walker, by the medieval hagiographic tradition, which glorifies the miraculous deeds of nomadic saints (Pupo-Walker 1987, 535). This climactic phase of the text shows the greatest concentration of fantastic elements, such as Mala Cosa and the Mora de Hornachos prophecy.

According to Pupo-Walker, two factors may account for this accumulation of dissimilar narrative strata: the work's process of composition, which was the result of successive and distinct rewritings carried out over a period of twenty-five years, and a search for a rhetorical impact on its addressee by means of intensification. The diverse literary models that are evident in *Naufragios* (medieval chronicles, classic texts of antiquity, the Bible, medieval hagiography, travelogues, chivalry romances, picaresque novels, and the Arcadian tradition) serve a pragmatic purpose: to make the account as convincing as possible in order for Cabeza de Vaca to secure the command over a new expedition to Florida (Pupo-Walker 1987, 536). This interaction of these diverse models results from the use of conflicting rhetorical mechanisms, from which ambiguity, but also poetic richness, derive.

All critical perspectives reviewed thus far clearly privilege the imaginative realm of fiction over the realm of facts. According to Lewis and Pupo-Walker, some of the chronicles and *relaciones* of the conquest, and especially Cabeza de Vaca's *Naufragios,* make use of fictional conventions in order to be more convincing and to elevate their persuasive potential, connecting these works with the novelistic tradition that was beginning to develop in the sixteenth century. In Carreño's view, the saturation of the "I" that characterizes *Naufragios* moves the narrative away from the objectivity associated with historiography (Carreño 1987, 507). The work favors fictional prose for its rhetorical impact, causing critics to fall into the obsolete distinction between historical objectivism and literary subjectivism.

The explanation for this compulsive search for literary models in *Naufragios* should be traced to the intrinsic character of Spanish American literary history, rather than to the logic of discourse itself. Rolena Adorno has pointed out that since the generation of Alfonso Reyes and Pedro Henríquez Ureña, Spanish American critics have conferred a "literary vocation" upon the historiographic writings of the conquest, which represent for many the foundations of Spanish American literature. Among the reasons that would account for this attitude, Adorno and Mignolo suggest the search for an autochthonous cultural space in which colonial texts, originally considered as deficient imitations of metropolitan culture, have been recovered and incorporated into the literary canon (Adorno 1990, 175; Mignolo 1982, 157).

Themes and Motifs

Among the numerous themes analyzed in *Naufragios,* three are intimately related and continue to provoke the most perspicacious approaches to this work: the construction of an identity based upon the dialogue with the native Other, the interaction between the Spaniards and the Amerindian cultures, and the role of the miraculous healing practices as an expression of cultural and religious syncretism. In my brief survey of the treatment received by these themes, I will focus on essays written by Silvia Molloy, Rolena Adorno, and Jacques Lafaye.

According to Molloy, the construction of the first-person narrator/protagonist in *Naufragios* is carried out by means of a process of differentiation, dispossession, and displacement (Molloy 1987, 428). On the formal level, differentiation is exemplified by a fluctuating use of pronouns. The initial plural *nosotros* ["we"] is quickly replaced by the use of the singular *yo* ["I"]. The incipient "I" of this initial stage allows Cabeza de Vaca to establish a discursive space of his own in relation to Pánfilo de Narváez, who at the beginning of the narrative represents the highest authority. The confrontations with the expedition leader culminate in the transmission of power, symbolized by the "taking of the rudder" [*toma de leme*]. This act implies, in Molloy's view, a double liberation: for the Cabeza de Vaca-author (at the plane of events), the subaltern is emancipated and assumes the leadership of the expedition; for the Cabeza de Vaca-narrator (at the plane of writing), the main narrative agency gains authority and the role of protagonist (Molloy 1987, 431). The overturning of the original expeditionary purpose forces the conquistadors into confronting a radically different aboriginal culture of which they know nothing. At this early stage of their journey, their physical nakedness emblematizes the need to renounce their own world in order to survive in an alien space controlled by unknown cultural codes. In Molloy's description of this process, learning of the Other ends in dispossession, and the tensions between the participant "I" and the witnessing "I" reveal the extreme difficulty of that learning (Molloy 1987, 434).

The third stage or level in the construction of identity—displacement (*el traslado*)—plays a dominant role in Molloy's essay. Spatial displacements, the structural backbone of *Naufragios,* are manifested in relation to Cabeza de Vaca's destiny, culture, and identity. In these displacements the "I" becomes a link between opposite poles. The professions Cabeza de Vaca undertakes in the second stage of his journey (peddler and nomadic shaman) symbolize this mediating position (Molloy 1987, 437). Of particular interest is Molloy's description of the ritualization of the healing journey. The occasional healing practices of the earlier stage rapidly acquire a sacred value. Their reach and scope are broadened: the simple presence of the shamans becomes a guarantee against evil; relations among aboriginal peoples are altered; the ritual journey evolves into a lucrative enterprise for the ethnic groups that accompany the Spaniards, degenerating eventually into simple looting; and, finally, the initial healing and prevention of evil achieves consecratory stature. For Molloy, this progressive ritualization of the journey culminates in the final evangelical vision, a moment in which the man of action and the first-person narrator achieve their highest authority. The dispossessed and humble "I" of the initial chapters recovers part of his original cultural legacy, utilizes it to establish differences in relation to Amerindian culture, and prepares in this way his reincorporation into the world to which he belongs. Correspondingly, as soon as the text is inscribed into the program of spiritual conquest of the chronicles, it is instantly institutionalized (Molloy 1987, 444).

The cultural adaptation process in *Naufragios* has also been analyzed by Rolena Adorno from the perspective of the exchange strategies between Europeans and Amerindians. Adorno focuses on the use of fear as a weapon employed by both sides. The so-called "negotiation of fear" can be read, according to Adorno, in three different ways: the fear that the aboriginal groups inspired among the Spaniards, the fear that the latter, in turn, caused among aboriginal peoples, and the control of indigenous fear that Cabeza de Vaca and his travel mates came to possess during the final stage of their journey (Adorno 1991, 167).

Initially, fear is manifested through the terror Cabeza de Vaca's group experience on the Island of Malhado. Their learning of the techniques of fear production and control at this early stage proves to be crucial in subsequent events. The cycle of healing practices shows, however, an inversion of the agency of fear. Now it is the Spanish presence that unleashes fear in the ethnic population. The origin itself of the healing practices, Adorno suggests, may be found in this generalized fear. Like Molloy, Adorno utilizes the theories of Lévi-Strauss to justify her hypothesis. According to Lévi-Strauss in his article "The Sorcerer and His Magic," the shamanic complex is composed of three elements (shaman, sick individual, and consensual group). In order for healing to be effective, three conditions must be met: the shaman must trust his techniques; the sick person must believe in the shaman's power, and the community must manifest its consensus (Adorno 1991, 174; Lévi-Strauss 1963, 168). Nevertheless, as Molloy and Adorno suggest, *Naufragios* inverts this sequence: the communal demands make the sick person trust the shaman; such trust provokes, in turn, the shaman's belief in his own powers, even though he initially rejects this practice as ludicrous. The problem begs a question: Why do they have to function as shamans? Why they and not others? Molloy forwards the hypothesis that it is precisely their "different" nature that leads Amerindians to place the Spaniards at the extreme poles of privilege and submission (Molloy 1987, 439–40). Adorno finds in the aboriginal peoples' decision an attempt to compensate for the potential threat implied by the presence of a white man in their territory (Adorno 1991, 173). To this effect, Adorno suggestively connects healing practices with the legend of *Mala Cosa* ["Evil Thing"]. This legend, whose narrative features coincide with the traditions of the central valley of Mexico, may well be a fantastic materialization of the indigenous fear of the Spaniards. The analogies between this devilish representation (a bearded being who receives food and offerings that he refuses to consume) and the activities of the Spaniards as destroyers (Nuño de Guzmán) and healers (Cabeza de Vaca), make *Mala Cosa* into an expression of the Spanish presence in the region (Adorno 1991, 174).

The episodes concerning healing practices make more evident the negotiation of fear of which Adorno writes. In their pilgrimage and/or ritual looting, the Spaniards were preceded by ethnic groups who, in order to obtain offerings, terrorized those who were unaware of the conquistadors' presence. Fear is generated by force and subjected to the manipulation of those familiar with the Spaniards.

The third stage in this negotiation of fear transforms Cabeza de Vaca into a useful agent of empire. He is called on to contribute to the pacification and repopulation of the lands abandoned by the aboriginal groups. The tribes of Nueva Galicia had escaped to the mountains after being terrorized by Nuño de Guzmán's campaigns. Cabeza de Vaca undertakes the mission of appeasing the natives' fears and persuading them to return to their lands, where they could be useful to the Spanish settlers. In the execution of this task, Cabeza de Vaca presents, according to Adorno, a pacific alternative to the violent conquest and evangelization practiced thus far. In Adorno's opinion, the success of this action represents the triumph of negotiation and exchange over the conquistadors' rampant hostility.

The new perspectives offered by Molloy and Adorno represent two of the most valuable critical contributions to the modern bibliography on *Naufragios*. However, Cabeza de Vaca's activities in Florida and New Spain have been the object of disproportionate idealization throughout the centuries. In a memorable essay, Jacques Lafaye offers a brief review of the treatment the miraculous healing practices have received through the centuries. For Lafaye, the legend of a miracle-maker Cabeza de Vaca originates not in his narrative itself, but in López de Gómara's *Historia General*. Gómara was the first to use the expression *milagro* to refer to the healing practices performed by Cabeza de Vaca, thus laying the groundwork for a legend that would be enriched (and further distorted) by the contributions of later historians. Lafaye's methodology consists of a systematic trace of the existing documentation of this topic, from Motolinía's *Epístola proemial* (1541), where miracles are not even directly mentioned, to the French Jesuit Charlevoix's *Histoire du Paraguay* (1756), which represents the maximum degree of evolution of the legend. Between these two poles, we can witness the genesis of a mythic legend in which the figure of Cabeza de Vaca as a holy miracle-maker has been progressively amplified and distorted.

There is no evidence that even Cabeza de Vaca believed himself to be endowed with supernatural powers. On the contrary, in most cases the first-person narrator considers the healing of sick people and the expression "children of the sun" [*hijos del sol*] as "great lies" [*mentiras mayores*]. What is clear is that the Spanish conquistador believed himself to be a mediator or privileged instrument of divine grace (Lafaye 1984, 70). This is something that can be explained in light of the providentialist spirit that thrived in the minds of sixteenth-century conquistadors and evangelists, who saw themselves as agents of a divine plan: the propagation of the Catholic faith beyond the known horizon. A careful reading of the most conflictive passages, such as the one dealing with the seeming resurrection of a dead man, reveals a high degree of ambiguity. The miracles could very well be due to the active propaganda effected by those indigenous people who accompanied Cabeza de Vaca and who benefited from the healing practices.

However, while the terms in which Cabeza de Vaca describes these events are ambiguous, those in which later historians pronounced themselves where less and less so, eventually becoming certitudes. As Lafaye mentions, Gómara refers to these events as miracles, although when he mentions the supposed resurrection he adds an ambiguous "as they said" [*según ellos dijeron*]. (Lafaye 1984, 76). The Inca Garcilaso eliminates, in turn, Gómara's expressions of ambiguity, replacing the expression "children of the sun" [*hijos del sol*], given by the Amerindians to the Spaniards, with "gods" [*dioses*]. The same dynamics are repeated in later versions by Antonio de Herrera, the Marquis of Sorito, Andrés Pérez Ribas, Father Nichole du Toit, and the already-mentioned Father Charlevoix. One hundred and twenty years later, the legend continued to adopt the most absurd forms that had little to do with the original model. As Lafaye points out, "it is no longer Álvar Núñez who has made the miracles, it is the miracles which have made Álvar Núñez" (Lafaye 1984, 80).

Lafaye's final reflections serve to orient future approaches to *Naufragios*. Lafaye insists upon understanding Cabeza de Vaca in the context of sixteenth-century historiography, a discipline that was less interested in objectivity than in constructing edifying models and in glorifying characters or exalting spiritual values of national and political transcendence. This explains the process of myth-amplification and may also account for both the attitude of many contemporary critics obsessed with finding the characteristics of historiographic practices of the time in literary models, and the tendency of creative writers fascinated—when not totally blinded—by the fantastic possibilities of the Cabeza de Vaca legend.

II. Cabeza de Vaca in Contemporary Theater and Film

Nicolás Echevarría, Cabeza de Vaca (1990)

Nicolás Echevarría's film *Cabeza de Vaca* is a part of the revisionist trend dominant during the years surrounding the Columbus quincentennial. The film, which took ten years to complete, was coproduced by Mexico and Spain in association with Channel Four (Britain) and PBS, and was broadcast as part of the American Playhouse Theater series. Funding came to a large extent from the commission in charge of quincentennial events—hence, the advantages and limitations of this kind of institutionally financed project. The film purports to be historically and anthropologically rigorous, and benefits from a display of backing that is unusual in Hispanic cinema. However, such an apparent faithfulness to the historical record collapses as soon as one takes a closer look at Cabeza de Vaca's text. Although the film presents a revisionist view of the conquistador as a transcultural subject, it continues to present Cabeza de Vaca as the mythical cultural hero produced by five centuries of pseudo-historiographic magnification.

Among the numerous themes that have led to the popularizing of *Naufragios,* I would like to focus on the cinematic and theatrical transpositions of two of the topics discussed in the previous sections of this essay: the construction of identity on the basis of a dialogue with the native Other (which implies an analysis of the interaction between Spaniards and Amerindian cultures) and the role of the miraculous cures as an expression of cultural, as well as religious, syncretism.

From the beginning, Echevarría's film follows the self-mythicizing view that Cabeza de Vaca offers in his account: a view aimed at justifying his rebellion against Narváez, as well as the military failure of the expedition. Álvar is thus presented as the honest and sensible *hidalgo,* who is critical of the actions of other conquistadors. His long period as a slave on the *Isla del Malhado* ["Island of Misfortune"] provides him with an initiation into the indigenous world that prepares him for a new transmission of power. Just as he had previously replaced Narváez in the command of the expedition, he now replaces the Indian shaman in curative practices, thus launching his career as a holy man, a kind of syncretic Messiah. From then on, the film portrays all events as being controlled by the shaman's supernatural powers. The idea of a shaman controlling the conquistador's steps does not seem incongruent within the context of cinematic fiction, where it can be understood as an attempt to endow the colonized subject with a central role. What is more questionable is the acritical mythicizing of Cabeza de Vaca, a mythicizing that has its origin in Cabeza de Vaca's own manipulations and their distortion by later historians. For many contemporary scholars, Cabeza de Vaca is a multicultural hero, a forerunner of the Chicano movement, a humanitarian and altruistic conquistador, and a predecessor of the modern anthropologist, one with a scientific interest in knowing the indigenous Other. This hagiographic portrayal is the result of a decontextualized misreading of sixteenth-century historical sources. This tendency to look into the past for cultural heroes who can appease our own ideological anxieties nevertheless ignores a fundamental aspect in the genesis of the text: the fact that the image that stems from *Naufragios* is the result of the self-mythicizing that Cabeza de Vaca so thoroughly pursues throughout his journal. His self-representation as the loyal conqueror and pacific evangelist endowed with the attributes of a religious and political leader, his geographic and ethnological knowledge of the territory, and his rhetorical ability to enlighten his readers' imagination reveal a goal that is not primarily ethnic, scientific, or even literary, but rather political and military: to justify his actions during the journey and request new *mercedes* from the king (most probably an appointment as the leader of a new expedition to the region).

José Sanchis Sinisterra, *Naufragios o la herida del Otro* (1990)

Ideologically, the theatrical adaptation carried out by the Spanish playwright José Sanchis Sinisterra substantially departs from the film adaptation and its historiographic models. While Álvar Núñez's chronicle unconsciously (but recurrently) expresses the protagonist's difficulty in establishing an identity space of his own, Sanchis Sinisterra's play lends a transcendental value to this progressive "discovery" of the native Other.

Sanchis Sinisterra's work literally offers a re-presentation of the facts as narrated by Cabeza de Vaca from an ideological perspective that questions both the protagonist's narrative and the mythicizing of the account that began to evolve in the sixteenth century and is still at work today. The first act of the play opens with Álvar fully integrated into the bourgeois life of twentieth-century urban Spanish society. However, he listens with remorse to complaints expressed by other characters in the play. One of these characters is soon identified as Shila, his apocryphal indigenous wife, who castigates Álvar not only for repudiating her and their child, but also for ignoring them in his account. The other three characters (Castillo, Dorantes, and Esteban) show themselves equally upset by Álvar's version of history, and force him to represent his role again, to reenact the events narrated in the chronicle, but this time from their own perspectives. It is noteworthy that the voices most marginalized in *Naufragios* are the ones that progressively monopolize the play: the voice of women—who obviously must have played a part during the long stay of the Spaniards among the southern native peoples—and the voice of the African slave Esteban (or Estebanico). Some of the most significant episodes in Cabeza de Vaca's New World experience follow one another on the stage, but they are viewed in a different light, one that deconstructs the historical record: Narváez's stubbornness, Álvar's enslavement, his questionable role as shaman, the prophecy of disaster made by a Moorish woman back in Spain, and other well-known events.

Thus, Álvar's interpretation is systematically questioned by the characters. They accuse Cabeza de Vaca of monopolizing his role as shaman (when it was really Castillo who first began the miraculous healing practices), of ignoring the sufferings of his companions, of repudiating his indigenous wife and son, and of omitting all those events that did not contribute to magnifying his mythical image. In the end, the play is revealed to be a dream, not Álvar's, but that of Shila, who ends the work with these words: "I don't know what you're talking to me about. These words . . . 'final' . . . 'history' . . . are not in my language. (*Indicates the back of the set.*) There's nothing over there. (*Looks around.*) Well . . . There isn't anything anywhere . . . (*Pauses.*) All of this . . . everything that has happened . . . I'm dreaming it" (Sanchis Sinisterra 1992, 238).

Sanchis Sinisterra's play is thus presented not only as a reaction to the phenomenon of the conquest, but also to the contemporary "official" revisionism of the period. Although it attempts to put Cabeza de Vaca in his historical place, it instead vindicates an apochryphal character (Shila). Paradoxically, however, it more accurately depicts history in that it presents the view of the conquest through the eyes of an imaginary character, who by her own condition as a native and as a woman is doubly marginal.

Unlike Álvar Núñez's monologist discourse, apparently addressed to the king in search of reward, Sanchis Sinisterra makes the Other speak through a character who is absent in *Naufragios.* Unlike the chronicle and its cinematic adaptation, Sanchis Sinisterra's play provides us with the possibility of listening to a discourse not *on* but *of* the Other. The Other thus becomes not a subaltern object, but a colonial subject, not just the observed one, but the observer. The final inversion generated by Shila's words corresponds with one of the techniques of appropriation and resistance that characterize anticolonial discourse. From these words follow that all past events have been (continue being) part of her own dream. The history of the conquest turns out to be the fantasy of an indigenous woman. Power is thus displaced from metropolitan empire to colony, from center to periphery.

In contrast to the evident military failure of Cabeza de Vaca's expedition, Sanchis Sinisterra proposes a triumph, one that is barely glimpsed by either Álvar Núñez or Nicolás Echevarría: the birth of a third type of alterity, or, as the author himself has expressed, "the access to a mixed, border identity, not being from anywhere and thus from everywhere" (Antón 1991, 7).

Bibliography

Adorno, Rolena. 1990. "New Perspectives in Colonial Spanish American Literary Studies." *Journal of the Southwest* 32, no. 2: 173–91.

——— 1991. "The Negotiation of Fear in Cabeza de Vaca's *Naufragios.*" *Representations* 33: 163–99.

Antón, Jacinto. 1991. "Brecht en Macondo." *El país/Babelia,* 16 November, 7.

Barrera, Trinidad. 1985. Introduction to *Naufragios,* by Álvar Núñez Cabeza de Vaca, 7–55. Madrid: Alianza.

Bruce-Novoa, Juan. 1990. "Naufragios en los mares de la significación: De la relación de Cabeza de Vaca a la literatura chicana." *Plural* 221: 12–21.

Carreño, Antonio. 1987. "*Naufragios* de Álvar Núñez Cabeza de Vaca: Una retórica de la crónica colonial." *Revista Iberoamericana* 53, no. 140: 499–516.

Covey, Cyclone. 1961. *Cabeza de Vaca's Adventures in the Unknown Interior of America.* New York: Collier Books.

Echevarría, Nicolás, dir. 1990. *Cabeza de Vaca.* Producciones Iguana.

Hallenbeck, Cleve. 1940. *Álvar Núñez Cabeza de Vaca: The Journey and Route of the First European to Cross the Continent of North America, 1534–1536.* Glendale: Arthur Clark.

Jenkins, Keith. 1991. *Re-thinking History.* London: Routledge.

LaCapra, Dominick. 1985. *History and Criticism.* Ithaca: Cornell University Press.

Lafaye, Jacques. 1984. *Mesías, cruzadas, utopías: El judeo-cristianismo en las sociedades ibéricas.* Translated by Juan José Utrilla. México: Fondo de Cultura Económica.

Lagmanovich, David. 1978. "Los *Naufragios* de Álvar Núñez como construcción narrativa." *Kentucky Romance Quarterly* 25, no. 1: 27–37.

Lévi-Strauss, Claude. 1963. *Structural Anthropology.* Translated by Claire Jacobson and Brooke Grundfest Schoepf. New York: Basic.

Lewis, Robert E. 1982. "Los *Naufragios* de Álvar Núñez: Historia y ficción." *Revista Iberoamericana* 48, no. 120–21: 681–94.

Mignolo, Walter. 1982. "Cartas, crónicas y relaciones del descubrimiento y la conquista." In *Historia de la literatura hispanoamericana: Época colonial,* edited by Iñigo Madrigal, 57–116. Vol. 1. Madrid: Cátedra.

Molloy, Silvia. 1987. "Alteridad y reconocimiento en los *Naufragios* de Alvar Núñez Cabeza de Vaca." *Nueva Revista de Filología Hispánica* 35, no. 2: 425–49.

Núñez Cabeza de Vaca, Álvar. 1985. *Naufragios.* Madrid: Alianza.

Pupo-Walker, Enrique. 1982. *La vocación literaria del pensamiento histórico en América. Desarrollo de la prosa de la prosa de ficción: Siglos XVI, XVII, XVII y XIX.* Madrid: Gredos.

——— 1987. "Pesquisas para una nueva lectura de los *Naufragios* de Álvar Núñez Cabeza de Vaca." *Revista Iberoamericana* 53, no. 140: 517–39.

——— 1989. "Los *Naufragios* de Álvar Núñez Cabeza de Vaca y la narrativa de viajes: Ecos de la codificación literaria." In *Los hallazgos de la lectura: Estudio dedicado a Miguel Enguidanos,* 63–83. Madrid: Porrúa.

——— 1990a. "Notas para una caracterización de un texto seminal: Los *Naufragios* de Álvar Núñez Cabeza de Vaca." *Nueva Revista de Filología Hispánica* 38, no. 1: 163–96.

——— 1990b. "Versiones equívocas de lo fáctico: los *Naufragios* de Álvar Núñez Cabeza de Vaca." *Ideas '92* 6: 77–84.

——— 1996. "El libro de viajes, la ficción y sus legados en los *Naufragios.*" *Annali d'italianistica* 14: 131–44.

Sanchis Sinisterra, José. 1992. *Trilogía americana.* Madrid: El Público.

White, Hayden. 1973. *Metahistory: The Historical Imagination in Nineteenth-Century Europe.* Baltimore: Johns Hopkins University Press.

——— 1978. *Tropics of Discourse: Essays in Cultural Criticism.* Baltimore: Johns Hopkins University Press.

——— 1987. *The Content of the Form: Narrative Discourse and Historical Representation.* Baltimore: Johns Hopkins University Press.

You Are What You Eat: *Tropicalismo* and *How Tasty Was My Little Frenchman*

THEODORE ROBERT YOUNG

> Contra Anchieta cantando as onze mil virgens do céu, na terra de Iracema, —o patriarca João Ramalho fundador de São Paulo.
>
> [Against Anchieta praising the eleven thousand virgins of heaven, in the land of Iracema, —the patriarch João Ramalho, founder of São Paulo.]
>
> —Oswald de Andrade, "Manifesto antropófago"

In 1971, during the height of Brazil's political repression, while the left-wing intelligentsia ardently "sought to mobilize workers and students through 'revolutionary and consequential' art" (Dunn 1993, 16), filmmaker Nelson Pereira dos Santos directed a period piece inspired by the 1557 account of a German captive among the Brazilian Tupinambás. Pereira dos Santos's film, *How Tasty Was My Little Frenchman* (*Como era gostoso meu francês*), at first glance could appear anachronistic for the turbulent and engagé artistic climate of the time. However, the motion picture in fact incorporates *tropicália* aesthetic of the late 1960s into a cinematographic idiom. In essence, the filmmaker "cannibalizes" *tropicalismo*'s musical stylistics along the lines of modernism's "Manifesto antropófago" while juxtaposing an "official" history with an irreverent reinvention of Brazil's colonial period. Ultimately, this revisionist technique purposefully undermines the authoritative self-representation of the military regime after the Fifth Institutional Act of 1968.

In 1556,[1] the German adventurer Hans Staden published a book of his travels, focusing on his nine months as a captive among Brazil's anthropophagic Tupinambá tribe.[2] The issue of Brazil's ritualistic cannibalism is essential to understanding Staden's experience, the indigenous totemic system, and later attempts to create a Brazilian cultural identity. Indeed, the frontispiece of the 1557 Marpurg edition reads: "A true description of a land of naked, fierce and cannibalistic savages" [*Descripção verdadeira de um paiz de selvagens nús, ferozes e cannibaes*] (Staden 1930, 13). According to his account, Staden was held prisoner by the Tupinambás, waiting to be eaten by his captors. Similar to the pre-Colombian Caribs, whose "cannibalistic practices were limited to occasional consumption of their prisoners of war" (Boucher 1992, 6), various peoples of the Tupi culture frequently ate enemies captured in battle, literally incorporating part of the ingested individual's identity and acquiring in the process a new name (Staden 1930, 68).[3] The renaming of an individual after the ingestion of an Other is part of the totemic belief system of Brazil's pre-Cabralian inhabitants. People's names frequently reflected their totem, a nature spirit that expressed the individual's or the clan's identity. In *The Elementary Structures of Kinship,* Claude Lévi-Strauss affirms, "the religious life of these [primitive] societies is dominated by beliefs affirming an identity of substance between the clan and the eponymous totem" (1969, 20). He continues, "We know that this belief poses no obstacle to the eating of the totem, but merely confers some ceremonial significance upon this eating" (21). In devouring a foreign body, that Other's traits become incorporated into the devourer's Self. In *Tristes tropiques,* without explicitly referring to exocannibalism, Lévi-Strauss corraborates Staden's observation about renaming after the killing of a prisoner, adding that the Tupi "also acquire names on passing from childhood into adolescence, and then again when they reach adulthood" (Lévi-Strauss 1992, 353).

According to anthropologist Edmund Leach, the question of what you eat is closely related to whom you can have sex with in many preindustrial, rural societies (Shipman 1987, 71, 72). The defining elements are more or less proximity to self and familiar alterity. For example, most carnivorous humans eat specific domesticated animals raised expressly for slaughter. In contrast, pets, such as dogs and cats in European and Euro-American societies, are not eaten by people, being perceived as more self (human) than other (animal). Nondomesticated game is also eaten; however, strange, unfamiliar animals are not readily consumed, thus avoiding possible poisoning or other hazards.[4] Similarly, siblings do not marry; cousins can in some societies; and neighbors (known others) are ideal mates, while strangers are not immediately selected until their qualities can be discerned. Both eating and mating tendencies vary across cultural lines, with some peoples consuming cats, dogs, and monkeys, and some communities permitting the marriage of cousins. Most societies make important distinctions between first cousins and more distant relatives. Consequently, in Portuguese, similar to other Romance languages, a first cousin is known as a "brother-cousin" [*primo-irmão*] or a "sister-cousin" [*prima-irmã*]. The codification of these tendencies constitutes social taboos, the strongest of which are against incest and cannibalism. As paleontologist Pat Shipman indicates: "Because both cannibalism and incest violate rules of accepted distances, the two are often believed to be practiced together. Thus to accuse a group of both cannibalism and incest is tantamount to denying their humanity" (Shipman 1987, 72).[5]

In his 1979 book *The Man-Eating Myth: Anthropology and Anthropophagy*, William Arens attacks "the very notion of cannibalism, calling it a myth generated to enslave or otherwise oppress a hostile 'other' " (Boucher 1992, 6). Shipman points out that accusations of cannibalism serve to distance the accuser (self) from the accused (other), and may contrast one's own "civilized state" to animalistic barbarism, or may justify one's own inhuman behavior in time of war.[6] The denying of humanity to another group can rationalize such acts as slavery, genocide, and appropriation of lands. Beginning with Columbus's *Diaries* (1492) and Caminha's *Carta do Achamento* (1500), many descriptions of the indigenous inhabitants of the Americas in some way animalize the so-called "savages," much as in Staden's account. Columbus himself urged Ferdinand and Isabella to enslave "these cannibals, a people very savage and suitable for the purpose" (Boucher 1992, 16)—not coincidentally a move that would add capital value to the explorer's newly claimed territories.

For whatever the motivations, the legacy of cannibalism heavily marked the iconography of colonial Brazil, and thus the identity of the nation that eventually developed. In 1928, Oswald de Andrade published his modernist "Manifesto antropófago," a declaration of Brazilianness through cultural cannibalism. Andrade acknowledges the historical occurence of anthropophagy not as a stigma, but rather with pride. In reference to the indigenous ritual of devouring captured enemies, Andrade writes: "We had justice, codification of vengeance. Science, codification of Magic. Anthropophagy. The permanent transformation of the Taboo into totem" [*Tínhamos a justiça codificação da vingança. A ciência codificação da Magia. Antropofagia. A transformação permanente do Tabu em totem*] (Andrade 1970, 15). In the social and cultural sense, Andrade views the identity of the former colony as a conglomerate of diverse elements, incorporated (brought into the body) from foreign cultures. A society creates its own body by ingesting and internalizing pieces of other cultures, just as a human body produces its own protein from enzymes of the plants and animals consumed.

Andrade goes on to justify this consumption of other cultural elements, stating: "I am only interested in what is not mine. The law of man. The law of the cannibal" [*Só me interessa o que não é meu. Lei do homem. Lei do antropófago*] (Andrade 1970, 13). He adds: "From the equation *I* part of the *Cosmos* to the axiom *Cosmos* part of the *I*. Subsistence. Knowledge. Anthropophagy" [*Da equação eu parte do Cosmos ao axioma Cosmos parte do eu. Subsistência. Conhecimento. Antropofagia*] (Andrade 1970, 15). Haroldo de Campos classifies the "Manifesto antropófago" as: "heading towards a Brazilian vision of the world as ingestion, towards a critical assimilation of the foreign experience and its re-elaboration in national terms and circumstances, allegorizing in this way the cannibalism of our savages" (Perrone 1988, 65).

The notion of devouring and assimilating foreign influences into Brazilian culture resurfaced forty years after the manifesto. In 1968, musicians Caetano Veloso and Gilberto Gil released their album *Tropicália,* which simultaneously criticized the Brazilian sociopolitical status quo and mixed musical styles from around the world to form a new, Brazilian artistic expression (Perrone 1988, 65). Veloso himself explains: "We took the example of cultural cannibalism, created . . . by the Modernists, especially Oswald de Andrade, who had invented this idea that you devour everything that comes from anywhere in the world and digest it however you like in order to produce something new" (Dunn 1993, 17). The album's complete title, *Tropicália; ou, Panis et Circensis,* combines the notion of Brazil as a tropical country with *panem et circenses,* the classical Roman concept of appeasing discontent in the general populace by means of food and entertainment, elaborated by Juvenal in his indignant satiric attack on imperial Roman corruption and decadence. Veloso and Gil's work is thus a critical commentary on Brazil's situation under the military rule of the late 1960s. The musicians also responded to the extreme censorship of the military government of President Arthur da Costa e Silva, which enacted the Fifth Institutional Act in December of 1968. The resulting *tropicália* aesthetic was a "juxtaposition of contradictory elements, irregular metrification, incorporation of noises from the industrialized city, etc." (Franchetti 1988, 138). Furthermore, the *tropicalistas* rebelled against all forms of musical limitations by taking from pop, traditional Brazilian samba, bossa nova, baião, and Caribbean rhythms, among other influences (Perrone 1988, 65). By mixing various styles from diverse locations and periods, and by consciously ignoring the political implications of modern electronic music (emanating from the "First World") vis-à-vis traditional, "Third World" expressions, the *tropicalistas* developed anachronisms that undermined the cultural imperialism of modernized Western society by breaking the boundaries between developed and under-developed cultures. According to Roberto Schwarz, these anachronisms result in an allegory of Brazil insofar as the juxtaposition of the old and the new, the antiquated "Third World" and the modern "First World," form a social and a political absurdity (Schwarz 1978, 74, 76). He explains: "we, the modernized ones, the ones articulated with the circuit of capital, given the failure of the attempt at social modernization enacted from above, recognize that absurdity is the country's soul, and ours" (Schwarz 1978, 77).

Influenced by both Oswald de Andrade's modernist notion of cannibalism and the *tropicalista's* postmodern destruction of history, Nelson Pereira dos Santos re-created the conflicts of cultures exemplified in the story of Staden's captivity. The backdrop for *How Tasty Was My Little Frenchman* are the wars between the Portuguese and the French in the area of Guanabara Bay and São Vicente. Both European countries established alliances with rival indigenous tribes, among them the Tupiniquins and the Tupinambás. The title character, transformed from Germanic Staden into a nameless Frenchman, is a prisoner of the Portuguese when these are overrun by Tupinambás who take him captive, mistaking him for an enemy Portuguese. He lives among the tribe for almost a year until he is eaten.

From the opening scene, Pereira dos Santos juxtaposes official history with revisionist questioning. The film's first sequence shows French authorities punishing supposedly rebellious soldiers. The voice-over narration, a letter from the commander to the king, describes the official version of events, in striking contrast to the images on the screen. The scene closes with the voice-over elaborating a failed gesture of clemency on the part of the authorities: "We unshackled his hands so that he might better express himself, but the prisoner inexplicably ran and threw himself into the sea." At the same time, the audience views the prisoner, in irons, being pushed off a cliff into the surf after a priest performs an unceremonious sign of the cross.

Throughout the motion picture, Pereira dos Santos provokes the audience with a clash of cultural standards. After the first scene, almost the entire film is spoken in the Tupi language, with subtitles in Portuguese for the Brazilian audience. Given that the vast majority of cinema viewed in Brazil is from either the United States or Europe, Brazilian viewers would be readily accustomed to the reading of subtitles. Nevertheless, in *How Tasty Was My Little Frenchman,* the filmmaker polemicizes the distancing inherent in subtitles (written text that necessarily must translate only part of the spoken dialogue), separating the viewer from the aurality of the cinematographic experience. (Obviously, silent films depended on written text to transmit dialogue, but the entire filmic idiom was correspondingly distinct: directors of the silent era created motion pictures precisely as moving images that incorporated the written text, while makers of "talkies" develop their product/art form with the aural experience of the audience included organically into the medium.)

Pereira dos Santos accentuates Third World audiences' constant loss of information due to subtitles by forcing Brazilian audiences to view a Brazilian film about indigenous Brazilian people while facing the filter of subtitles. In contrast, most films set in a linguistic environment other than that of the intended audience present the dialogue in the audience's home language. When a few foreign characters are present as a minority among the overall cast, they may speak normally in the audience's language, heavily accented in the audience's language, in a foreign tongue with subtitles, or in the foreign tongue with partial or no subtitles at all. Through these options, the director gives the viewer more or less information, emphasizing the role of verbal communication. In *How Tasty Was My Little Frenchman,* only a couple of lines of Portuguese are spoken, the vast majority of the dialogues being in Tupi, with a few lines in French. Besides evoking the "First World" vs. "Third World" information chasm, Pereira dos Santos also reiterates the "Old World" vs. "New World" problematic manifest by the imposition of the European languages in the cultural landscape of the Americas. By making the indigenous Tupi language the dominant tongue in the film, the director raises the issue that Portuguese, and not Tupi, is the dominant language of Brazil today.

Pereira dos Santos also presents clashing cultural norms in regards to clothing, treatment of captives, sex, and, of course, death and cannibalism. Both the Frenchman and the Euro-American audience encounter difficulties in understanding the behavior of the Tupinambás in the film. One of the first obvious cultural differences is the nakedness of the indigenous characters.[7] Indeed, throughout the movie, only a handful of French characters appear clothed. Even the title character soon strips off his European garments. The director immediately and constantly confronts the audience with an entirely unclothed cast, calling into question the social norms of dress, especially in a tropical climate.

More confusing to the Euro-American mind-set is the Tupinambás' treatment of their captive. The captors give their prisoner a wife, the young widow of a warrior killed by the Portuguese, and allow him to roam freely not only within the village compound, but also around the surrounding lands. As the Frenchman transforms his own appearances to conform to that of the Tupinambás, he also becomes hunting partner to the chief, eventually even fighting and killing two Portuguese alongside his master. While never giving up hope of a return to French soil, the European begins to view himself as integrated into the Tupinambá society, to the extent of having his indigenous wife refer to him as her husband. Subtly, Pereira dos Santos demonstrates the difference in the two characters' perceptions when the Tupinambá woman calls her dead husband by the indigenous word for spouse while adopting the French word *mari* for her European partner. Presented with an opportunity to escape, the Frenchman loses his chance at freedom when the ship sets sail while he is trying to convince his indigenous wife to accompany him. Soon afterwards, he is scheduled to be killed and devoured, his wife indicating that she will eat his neck. As she prepares him for the ritual of death, he clearly does not believe in his impending fate, choosing to have sex instead of fleeing. The director thus eroticizes the scene, fusing sexuality with the act of eating.[8] The double entendre of the film's original title in Portuguese, *Como era gostoso meu francês,* itself accentuates the association between sex and eating: *gostoso,* meaning "flavorful" or "tasty," is a common adjective to refer to an individual who is sexually appealing. In popular Brazilian speech, the sexual partner who penetrates "eats" ["*come*"] his partner; ironically, in Pereira dos Santos's film it is the woman who literally eats the man.

Thus, contrary to Staden's experience, in the film's final scene, the Tupinambás indeed kill the Frenchman, his hunting partner and wife presumably eating their allotted portions. In this manner, Pereira dos Santos demonstrates the misunderstanding across cultural lines: the Frenchman viewed his interactions with the chief and especially with his supposed wife as interpersonal relations, an emotional bonding, while in the eyes of his captors he was at all times something to be eaten.[9] Indeed, his wife's pet name for the Frenchman was "my little neck"; he was a substitute for the husband killed in battle, serving her while awaiting death.

The murder and consumption of the Frenchman is disturbing to Euro-American audiences. It is barbaric by definition, according to the criteria indicated by Shipman, Leach, and others. Yet Pereira dos Santos seeks more than a portrayal of historic customs: he demonstrates the indigenous cannibalistic foundation of Brazilian culture while simultaneously undermining the supposed nobility of European society in the Americas. Much as the *tropicalista* music of Caetano Veloso mixed clashing sonorous elements, *How Tasty Was My Little Frenchman* presents the audience with a series of internal oppositions: the voice-over and the visual images; the expected relationship-based outcome and the film's actual conclusion; even the incongruous behavior of the European characters. In one telling scene, a French merchant ship comes to trade with their Tupinambá allies. The captive Frenchman implores the ship's captain to properly identify him as French and thus not subject to exocannibalism, having been initially taken for a Portuguese when he was captured. The captain, however, purposefully perpetuates the Frenchman's mistaken identity, stating: "He's Portuguese. Go ahead and eat him." The reason for the condemning lie is so that the captain will have a dependent, exploitable worker inside the indigenous compound. The audience must question what is more barbaric: a society that adheres to a commonly accepted anthropophagic totemic system, or an individual who knowingly breaks his own society's ethical code, sacrificing an innocent victim to probable death for the possibility of material gain. Pereira dos Santos emphasizes the barbarism of the supposedly civilized Europeans when in a later scene the Frenchman slays the captain with a shovel in a dispute not over his betrayal but rather over gold and gems discovered by the captive. Moreover, the Frenchman discovers the treasure by plundering the grave of his indigenous wife's deceased husband. The immoral (by the Europeans' own standards) and greed-driven behavior of the two Europeans serves to further undermine the official, European version of the struggle between "civilization" and "barbarism."

Pereira dos Santos made *How Tasty Was My Little Frenchman* at a time of extreme governmental control of state iconography and means of mass communication. By contrasting indigenous and European cultures, the filmmaker could question traditional, "First World" oriented images of Brazilian society while avoiding censorship. He did so in a way that followed the compositional style of the *tropicália* movement. As Charles Perrone indicates: "Such compositions juxtapose the old (primitive, native, savage, under-developed) and the new (modern, industrialized, developed) in order to ridicule social values and criticize the statute of Brazilian subject" (Perrone 1988, 72). In *How Tasty Was My Little Frenchman,* Nelson Pereira dos Santos cannibalizes this *tropicalista* aesthetic, digesting it to produce a new, filmic expression of its at once serious and satiric attack on oppression and the status quo.

Notes

1. A first, although perhaps not definitive, edition appears to have been published in Frankfurt in 1556. There is no date on the book, but the preface is from that year. According to J. C. Rodrigues in his *Bibliotheca brasiliense* (Rio: 1907, 590), Staden likely switched to a Marpurg publisher in order to improve the historic accuracy (at the expense of artistic quality) of the woodcut engravings that illustrated the book (Staden 1930, 9, n. 1).

2. In his preface to the Marpurg edition, Staden indicates nine months (Staden 1930, 16), while the book's contents indicate ten and a half months (Staden 1930, 25).

3. This form of exocannibalism—the eating of outsiders or foreigners—should be distinguished from autocannibalism (eating of one's self) and especially endocannibalism, the eating of one's own social group (Shipman 1987, 70). The latter is well documented as survival cannibalism (plane wrecks in the Andes, etc.), and is present in some cases as ritualistic preservation of ancestors through ingestion (Boucher 1992, and Lévi-Strauss 1992, 387).

4. One wonders who was the first person to eat a lobster.

5. In chapter 2 of *The Elementary Structures of Kinship,* Lévi-Strauss discusses "The Problem of Incest," referring to the similarities of the totems and taboos of sex and eating: "Marriage and, in very many societies, the sexual act itself have a ceremonial and ritualistic significance in no way incompatible with the claim that they represent a form of totemic communion" (Lévi-Strauss 1969, 21).

6. Along these lines, it suffices to recall Allied propoganda posters from World War II that depicted Germans as salivating wolves and Japanese as devious rats.

7. Anthropologist James Ito-Adler, an extra in the film who played one of the French soldiers in the opening scene, indicated the filmmaker's difficulty in recruiting actresses on location in Parati (a small, coastal resort community) to play the unclothed indigenous women.

8. As Pat Shipman indicates, "Sex and eating are, of course, closely associated in many societies, including our own [American]" (Shipman 1987, 71).

9. Similar contrast can be found in the Hollywood production *City Slickers,* when the dude ranchers playing cowboy come to the realization that the calf they have cared for will, like all the cattle, soon be slaughtered. The Australian animal rights film *Babe* also creates such a situation. The purpose and outcome of these two English-language films, however, are radically different from those of *How Tasty Was My Little Frenchman.*

Bibliography

Andrade, Oswald de. 1970. *Do Pau-Brasil à antropofagia e às utopias: Manifestos, teses de concursos e ensaios.* In *Obras completas.* Vol. 6. Rio de Janeiro: Civilização Brasileira.

Arens, William. 1979. *The Man-Eating Myth: Anthropology and Anthropophagy.* Oxford: Oxford University Press.

Boucher, Philip P. 1992. *Cannibal Encounters: Europeans and Island Caribs, 1492–1763.* Baltimore: Johns Hopkins University Press.

Brito, Antônio Carlos de. 1972. "Tropicalismo: sua estética, sua história." *Vozes* 66, no. 9: 693–702.

Campos, Haroldo. 1977. Preface to *Trechos escolhidos,* by Oswald de Andrade. Rio de Janeiro: Agir.

Dunn, Christopher. 1993. "It's Forbidden to Forbid." *Americas* 45, no. 5: 14–21.

Franchetti, Paulo e Alcyr Pécora. 1988. *Caetano Veloso.* São Paulo: Nova Cultural.

Lévi-Strauss, Claude. 1969. *The Elementary Structures of Kinship.* Boston: Beacon Press.

——— 1992. *Tristes tropiques.* Translated by John Weightman and Doreen Weightman. New York: Penguin Books.

Pereira dos Santos, Nelson, dir. 1971. *How Tasty Was My Little Frenchman.* (*Como era gostoso meu francês.*) Condor Films.

Perrone, Charles A. 1988. *Letras e letras da música popular brasileira.* Translated by José Luiz Paulo Machado. Rio de Janeiro: Elo Editora.

Schwarz, Roberto. 1978. "Cultura e política, 1964–1969." In *O pai de família e outros estudos.* Rio de Janeiro: Paz e Terra.

Shipman, Pat. 1987. "The Myths and Perturbing Realities of Cannibalism." *Discover* 8, no. 3: 70–76.

Staden, Hans. 1930. *Viagem ao Brasil.* Edited by Theodoro Sampaio. Translated by Alberto Löfgren. Rio de Janeiro: Officina Industrial Graphica.

Part Three
Sexual Differences and Textual Politics

Transhistorical and Transgeographical Seductions in Rosa Montero's *Te trataré como a una reina*

WA-KÍ FRASER DE ZAMBRANO

A VIOLENT AND RANDOM SEXUALITY THREATENS TO SURGE AT ANY MOMENT in *Te trataré como a una reina* (*I Shall Treat You Like a Queen*), (1983) the tragicomic novel by Spanish writer Rosa Montero.[1] This pervasive textual apprehension puts into play popular representations of demonized men, masculine mystique and sexuality; and of victimized women, female sexuality, complicity, and contingency—all of which orient themselves upon the codification of tropes associated with the encounter, conquest, and colonization of America: a "New World" that promised the fulfillment of unlimited erotic possibilities.[2] Not only do these sexual paradigms constitute a historical and textual hybridization[3] of popular and mass culutre, but they also condense distinct intercultural combinations of the traditional, the modern, and the erudite, in a multitemporal and multicultural amalgam. Among various cultural products, the novel integrates the chronicles of the New World, *costumbrismo,*[4] the age of the sex crime[5] and criminologic journalism, film noir, comic strips and graphic novels for adults, soap opera and melodrama, the perfume industry, psychoanalysis, cabaret theater, and the music of the bolero.

In the midst of an ample cast of secondary and anonymous figures, nine principal protagonists are presented. Although they are imbued with the grainy, grotesque stamp of the twentieth-century comic strip and graphic novel, as well as the kitsch of soap opera, they compose a gallery of popular social types from the Spanish capital and from the cities and provinces, extracted from nineteenth-century Madrid and conserved in *Los españoles pintados por sí mismos* (1843).[6] These motley caricatural characters inhabit a seedy, contemporary barrio of Madrid, Spain, where they traverse the same solitary steps, day after day, year after year, in monotonous cycles that seem to mark their passive decomposition. "Old World–New World" sexual models unfold here through a series of interlaced and mirrorlike human relationships—of doublings, repetitions, and reversals—within a framework of contextual signs and specific textual markers that work together to create the displacement of colonial identification. Within this space of difference and otherness, the site of congregation is a sleazy, broken-down, malodorous nightclub called the Desiré, which exudes the clichés of Caribbean libidinousness.[7]

Even though the novelistic setting is geographically distant from the Caribbean, *Te trataré como a una reina* amplifies space and time as if it were a discursive habitation that entails and is entailed in the radical entwining of culture and colony (Kadir 1993, 20). This milieu integrates parodically a Madrilenian environment and its "types," with the allusion to Cuba and Caribbean "types," as well as to certain events and actors of the fifteenth, sixteenth, ninetenth,[8] and twentieth centuries on both sides of the Atlantic. The hybridized protagonists dredge up the first European social specimens that populated the streets during the early colonization of America: the military lawyer, the soldier without war, the scribe, the mercenary, the recently disembarked adventurer, the royal envoy, the peace officer, the servant, the concubine on her litter, the halberdiers with lances on their shoulders (Fernando Benítez, cited in Careaga 1987, 34; my paraphrased translation). In particular, the mirroring effect of the novel embraces at once a retrogradation-projection toward the Cuban Independence of 1898 and its Revolution of 1959. Behind the advertence to this revolutionary process exists the awareness that nominal political independence does not dismantle internal colonialism. Cuban Revolution or not, Spanish democracy or not, the composite identities of *Te trataré como a una reina* represent, economically, the straitened to the modest; politically, the disenfranchised and discounted; and culturally, the frustrated and flashy, ignorant and coarse (Colás 1995, 388–89). In this textual grid of colonial relationships, feminist movement or not, the female protagonists continue to be the victims of sexual violence.

In order to insinuate the ciphers of a tropical, colonial context, the novel insists on "exoticisms" such as the insular quality of its marginalized urban space; the relentless heat and humidity that introduces morning "like a broth" (Montero 1983, 42) and night as "thick and asphyxiating" (126); the typical sour stench of the Club Desiré, which reeks of "rotten orange peel" and incites "a certain coprophilic pleasure" (130); the remains of viceroyal bureaucracy in the mania of a ministerial office; an inquisitorial morality, made manifest by raving policial propriety; the anxious competition among the heterogenous members of the middle class to create a distinct identity; the boleros that are warmed with the sound of Spanish American "s's . . . [to give] the matter a chic and tropical flair" (28); the trompe l'oeil of the "Cuban scenography" (218) in the Club Desiré, with its faded, cardboard palm trees and naive tropical mural behind the bar: "a beach, coconut trees, three naked black women with colossal, smudgy breasts . . . sea gulls . . . and a little boat that was disappearing on the horizon" (29); the picturesque "types" that frequent the club and the port-flavored night life, particularly in relationship to the seething Barrio Chino; the evocation of sensual, peregrine fragrances, like "the dizzying sweetness of vanilla . . . the dry burst of *especanardo*" (46) and "the splendor of hesperidium . . . civet . . . musk . . . and patchouli" (188–89). The novel also sustains the persistent leitmotif of Cuba, with references to the Tropicana Club in Havana; to the interpretation of specific boleros; to Olga Guillot,[9] the famous Cuban *bolerista;* to the 1954 postmark on an envelope, a year that predates the Cuban Revolution; to the cocktail called Cuba libre, "free Cuba," which was once the toast pronounced by rum-drinking revolutionists; to the nostalgic and erotic illusion of an escape to the island.

Any doubt about the existence of a Caribbean backdrop evaporates with the introduction of a linguistic trigger of unquestionable American origin. The fury of high winds, "as if in the interior of the Desiré a hurricane were to blow" (Montero 1983, 33), recalls the Arawakan word *hurakan,* "the first American word that passed into universal language, picked up by the sailors of the discovery" (Chao 1984, 19); and the fact that Christopher Columbus, while returning to Spain after his maiden voyage to the "New World," was the first to record the difficulties and terrors of this tropical storm in his *Diario.*[10] Referring to the hurricane, Peter Hulme states in *Colonial Encounters:* "Arguably no phenomenon—not even the natives themselves—characterized so well the novelty of the New World for Europeans" (Hulme 1986, 94). The mere suggestion of such an incongruous force of nature in the Club Desiré dispels any doubt about whether *Te trataré como a una reina* is a staging of America.

To facilitate this montage, a novelistic guide joins the cast of characters. She incarnates only through the omniscient presence of a *voz costumbrista,* defined here as a narrative voice. This voice dominates the *cuadros costumbristas,* scenes or portraits of social types, customs, and manners, into which the novel is divided. The textual structuration in scenes of local color situates the protagonists within a classifying and defining system. Like a cultural condensation, this system is also an interpretation directly linked to the authorial project. The spokesperson of these intentions is the narrative voice, which insistently recuperates history and makes it intelligible for the reader. Since the carelessness of memory is a key point in *Te trataré como a una reina,* as witnessed in the protagonists who live in a state of historical amnesia, and do not know, cannot remember, cannot process history, the voice performs a critical function in the interpretation and comprehension of the novel. By commenting, criticizing, and overturning the cultural constructions exhibited by the novel, it frames these scenes, which, like historical-cultural theaters of memory,[11] put on stage an archive of persistent values in the construction of gender, subjectivity, eroticism, and desire (García Canclini 1990, 99).

The positioning of "types" in specific settings also has a museographic effect.[12] Like a museum that groups people, objects, and images by exhibition halls, one for each century or period, the novel accomplishes the same, with the distinction of turning the ensemble into an almost synchronic sequence. It places its Spanish cast in their daily habitat, in the ritualistic headquarters of their historical-cultural patrimony, and constructs relationships of continuity with antecedents of the same society. *Te trataré como a una reina* not only installs a twentieth century Spanish society in relationship to its colonial beginnings, but creates, in the cultural production, connections of filiation and replica with discursive practices, from the past and the present, from national and foreign cultural archives (García Canclini 1990, 134, 158–59, 184, 187).

Even though the narrative voice belongs to Spain, it remains separate. Ridiculing, brusque, ludic, biting, and agitative in its critique, it demonstrates that socially constructed identity is arbitrary and that values and conventions demand revision. This feminist and postcolonial voice,[13] curator of the effects of colonization with specifically evaluative and anticolonial intentions, helps the reader enter the crumbling barrio of the Club Desiré and the unlegitimated lives of its inhabitants.

Having set forth *Te trataré como a una reina* as an ensemble, this essay will now focus upon the novel's first *cuadro costumbrista,* or portrait. The reader is introduced to Antonia Ortiz, an adipose, dowdy, timid, silent, "good Catholic woman," who has been relegated to the domestic charges of her bachelor brother Antonio. She represents the female who has exchanged her independence and autonomy for socioeconomic support and familial protection. Although her parodic characterization might suggest an organic retardation, Antonia epitomizes the woman who has been truncated in her mental and emotional growth because of patriarchal conditioning and constraints. Dominated by the rigid and tyrannical regimen of her brother, she occasionally rebels with a private, domestic noncompliance. As if she were to debut in a television commercial,[14] she scours valiantly ("with detergent until getting rid of the burned-on grease" [Montero 1983, 14] the frying pans her brother claims should never be subjected to soap. In terms of the nineteenth century archive of social types from Madrid, Antonia is the direct descendent of the *ama de llaves,* or housekeeper, described in *Los españoles pintados por sí mismos:*

> Every Spaniard knows what the words *ama de llaves* mean . . . : "a servant in charge of the keys and domestic economy" . . . to whom one entrusts the clothing, utensils, and provisions. . . . [T]hese aristocrats of servitude

> . . . [attend to] a bachelor. . . . [T]hey cook . . . sew . . . scrub. . . . [T]he true *ama de llaves* ought to be middle-aged, buxom, and rather ugly. Being, well, in her most genuine form, a woman of forty to fifty, and finding herself at present in the year of 1843. . . . (Hartzenbusch 1950, 1,043)[15]

Being a lonely, single, virginal, forty-four-year-old woman, Antonia would like nothing more than to love and be loved by a good man. The narrative voice confides that this reticent female talks to herself, while reminiscing and fondling items from her collection of phallic fetishes.[16] These carefully labeled bits and pieces of paraphernalia trace her slightest contact with the opposite sex. Sometimes, to pass the time, she seduces herself. First, Antonia applies make-up, darkening with "deep blue the fold of her eyelids" and outlining "her lips with a discreet carmine" (Montero 1983, 20). Then, narcissistically, she presses her lips to her image in her bedroom mirror. Immersed in this irrepressible erotic ritual, she takes off her housedress, tumbles onto her bed, discards her underwear, spreads her legs, and masturbates.

This episode of *Te trataré como a una reina* targets a woman's masturbatory intimacy and converts it into a spectacle. By means of this representative anecdote, the narrative voice gestures toward Columbian and Vespuccian history and the protocolonialist discourse of discovery, which refers specifically to the assignment of feminine gender to the New World and the sexualization of its exploration, conquest, and colonization (Montrose 1993, 178).

Starting with the vision of Antonia's recumbent nakedness, the narrative voice evokes the allegorical personifications of America that by the year 1570 began to appear in engravings and paintings, on maps and title pages of western Europe. Perhaps the most circulated image of this allegory is the drawing by Jan van der Straet that interprets the "discovery" of America by Vespucci. At the end of the sixteenth century, this drawing was amply disseminated through the engraving of Theodor Galle (Montrose 1993, 179). It reveals a nude and hammocked indigenous woman in a lush, tropical environment, who appears to be beckoning ambiguously[17] to an armed, heavily outfitted, and erect European. Although the visual impression is laden with a sexual dimension, the temporal adverbs of the engraving's inscription, "Semel . . . inde semper . . ." ("Once . . . from then always . . .") also register this "inaugural scene" as an erotic possession that will endure in the Occidental archives of cultural consciousness (Hulme 1986, xii, 1). By bringing into focus the sexual self-gratification of a forlorn housekeeper from Madrid, *Te trataré como a una reina* will uncover the erotic stamp of the encounter, conquest, and colonization of America on the construction of this woman's subjectivity and desire.[18]

The narrative voice relates that, during one especially hot afternoon, Antonia throws herself across her pink imitation silk bedspread. Intensely made-up and dressed only in underwear, she unhooks her garters, ceremoniously unrolls "her stockings little by little," removes her brassière and her "very decent panties, of notable dimensions" (Montero 1983, 21). Once the voice has Antonia disrobed and supine, it fixes itself upon the monumental exposition of her breasts: "The breasts spread out blandly, looking for their arrangement over the ribs, and the nipples, normally so secret, began to tingle like crazy as soon as they found themselves free. So much heat and so much body, protagonist skin in the sultry weather, an apotheosis of epidermis" (Montero 1983, 21).

As if it were a vaporous tropical mass, composed of enormous breasts that are suddenly crowned by trembling nipples, the body of Antonia is thrown into relief. This "protagonist skin," in the shape of a female breast, also characterizes "el otro mundo" of the "Relación del tercer viaje" by Christopher Columbus. Referring to the new lands encountered as "the other world," the admiral declares that the hemisphere is not round, as the majority of cosmographers have believed, but formed like a pear or the breast of a woman: "It would be like half of a very round pear, which would have a tall nipple . . . like the teat of a woman on a round ball" (Varela 1992, 377). Upon navigating the slope of the breast, one arrives at Earthly Paradise, exalted by a Celestial Garden that, according to Columbus, locates itself suitably on top of the nipple: "[A] part of this world must be more near and noble to heaven than another" (Varela 1992, 379). This extravagant identification of the new lands with a paradisiacal female anatomy, "significantly anchored to the term 'other world,'" represents the culmination of a hermeneutic process of feminization and eroticization of the sign "Indies," which was initiated in Columbus's *Diario* with the landfall of 12 October, 1492 (Zamora 1993, 175).[19] By premiering the abundance of Antonia's lavish breasts, the novel works representation and repetition that parodically spin on Columbian excess.

Even though masturbation is a flagrant act of autonomy, one defined by autosatisfaction, this intimacy in Antonia does not escape the weight of her Catholic indoctrination. In order to free herself from prohibitive patriarchal and religious agencies, she has to follow an evasive plan of action. Aware that Catholicism ironically measures guilt by degrees, she never masturbates with her hand "(that would have been a very grave indecency)" (Montero 1983, 22). Instead, she engages her stuffed toy dog, Lulú. This docile female accomplice "rubs over and over her tousled back against the moist and swollen groove . . . down, up, down, ay" (Montero 1983, 23). Secondly, she always limits herself to fantasizing that she is being raped, "because she judge[s] that the acceptance of sex, even imaginary, ha[s] to be a terrible sin" (Montero 1983, 22). Her final gesture is to turn "toward the wall the portrait of her brother, Antonio, who contemplates her . . . fiercely from the bedside table" (Montero 1983, 22). As an image of institutional authority, the photograph of his masculine figure represents the "Law of the Father"[20] that defines sexuality and governs desire. The burlesque grace of "giving him the wall" recapitulates Antonia's real sin: the assertion of autonomy. Having applied various subterfuges, she becomes the agent of her own desire, a prerogative historically reserved for the male.

As the narrative voice informs us, Antonia closes her eyes and feels herself to be "all sweat and flesh, her conscience abandoned far away and she floating in an immense sea of sexual excitement" (Montero 1983, 22). With the distancing effect of a soap opera set, the "fixed setting" of Antonia's bedroom transforms itself into a metaphorical space that suggests the Caribbean Sea. In the midst of this sultry immensity, Antonia floats. Passing "the little threadbare feet of Lulú over her already enlarged nipples," she allows "to surface the phantoms that she was guarding . . . secretly within herself" (Montero 1983, 22). These specters elicit certain European representations of gender and sexual conduct in America, that have equated terra firma with a virgin of paradisiacal delights and the discoverer-explorer-conquistador with the ravisher and reclaimer of rights of possession.[21] In her imagination, Antonia opens the door of her apartment and ingenuously allows an unknown man to enter:

> a big, lusty, he-man that assures he is the plumber . . . that abruptly hurls himself on her, that grabs her breasts (ay, the tits), she struggles, he tears the buttons from her housedress, she begs, he throws her without mercy onto the bed . . . she fights, he rips off her clothes as if he were skinning an animal, she screams, he opens her legs, she wails and writhes, he lowers his pants and takes out an enormous sex, she is terrified, he holds her open and offered up[22] . . . he kneels, he sticks it in . . . he wags, bellowing barbarities that Antonia does not dare to formulate . . . he possesses her and Antonia does not know what that is, she struggles to invent it for herself . . . he possesses her and she is not able to imagine it. (Montero 1983, 22–23)

Making use of a discourse of desire that plays unconsciously, Antonia mixes self-love with matters of erotic domination and subjugation. The fact that a big, lusty he-man plumber, described in Spanish as "un hombrón . . . fontanero," appears at the door not only emphasizes the caricatural quality of her fantasy, in agreement with the comic strips, graphic novels, and soap operas that *Te trataré como a una reina* intentionally theatricalizes, but also *fontanero,* as an adjective, signifies belonging to sources or origins (*perteneciente a las fuentes*). Even etymologically, this sexual fantasy signals a protocolonialist discourse.

If we refer to Columbus's *Diario,* Antonia's imaginary candor alludes to the innocence and gentility of the islanders who greeted the Europeans. The entry for 12 October, 1492 paints them as effeminate, passive, naked, and unarmed.[23] Opening metaphorically their door to strangers, the indigenous people make gifts of "parrots and balls of cotton thread and javelins and many other things," and for their graciousness, Columbus rates them as "good servants and of good humor" (Varela 1992, 110–11). Their hospitality is followed by European cupidity and brutality.

In their initial act of possession, the Europeans bellowed what must have seemed like barbarities to the Amerindians. The *Diario* glosses over this "legal" ritual, referring to the "royal flag and . . . two flags of the Green Cross" that are planted in the sand, at the arrival of the scribe, Rodrigo d'Escobedo, and, later, to the acts of Columbus: "that they might give by faith and testimony how he in front of everyone took, as he in fact took, possession of the said island for the King and for the Queen, his masters, executing the required reclamations, as it is contained more extensively in the testimonies done there in writing. Later many of the islanders gathered there" (Varela 1992, 110).

Each time they stepped upon new land, the Europeans carried out this process, formulating it as they went until 1514, when Doctor Palacios Rubios composed the obligatory text that they had to follow. Supposedly, the conquistadors read the "Requerimiento" in each taking of possession.[24] This document, in Spanish, informed the indigenous populations of their rights and obligations as vassals of the Spanish monarchs. Supported by a papal donation, the possessors also indicated to them that they would be instructed in the Catholic faith. Immediate obedience was rewarded, while any resistance was severely punished (Camps 1989, 17; Greenblatt 1991, 97–98).

The "Requerimiento" assumed not only a commonality of language between the indigenous populations and the conquistadors, but also that the lands of the New World could be claimed by Spain with impunity. In reference to this official document and the absurd belief that no idiomatic difficulties could possibly exist, Bartolomé de Las Casas in his *Historia de las Indias* writes that he does not know "whether to laugh or cry at the 'Requerimiento' " (cited in Greenblatt 1991, 98).

Antonia's virginity would permit the narrative voice to state that personally this protagonist does not know what sexual intercourse is, but the final words of the fantasy also suggest the incoherence of such an act of seizure. Confluent with a metaphorical Amerindian position,[25] Antonia does not understand what the invader articulates or intends: "he possesses her and [she] does not know what that is" (Montero 1983, 23). Indeed, Antonia's colonial fantasy puts on stage a rape that points to the conquest of America.[26] From the beginning, it integrates eroticism with violence, and Woman with the racial Other.

Since this assault is a daydream, it must be classified as rational violence, that is to say, a form of controlled, ritualized, and voluntary rape. It composes a part of Antonia's masturbatory ritual and, as if she were to perform in a segment of a soap opera, with a certain sequence, tone, and appearance, she abandons herself melodramatically to her figment of erotic coercion in order to achieve her orgasm. From a psychoanalytical point of view, this fiction embodies the desire for autonomy and transcendence. The desperation to liberate herself from her numbing confinement in order to obtain support, encouragement, and affirmation in an ordinary human relationship supposedly provokes the brutality of this sexual reverie (Benjamin 1984, 292–93). However, the psychology of this imaginary violation has political implications,[27] inseparable from the erotic, that are tangled up in the construction of femininity and masculinity, gender difference, phallologocentric attitudes,[28] domination, and dependence.

Condemned to a life of soapsuds, where no type of recognition and independence exists within the patriarchal censorship of her brother, it is not surprising that Antonia invents an escape. What fouls all the feminist expectations is that such a brazenly overpowering, conventional, male sexual fantasy transfixes this woman. Although this ironic inversion may provoke repulsion,[29] it is certain that Antonia effectively takes advantage of a discourse of appropriation and domination in order to convert her body into a knowable, desirable, and acquirable—that is, rapable—object. Her female sexual identity has not developed in relationship to sexuality, but in the necessity of being chosen by a man. Upon being selected by an unknown man who ripples with masculine mystique, she receives the essential proof of her value—based on gender—as a woman, in her own eyes and in her imagination of others (Olsson, cited in Heise 1995, 130). With the suggestion of a Caribbean context, the narrative voice situates this body in a protocolonialist discourse and, consequently, makes it yet another representation of America.

Since *Te trataré como a una reina* insinuates a brutal and anonymous sexuality and makes clear that all its female protagonists are besieged by dangerous men, an undeniable fact that the novel installs by means of its "ripper formula,"[30] a romanticized narrative of an imagined violation hangs disturbingly over the presentation of Antonia's masturbation. Her eroticism, a key to her autonomy, proves to be the essence of a configuration of power and control, the reductio ad absurdum of patriarchal attitudes toward women (Nochimson 1992, 80). No doubt exists that a ravaged vision of the woman as a conquered possession mars Antonia's sexual pleasure for the feminist reader[31] and provokes an intricate questioning of the text. Why does this scene position contextually the polarities of masturbatory intimacy and sexual violation? Does it reveal, perhaps, that Antonia, with her indoctrination in a "New World-Old World" sexual paradigm, interlaced by various cultural industries and Catholicism, has no other language to describe her voluptuosity than one that links masculine force with eroticism? What does it say about Antonia's complicity within her colonial context? Does it point out that in the most recondite aspect of her being and in the most secluded domestic space, the most complex conquests of History are able to unfold in a transhistorical and transgeographical convergence? Does Antonia's bed convert itself into a stage for traumatic ambivalences of a personal, psychic, and corporeal history, which relate to the wider disjunctions of political existence (Bhabha 1994, 9–11)?

The questioning of the text (and certainly more inquiries could be stimulated) grows out of the ironic and inherent complicity in this scene, which generates a sense of estrangement. Although it is debatable whether the subtleties of irony are able to compete with the power of the images of subjugation (Hutcheon 1994a, 193), the reader must not forget that this representation is a staging and, for that reason, its theatricality must be part of its critical significance and not simply the vehicle for a preestablished content. Antonia's heavily made-up face; the parodic nature of her striptease, with the languorous unrolling of her stockings and the elimination of her burlesque-sized underpants; the outlandish masturbatory accomplice of the stuffed dog; the synthetic character of the "soapish" studio setting and the "bad taste" of all the gestures and movements point to a stylized and antirealist register. This stylization does not, in any form, try to transcend the material reality of extratextual male domination (Smith 1994, 68–69), but it does, at least, try to denote the layers of entangled ambiguities that define subjectivity and desire.

Immediately after the orgasmic climax of this episode, the narrative voice returns a disoriented and compunctious woman to the usual space of her bedroom: "Antonia recuperated the environment with bewilderment: the tedious drip of the broken water tank, the hot afternoon, the synthetic touch of the bedspread, the trotting of her heart inside her chest, the sticky dampness of sweat. . . . The vertigo was disappearing and its place was being occupied by dirtiness and by guilt" (Montero 1983, 23).

Her postmasturbatory remorse, however, rapidly yields to the enormity of the recognition that she has been spied on: "The sun was already low, night was approaching. And then, upon glancing through the window, Antonia realized the horror: on the roof, barely a couple of meters of distance, his frail adolescent body standing out against the sky, staring at her very cross-eyed, exorbitant, and motionless, was Damián, the silent nephew of the doorman" (Montero 1983, 23).

Just as Antonia becomes aware of the "horror," the scene arrives at a liminal moment. The "New World-Old World" sexual paradigm of discovery, conquest, and colonization returns to its inaugural moment with an allusion to the Columbian encounter with America. Performing a mirror-like reversal, the novel changes the backdrop of a contemporary dusk in Madrid to a metaphorical morning, facing the coasts of Guanahaní, at 2 A.M., 12 October, 1492. The faint light and the appearance in silhouette of a body against the sky echoes the sailor, the look-out on the Pinta's forecastle, who was the first to shout: *¡Tierra!* The *Diario* reports: "After the setting of the sun, [the vessel] navigated its first route to the West . . . and until two hours after midnight it covered ninety miles. . . . And because the caravel Pinta was faster and was in front of the admiral, it found land and made the signs that the admiral had ordered. The first to see this land was a sailor named Rodrigo de Triana" (Varela 1992, 109).

The visual introduction of this "peeping tom–ship's boy" foreshadows the sexual relationship that Damián will have with Antonia and casts light on the erotic possession of the female by the male who gazes at her. Intertwining the protocolonialist discourse of the Columbian encounter with a woman's intimacy, this example of active scopophilia compares the initial sighting of the New World with a first titillating view of naked femaleness.[32] The conclusion of this scene arrives at the original point of departure, in which Antonia, afloat in an immense Caribbean Sea, represents in effect the exaltation of body, gender, and sexuality. Dazzling in its reflection, it gestures at once to the beginnings of colony in America and to the last five hundred years on both sides of the Atlantic.

Antonia's sexual fantasy demonstrates that the ritualization of certain fictions and myths continues to generate relationships that resemble traditional ones of power between colonizer and colonized. Inseparable from the construction of Woman and Man, this historical-cultural legacy exhibits links between identity and masculine desire and the domination, subordination, and violent subjugation of women.

By problematizing the representations of the categories of identity, *Te trataré como a una reina* articulates diverse "subjects" of differentiation, the multiplication of identities, and the intersection of nation, gender, sexuality, social class, race, history, and language. Just as in the other portraits or scenes into which the novel is divided, its multitemporal and multicultural mirroring not only points to decisive stages in the foundation and the alteration of nations that share the same historical-cultural patrimony, but brings to light the underside or reverse of colony: the dual identity of a nation as colony and colonial power (Hutcheon and A. R. JanMohamed, in Hutcheon 1994a, 184).[33] The most intimate manifestation of this duality occurs between the novel's "couples," in what can be defined as exchange based on libido and gender between the colonizer and the colonized. Staged in a Spanish "housekeeper's" bed, an aestheticized, imaginary rape disturbingly exposes this doubling.

In order to shatter these colonial relationships of power, *Te trataré como a una reina* turns its historical-cultural theater of memory into one of parody, which includes a repertoire of positions of power and resistance, domination and dependency. Through colonial representations, whose crucible is gender, the novel sets up ironic tensions in the model of the conquering hero, male mystique, the paradisiacal virgin, female complicity and contingency: all cultural values with which the protagonists so deeply identify. Appropriating stereotypes and anonymity, linguistic triggers, mimicry, farce and caricature, engenderment and sexualization, "bad taste," strategies of illusion, repetition, doublings, and reversals, ambivalence and ambiguity, the novel inverts, subverts, and displaces political power and constructed identities. By working irony to its uneasy limits,[34] the novel's transhistorical and transgeographical seductions are converted into subversive, postcolonial spectacles.

Notes

1. This and all subsequent translations of *Te trataré como a una reina* are mine. Although other novels by Rosa Montero have been translated into English, to my knowledge this novel has not been.

2. Tourist propaganda for the modern Caribbean continues to equate it with Terrestrial Paradise, where there is an open invitation to experiment with sensual pleasures, mystical states, and libidinous urges. For a comparison between the vocabulary of the "New World" Columbian encounter and the popular, symbolic language of Caribbean tourist slogans, see Zamora 1993, 132–33.

3. According to Néstor García Canclini, the process of hybridization constitutes a recombination of forms and symbols, separated from their existent contextual practices, with new forms in new practices. Hybridization is accompanied by "deterritorialization," or the liberation of cultural signs from their fixed spatial-temporal sites. This liberation involves a rupture with tradition, in which elements of distinct territories and histories are able to combine. These elements compose phenomena that began with, or before, the conquest of America. With the development of cultural vanguards and the proliferation of mass media, the process of hybridization has accelerated. See García Canclini 1990, 15, 288; and Zimmerman 1994, 76–77.

4. The literary genre known as *costumbrismo* studies the peculiar and distinctive of the human type: institutions, dress, speech patterns, gestures, occupations, objects, and utensils in their typical locales. It frames these lifestyles with the purpose of conserving specific aspects of daily life or of exposing certain oddities, in contrast to the apparent normality in which they exist. The point of departure for this literature resides in self-recognition.

5. The age of the sex crime began in London in 1888, with the unprecedented crimes of Jack the Ripper. From the end of the nineteenth century to the present day, rippers, stranglers, mutilators, and other types of sexual assassins have become more common. See Caputi 1987, 4.

6. The popular social types of *Te trataré como a una reina* have progenitors in *Los españoles pintados por sí mismos* (1843), a two-volume compendium of nineteenth-century human stereotypes, manners, and picturesque customs. The majority of these figures gravitate to the margin of society and make up the *bajo pueblo.* The same subalterns exist in *Te trataré* . . . , however, not only as singular "types," but also as composites: *el ama de llaves,* Antonia; *el conscripto-grumete,* Damián; *el elegante oficinista-cazador,* Antonio; *el arcaizante esbirro-cesante,* Benigno; *la cantante-mujer del mundo,* Bella; *la actriz aspirante-mujer del mundo,* Vanessa; *el cantinero,* Menéndez; *el indiano-matón,* el Poco; *el sereno,* García; *el pícaro,* el macarrita; *el periodista,* Mancebo. The Boix Press of Madrid began to publish *Los españoles pintados por sí mismos* in 1843, with the collaboration of the most distinguished writers of the epoch, such as the romantic-realists Ramón de Mesonero Romanos, Mariano José de Larra, Serafin Estébanez Calderón, Duque de Rivas, and Eugenio de Ochoa, and a great number of lesser-known journalists. This anthology has turned out to be "one of the most curious productions of that period, and one of the most fecund in consequences" (Montesinos 1960, 106).

7. The expression "Caribbean libidinousness" is sparked by the colonial/postcolonial essay "Loving Columbus," by José Piedra. This essay signals libidinous clichés associated with the Caribbean, which are rooted in stereotypical ideas concerning gender and sexuality (Piedra 1992, 232–33).

8. Among the best Latin American writers of nineteenth-century *costumbrismo* is the Cuban Cirilio Villaverde (1812–1894), who delineated the colonial social classes of Cuban society in *Cecilia Valdés* (1839–1879).

9. Born in Havana in 1925, Olga Guillot was labeled the first popular singer on the island. In 1950, Cuban President Carlos Prío Socarras crowned her "Queen of the Radio," declaring her "one of the most pride-inspiring of Cuban possessions" (*una de las posesiones cubanas más enorgullecedoras*). While on a European tour in 1951, she danced and sang boleros and mambos. Until then, she was best known for a Spanish version of *Stormy Weather* (Smith 1991, 5). Since a hurricane threatens to level the Club Desiré, where reference to Guillot occurs, this extratextual detail of inclement weather is humorously fitting.

10. Citing the increase in winds and waves, and prayers and vows, the *Diario* of Christopher Columbus parallels the growth of the hurricane and the terror of the crew in the entries for 12–14 February 1493. In terms of the codification of America in *Te trataré como a una reina,* this inaugural documentation of the storm activity of the Caribbean basin also holds specific reference to the "nuevas tan grandes," the big news, of the initial encounter with the "New World" in the entry for 14 February. Fearing the loss of his own life on this day, Columbus took the precautions of writing the account of his "discovery" of America on parchment, sealing it in a waxed cloth, stuffing it into a wooden barrel, and casting it into the sea, with the hope that the news would eventually reach the Spanish monarchs (Varela 1992, 205–8).

11. This same concept, applied to museums instead of to *cuadros costumbristas,* comes from James Clifford (cited in Hutcheon 1994b, 225).

12. For studies about the postmodern and postcolonial implications of collections and exhibitions in museums that are applicable to textual analysis in a museographic sense, see García Canclini 1990, 82–83, 98–101, 133–41, 171–77, 197–98, 280, 283, 333; Hutcheon 1994b, 205–38 and 1994a, 176–209; and Huyssen 1995, 1–35.

13. The prefix *post,* attached to colonial, can refer to the dynamics of cultural resistance and retention. Effectively, *post* has come to mean "after," "because of," and, inevitably, "inclusive of" the colonial; it also signifies resistance and

opposition—the anticolonial. Postcolonial in this essay refers to the representation of certain ritualized, traditional, colonial discourses in *Te trataré como a una reina,* which Montero, through the narrative voice, explicitly exhibits, judges, and overturns. See Hutcheon 1995, 10; 1994a, 198.

14. The parodic trivialization of the female protagonist in this scene refers to the soap opera. This cultural medium, which concerns itself with women and desire, came into being at the same time that radio propaganda in the United States began to experiment with the dramatic script. Its first narrative series, entitled *Painted Dreams,* was a program of daily episodes that briefly aired in 1930. Concentrating on a family aptly named the Suddes, the program hoped to attract the company Super-Suds as a sponsor. Today, second-class Venezuelan productions are favored by Spanish-speaking soap opera fans. See Nochimson 1992, 12–13; and Smith 1994, 127.

15. Although Juan Eugenio Hartzenbusch (1806–1880) is among the Spanish authors of *Los españoles pintados por sí mismos,* he is best known for his romantic dramas on historical themes.

16. For a museological study that makes connections between the historical manner of collecting based on gender—that considers the passion of collecting, preserving, and exhibiting—in relationship to Occidental processes of identity formation, to representativeness and presentation of collections, see J. Clifford, "On Collecting Art and Culture," in *Out There: Marginalization and Contemporary Culture,* ed. M. Ferguson, M. Gever, Trinh T. Minh-ha, and C. West (New York: New Museum of Contemporary Art; Cambridge: Massachusetts Institute of Technology Press, 1990). Cited in Hutcheon 1994a, 197.

17. For an essay about the feminization and eroticization of the "discovery" of America that begins with an analysis of the drawing by van der Straet and that notes the ambiguous gesture of the Amerindian woman's hand (152), see Zamora 1993, 152–79.

18. Antonia's masturbatory scene is one particular, micropolitical example of a Madrilenian locale in which protocolonialist discourse reproduces itself. As an analytical model, this discourse is flexible because it is able to conceptualize gender in its reciprocally constituted and historically variable categories of Man and Woman and to comprehend that gender systems themselves are reciprocally related, in many shifting ways, to other modes of cultural, political, and economic organization and experience. Since gender representations display many ideological facets, they generate, constrain, and contest cultural meanings and values. Indeed, beneath their manifest surface stability and consistency of collective structures exist innumerable local and individual sites of social reproduction, variation, and change (Montrose 1993, 177–78).

19. Zamora's essay analyzes in detail the feminization and eroticization of the "Indies" in Columbus's *Diario,* as well as his provocative observation in the "Relación del tercer viaje" that equates the "other world" to a woman's breast. See Pastor, who refers to Columbus's "breast theory" as the "maximum point of [an] identifying delirium" (Pastor 1988, 29–31).

20. The "Law of the Father," a concept of Jacques Lacan, refers to the figure of the father as an institutional authority, which comprises sexual definition and the control of desire.

21. The English poet and clergyman John Donne (1573–1631) wrote in his "Elegy 19": "Licence my roaving hands, and let them go, / Before, behind, between, above, below. / O my America! my new-found-land, / My kingdome, safeliest when with one man man'd, / My Myne of precious stones, My Emperie, / How blest am I

in this discovering thee!" Cited in Sale 1990, 258. The North American historian Samuel Eliot Morison sums up the same idea in his *Admiral of the Ocean Sea:* "Never again may mortal men hope to recapture the amazement, the wonder, the delight of those October days in 1492 when the New World gracefully yielded her virginity to the conquering Castilians" (Morison 1942, 236).

22. The "spread-eagling" [*el despatarrar*] of naked women is endemic in patriarchal cultures and points to the implacable and systematic humiliation of the female. With this ignominious pose, the contemporary sexual criminal and the pornographer, among others, instantly communicate female defeat, degradation, and destruction. This forced posture is also that of the derogated eagle seen on the Great Seal of the United States, which, even as a patriotic icon, symbolizes the violation of the national wilderness (Caputi 1987, 8). In this stylized scene from *Te trataré como a una reina,* Antonia, naked and open-legged, summons up the New World equation of the rape of the land and of Woman.

23. Beginning with the landfall, Columbus portrays an edenic encounter with America, nuanced with feminine and erotic countenances. He describes a sensual green land, adorned by many waters, fruits, and natives with fascinating canary-colored skin. He also reports that they are "very well formed, of very beautiful bodies and very good faces," with "thick hair almost like silks of horses' tails . . . that [some] never cut" (Varela 1992, 111). See Zamora 1993 for a study of Columbus's feminized and eroticized discourse.

24. The "Requerimiento" read by the conquistadors declares: "And we protest that the deaths and losses which shall accrue from this are your fault, and not that of their Highnesses, or ours, nor of these cavaliers who come with us. And that we have said this to you and made this Requisition, we request the notary here present to give us his testimony in writing, and we ask the rest who are present that they should be witnesses of this Requisition." Cited in Greenblatt 1991, 97–98.

25. For an article that treats the colonial metaphorical confluence of the non-European and Woman, see Carr 1984, 46–60.

26. It should not be assumed that Amerindian women were yielding and compliant to the sexual caprices of the Europeans. The first documentation of New World-Old World sexual intercourse was written by Michele Cuneo, an Italian nobleman who traveled with Christopher Columbus on his second voyage. With sadistic and erotogenic pleasure, Cuneo, in Santa Cruz, recorded how he affirmed his power and control by whipping and raping a young Caribe woman. In order to cleverly justify his lust, he attributes a seductive expertise to his prey. For an English version of this sexual violation, see Sale 1990, 140.

27. From a psychoanalytical point of view, fantasized erotic domination is a calculated violence in which participation is voluntary. It does not refer to all forms of violence, nor to all the violence perpetrated by men against women, of which assaults principally figure. Feminism perceives rape as a social conflict between individuals, while psychoanalysis sees it as a conflict within the individual's unconscious realm. Feminism accuses psychoanalysis of inadequate theorization, which does not take into account the psychoanalysts' own complicity in the cultural construction of femininity and masculinity. According to feminism, sexual violation is not a matter of fantasy but of domination. For an essay that analyzes the imagination of violent eroticism in *The Story of O,* by Pauline Réage, see Benjamin 1984, 292–311. For a dictionary entry that aligns the different points of view of feminism and psychoanalysis, see Whitford 1992, 364–66.

28. The term "phallologocentrism," coined by Jacques Derrida, conflates the monolithic systems of "phallocentrism" and "logocentrism." The first privileges the

phallus as universal arbiter of sexuality, the latter privileges the Word as ultimate truth. This equation has brought together the feminist critique of patriarchy and the deconstructionist critique of language. It now extends to many new areas of intersecting critical theories, where feminism is at the forefront of other political struggles. See Smith 1992, 316–18; Spivak 1988, 144; and Ordóñez 1991, 211 n. 53.

29. The strange union of rationality and violence abounds in sexual imagery. All one has to do is stroll by a kiosk of newspapers, magazines, and pulp fiction to be able to see the propagandistic covers that represent sexual bondage. Of course, this theme, which is not exclusive to heterosexuality, is also common in the film, television, and musical industries.

30. Based upon the atrocities of Jack the Ripper and other serial sex criminals, *Te trataré como a una reina* indirectly installs a "ripper formula." Instead of bringing to the forefront one ripper, it includes a woman, in an ironic reversal; almost all the men, by implication; and an unknown youth, nicknamed the Ripper of Cabrerillo, who is determined to be guilty of killing women and whose story is not developed in the novel.

31. The feminist reader, of course, includes male and female readers.

32. "Scopophilia," a psychiatric term, is the active instinct to see (voyeurism) and the passive instinct to be seen (exhibitionism). Although it refers to the attainment of sexual pleasure by looking at naked bodies and erotic photographs, and by being looked at, scopophilic impulses figure prominently in the quest for knowledge and mastery of the world. Voyeurism and exhibitionism are linked to each other; the first has become associated with masculinity and the latter with femininity. See Wright 447–49. In the novel, Antonia and Damián enter into a nonverbal erotic pact of voyeurism and exhibitionism. Sprawled out on the bed, in front of the window and in plain view from above, Antonia begins to masturbate at the same time every day. Up on the roof, Damián follows suit.

33. In Hutcheon's essay "The Ends of Irony: The Politics of Appropriateness," the duality of colony is applied to Canada in relationship to an exhibition, "Into the Heart of Africa," in the Royal Ontario Museum, Toronto (16 November 1989 to 6 August 1990). See Hutcheon 1994a, 176–204.

34. One supposes that irony is what gives parody its bite. However, irony is distressing for many, especially in terms of a postcolonial posture. What is experienced by some as marvelously problematizing and transgressive, in the sense of gender, race, class, and sexuality, for others is simply insulting, abusive, and threatening. Irony is "tricky." For a study about irony's subversive potential and its inherent risks, see Hutcheon 1994a.

Bibliography

Benjamin, Jessica. 1984. "Master and Slave: The Fantasy of Erotic Domination." In *Desire: The Politics of Sexuality,* edited by Ann Snitow, Chistine Stansell, and Sharon Thompson. London: Virago.

Bhabha, Homi K. 1994. *The Location of Culture.* London: Routledge.

Camps, Olga. 1989. Introduction to *Brevísima relación de la destrucción de Las Indias,* by Bartolomé de las Casas. Mexico: Fontamara.

Caputi, Jane. 1987. *The Age of Sex Crime.* Bowling Green: Bowling Green State University Press.

Careaga, Gabriel. 1987. *Mitos y fantasías de la clase media en México.* Mexico: Océano.

Carr, Helen. 1984. "Woman/Indian: 'The American' and His Others." In *Essex Conference on the Sociology of Literature,* 46–60. Colchester: University of Essex.

Chao, Ramon, ed. 1984. *Palabras en el tiempo de Alejo Carpentier.* Barcelona: Argos Vergara.

Colás, Santiago. 1995. "Of Creole Symptoms, Cuban Fantasies, and Other Latin American Postcolonial Ideologies." *PMLA* 110: 382–96.

Ferguson, Moira. 1993. *Colonialism and Gender Relations: From Mary Wollstonecraft to Jamaica Kincaid: East Caribbean Connections.* New York: Columbia University Press.

García Canclini, Néstor. 1990. *Culturas híbridas: Estrategías para entrar y salir de la modernidad.* Mexico: Grijalbo.

Greenblatt, Stephen. 1991. *Marvelous Possessions: The Wonder of the New World.* Chicago: University of Chicago Press.

Hartzenbusch, Juan Eugenio. 1950. "El ama de llaves." In *Los españoles pintados por sí mismos. Costumbristas españoles: I,* 1,043–55. Madrid: Aguilar.

Heise, Lori L. 1995. "Violence, Sexuality, and Women's Lives." In *Conceiving Sexuality: Approaches to Sex Research in a Postmodern World,* edited by Richard G. Parker and John H. Gagnon, 109–34. New York: Routledge.

Hulme, Peter. 1986. *Colonial Encounters: Europe and the Native Caribbean, 1492–1797.* London: Methuen.

Hutcheon, Linda. 1994a. *Irony's Edge: The Theory and Politics of Irony.* London: Routledge.

———. 1994b. "The Post Always Rings Twice: The Postmodern and the Postcolonial." *Textual Practice* 8, no. 2: 205–38.

———. 1995. "Introduction: Colonial and the Postcolonial Condition: Complexities Abounding." *PMLA* 110: 7–16.

Huyssen, Andreas. 1995. *Twilight Memories: Marking Time in a Culture of Amnesia.* New York: Routledge.

Kadir, Djelal. 1993. *The Other Writing: Postcolonial Essays in Latin America's Writing Culture.* West Lafayette: Purdue University Press.

Montero, Rosa. 1983. *Te trataré como a una reina.* Barcelona: Seix Barral.

Montesinos, José F. 1960. *Costumbrismo y novela: Ensayo sobre el redescubrimiento de la realidad española.* Madrid: Castalia.

Montrose, Louis. 1993. "The Work of Gender in the Discourse of Discovery." In *New World Encounters,* edited by Stephen Greenblatt, 177–217. Berkeley: University of California Press.

Morison, Samuel Eliot. 1942. *Admiral of the Ocean Sea: A Life of Christopher Columbus.* Boston: Little, Brown.

Nochimson, Martha. 1992. *No End to Her: Soap Opera and the Female Subject.* Berkeley: University of California Press.

Ordóñez, Elizabeth J. 1991. *Voices of Their Own: Contemporary Spanish Narrative by Women.* Lewisburg: Bucknell University Press.

Pastor, Beatriz. 1988. *Discursos narrativos de la conquista: mitificación y emergencia.* Hanover: Ediciones del Norte.

Piedra, José. 1992. "Loving Columbus." In *Amerindian Images and the Legacy of Columbus,* edited by René Jara and Nicholas Spadaccini, 230–65. Minneapolis: University of Minnesota Press.

Sale, Kirkpatrick. 1990. *The Conquest of Paradise: Christopher Columbus and the Columbian Legacy.* New York: Plume-Penguin.

Smith, Paul Julian. 1991. "Speaking of People: Lena Horne of Cuba (Olga Guillot)." *Ebony* (May): 5.

———. 1992. "Phallologocentrism." In *Feminism and Psychoanalysis: A Critical Dictionary,* edited by Elizabeth Wright, 316–18. Oxford: Blackwell.

———. 1994. *Desire Unlimited: The Cinema of Pedro Almodóvar.* London: Verso.

Spivak, Gayatri Chakravorty. 1988. "French Feminism in an International Frame." In *Other Worlds: Essays in Cultural Politics,* 134–53. New York: Routledge.

Varela, Consuelo, ed. 1992. *Cristóbal Colón: Textos y documentos completos.* Madrid: Alianza.

Whitford, Margaret. 1992. "Rape: Political Perspectives." In *Feminism and Psychoanalysis: A Critical Dictionary,* edited by Elizabeth Wright, 364–66. Oxford: Blackwell.

Wright, Elizabeth. 1992. *Feminism and Psychoanalysis: A Critical Dictionary.* Oxford: Blackwell.

Zamora, Margarita. 1993. *Reading Columbus.* Berkeley: University of California Press.

Zimmerman, Marc. 1994. "Postmodernity and Popular Culture in Latin America." In *Columbus Quincentenary: Encounter and Aftermath, 1492–1992,* edited by George DeMello and Nora Gonzalez, 59–86. Iowa City: Center for International and Comparative Studies.

Marina: A Woman before the Mirror of Her Time in Carlos Fuentes's *Ceremonias del Alba*

GLADYS M. ILARREGUI

> MARINA: Todos han querido deshacerse de mí. Mis padres primero, ahora los caciques. Es que nací bajo el signo de la mala fortuna, la revuelta, la riña y la impaciencia. Mi nombre es Malitzin, que significa todo esto. Mis padres eran príncipes. Pero no me querían.
>
> [MARINA: Everyone has wanted to get rid of me. First my parents, now the chiefs. It's that I was born under the sign of bad fortune, of disturbance, of quarrel, and of impatience. My name is Malitzin, which means all this. My parents were princes. But they didn't want me.]
>
> —Carlos Fuentes, *Ceremonias del Alba*

THE FOUNDING OF NUEVA ESPAÑA SHOULD BE CONSIDERED AS SOMETHING more than the appropriation of Mesoamerica's territory, despite its being the colonization of a mosaic of indigenous people subjected to the European invader. It dealt, above all, with a textual foundation that enacted the active creation of doctrinaire-anthropological texts that opened the native world to transatlantic readers. This enterprise, carried out especially by religious orders, promoted the pragmatic inquiry into the religious and local life of prehispanic Mexico. The chronicler monks started some of the most prodigious research on an exotic and subdued culture by developing active programs of Indian-religious collaboration in order to gather and restructure the historical data of the new colony.[1] The textual phenomena produced two alternative movements during the first half of the sixteenth century. On the one hand, European texts were invading the world of Mesoamerican glyphs with the objective of teaching Mediterranean moral principles, while at the same time the European emigrants concerned themselves—in humanist and religious circles—with understanding of the subdued culture: its practices, history, and cosmology.

In this climate of textual creation, the prodigious collection of Friar Bernardino de Sahagún is found. His ethnographical reports of direct interviews with the survivors of Tlatelolco retell the different points of view of a world whose customs the missionaries were trying to change. In particular, the "Libro de la conquista" (Book XII) of his prodigious *Códice Florentino*[2] articulates the confrontation between two cultural models in which the Amerindian account projects the growing frustration with regard to the misunderstanding of a new political-religious symbolism imported by the Europeans. The discourse articulated by the collector, his *nahuatlatos,*[3] and the native informants proposes an ambiguous reading about the status of the Nahuas within the colonization framework. Narrating the final defeat—one that eliminates the cultural diversity from a material standpoint: clothes, food, arms and even the configuration of the historic space that is symbolic, ritual, and identifiable of a group—the text invites one to a complex reading of the protagonists: the writer/the survivors. The language, a crucial topic to Sahagún, who is interested in linguistic curiosities, becomes the invaded space par excellence, insofar as the metaphors, their synthetical movements, and the rudimentary hieroglyphic apparatus of the oral culture are reduced within the colonizing translation, producing a text already edited at a verbal level that is decontextualized from the identity of the local Mexican group.

This is the moment to which Carlos Fuentes elects to transport himself in *Ceremonia del Alba* (first version 1968, second 1991), a play that confronts us with the last days of the history of the conquest by taking almost verbatim the passages of the Sahaguntine *Códice.*[4] The play has such an impact because in spite of its faithfulness to a document produced in the sixteenth century in classical Nahuatl and Renaissance Spanish, it is still capable of procuring—as in Fuentes's other narrative productions—a reflection of the past, a reflection that really marks the presence of the text in the Mexican present, since the historical characters have a notion of the fate that awaits them. Thus, two ages dialogue: the present and the past; Malinche and Marina, the world of the conquered conqueror, the force of the chaos that befalls after the fall of the Aztec empire. The leading role of Marina in Fuentes's work is a contemporary addition, since in the *Códice,* Malinche is only alluded to although she is a key protagonist in the history of the conquest. Her presence within early colonial texts and in the correspondence of the Corpus Cortesianum (1519–1526) occupies only a few brief lines to the king. As Baudot says in *México y los albores del discurso colonial:*

> The only thing that the conqueror concedes is a fleeting allusion to the role of intermediary, which Malitzin was obliged to assume during the political conversations with the populace or with the Amerindian authorities, and this with the inoffensive qualifier of "our language" or of "the language." Written by such a rational pen, one so concerned with the degree of the narrator's proximity to the narrative and with her voluntary and supposed objectivity, this messenger of the conqueror already is deeply significant within her verbal strategy. In the process of fictionalization that will mold her representation of the conquest, the role attributed

> (without insistence) to Malitzin's word is, nonetheless, that of the crucial distribution of the discourse, the political and verbal allocation that implies a central situation, even though this was not Cortés's intention on an immediate level, due to the tactical charge that is present in the *Cartas de relación*. Yet, also on an immediate level, this seems to all of us to be little, indeed very little, given that this was a woman who offered him the keys to an empire. (Baudot 1996, 288)

Carlos Fuentes makes Marina enter the stage as the true translator of this history of two worlds. He does not neglect her or treat her with hostility, as did her contemporaries, but instead identifies her as the woman with the great enigma of the Mexican identity, of the *nepantla,* a Nahuatl term used to name an in-between situation. Marina wears the embroidered *huipil* of her culture and appears in total darkness on stage; in the meantime the murmur of a broom sweeping is heard in the background. When she addresses the audience, she asks questions that introduce us to the conflict of her identity, an identity that, like the prehispanic group culture, represents more than an "I," and that extends to Mexican territorial and political conflicts. Malitzin, the name given to her by her parents who abandoned her, and Marina, a name that evokes the oceanic transit route by which the Spaniards came to break up the native power, relate to each other in a complex way. With these two names, two men are trapped in their own identity: Moctezuma Xocoyotzin, great *tlatoani* of Mexico, and Fernando Cortés, a Spanish captain and noble of little account. Cortés's biography, succinctly given in the sketch, is in spite of its brevity, sufficient to let us know about his past:

> Hernán Cortés. Born in Medellín, in Extremadura, son of millers who gathered scant resources to send me to Salamanca, where I was a sponger and a wastrel, letting down my parents. A little Latin, yes, and some law, but mostly books of chivalric deeds that teach the norms of boldness and of honor, and tales of the new world that teach one to dream of cities of gold and the bellicose Amazons. . . . Don't you see? I was seven years old when Columbus discovered the New World. (Fuentes 1991, 60)

Moctezuma Xocoyotzin, the other key man in Marina's life, is, on the other hand, a leader whose power surpasses that of any other man. Of him Marina says: "No one can look him in the face, such is his resplendence. Moctezuma is the sun on the earth. More than three thousand servants wait on him in his palace, and he has thirty women with whom to amuse himself" (Fuentes 1991, 64).

Confronted with a war in which to translate is to facilitate the knowledge of the Other, Marina negotiates a new conception of herself. Through the contrast between the men of two symbolic worlds, she understands that her own identity is also opening to new and unexpected events, responding to invisible forces present in the person of Cortés: a king and a Christian, European god. Cortés, being the negotiating figure par excellence, prepared for the bitterness and exhaustion of endless expeditions to find gold, reflects: "You can't go home miserable. The future is here. . . . We can't go back empty-handed" (Fuentes 1991, 74). His political ambition installs Malinche inside his own game—a game destined toward her personal fortune, being about a woman who at a certain moment assumes a state of submission in front of the commander of an expedition full of ambition and violence[5]—because in one of the notations for the play Fuentes says that "Marina helps Cortes to undress, removing the armor. There is a parallelism with the gestures of the maidens dressing Moctezuma" (Fuentes 1991, 90). This gesture can also be read as anticipating the transference of power that will take place in Tenochtitlán, in great part because of the linguistic and valiant help of Marina.

As we see in the "Libro de la conquista," the unique objects sent by Moctezuma to Cortés are a sign of welcome. The men, not the women, are the ones who appear to be preoccupied with their appearance in the retelling of the conquest. They are the ones who worry that the body, as the seat of authority, assumes an ideal presence. In chapter IV the luxury goods sent to the Spanish conqueror are described.

> They also brought golden earflaps: they brought little golden dangling bells, and strings of beautiful little white shells. From these strings there hung leather that was like a breastplate, and they carried it cinched in such a way that it covered the entire chest to the waist: this breastplate has many shells pinned all over it; they also brought a corset of white, painted cloth, the lower hem of this corset was embroidered with white feathers in three rows all the way around: they brought a rich cape, the cloth was of a light blue and was worked all over with much fine blue needlework. (Sahagún 1988, 726)

The articles given vary from sheets to masks, hats, and precious feathers mounted with jade or obsidian, all favorites of the Aztec emperor. Bernal Díaz, who appears in Fuentes's play as a beginning chronicler, the man who later would retell and expound the conquest, giving Marina the role of a brave and exceptional translator, reminds Cortés of the importance of clothes when, upon opening the trunk, Marina starts to take out gentleman's clothing that Cortés will wear when he is named chief of the Cuban expedition. Marina celebrates these clothes—even though we never see her beautify herself—as she places plumes, necklaces, and golden medals on Cortés next to the velvet garments that recall the world of Iberian splendor.

In these cultural signs we notice that the feminine presence is fundamental within the ideological and political duality that the confrontation of these two worlds creates. Although it should be remembered that this confrontation was directed, above all, toward the European domination of the materialistic culture,[6] the Aztec abundance would eventually result in an identity problem with Cortés, confronting him with the Spain he left behind, and the one he wanted to conquer by means of economic glory. As the translator of these material signs, Marina appears on a secondary level during Cortés's narration, only to reappear when the conquistador sleeps. This dream, which we never see in the "Libro de la conquista," gives some respite to her court-breeding ambitions, as Marina reflects on Mexico, the Mexico that in a way is beginning to be torn apart. With these thoughts in mind, Marina addresses Cortés as he sleeps hugging her: "Be in truth the Feathered Serpent; in truth give back unity and happiness to these disintegrated and subjected people. . . . Do not destroy this garden" (Sahagún 1988, 106).

This protective thought for the splendorous city that she has seen for the first time suggests that Marina wanted to believe, like the Mexicas, that Cortés was indeed the god, the *teúl* who would grant an opportunity for reconciliation to the people, tired of Moctezuma's demands for human sacrifices and taxes. But the alliances that Cortés establishes (as told in the "Libro de la conquista" when Tlaxcala fulfills an important role in chapter XXVII), give an idea of the divided territory that would permit the entrance and defeat of Tenochtitlan. As suggested by Rysard Tomicki,[7] at this point in time in sixteenth-Century Mesoamerica, it is not rare that anti-Moctezuma and anti-tenochas prophecies would circulate, stemming from the subjugation of these people by the great empire of the Valley of Mexico. Of Moctezuma it is said: "Blessed Moctezuma does not address anyone: not the mortals, who are unworthy; nor the gods, for he already knows their thoughts. There is an abundance of reasons" (Fuentes 1991, 112).

Marina, reared amid sages and fortune-tellers with a circular and thus repetitive religious conception, must contrast the expectation of the Hispanic universe based on divine interpretation and superstitious signs to the tactile and expansive world of the men with whom she shares this territorial advance. In them, the enchanted signs and the calendars are fabrications that can be conquered not by mere suggestion, but by reason and war. The displacement that occurs between the historical authenticity of the Mexica memory and the implantation of new symbolic conditions accounts for the fact of naming, being *la lengua.* The Marina of Fuentes reflects upon the conditions of the language when this is also a trap, and produces a force that disarticulates space and time through the modification between Spanish and Nahuatl. She says: "What was this mountain called before? What will this river be called now? Do you remember the old name for this bird? What name will we give to this new city? What is your name? How do you speak? Who speaks for you? Which are your words?" (Fuentes 1991, 119).

In another tender moment—of the many between the young conquistador and Marina—she asks: "Do you want to know what your tongue says?" and Cortés kisses her passionately, as she pushes him away and tells him: "Your tongue says that the language of this land names you as a god" (Fuentes 1991, 127). Undoubtedly, Marina rearticulates these two worlds, which are unknown to each other. This is a problem, if it is considered that Cortés cannot communicate with any of the important emperors of his time: not with Moctezuma, since he can't exchange with him a word in Nahuatl, and not with Carlos V, because the emperor cannot speak Spanish.

> No, by my faith, my young king Carlos has led a placid life outside of Spain; a son of Flanders, he doesn't even know how to speak Spanish, son of Juana, the crazy queen, he has cloistered himself like his mother, between preceptors, physicians, and courtiers. . . . From now on I bet you, woman: a Spanish king will never put his feet on these lands won by us for your lineage. I, on the other hand . . . ever since a child, I have lived with my eyes filled with visions of the new world. (Fuentes 1991, 128)

There did not exist in Mesoamerica the possibility of a biculturalism that would teach the prospective convert the new doctrine. Those persistent texts that blossom from Christian ideology contain the possibility of reordering the chaotic world of language, a world in whose richness and perpetual amazement Marina lives. The destruction of Mesoamerica appears to her as the destruction of those fabulous constructions, fictional constructions, rich in fantasy like chivalric novels. The language that Marina represents is undergoing a crisis, inasmuch as the Church would promote brilliant and dedicated linguists who would demarcate the indigenous culture within the parameters of a diabolic ideology. Those words, texts, and glyphs, paintings and memories, that Sahagún is bent on gathering in his *Códice* achieve the status of prohibited texts, texts that the Inquisition will prosecute during the second half of the century. What Marina pronounces and translates does not erase the status of *nepantla,* since Olmedo, as representative of the rigid Church, confronts Marina and Cortés in *Ceremonias,* anticipating the future role of the clerics in matters pertaining to the legislation of moral and Christian usages. At the time in which Marina exalts Cortés for the virtues of his expansionist dream, Olmedo says: "Be silent, diabolical woman, because even though you have received from my hands the waters of baptism and the sign of the cross, your pagan soul continues to belong to these filthy stone idols, which we will destroy in our path" (Fuentes 1991, 129).

Olmedo scolds Cortés, promising a future revenge because the conquest is not only for the king, but also for the Church. This church will plan an appropriation of the Mexicans through rhetorical and obsessive spiritual conquest of these manifestations of pagan idolatry that the same Sahagún describes in his preface to the reader. The native recollections—produced from the genuine effort of these religious orders—are the clearest manifestations of a textual war between the vanquished oral text and the appropriation of a writing that fractures the world and returns it apparently intact. In the work, Olmedo anticipates that manipulation of pagan, pre-Christian, polytheistic history.

The Defeat

> MOCTEZUMA: Llegamos a esta tierra con un solo dios, Huitzilopochtli, deidad de la guerra. Pero para legitimarnos tuvimos que apropiarnos de un segundo dios, Quetzalcóatl, deidad de la moral. ¿A quién debo honrar ahora?
>
> [MOCTEZUMA: We arrived at this land with only one god, Huitzilopochtli, the deity of war. But to make ourselves legitimate we had to appropriate a second god, Quetzalcóatl, the deity of morality. Who should I honor now?]
>
> —Carlos Fuentes, *Ceremonias del Alba*

In this piece, not divided in scenes, takes place the bloody defeat of the Mexican people. After the invasion of Moctezuma's palace, with the violent death of the Mexicans, what was the garden between lakes that Marina wanted to preserve has been converted by the Spaniards and pestilence to a cruel battlefield where Malinche recognizes in a loud voice the new tyranny, that of Cortés. Upon hearing these words, Cortés throws Marina on the ground, mistreating her physically for the first time. The words that gave him an empire are converted to words that weigh him down: "Watch your words, witch, lest I return you to the slavery from which I delivered you, or give you to the lowest of my soldiers" (Fuentes 1991, 158).

Marina then intensifies her protective discourse toward the Mexican people, maybe because she understands that her own identity is fragmented in this market of slaves and dead in which she is forced to remain after Cortés's actions. Her discourse invites one to reflect after the fulminating action that leaves Tenochtitlan in ruins. Marina asks herself and her companion:

> What would we have found in your house had this story been reversed? What evil, what horror, what sacrifices, what tyrannies, sir, in your own home? Try to understand us. Give us a chance. Don't kill the goodness of my people in trying to kill your own evils. Don't destroy or fragile identity. Take what is constructed here and construct something beside us. Don't assassinate my homeland. Don't take away our history, since it is also thanks to it you are who you are. Somebody, somebody, never again a nobody. (Fuentes 1991, 159)

The passionate dialogue between the main protagonists of this story makes one understand that Cortés, young, powerful, and rich, finally finds in the conquest the main thread of his personal and social security. Mesoamerica is the land that gives him back a different image, one in which he can recognize himself. But Marina intuitively describes her fears to Cortés: "I love you and I don't fear your death but rather your destiny, for destiny is always briefer than life, and death is to go on living after destiny has already been fulfilled" (Fuentes 1991, 161).

This anticipation by way of an omen will mark in reality the lives of Cortés and Marina after the conquest. Their roles will disappear in a new network of political relationship, in which the accomplished destiny will be subdued to the guidelines of a first viceroyalty and in the midst of the Church's didactic and evangelical methodology. Not even the son Marina gives birth to, who has a long monologue in the piece, can create the security of a common space for both of them. This son is born after the indigenous defeat. Marina warns him that he will not be able to enjoy the privileges of those born among Spaniards, because her son is white and brown, a son of the *mestizaje,* who occupies the space of *nepantla,* which is his own space from the moment in which he was baptized as Cortés's son. She foretells for her son unhappiness, as a known and resented bastard, and cleverness, cleverness such as Marina's own, earned through the language, through the traps of the language and its mutations. Now she begs her son to become the Feathered Serpent, the one who returns: "my little son of a whore, you must be the feathered serpent, the land with wings, the bird of clay, the cuckold [*cabrón*] and the bastard son [*encabronado hijo*] of Mexico and Spain: you are my only legacy, the legacy of Malitzin, the goddess, of Marina, the whore, and of Malinche, the mother" (Fuentes 1991, 178).

Her repetition of her name in the different stages indicates the fragmentation that has taken place because she cannot give birth to a unity, just as she cannot give birth to herself within this space as a new woman. The past is latent, and she fractures that past before the vanquished. At the same time, as a mother she assumes an attitude of revenge before that fragmentation that condemns her in the Mexican culture. Judy McInnis, in her article "La Malinche as Symbol of Illegitimacy and Betrayal," discusses this battle of ideologies vis-à-vis Malitzin/Marina/Malinche as a Mexican icon.

> As Sandra Cypess points out in her book *La Malinche in Mexican Literature,* Paz denied Malinche the "sacredness . . . as mother of the Mexican people" that his grandfather Ireneo Paz has developed in the novel *Doña Marina.* While Ireneo developed her as embodiment of the Virgin Mary archetype possessing beauty, courage, valor, a good heart and compassion, Octavio assimilated her to Eve, the woman who betrays and brings the downfall of her people. Octavio Paz's identification of Malinche with "la chingada" and "la llorona" reduced her to an example of female passivity yet more abject than Eve. (McInnis 1995, 53)

Within the complexity of the mystifying historiography, there is no doubt that Marina was an efficient participant in the Cortesian and Spanish purposes, to which Georges Baudot adds:

> It should be added that her physical intimacy with Cortés has facilitated and even permitted this central role for her, in which the decisive process of the conquest is elaborated. We can thus note, in effect, that Malitzin only was the conqueror's lover during the determining period of the enterprise, that is, from the arrival at Tlaxcala until the fall of Mexico (more or less over the course of two years), and that their love-child, Martín Cortés, was born in the spring of 1522, which places the moment of his conception in the final phase of the conquest: during the siege of Mexico when destiny at last seemed to undergo a definitive turnabout. It must be emphasized as well that this love affair grew distant, at times turbulent, after the final victory, as if the project that governed it no longer existed. (Baudot 1996, 297)

At the end of the work, Bernal Díaz's account, written when this former soldier of Cortés was in old age, is profiled as the future chronicle that will offer a fresh view of these culminating moments in the life of Mesoamerica. With his pen he will exercise a unique power: that of examining his own history and those of the important persons of his time with a benevolent look for Malinche and the Mexican culture in general. His pages will do nothing less than deny all that was written earlier.

If the identity of Cortés is a problem during the entire work, the search for Marina's identity is unceasing, exacerbated by the proximity of the fall of an imaginary social and ideological order that she anticipates at the age of twenty-five. The questions that the characters expound at the end are questions that situate them as protagonists and spectators at the same time: Where are the names of the things? Whom will these new subjects serve? In what way will these local realities be articulated—by articulating them? Therefore, the bottom mirror, the mirror that has dominated the whole piece and that reflects these different moments of Marina/Malinche, is broken and falls shattered. This is perhaps the metaphor of a definite rupture of Marina's main character at the end of the warlike encounter and before the rapid territorial appropriation that the religious orders carried out to subjugate the world of the Amerindian rituals: building convents over the old temples, burning or prohibiting sacred paintings, translating.

For the contemporary reader, Carlos Fuentes created a new Malinche with a voice and a conscience that the sixteenth-century reader couldn't have imagined. She is part of a new cultural model within contemporary historiographic search. Fuentes originally wrote the piece in 1968 as a forceful public protest in regards to the problems of Mexican identity, the eternal *nepantla,* the tradition of a defeat. From this same angle, the translating woman acts, in this play, as the true link to matters that still affect Mexican history. As a contemporary chronicler, Fuentes initiates the search for that same feminine sensitivity that, in a parallel manner, Baudot looks for in the archives and investigations. Baudot thinks that:

> That long voyage to rediscover herself appears to have lasted twenty-four years, a quarter of a century of loneliness in New Spain, after a quarter of a century of icy rebellion in the Mexico of the Aztecs. It is a life that is bisected into two almost equal, yet both equally marginalized, spaces, outside of all foreseeable trajectories, beyond the Others. The silence that Malitzin imposes on the last half of her existence is surprising; she was probably entirely dedicated to her husband, Juan Jaramillo, and to her two children, Martín Cortés and María Jaramillo, shunning honors and all sorts of social success. Perhaps her memories haunted her? Perhaps she fled from the eyes of a destroyed people, of those Indians who in Tlatelolco or in Texcoco saw her in their dreams burning in the deepest of hells, as Bernal Diaz remembers: "near Tlatelolco . . . he saw in the patio that the souls of Cortés and Doña Marina burned in open flames" or even "some evil things wandered in the patios of Texcoco, which the Indians said were the souls of Doña Marina and of Cortés." (Baudot 1996, 330)

My essay, undoubtedly, does not conclude the search for the always-fictionalized Marina of the nineteenth and twentieth centuries.[8] I want to believe that, rather, it joins the body of speculative constructions around that woman who with exceptional courage simultaneously resisted and supported battle, pregnancy, and ideological colonialism. I do not believe it is possible to identify Malinche from only a Eurocentric perspective, since a circular culture, a ritual culture, saw her birth and gave sense to her life. Fuentes's mirror offers an alternative vision from a particular premise: the entrance of a woman as a subject of autobiography, investigation, and analysis.[9] As works dealing with elements of cultural synthesis, *Ceremonias del Alba* and the *Códice florentino* resemble each other and distance themselves in the development of the same topics. In the first, there is already a Mexican writer confronting his own past (and perhaps his own cultural search), while the Sahaguntine document inserts itself in the ideological complexities of the sixteenth century. According to Fuentes, in his written preface to the second version of his work: "As long as Mexico does not eliminate colonialism, both from abroad and that which some Mexicans exercise over and against millions of Mexicans, the conquest will continue to be our historical trauma and nightmare: the sign of an insurmountable fatalism and of a frustrated will. La Malinche's clamor is the warning of a new human sacrifice and of the new human necessity of the Mexico born of the conquest" (Fuentes 1991, 12).

Within the bellicose pages of a unique encounter, Malinche, in fiction and ethnography, remains still as that woman who occupies the *Lienzo de Tlaxcala,*[10] the one who spoke for many years from her persistent curiosity and daring, rich with words, powerful in the linguistic interpretations of two cultures, but dumb from the iconography in which we again find her as the young Mexican woman who still amazes us. The extraordinary force of her myth still reveals to us the fresh academic space of women in historiography and the need to enter the subjective games of the old and doctrinaire texts as Fuentes does in this contemporary play.

Notes

1. Fernando Aínsa expounds in his essay "Los signos imaginarios del encuentro y la invención de la utopía," an analysis of the pragmatical procedures that American utopia acquired through social and anthropological discourse generated by religious orders. Through the critique of the prevailing historical model in Spain, the missionaries projected a model of primitive Christianity in the native world, hence the need they felt to structure the knowledge of local Mexico, as a first step to build up their religious utopia. At the same time that this was happening, the production of an ethnographic literature did not have major importance to the secular writers. Their objectives were related to the recording of Spanish feats in the new land. For them, the textual world was also the world of social claim. The written word granted preeminent prestige to private soldiers that had departed from Spanish coasts many years ago.

2. Sahagún's work is normally called *La historia general de las cosas de la Nueva España.* This error is due to the fact that the page with a more detailed version of the title *Códice florentino* was lost. Nevertheless, other versions of this work do not omit this title. For a rectification of this error, see García Bustamante 1990.

3. The *nahuatlatos,* or interpreters, reconciled the prohibitive side of their past with the inevitable colonial reality. The functions they fulfilled were fundamental, if the multiple forms that they had to adapt to new knowledge and strange techniques are considered. In Gruzinski's words: "There were a multiplicity of expressive media: glyphs rubbed shoulders with the alphabet and musical notation; the painted picture met the engraving; oral transmission oscillated between pre-hispanic or Christianized forms; plain chat, polyphony followed upon ancestral dances. Multiplicity also of languages: Latin and Spanish were added to the Indian languages, dominated by Nahuatl, which served everywhere as lingua franca. Multiplicity of calendar in the Annals, which recorded the Indian and the christian year at the same time" (Gruzinski 1993, 62). The *nahuatlatos,* besides articulating the complexity of the alphabetic/oratory world of the first colonial period, salvaged the oratory of the ancient Nahuas, based on the *huehuetlatolli.* The Mexican cultural universe came from these oral testimonials collected ethnographically both by Fray Andrés de Olmos and by Bernardino de Sahagún. The *huehuetlatolli* constituted the core of the ceremonial, political, religious, social and quotidian discourses of the Nahuas. For a detailed study of the construction and content of the *huehuetlatolli* and for a metaphoric analysis of the structures of Nahuatl, see Carmen Espinoza's *Huehuetlatolli. Discursos de los antiguos nahuas.* Another highly important work on the question of orality reinterpreted by the Spaniards is Patrick Johansson's *Voces distantes de los*

aztecas. This linguistic study opens a multifaceted and complex universe to whomever desires to know more about the oral culture that Malinche was able to translate, seduce, and dominate.

4. Carlos Fuentes develops a close historical parallelism to the Sahaguntine *Códice.* As with his other works, such as *Terra nostra* or *Cristobal Nonato,* the past establishes its weave of relationships, and history becomes the original text for the search of a Mexican and Latin American identity. In the crisscrossing of passions—at many levels—that expounds the history of conquest, as a writer he finds the joy and the tragedy of a conquered region that is, at the same time, ready to be born. This is expressed by Bernardo Ezequiel Koremblit in "Tragedia y humor en el Nuevo Mundo: La narrativa de Carlos Fuentes."

5. After the conquest, Cortés progressively negotiated his economic advantages and his titles. In a letter addressed to Charles V dated 1 April 1529, he expanded his title of "Captain General" to "Captain General of all of New Spain and provinces and coast of the South Sea." The queen ordained on 5 April 1529 that honors should be granted to Cortés, Marquis of del Valle, during his return voyage to Nueva España. On 16 April 1529, Pope Clement VII legitimated Cortés's three illegitimate children: Martin Cortés (Malitzin's son), Luis de Altamirano (son of Antonia or Elvira Hermosillo), and Catalina Pizarro (daughter of Leonor Pizarro, perhaps a relative of Cortés). In another royal warrant that same year, Charles V and Queen Juana awarded him twenty-three thousand vassals. This rising power initiated another battle in Cortés's life between the Church and his ex-comrades-in-arms, a recurring battle that plagued him for the rest of his life in Mexico, as the *Documentos cortesianos* (1528–32) (Mexico:UNAM, 1991) testify.

6. The difference of Spanish materialistic culture cannot be sufficiently emphasized. The domination of certain metals like steel, shining on their bodies, from the beginning gave the Spaniards that psychological halo of gods. In *El encuentro de la piedra y el acero,* José Lameiras Olvera finds another difference between the Renaissance man and the Mesoamerican man—the materialistic culture included in the symbolic cycle in which celebrating and fighting were part of the indigenous calendar. The Mesoamerican sociopolitical conformation was sustained by war: "The case of the Mexica, Tepaneca, Acolhua, Colhua, Chalca, Huejotzinca, Xochimilca, Coyuaque, Tlaxcalteca, and other groups from the Central High Plateau; the Mixtecos and Zapotecos, Mayas and Huastecos, Totonacos, Chontales, and other southern and oriental ethnic groups, constituted stratified societies with the nobility at the head. Wars fought for and among them throughout eleven centuries would place the military in superior stratas" (Lameiras Olvera 1994, 86). Spanish weapons played a prominent role in Cortés's final defeat of Moctezuma. In his novelistic chronicle *Gonzalo Guerrero: Memoria Olvidada,* Carlos Villa Roiz clearly relates the indigenous defeat by force of arms and describes the scene of the conflict, after which twenty indigenous women were turned over to Cortés to perform services such as preparing tortillas. In reality, the women were pressed into forced sexual service for the sailors, and the tale shows the drama of a technically beaten people: "March 15, 1519. The Ides of March. We said it, the field was bloody, the cadavers scattered, the vultures gathered all about. The flint rarely could pierce the soldier's armor, just as it is difficult to break with one's hands a tortoise's shell. The iron breastplate was resistant to obsidian, jade, and serpentina" (Villa Roiz 1995, 391).

7. Tomicki questions the information from the records of the sixteenth century, arguing that the real historical facts have been concealed by a series of subsequent political legends. In *Sahagún's Historia General,* Moctezuma's weakness could have been recreated at a later date; men are treated as women who are afraid of the

unknown. But Moctezuma's unpopularity is evident before the arrival of the Spaniards to Mesoamerican territory. The emperor's absolutist aspiration was reflected in the way he perceived the subjugated people from the Mexican complex, and also contributed to this perception. With Moctezuma Xocoyotzin, the control of the Mexica-Colhua-Tenocha was secured, but his military, religious, and political authority took on absolutist characteristics as described by Diego Durán in *Historia de las Indias de Nueva España.*

8. In my article "Itoca Malitzin/Doña Marina: Biografía de una mujer indígena," I explore the different versions of the name and figure of Malitzin before and after the conquest from a contemporary ethnographic perspective. This revision passes through the archival documentation after 1521, and continues through the investigatory process around the figure of a mythical woman from a new post-structuralist historical conception. Regarding the articulation of women's space in the sixteenth century, see also Susan Kellog 1993, 1995; and Cecelia Klein 1994.

9. In the chapter "Toward Intimacy: The Fourteenth and Fifteenth Centuries," Philippe Aries and Georges Duby comment on the phenomenon of auto-conscience and the diaries, letters, and private chronicles that begin to flourish during this period. The progressive emergence of autobiographical narrative is something that the European is already familiar with when he enters Mesoamerica. But the private feelings are unknown in the pre-Hispanic codex, except for areas dealing with pain, failure, happiness, and common pain related to the group at issue. Of course, women have limited access to this process of personal individualization and projection. Marina speaks through Fuentes, who intuitively projects her from a society in search of a feminine history.

10. As Serge Gruzinski says: "The *Lienzo of Tlaxcala* was probably painted to order for the viceroy don Luis de Velazco between 1550 and 1564. It is thus a commissioned work, 7 by 2.5 meters, which reconstructs the Tlxcaltec version of events in 87 pictures. For these Indians it was also a political manifesto that did not hesitate to disguise events when they might refute the irreductible attachment of the Indians of Tlaxcala to the cause of conquistadores. . . . Although colonial in content, the Lienzo still in many respects belongs to the native tradition. Names of places and protagonists and dates were indicated according to custom by glyphs. The Indians were represented in profile with the attributes of their functions, the signs of their power—the icpalli seat—the clothes of their rank, the hairdos of their tribes" (Gruzinski 1993, 21).

Bibliography

Aínsa, Fernando. 1992. "Los signos imaginarios del encuentro y la invención de la utopía." In *Utopias of the New World,* edited by Anna Houzková and Martin Procházka. Prague: Institute of Czech and World Literature.

Baudot, Georges. 1996. *México y los albores del discurso colonial.* Mexico: Editorial Patria.

Cypess, Sandra Messinger. 1991. *La Malinche in Mexican Literature: From History to Myth.* Austin: University of Texas Press.

Durán, Diego. 1967. *Historia de las Indias de Nueva España.* 2 vols. Mexico: Edina.

Espinoza, Carmen. 1997. *Huehuetlatolli. Discursos de los antiguos nahuas.* Mexico: Instituto Michoacano de Cultura.

Fuentes, Carlos. 1991. *Ceremonias del Alba.* Mexico: Siglo XXI.

García Bustamante, Jesús. 1990. *Fray Bernardino de Sahagún: Una revisión crítica de los manuscritos y su proceso de composición.* Mexico: UNAM.

Gruzinski, Serge. 1993. *The Conquest of Mexico: The Incorporation of Indian Societies into the Western World, 16th–18th Centuries.* Cambridge: Polity Press.

Johansson, Patrick. 1994. *Voces distantes de los aztecas. Estudio sobre la expresión nahuatl prehispánica.* Mexico: Fernandez Editores.

Kellog, Susan. 1993. "The Social Organization of Households among the Tenochca Mexica before and after the Conquest." In *Prehispanic Domestic Units in Western Mesoamerica: Studies of the Household,* edited by Robert Stanley and Kenneth Hirth. Boca Raton: CRS Press.

———. 1995. "The Woman's Room: Some Aspects of Gender Relations in Tenochtitlan in the Late Pre-Hispanic Period." *Ethnography* 42, no. 4: 563.

Klein, Cecelia. 1994. "Fighting with Femininity: Gender and War in Aztec Mexico." *Estudios de la Cultura Nahuatl* 24: 219–53.

Koremblit, Bernardo Ezequiel. 1988. "Tragedia y humor en el Nuevo Mundo: La narrativa de Carlos Fuentes." *La Prensa* [Buenos Aires] 20 March.

Lameiras Olvera, José. 1994. *El encuentro de la piedra y el acero: La Mesoamérica militarista del Siglo XVI que se opuso a la irrupción europea.* Mexico: El Colegio de Michoacán.

McInnis, Judy. 1995. "La Malinche as Symbol of Illegitimacy and Betrayal." *MACLAS: Latin American Essays* 8: 51–56.

Sahagún, Bernardino de. 1988. *Historia general de las cosas de la Nueva España.* Edited by A. López Austin and J. García Quintana. Madrid: Alianza.

Tomicki, Ryszard. 1986. "Augurios de la conquista Española entre los Aztecas: El problema de la credibilidad de las fuentes históricas." *Etnología Polona* 12: 51–78.

Villa Roiz, Carlos. 1995. *Gonzalo Guerrero: Memoria Olvidada.* Mexico: Plaza y Valdez Editores.

Daimón and the Eroticism of the Conquest

TERRY SEYMOUR

According to Abel Posse, the Spanish conquest of Latin America was motivated as much by eroticism as by a search for wealth, because the relative openness of the Indians in sexual matters became a consolation for the conquistadors' failure to find the riches they had originally sought: "The gold and the pearls were no longer the only attraction; from then on the invaders would find a great consolation. The other gold were the bodies" (Posse 1989, 200). However, Posse argues, the chronicles hushed up the conquistadors' erotic motivation in order to conform with the strictures of Judeo-Christian morality: "For centuries the official and academic chronicle silenced the erotic motive with all that it had of nakedness and of savage freedom for people who did not see a woman naked even on their wedding night" (Posse 1989, 200).

One of Posse's stated objectives in writing *Daimón* and *Los perros del paraíso* was to present the clash between two different ways of viewing eroticism. In *Daimón* these are the repressive strictures of Judeo-Christian morality and the idyllic sexual freedom of Latin American paganism (Posse 1989, 200). As the quotation above suggests, Posse's novel interprets the conquest as the male search for the female Other. The conquistador Lope de Aguirre comes back to life and carries on a series of often unsatisfactory or perverse sexual encounters that are not mentioned in the chronicles, including rape, necrophilia, incest, and prostitution. Moreover, the conquistador's erotic adventures parallel political and cultural developments in Latin America, because, like other conquest novels of the sixties and seventies, *Daimón* seeks to show how contemporary problems are rooted in Latin American history. The novel criticizes what Posse calls the "eternal adolescence" of the region (García Pinto 1989, 500), by discovering in its history and culture a failure to resolve the Oedipus complex.

But Posse's treatment of eroticism in *Daimón* is problematic. Through a process of parodic inversion, he associates sexual repression with "barbarism," and "civilization" with sexual freedom. However, although he parodies Freud's contention that erotic repression is a necessary prerequisite to civilization, he portrays eroticism as a dangerously rebellious impulse associated with the will to power. Posse's treatment of the female characters is even more ambiguous. Although he inverts the evaluation of the virgin-whore archetype, presenting the figure of the prostitute in a positive light, his use of parodic degradation serves to reinforce misogynistic stereotypes.

One cause of this problem is the use of "postmodern parody" (abundant parodic allusions to other texts, often cited in radically different contexts), a characteristic of the postmodern narratives Linda Hutcheon calls historiographic metafiction.[1] These are novels that use the conventions of history and realist fiction in order to subvert them, include major historical figures as characters, deliberately falsify known historical details, include "mass" or "low" culture, and are concerned (Hutcheon argues they are "obsessed") with the question of "*whose* history survives" (Hutcheon 1988, 49–50). Hutcheon argues that the ironic tone of "postmodern parody" makes historiographic metafiction inherently ambiguous. Posse has stressed the importance of eroticism in the conquest, and his primary technique for elaborating on the hints of eroticism in earlier historical and fictional accounts of Aguirre's expedition is parody. By examining the relationship between eroticism and history in *Daimón,* we can better understand the ambiguity inherent in Posse's use of parody in this novel.

Posse makes no pretense of operating in a literary or historical vacuum; instead, he delights in drawing attention to his models. For example, he underlines the relationship of *Daimón* to the chronicles of the Orellana and Ursúa expeditions to the Amazon. The Scribe is engaged in writing his own chronicle, which includes passages from Francisco Vázquez's *Relación de la jornada de Pedro de Orsua a Omagua y al Dorado;*[2] other references suggest a familiarity with either Toribio de Ortiguera's history or an anonymous *relación* thought to have been written by a survivor of the expedition, and the description of Aguirre's encounter with the Amazons suggests Posse has read Gaspar de Carvajal's chronicle of the Orellana expedition.[3]

It is true that these *relaciones* are not explicit about the role of eroticisim in the conquest, particularly not in the sense of presenting an erotic motivation for the conquistadors. This is not surprising, since they were written in compliance with an obligation to inform the king of actions taken on his behalf in the Americas (Mignolo 1982, 71) or in order to excuse the author's participation in a rebellion against the king (Pastor 1983, 412). Nevertheless, an element of eroticism is hardly absent. The chronicles of the Ursúa expedition describe a movement from order to disorder and end with the apparent restoration of order.[4] The source of the disturbance is the presence of Inés de Atienza, Pedro de Ursúa's consort. As Pastor notes, the chronicles present her as a possible cause of Ursúa's transformation from a model conquistador to one who neglects his military obligations in order to satisfy his personal desires.[5]

The soldiers on the expedition believed that either Inés had bewitched Ursúa, causing him to neglect his duties and ultimately leading to his death, or she was responsible because she was a "bad" or immoral woman: "one called her a whore and another said that she had killed the governor with a spell" (*Crónicas* 194). Aguirre himself seems to have viewed dishonorable women as the root of all evil. Both Vázquez and Zúñiga attribute this sentiment to him: "This tyrant would say . . . that all the evil-bodied women had to be killed because they were the cause of great evils and scandals in the world, and because of one whom governor Ursúa had taken with him, he and many others whom had been killed" (*Crónicas* 238; c.f. 22).

While the chronicles present Inés as the cause of jealous disputes among the soldiers after Ursúa's death, they seem at times unsure whether Inés was a "bad" woman or whether the "problem" was simply her great beauty. The degree of understanding they show her varies from Hernández, who clearly sympathizes with her uncomfortable position after Ursúa's death (*Crónicas* 194), to Ortiguera, who takes a more vindictive tone and explicitly structures his history around the theme of female honor/dishonor. Inés de Atienza is a model of dishonor and the cause of great evil: "and correctly it is believed that if Pedro de Ursúa had not taken with him this Doña Inés, the land would have been populated and great harm would have been excused, . . . and in effect it was the whole beginning and destruction of the journey, and in the end he died cruelly and tyrannized, stabbed to death and without confession, because he could not escape punishment" (*Crónicas* 46).

Aguirre's daughter Elvira, on the other hand, clearly embodies female honor. She is generally identified as a young *mestiza,* or as a virgin (*doncella*), or as innocent (*Crónicas* 279)—occasionally as a humanizing influence (*Crónicas* 253). Aguirre's murder of her is his most perverse cruelty; he is a tyrant and a demon (*Crónicas* 149–50, 268). In Ortiguera's version, the demonic Aguirre explains to his maiden daughter that he is going to kill her to preserve her virtue ("so that no scoundrel enjoys your loveliness and beauty" [*Crónicas* 149]). The unfortunate victim falls to her knees, begging for mercy and offering to enter a convent and pray for him, but instead the cruel tyrant stabs her to death, because he equates female virginity with honor. Thus, Doña Inés's dishonorable presence on the expedition leads ultimately to the sacrifice of the innocent victim, Elvira.[6] Unbridled female sexuality and the erotic feelings it arouses in the male members of the expedition lie at the root of the disorder and the rebellion, but even a virgin like Elvira is cause for concern. The theme of female honor is not developed in the anonymous *relación,* but it is suggested in all the other chronicles I have examined.

Posse ultimately inverts the idea that female eroticism is the root of all evil (particularly through his treatment of the prostitute la Mora), but he shares with the chroniclers a view of eroticism as a source of disorder. In fact, Posse filters the theme of eroticism suggested by the chronicles through a post-Freudian and postmodern sensibility, revising it for his own parodic ends. In

Daimón, sexual desire is a challenge to all forms of order, a subversive force locked in eternal battle with forces of political and sexual repression. Through a process of inversion and hyperbolic elaboration, Posse parodies the historical accounts of Aguirre's rebellion and the fictional accounts based on them. For example, the character Elvira is modeled on Aguirre's daughter; she is *mestiza,* like the historical figure, and approximately the same age as the historical Elvira at the time of her death. Ortiguera has Aguirre claim that he is killing her because of his great love for her ("so that things that I love so much don't come to be a mattress for scoundrels" [Posse 1981, 279]). Posse takes that love literally, interpreting her murder as an extreme result of repressed incestuous desire, and has his Aguirre give in to that lust.

A similar idea appears in Werner Herzog's movie *Aguirre, Wrath of God,* but there are important differences between the two works. As Aleida Anselma Rodríguez points out, in the movie, Flora (Aguirre's daughter) dies, her breast pierced by an Indian arrow, in an allusion to Catholic iconography for Divine Love. Aguirre not only fails to kill his daughter, he also declares that he wants to marry her and found the purest dynasty the earth has ever seen. He thus seeks to take the place of God who, through the Virgin, will give birth to a son (Rodríguez 1989, 236). Posse's version is the antithesis: Aguirre is not possessed by God but by the devil. He becomes a figure of American rebellion rather than a representative of European imperialism. And Elvira, who in Herzog's movie, as in the chronicles, was the embodiment of innocence, is instead an example of perverse complicity.

When Aguirre meets up with her again around the time of Latin American independence, he looks at the stab wounds on her throat and, in a clear parody of the pathos of nineteenth-century romantic novels, he is moved to tenderness and tries to excuse the past: "Maybe I haven't been the best father . . . I don't deny it," he begins, like a rueful *paterfamilias* who has been somewhat amiss in his duties. Elvira gazes at him intently in a way the narrator characterizes as inappropriate and speaks "with a voice perhaps too intimate and not filial" (Posse 1981, 178).

Elvira's eternal adolescence is apparent in her ever-youthful body, which the narrator insistently, but humorously, compares to the beauties of nature. It is also clear from her reaction to the world around her. She loudly proclaims her support for racial equality, while quietly excluding Indians, blacks, and mulattoes from her home. And when her husband is jailed and tortured under the twentieth-century military dictatorship, she cheerfully packs her bag for exile in Europe, looking forward to the opportunity to study *bel canto.*

Elvira's fascination with European culture is another mark of her lack of true independence, as is her continued complicity in the incestuous past that links her with her father. Freud viewed this kind of childlike adoration of the father on the part of a grown daughter as the mark of an unresolved Oedipus complex (Freud 1989, 673). In his view, it culminates in her wish to have a child by the father. In the case of Elvira, this "wish" is fulfilled, another sign that she remains in a perpetual state of adolescence. Elvira's immaturity and guilty complicity represent a commentary on the members of the liberal *mestizo* elites in Latin America. Not only do they lack both political and cultural maturity, but also the European models they worship cannot disguise their responsibility for the unjust systems they claim to despise. Nevertheless, the well-intentioned parody of the virtuous Elvira of the chronicles is based on the idea that the adolescent is complicit in her own victimization. There would be no humor if the narrator emphasized Elvira's suffering, but the idea that she cherishes the memory of the incestuous relationship leads to the old canard that women secretly enjoy being abused.

Posse carries out a similar process of parodic degradation with Inés de Atienza, Ursúa's consort. As we have seen, Inés is not an idealized figure in the chronicles. Though routinely praised for her great beauty, she is presented as a woman of unsettling erotic charms or even as loose or manipulative. Posse inverts this situation. His Aguirre idealizes Inés as a cool, aristocratic beauty,[7] but when he discovers she is having an affair with the vulgar dictator and torturer Carrión (her social opposite), he degrades her with fantasies of sadomasochistic rape. On the level of social criticism, the result seems clear: Inés represents the moralistic right-wing aristocrats who support military dictatorships. The novel suggests their sermonizing masks a secret love of sadistic tyrants.

This treatment of Inés is carried out through literary parody, through the manipulation of the ideal of courtly love and the conventions of courtly love poetry, *modernismo,* and the novels of romanticism. Posse shows us the romantic tendency in Latin American literature as a thin veil over a degraded reality of necrophiliac and sadomasochistic rape. For example, we learn that Aguirre has murdered the beautiful Inés because he was unable to express his love for her. The theme of miscommunication continues as the reborn Inés plays a "wordless" game with Aguirre. Like the pale, passive heroines of romantic novels, she waits for him, bleeding "sweetly," with her "marvelous thighs" (*marvellosos muslos*) shimmering in the moonlight and an indecipherable expression on her face. When Aguirre rapes her, she accepts this posthumous "homage" of a clumsily timid lover. In fact, his shyness caused her death; he was too timid to declare his love ("You should have spoken sooner!" [Posse 1981, 41]). The act of necrophiliac rape becomes a gentle "extending himself over her." As she lies in the serene pool, Aguirre struggles in vain to reach "the greatest delight," against the heat from the flames of her burning hut and the imminent coldness of rigor mortis. The end result is "*Coitus interruptus in aeternis*" (Posse 1981, 41).

Posse's use of the conventions of courtly love poetry (the flames and wounds of love, homage, aristocratic nobility) and of romanticism (the passive victim of love and the hero's love of her beyond death; moonlight) suggest that he is concerned with a broader tendency in Hispanic literature to sentimentalize a brutal past by presenting it as pure love. Posse writes sex ("the body") back into the apparently chaste texts of Latin American literature (and history) in part to ridicule the idea that necrophiliac rape is true love in disguise, love that has not been allowed to speak its name. The problem of Inés and Aguirre is indeed a problem of communication. However, it is not she that has misread his intentions, but Latin American literature, by trying to turn corpses into evidence of undeclared love.

The parodic stereotype of the degraded aristocrat is meant to be amusing. After all, the narrator is not presenting his own point of view but the character's; it is because Aguirre idealizes Inés that he gives in to his angry rape fantasies. But the game is ultimately in the service of Posse's allegorical intentions. He needs to show the aristocracy "in bed" [*entrepernarse*] with the tyrant. For the same reason, Inés must seek out Carrión and enjoy her own rape. The allegory requires that both female characters be degraded through a parodic use of incest and sadoeroticism. But the reader is not led to question the misogynistic ideas on which the parody is based, since to suggest the characters might be suffering or might not agree with the treatment they receive would ruin the humorous effect Posse is seeking.

Even when the novel apparently treats female characters positively, as in the case of the Amazons, they are linked with stereotypically "female" qualities. Since the chronicles of the Ursúa expedition, in which Aguirre participated, have little to say about the warrior women, Posse uses Carvajal's chronicle of the earlier Orellana expedition and Ramón Sender's novel *La aventura equinoccial de Lope de Aguirre* as a pretext for including them in the novel. Carvajal claims to have fought against some fierce Amazon warriors, tall white women who "go about naked, their privy parts covered" (Leonard 1949, 59). When the characters in Sender's novel arrive at the place where Orellana and his men are supposed to have encountered the Amazons, they find a skeleton, which they take to be that of an Amazon. This leads the characters to criticize the Spaniards' reaction to them. "It was necessary to be careful, not the way that Orellana was, but another very different way," comments the narrator (Sender 1962, 261). But while in Sender's version the possibilities of an erotic encounter with the Amazons remain pure speculation, in *Daimón,* the Spaniards live out the fantasy.

The Amazons they meet are a composite of male fantasies come true. They go around almost completely naked, showing off their firm breasts; they worship under a full moon at what initially seems to be a phallic monument, and they long to become pregnant. Their queen is "Cuñan (who others called Coñori)" (Posse 1981, 61), whose very name links her with female genitalia.[8] In an inversion of traditional gender roles, the Amazons "conquer" the sexually repressed Spaniards. The queen and her princesses know the "art" of kissing and the "science" of love, and they leave their fearful, guilt-ridden Spanish partners moaning with pleasure (Posse 1981, 66).

Although at first the Spaniards manage to calm their anxieties, they suffer from a great fear of castration. Rumor has it that once the Amazons become pregnant, the soldiers will be forced to join the ranks of enslaved eunuchs who serve the women warriors (another invention of Posse's). "Once they are fertilized they will devour us!" warns the torturer Antón Llamoso (Posse 1981, 60); "(would they do it with their teeth, as rumor had it?)," asks the narrator, tongue in cheek (Posse 1981, 57). In the world of the Amazons with its enslaved eunuchs, castration might appear to be a realistic danger, yet there is nothing in the extremely passive behavior of Posse's Amazons to make the threat believable.[9] Despite the presence of the eunuchs, the narrator treats the threat of castration with ironic amusement.

Actually, according to the indigenous groups, it is Christianity that castrates the Spaniards: "their stupid god seemed to have them grabbed by the genitals" (Posse 1981, 58–59). Like Freud in *Civilization and Its Discontents,* they recognize the role of religion in sexual repression, but they do not share his belief that it is a necessary first step toward civilization. Although the soldiers manage for a time to suppress their exaggerated fear of castration and the guilt feelings inspired by their religion, they eventually succumb to them. The lack of obstacles upsets them: they want to be the initiators and the transgressors; women should be forbidden—or at least they should resist. The Amazons' nudity eventually ceases to excite them and instead diminishes their erotic fantasies. Bored with sex (or afraid of it), the soldiers turn to pursuits they are more comfortable with: card games and war. Finally, although the Amazons remain passive in the face of Spanish aggressions, the soldiers abandon the paradise of sexual pleasure, citing their fear of "a shocking ritual castration" (Posse 1981, 75). Thus, Posse parodies Hispanic attitudes of machismo, suggesting that despite their posturing the soldiers actually prefer male camaraderie to sex with women. Just as the mythic Amazons eschew the company of men except to procreate, these soldiers seek female company only for brief sexual encounters.

Thus, Posse portrays Amazon culture as the inversion of Spanish patriarchal culture, a portrayal that, according to Alison Taufer, is typical of the Amazon tradition in Western culture. In her analysis of the Amazons in the Amadís cycle, Taufer argues that "the Amazon figure provided the Spaniards with a model for understanding and dealing with alien cultures by portraying these cultures as the inversion of European civilization" (Taufer 1991, 36). She maintains that this model was later adopted by the Spanish explorers to conceptualize the New World.

At first it seems that Posse has gone a step further by portraying the refined culture of the Amazons as superior to that of the Spaniards. But if the Spaniards are hobbled by their baseless fear of female sexuality and their inability to experience erotic pleasure without transgression, the queen of the Amazons is fatally flawed by her passivity. Despite all the evidence the text provides of the cultural superiority of Amazon civilization, Cuñan, like all the indigenous characters in the novel, is linked with an exaggerated passivity that is ultimately suicidal. However, the form this passivity takes depends on the gender of the character. Huamán, the Inca *amauta* and guru, intitiates Aguirre into a philosophy of passive resistance, while Coñori, true to her name, can only teach him about sex. The queen is rendered so passive by her own emotions ("she had become fond of [the Spaniards]" [Posse 1981, 75]) that her civilization becomes extinct. When, years later, Aguirre returns to the Amazons' lagoon, he finds it has been completely polluted by the latrines of the rubber tappers and the Amazons are nowhere to be found.

Despite Posse's frequent use of parodic inversion in *Daimón,* the novel almost invariably falls back into traditional gender stereotypes of this kind. However, there is at least one exception, namely the eroticization of the physical environment. In this case, although the parody is based on gender stereotypes, it works to question ingrained cultural myths. Pastor notes that in their chronicles, the survivors of the Ursúa expedition emphasize the difficulties caused by the hostile jungle environment (Pastor 1983, 391–92). Posse transforms this hostile force into an erotic stimulus that acquires an obsessive character. For example, when Aguirre's soldiers reach El Dorado, they find golden dunes shaped like huge breasts: "Smooth and sleek dunes. Immense golden teats" (*Inmensos tetones áureos*) (Posse 1981, 128), which they kiss (and this like all forms of sexuality, makes them feel guilty). It is the New World as experienced by the conquistadors, who are amazed by its beauty and scared of its incredible fertility.

An important model for this eroticizing and gendering of nature is José Eustasio Rivera's novel *La vorágine* (1924). Posse's predecessor associated the jungle with procreation and sexuality, and Posse both echoes and goes beyond him. For example, while Rivera describes "filthy flowers that contract with sexual palpitations and whose sticky smell inebriates like a drug" (Rivera 1942, 182), Posse has the Priest and Scribe actually copulate with such flowers: "The silent expeditions of the Priest and the Scribe . . . to copulate with the waxy, contractive orchids that would return them languid at dawn" (Posse 1981, 40), but his description omits the negative evaluation ("filthy") and shifts the moral question from the jungle to the actions of the otherwise prudish leader.

Posse reevaluates Rivera's portrayal of the jungle as a hell of vile, sadistic, impure, and even perverse sex, the place that encourages men to give in to their basest impulses.[10] One reference in particular shows how Posse's view differs from that of his predecessor. In *La vorágine,* when the characters realize they are lost in the Amazon jungle, they see "the vision of a cannibalistic abyss, the jungle itself, open before the soul like a mouth that swallows the men who are placed between its jaws by hunger and despair" (Rivera 1942, 192).[11] Posse sexualizes this vision of the cannibalistic abyss. When Aguirre and his men enjoy oral sex with the Amazons, the narrator of *Daimón* describes their reaction as follows: "They gave into the temptation of delight overcoming the abyss of fear—ancestral in the white man—of cannibalism, the fear of the treacherous castration of the legend or of the sinful magnitude of the deed" (Posse 1981, 66). This description both evokes and contradicts Rivera's "cannibalistic abyss." First, Posse transforms a metaphoric abyss yawning wide before the souls of lost men into a woman's mouth open in the act of fellatio. The fear of being devoured by the jungle becomes a baseless fear of castration induced by religious notions of sin and temptation. The soldiers suffer from religious strictures that turn pleasure ("delight") into sin or temptation, and from the incomplete Oedipus complex that has left them with an "ancestral fear of castration."

Posse's parodic reworking of *La vorágine*'s nature descriptions emphasizes the idea that his predecessor got it wrong. Nature has a "corrupting" effect on the Europeans, but that effect is salutory. It encourages them to escape from "barbaric" sexual repression. The problem is not the Amazons, sexuality, or the jungle, but the religious strictures of European civilization. This, of course, is radically opposed to Rivera's idea of the positive role of civilization in curbing the dangerous excesses of the untamed heart.[12]

However, despite Posse's comments on the importance of the "savage" erotic freedom the conquistadors experienced, *Daimón* presents unchecked eroticism as a dangerous force. This is particularly clear from Aguirre's final encounter with the prostitute la Mora, an archetypal character not found in the chronicles, but who (with her opposite, the virginal Sor Angela) is another avatar of the virgin-whore dichotomy. In the final chapter of the novel, Posse links Aguirre with Che Guevara, and la Mora with the guerrilla fighter Tania (Tamara Bunke), who worked with Guevara and his guerrillas in Bolivia in the late 1960s. Posse is concerned here with the mythic Guevara of popular legend. Aguirre's affair with la Mora parallels the supposed romance between Guevara and Tania. After their deaths in 1967, there was much speculation as to the nature of their relationship. Rumors abounded of her possible complicity in his death. According to some, Tania was a beautiful Soviet spy who deliberately betrayed Guevara; others depicted her as Guevara's mistress who betrayed him inadvertently through "indiscretions" and "unprofessional conduct" (Welles 1968, 2).

The question of betrayal is fundamental to *Daimón,* but the situation appears to be the opposite of the historical one. It is not la Mora-Tania who betrays Aguirre-Che, but Aguirre who plans to betray la Mora.[13] He wants to use her to defeat his rival, the mystical revolutionary Diego de Torres, whose ascetic (repressive, life-negating) ideology Aguirre despises. By passing on his erotic demon to la Mora, who then presumably will "contaminate" Torres, Aguirre can defeat his rival.

La Mora functions here as Eve's descendant, as the instrument of the devil (Aguirre) in the "corruption" of Torres, except that here that corruption is presented as a largely positive thing. However, despite the exculpation of the sinner, the future is bleak. On the one hand, Aguirre's betrayal of la Mora shows he has not changed in any fundamental sense. The erotic impulse, it turns out, is a rebellious one precisely because it will never be permanently satisfied; it will never accept any limits, and holds nothing sacred. But it is as easily allied with retrograde impulses like Aguirre's as with la Mora's (or Posse's) supposedly revolutionary attempt to renovate literary codes: "renew a game of secret codes" (Posse 1981, 266).

Likewise, Posse's use of parody in *Daimón* can be characterized as an act of rebellion against fictional and historical models, a revolutionary attempt to write the body back into the supposedly chaste texts of the Latin American tradition. But, as the treatment of female characters in the novel makes clear, this parodic literary eroticism is as ambiguous as the physical and emotional impulse. While apparently intended as a liberating attempt at renovation, it can also inadvertently support traditional misogynistic gender stereotypes.

Notes

1. While it is true that postmodernism does not exist in Latin America in Jameson's sense of a cultural product that "expresses the inner truth of that newly emergent social order of late capitalism" (Jameson 1983, 113), because late capitalism does not exist there, many of the descriptions of postmodern practice (Hutcheon, Collins, Hassan) have been based on Latin American literature of the Boom and post-Boom (Ruffinelli 1990, 33). José Joaquín Brunner offers the most plausible explanation of this, namely that the Latin American experience of modernity is one of fragmentation expressed as pastiche: "that is, a heteroclitic configuration of elements taken from virtually anywhere, but always out of their original context" (Brunner 1988, 198). Although, according to Brunner, the Western culture of Latin America often takes the form of nonironic, nonparodic pastiche, it can also take a more independent, distanced stance toward the elements it adopts. Such works might correspond to what is called postmodernism.

2. Posse 1981, 18; Mampel González and Escandell 1981, 270. Subsequent references to this anthology will be indicated in the text as *Crónicas.*

3. Posse has stated that he did substantial historiographic work before writing the novel (García Pinto 1989, 500).

4. Pastor shows the transition from transgression of the established order to its "fictional restoration" in the Vázquez chronicle (Pastor 1983, 417–24).

5. In *Daimón,* Lope de Aguirre undergoes a similar transformation from warrior, in the first half of the novel ("La epopeya del guerrero"), to lover in the second half ("La vida personal").

6. While both women are stabbed to death, Ortiguera clearly distinguishes between Inés's death, which he considers just punishment for her role as the source of evil, and Elvira's, which was cruel and unnecessary, since she was innocent and could have entered a convent.

7. In Ramón J. Sender's *La aventura equinoccial de Lope de Aguirre,* the other characters look down on Inés because of her racial origins: "Doña Inés was one of those little Indian girls who come on to Saint Anthony himself and who wasn't born to be a wife or a mother like the females of Seville" (Sender 1962, 267). But in *Daimón* there is no mention of Inés's mixed-race ancestry. We see her only through the eyes of Aguirre, who has idealized her.

8. Posse apparently adopts the name Coñori from Sender's novel, where an Indian cacique warns the Spaniards to be suspicious of the Amazons. The narrator quotes him as saying: "Reciquié cuñan puiara" (Posse 1981, 261). The narrator goes on to explain that the name Coñori is based on a Spanish misunderstanding of the name of a tributary of the Amazon, the Conhuris River: "and their queen was called *coñopuira* (Friar Gaspar writes naively). Her real name was *Cuñanpu-iara*" (Posse 1981, 262–63). But the joke is Sender's, for this information does not appear in the chronicles.

9. Nor do Posse's historical sources suggest the Amazons castrated their enemies.

10. "The jungle transforms man, developing his most inhuman instincts" (Rivera 1942, 139).

11. Another possible reference is to the essay "De lo real maravilloso americano." Carpentier describes what happened when the French artist André Masson tried to draw the jungle of Martinique: "with . . . the obscene promiscuity of certain fruit, the marvelous truth of the subject devoured the painter, leaving him little less than impotent before the white page" (Carpentier 1967, 116). This suggests Posse is also parodying the idea that European artists suffer from Oedipal castration fears to which the American artist is not subject.

12. Hutcheon's definition of parody as "imitation characterized by ironic inversion" or "repetition with critical distance" is applicable here (Hutcheon 1985, 8). Posse is not engaged in the "nostalgic imitation of past models"; he carries out "a stylistic confrontation, a modern recoding which establishes difference at the heart of similarity" (Hutcheon 1985, 8).

13. As usual, the novel parodies "official history;" in this case, a famous news photograph of Che Guevara's corpse surrounded by the soldiers and other officials who had participated in his capture and execution (the photo appears in Jon Lee Anderson's biography). The narrator of *Daimón* mentions a photograph supposedly disseminated by the Associated Press, which shows Aguirre's former aide Nicéforo Méndez standing by Tania's corpse alongside a creek. Once again, Posse has inverted the historical situation so that the martyred hero is not Che-Aguirre, but Tania-la Mora.

Bibliography

Anderson, Jon Lee. 1997. *Che Guevara: A Revolutionary Life.* New York: Grove Press.

Brunner, José Joaquín. 1988. *Un espejo trizado: Ensayos sobre cultura y políticas culturales.* Santiago: Chile: FLASCO.

Carpentier, Alejo. 1967. "De lo real maravilloso americano." In *Tientos y diferencias,* 102–20. Montevideo: ARCA.

Carvajal, Gaspar de. 1972. "Relación del nuevo descubrimiento del Río Grande por el capitán Francisco de Orellana." In *Historiadores de Indias. América del Sur,* edited by Angeles Masia, 321–89. Mexico: Bruguera.

Freud, Sigmund. 1971. *Civilization and Its Discontents.* Edited and translated by James Strachey. New York: Norton.

———. 1989. *The Freud Reader.* Edited by Peter Gay. New York: Norton.

García Pinto, Magdalena. 1989. "Entrevista con Abel Posse." *Revista Iberoamericana* 146–47: 494–506.

Herzog, Werner, dir. 1972. *Aguirre, Wrath of God.* Werner Herzog Filmproduktion.

Hutcheon, Linda. 1985. *A Theory of Parody: The Teachings of Twentieth-Century Art Forms.* New York: Methuen.

———. 1988. *A Poetics of Postmodernism.* New York: Routledge.

Jameson, Fredric. 1983. "Postmodernism and Consumer Society." In *The Anti-Aesthetic. Essays on Postmodern Culture,* edited by Hal Foster, 111–25. Seattle: Bay Press.

Leonard, Irving A. 1949. *Books of the Brave.* Cambridge: Harvard University Press.

Mampel González, Elena, and Neus Escandell Tur, eds. 1981. *Lope de Aguirre: Crónicas 1559–1561.* Barcelona: Universidad de Barcelona.

Mignolo, Walter. 1982. "Cartas, crónicas y relaciones del descubrimiento y la conquista." In *Historia de la literatura hispanoamericana: Época colonial,* edited by Iñigo Madrigal, 57–116. Vol. 1. Madrid: Cátedra.

Pastor, Beatriz. 1983. *Discurso narrativo de la conquista de América.* La Habana: Casa de las Américas.

Posse, Abel. 1981. *Daimón.* Barcelona: Argos Vergara.

———. 1989. "El alucinante viaje del doble descubrimiento." In *1492–1992: A los 500 años del choque de dos mundos,* edited by Adolfo Colombres, 197–206. Buenos Aires: Ediciones del Sol.

Rivera, José Eustasio. 1942. *La vorágine.* Buenos Aires: Losada.

Rodríguez, Aleida Anselma. 1989. *Arqueología de Omagua y Dorado.* Ph.D. diss., University of Maryland.

Ruffinelli, Jorge. 1990. "Los 80: ¿Ingreso a la posmodernidad?" *Nuevo texto crítico* 6: 31–41.

Sender, Ramón. 1962. *La aventura equinoccial de Lope de Aguirre.* 2nd ed. Madrid: Magisterio Español.

Taufer, Alison. 1991. "The Only Good Amazon Is a Converted Amazon: The Woman Warrior and Christianity in the *Amadís Cycle.*" In *Playing with Gender: A Renaissance Pursuit,* edited by Jean R. Brink, Maryanne Horowitz, and Allison P. Coudert, 35–51. Urbana: University of Illinois Press.

Welles, Benjamin. 1968. "Woman Spy's Error Trapped Guevara." *New York Times,* 15 July, 1: 2.

Part Four
Mestizaje and Transculturation

From Cult to Comics: The Representation of Gonzalo Guerrero as a Cultural Hero in Mexican Popular Culture

ROSEANNA MUELLER

> Chetumal was the capital of a province of the same name, which was ruled by Nachan Can at the time of the first invasion of Yucatan. His principal captain was Gonzalo Guerrero, a Spaniard who had been shipwrecked off the coast in 1511. The story of this man's career seems incredibly romantic, but it is on the whole well substantiated. He was first enslaved. He turned completely native, piercing his nose and ears and tattooing his face and hands, rose to the position of war chief, and married an Indian woman of rank. He refused to be ransomed by Cortez in 1519 and later rejected Montejo's invitation to join him when he invaded the region. The Spaniards ascribed their failure here to Guerrero's opposition. Finally, he was killed when he took part in a native expedition to the Ulua river in northern Honduras to aid the natives there in their resistance to the Spaniards.
>
> —Scholes and Roys, *The Maya-Chontal Indians of Acalan-Tixchel*

THE SPANIARDS GONZALO GUERRERO AND GERÓNIMO AGUILAR WERE THE only long-term survivors of a shipwreck in 1511 that landed them on the Yucatan coast. Both were enslaved by Mayan lords. Aguilar was rescued by Cortés in 1519 and served as his interpreter during the conquest of Mexico. Guerrero eventually married a Mayan princess, had at least three children with her, became a Mayan warrior, and never rejoined his countrymen. Early chroniclers of the Spanish conquest, (Bernal Díaz del Castillo, Gómara, Tapia, Landa, and others) mention the two. Later historians of the colonization of Yucatan, such as Cogolludo, Solis, Chamberlain, and Cervantes de Salazar, integrated them into the larger history of the colonization of this difficult-to-conquer part of Mexico.

Although the outline of Guerrero's life is well-established historically, the conjectural details of his biography and the limited historical facts have tempted revisionists from the beginning. Guerrero's life touches central issues in Mexican history and culture—colonization, evangelism and miscegenation—and as attitudes toward these issues have changed, so have interpretations of his life. In the early chronicles, and even as late as Chamberlain's history (1948), Guerrero is described as a renegade, a turncoat, a traitor to his own kind; a bitter, dangerous enemy, and an idolater. Since the 1970s, however, Guerrero has been reconsidered, reevaluated, reenvisioned, and acclaimed the father of Mexican *mestizaje,* that is, the patriarch of those with mixed Indian and European blood.

Guerrero is first mentioned in Gómara's chronicle in 1552, and later by Bernal Díaz. Neither understood why Guerrero chose to stay behind, but both seem to agree that Guerrero fathered children of mixed blood. Gómara questioned Guerrero's love for a pagan woman, but accepted the love he showed for his children, as though biological *mestizaje* were a fait accompli. Bernal Díaz did not question Guerrero's refusal to abandon his family and suggested that Guerrero rejoined the Spanish along with his wife and children. He remarked on the beauty of the children and Guerrero's pride in his family.

Contemporary works reinterpret Guerrero as a cultural symbol of the fairly recent notion of *mestizaje.* Histories of Guerrero have been pieced together, and gaps have been filled to serve a political and social need: the need for an alternative model for *mestizaje.*

Guerrero ultimately became a symbol of resistance against the Spanish invaders, and by extension a symbol of resistance to all forms of colonialism and imperialism. He came into his own as a cultural hero in the 1970s. Populist Mexican President Luís Echeverría Álvarez, who held office from 1970 to 1976, struggled to make Mexico a leader among emerging nations and budgeted money for public works meant to rekindle ethnic pride and nationalism, emphasizing *mexicanidad.* This ethnic fervor, grounded in both European and American cultures, found a focal point in the story of Gonzalo Guerrero.

Early accounts of Guerrero differ slightly in detail but agree on the broader facts. Cortés's expedition learned of Guerrero and Aguilar in 1519 and picked up the latter after a near-miss in Cozumel. Aguilar's knowledge of the Mayan language was to make him invaluable as an interpreter in the conquest of Mexico, together with the celebrated Malinche. Guerrero, whom Aguilar apparently contacted after hearing from Cortés, refused to leave his Indian wife and children. It was believed in the sixteenth century, though on sparse evidence, that he was a leader of native resistance in the Yucatan area against the Spanish conquistadors. The Spaniards were so deeply disturbed by the idea that one of their own would go over to the side of the Indians, with their alien religion and practices of human sacrifice, that they demonized him and credited him with engineering the defeats they suffered in the conquest of the region.

Legends sprang up around Guerrero and Aguilar. As Cortés's indispensable aide, Aguilar came to symbolize the reintegrated captive, loyal to his culture, his church, and the Spanish crown. Some morality tales about Aguilar's captivity illustrate that loyalty in the face of hard tests. Both Guerrero and Aguilar escaped their original captors and went into the service of another Mayan lord. Guerrero escaped a second time and eventually turned up in Chetumal, where he spent thirty years as a Mayan warrior.

Landa recounts how he lived with Nachan Can Siu, "who placed him in command of the affairs of war. . . . He also showed the Indians how to fight, teaching them how to build fortresses and bastions. In this manner, and by behaving like an Indian, he built up a great reputation for himself and they married him to a very high-ranking lady by whom he had children. For this reason, he, unlike Aguilar, never made any attempt to escape. On the contrary, he tattooed his body, grew his hair long and pierced his ears so as to wear earrings like the Indians; and it is possible that he also became an idolater like them" (Landa 1975, 33). Landa reports total adaptation and consequent cultural integration, with Guerrero first "going over" and behaving like the Indians and receiving the noble lady as a reward.

The last contemporary news of Guerrero appears in a letter found in the general archives of the Indies. Written by the contador Andres de Cerezada, the letter reports that Gonzalo Guerrero was shot to death on 13 August 1536 in Puerto Caballos, Honduras, during a battle between the Mayan and the Spanish armies. "The Spaniard died thus in combat, who was nude, with tattoos on his body, who was dressed in scant clothing the Indians wear, was probably Gonzalo de Guerrero" (Chamberlain 1966, 178). The hardcover comic book, *La desaparicion de Gonzalo Guerrero,* includes this letter in its narrative.

I. The Comic Book

The twenty-five-volume hardcover comic book series published in 1992 by Planeta-deAgostini and Sociedad Estatal Quinto Centenario is devoted to early explorations and historical developments in the discovery of the New World. Each volume's introduction treats the historic event through lush and spectacular color illustrations. A *referencia histórica* includes maps, prints, and engravings, and each volume ends with a *cronología* and *bibliografía.* The topics in the series reflect the renewed interest in retelling the encounter in 1992, the quincentennial of Columbus's landfall in the New World. Each volume digests the encounter for a mass audience reared on illustrations, images, and murals, an exceptionally strong and continuing tradition in Latin America. The series is not simply an *Illustrated Classics* of the kind published in the United States. The reader, initially seduced by the vivid and often fantastic images, is educated in revisionist history.

The volume titled *Conquistadores en Yucatán: La desaparición de Gonzalo Guerrero* retells the story of the shipwrecked Spaniard who has become the "father of Mexican *mestizaje.*" Fernando Savater, in the *presentación,* introduces the book and asks the reader to ponder a question that lies at the heart of ethnic identity in general, and Mexican national identity in particular: "What is it that binds a man, any of us, to the social groups to which he *feels* he belongs? Necessity? Routine? A common language, race, beliefs? Whims? Is it not enough to ask, 'Where do you come from?' " According to Savater, the more interesting question is, "What are you or what have you become?"

The author of the narrative in *Conquistadores en Yucatán* uses Díaz del Castillo, Chamberlain, Oviedo, Landa, and Gómara as his sources to tell Guerrero's story. The *cronología* begins in 1511, with the shipwreck and the "adoption" of Aguilar and Guerrero by the Maya of Yucatan. It states that in 1517, Guerrero led the attack against Francisco Hernández de Córdoba, who had sailed from Cuba. Next, it is stated that in 1527, Francisco Montejo and Alonso Dávila disembarked on the north coast of Yucatan and were defeated by Gonzalo Guerrero's Mayas. Guerrero has been turned into a Mayan leader who defeats the Spaniards, something hinted at in the chronicles, but not known for a fact.

The story in this illustrated book opens with a flashback to a battle scene littered with the tattooed bodies of Mayan warriors. A Spanish conquistador, Pedro de Alvarado, proclaims, "Behold, the Jaguar and the Eagle are defeated. Search among the dead for the body of Gonzalo Guerrero. I want him to be an example of how a traitor meets his end" (Calatayud 1992, 8). Cerezada, the governor of Honduras, needs to report the skirmish to the crown and dispatches a soldier to find out what happened to the renegade Guerrero. This soldier, in turn, seeks out Aguilar, who proceeds to tell the story of the shipwreck. Aguilar's version, in keeping with similar reports in some of the chronicles, includes two women on board. In the flashback, Aguilar tells Guerrero that he has witnessed the death of their Captain Valdivia and has also witnessed their Mayan captors "devouring the remains." This grisly episode takes place off-page. Aguilar continues his story by recounting how his compatriot, Guerrero, eventually made his way to Chetumal and was put in charge of Mayan warriors. Guerrero appears, saying, "I'll teach the Mayan warriors that an attack is as important as a defense." Guerrero is also shown waging war off Cabo Catoche. He meets Aguilar, and as he refuses to go back with his compatriot, he explains that he is tattooed and has pierced his ears. Above all, he cannot leave "the jungle, the pyramids, the harmony, and the spell of all that surrounds him" (Calatayud 1992, 27). Dávila meets defeat after defeat, certain that Guerrero is behind it all. After the Copul uprising, Dávila is convinced that Guerrero organized the Indians and trained them to attack, "casting his shadow over the Spaniard's latest military defeat" (Calatayud 1992, 47).

Guerrero is now *jefe militar* of Chetumal and is depicted preparing for battle by painting his body. Chief Cicumba reports Guerrero's death to a Spaniard, noting that other Spaniards had failed to identify Guerrero's body because in death he looked like an Indian warrior. As the report is about to be written, Cerezada demands the truth from his informant, who says, "We will never know the truth. A renegade to some, a hero of legends for others, what was his real role in this madness?" (Calatayud 1992, 47). Cerezada instructs the reporter, "Add to the report that Guerrero was found dead, naked, his body painted so that he looked like an Indian" (Calatayud 1992, 53).

II. The Statues

Two statues of Gonzalo Guerrero and his family were created by Raúl Ayala Arellano in 1974 in Ciudad Juarez, Chihuaha. In both, Guerrero has European features and a beard, but his hair is cut and bound Mayan style and he is dressed in the *ex* (breechcloth) of the Mayan warrior. He holds a spear in his left hand; his wife is seated behind him, nursing an infant. Another child has made a toy of a Spanish helmet. A lance rests in Guerrero's left hand. The statues represent the first *mestizo* family. Guerrero is represented as an Indianized Spaniard through his vestments and adornments. His warrior status is represented by the lance. He is also presented as a loving father. The sculpture conflates Guerrero's many roles: he is a Spanish conqueror turned Mayan warrior, married to a noblewoman with whom he has had children of mixed blood.

The statue of Guerrero in Merida is situated on the Prolongación Pasejo Montejo on the outskirts of the city, seven kilometers from the center of town. The statue is on an island in the middle of a two-lane highway, and traffic proceeds at a fast clip past it. There is a modern high-rise commercial building to the right with dark, reflecting windows. No plaque or inscription appears on the statue's imposing tiered base. The statue is difficult to see, since traffic rushes by on either side of it, and a busy street must be crossed to gain access to the island. Once safely on the island, however, it is still difficult to see the statue since the viewer cannot stand back far enough to take in the whole in perspective. Guerrero has also lent his name to the neighborhood, or *colonia,* whose entrance is to the left of the statue. A large boulder at the entrance of Colonia Guerrero bears the inscription: "Gonzalo Guerrero, Father of Mexican mestizaje. He fought and died defending the freedom of the Mayan people" [*Gonzalo Guerrero Padre del mestizaje en México. Luchó y murió defendiendo la libertad del pueblo maya*].

Both statues include Guerrero's wife and three children. His Mayan wife (Ixpilotzama or Xzamil, depending on the source), smiles as she nurses and cradles an infant. She is represented as a noblewoman. Again depending on the source, she was a noblewoman, a princess, or a priestess. Her adornments include a large bracelet, large earrings, and a matching necklace. Guerrero appears very muscular, and since one must look up to see him, the articulation of the muscles seems prominent. This makes for an imposing effect, as though Guerrero continues to do battle. With his right hand he cups the chin of the child to his right. But these details are impossible to see unless one climbs up to the top of the platforms of the pedestal.

The setting of the statue in Akumal contrasts sharply with that of the statue in Merida. This grouping seems more at home in its natural setting of sand, sea, and palm trees. The Akumal statue lies approximately 150 kilometers south of Cancun on a crescent of white sand beach fringed with palms. The main tourist attraction here is the northernmost extension of the Palancar Reef, an attraction for divers, snorkelers, and sunseekers. The statue of Guerrero and his family is near the Club de Yates. One almost stumbles upon it. The statue is placed here because it was thought to have been the site where the shipwrecked members of the Valdivia expedition washed up after their ship broke up against the reefs known as *Las Viboras* or *Los Alacranes* on its way from Darien to Santo Domingo. This event is also documented in the early chronicles of the conquest.

The inscription on the plaque, placed there by the local historical society, reads: "Gonzalo de Guerrero of Palos de Noguer, Spain, a seaman, who in 1511 shipwrecked near this beach, married the Mayan princess Xzamil and thus founded the first Euro-American family."

The statue in Akumal represents a "social pact" entered into between the authorities of the central government and the inhabitants of the peninsula (Adorno 1996, 906). Both statues illustrate how Guerrero functions as a cultural icon, given the few concrete facts known about him. Adorno points out that historically, Guerrero is not known for any great deed, but because he makes an intriguing case study, he is constantly reelaborated (Adorno 1996, 911). Since he is open-ended and inconclusive, he becomes what the reader wishes him to be. When the Akumal statue was dedicated in 1975, the accompanying romanticized and poetic description appeared in a pamphlet published by the Club de Exploraciones y Deportes Acuáticos de México.

> Gonzalo contemplates the ocean, while the Caribbean breeze blows through his hair. He is a seaman whose glance is a mixture of melancholy and challenge. His accoutrements are not at all like he would have worn when he left the port of Palos. He is not alone, but is joined lovingly by his children, who are the result of his union with the noble Mayan who tranquilly and serenely glances at him while she nurses her youngest child. Part of the group is the daughter playing with her father's helmet.

She was born free and happy. She has parents to protect her and she belongs to the world that surrounds her. (Adorno 1996, 909)

Although both statues were executed by the same sculptor, there are subtle differences. In the Akumal statue, Guerrero's son to his left looks forward, in the same direction as his father, as Guerrero caresses him. In the Merida statue, Guerrero's earrings are like his wife's. In the Akumal version he wears pendant earrings. At Akumal the viewer does not have to look very high up to see the statue, since it sits on a simple pedestal, a plain white-washed stucco block placed a few feet off the ground. Not only is the setting a natural one, amidst palms, but it invites the viewer to walk around the statue and appreciate the symbolism in the adornments and poses of Guerrero's wife and children. Guerrero calmly looks out to the ocean. His son shares the same wistful expression. On his left, Guerrero's daughter plays with a Spanish soldier's helmet. Is the helmet meant to be a relic of Guerrero's former role as conqueror? The shipwrecked survivors probably had lost most of their possessions when they landed on the beach and were stripped of their remaining possessions when they were subsequently captured. Is the helmet a spoil from a local, more recent battle? In any event, it has become a plaything. Its new function can be read in two ways. The Spanish helmet toy mocks its origin and the people who brought it. The biblical admonition to turn weapons into plowshares has been taken a step further, and an implement of war has been turned into a plaything.

III. Murals and Paintings

The Fernando Castro Pacheco mural in the Governor's Palace in Merida continues the first *mestizo* family motif to a greater degree. Guerrero appears between his wife on the left and a child on the right. The pose borrows from holy family groupings of Mary and Joseph with the Christ child. This mural is entitled "Gonzalo Guerrero: father of the first Mexican *mestizos* in the domain of Chetumal" [*Gonzalo Guerrero: padre del los primeros mestizos mexicanos en el caciazgo de Chetemal*]. This is one of many murals in the hall of the Governor's Palace that tell the history of the region, beginning with a mural depicting how man was born of corn, according to the *Popul Vuh,* the Mayan creation story. The mural of Guerrero with wife and child places him squarely in the history of the Yucatan and its people, the Maya, and reinforces the important role he is assigned as the father of the first descendants of mixed blood, while locating him geographically in the powerful and important chiefdom of Chetumal, where he spent the longest portion of his life.

The mural, by S. Cuevas, is on the second floor of Merida's *Ayuntamiento,* or city hall. It was painted in December 1978, and is titled *Origen del Mestizaje.* The inscription translates: "Next to the robust Spaniard, lying beside him without submission, the Indian woman with languid gaze saw her companion arrive amidst the ocean waves, and their son, his eyes the color of corn and wheat, with the sorrow and the pride of mixed races."

The juxtaposition of the Mayan woman lying near Guerrero without shame or submission offers an alternative to the European model of miscegenation through domination. Guerrero's wife poetically sees her mate arrive from across the sea, not with fear, as she might feel for an invader, but with expectation. The child of this union will inherit the parents' blended coloring and will also inherit all the problems that will go with *mestizaje.* The inscription emphasizes that this mingling of the races, however, will also be a cause of pride.

An open book appears in the painting, and its text translates: "Ixchel, the goddess of fertility, descended to bless the man the color of the sun and the dark-skinned woman." Ixchel was the goddess associated with childbirth and the healing arts, and the consort of Itzamna, the greatest deity of the Maya. According to Aguirre Rosas, Guerrero was married to Ixpilotzama, who was named for Itzmna, in a Mayan ceremony. In San Buenaventura's version, Guerrero's marriage to the daughter of the chief of Chetumal takes place with the marriage of fourteen other couples (San Buenaventura 1994, xxv). Having Ixchel sanctify the marriage emphasizes that the union was legitimate in the eyes of the Maya. Guerrero is represented as fair-skinned, contrasting sharply with his dark-skinned wife. He gazes fondly on their nude *mestizo* child lying between them, the focal point of the painting.

IV. Novels

Several novels have been written with Guerrero as main character. *Gonzalo Guerrero: Novela histórica,* by Eugenio Aguirre (Mexico, 1980) won the Paris International Academy's Silver Medal in 1981. In *Gonzalo Guerrero: Memoria olvidada, trauma de México,* written by journalist Carlos Villa Roiz (Mexico, 1995), the novel's first chapter is written from the viewpoint of Guerrero's *mestiza* daughter. "I am *mestiza,*" claims the narrator proudly, "but I consider myself an Indian." In an exchange with some Spaniards, they refer to her as a "an ill-bred cross-eye" [*pizca mal nacida*] (Villa Roiz 1995, 22). She explains why she is cross-eyed and its significance, and the aesthetic appeal this had for the Maya. The narrator rails against Landa (at the beginning of this novel her son is working for the Bishop of Merida). Guerrero's daughter claims Landa lies and exaggerates, ignores some things, and hides others. She recounts her father's death. This is done through a narrative interspersed with excerpts from various chronicles, which appear throughout the novel and are highlighted in bold type.

The subtitle of the book (*Forgotten Memory, Mexico's Trauma*) eventually appears within the quote: "The profoundly religious indigenous world has fallen into hypocrisy and secrecy. The truth has become sectarian, occultist. This is the trauma of all of Mexico, the forgotten memory; they have forced us to lie, to hide our beliefs and feelings, to condemn what is ours and glorify what is foreign" (Villa Roiz 1995, 499). In other words, Guerrero's story recapitulates the destruction of Mayan civilization and the imposition of Christianity. This, says Villa Roiz, is the real blow to the indigenous culture. A whole culture has been forced to go underground, has been forced to lie, has been made to forget its beliefs, made to deny its truths and worship a totally alien religion. Villa Roiz states that the forced acceptance of Catholicism only reinforced the Mayans' faith. He includes Motolonía's suspicion that the Indians hid their pagan idols under crosses and statues.

Like the comic book, this novel repeats the idea that the sense of belonging, the sense of *patria,* is not where you are born but is rather where you die. The *mestiza* narrator explains that the Indians cannot grasp the concepts of Catholicism. The dogma is incomprehensible to the Maya. She points out the absurdity of some of the religious concepts for the neophytes. For example, she explains it is difficult to understand the notion of the Trinity in a society whose worldview is based on duality. She feels the need to write her father's story or others will write it in a *versión triunfalista,* that is, from the point of view of the winner. The narrative sets the background for the European voyages of discovery, explains how expeditions were assembled (this material is mostly from Chamberlain), covers the roles Nicuesa and Enciso played in the founding of Darien, and tells the events that occurred in 1510, one year prior to Guerrero's shipwreck (Villa Roiz 1995, 73). This part of the novel is told from Guerrero's viewpoint. It includes a description of how he fell in love with his Mayan wife. Villa Roiz's novel strings together historical sources to which the author adds his sense of what went wrong during the conquest and its implications for modern Mexico, which is still reeling from the blow.

This novel and others like it use the chronicles as the basis for the narrative thread. At the same time they reinterpret the events so that Guerrero emerges as a Mayan hero. The illustration on page 548 shows Guerrero as a Mayan warrior, with his wife and child in the background, overtaken by the events of the conquest as he futilely holds up his shield against the Spanish soldiers' lances.

Roiz's treatment is similar to those of many contemporary Latin American writers, who retell their nations' histories from the perspective of a marginalized protagonist in counterpoint to the histories written from the viewpoint of the antagonistic conqueror.

V. The Lost *Memorias*

A diary attributed to Guerrero was incorporated into two publications, the first by Aguirre Rosas in 1975, and the second by the editors of San Buenaventura's history in 1994. Both are of controversial authenticity. In 1975, a version of what purports to be a memoir written by Guerrero himself on deerskin vellum and paper Guerrero obtained from the Montejo expedition was published. There are problems determining the authenticity of the text, the original of which, at least in 1975, was reportedly in the hands of a private Mexico City collector.

In 1975, journalist Mario Aguirre Rosas, writing for the Mexico City daily newspaper *El universal,* published Guerrero's story in a series of articles as *Gonzalo de Guerrero: Padre del mestizaje iberomexicano* (Aguirre Rosas 1975, 5). This alleged transcript of Guerrero's manuscript contains elements of the story as it is recorded in the conventional histories, but told from Guerrero's perspective. The narrative is full of complications and ironies. It is an alternative view of history, with a suspiciously modern political message.

A second document of equally questionable provenance is *Historias de la conquista del Mayab, 1511–1697,* written between 1724 and 1725 by Fray Joseph de San Buenaventura (Merida 1994). Like the Aguirre Rosas novel, this purports to be memoirs written partly on deerskin and partly on European paper supplied later by conquerors.

The author was a Franciscan friar based in Merida. He says he lived in the land of the Itzaes, and in 1696 was taken prisoner in Alkin Xunib. He describes the *Relato de Gonzalo Guerrero,* and mentions that it was written on paper probably obtained through Cortés or Montejo, the rest being on deerskin. The account tells of the misfortunes of Guerrero, who arrived with other unfortunates in 1511. Buenaventura claims, "I have these writings and the skins with me, and it is a difficult task to verify and read. And from what I can read from these writings, this is what happened according to don Gonzalo de Guerrero" (San Buenaventura 1994, 9).

The friar formed a narrative around the "papers or writings" of Gonzalo Guerrero and other indigenous reports that reflect Spanish and Mayan history at the beginning of the Seventeenth century. Supposedly, a copy of this account was discovered 269 years later in the Centro de Estudios de Historia de Mexico CONDUMEX, in Mexico City. Again, there are doubts as to the authenticity of the work. But the "finding" of this document once again points to the quest for Guerrero and the need to enshrine him as a historical hero in the region.

Buenaventura claimed to have copied and reedited documentary sources, and to have taken down the oral histories and legends circulating in Merida. Among the writings Fray Joseph claimed passed through his hands are the alleged sheets of paper and deerskin hides on which Guerrero recorded his shipwreck and his life among the Maya in Yucatan. Buenaventura said Cortés gave Guerrero the paper to write on, and a Castilian knife, which concurs with Guerrero's *Memorias.* The author acknowledged that the Guerrero text is a copy, that the original was very difficult to read and decipher. He added he was offering an interpretation of what appeared before him, rather than a literal transcription, and that he had embellished the documents with oral history.

Did Buenaventura have the real thing? Or was the Guerrero manuscript a simple literary device, part of a broader fiction whose aim was to defend the Franciscans against the changing attitudes toward the order that were occurring between 1721 and 1723? Either way, "Guerrero was the perfect character from which to describe a savage yet wise society, born of the devil but basically Christianized, pacified but eternally subject to rebelliousness unless it subjected itself to the ministrations of the Franciscans" (San Buenaventura 1994, xvi).

VI. Conclusion

While primary and secondary sources sketched Guerrero's history during the colonial period, today he has become a political and literary icon and has been transformed into a national myth. There are images and interpretations of this emblematic figure not only in Yucatan, but in greater Mexico. He fills a void, a need for a hero who symbolizes an alternative and positive model of *mestizaje.*

Guerrero's continual redefinition in postcolonial discourse, as evidenced in artistic and literary products, is really an attempt to solve the current dilemma of cultural identity of *mestizo* Mexico. This concern applies to all of Hispanic America. The intellectual and psychological tension produced by the mingling of the cultural and genetic features of Europe and the Americas continues to be an important theme in Latin American writing today. The *mestizo* is a citizen of both the New World and the Old World, and of neither, and is still searching for his identity after five centuries of conquest and colonization.

A cultural icon is shaped in a social context. As today's symbol of Mexican *mestizaje,* Gonzalo Guerrero is alternately depicted as a misguided soldier, a Mayan warrior, the brave husband of a Mayan princess, and a loving father. Contemporary artists and writers have brought him out of the colonial period and into the present, as an exemplar of integration. Gonzalo Guerrero is an accumulation of stories and legends that have been pieced together to form a historical fiction. Unless Guerrero's own *memorias* and Buenaventura's account prove to be the real thing, most of what is being written about him is speculation. Nevertheless, historical fiction and other representations of Guerrero seek to incorporate the colonized conqueror into a new culture and describe a new consciousness of identity, which permits a radical departure from the demarcation of "us and them."

The relationship between fiction and history is always problematic. The manipulation of historical resources by contemporary Latin American writers and artists aims to reinvent the past for social and political ends—away from the "imperial eye" of European colonial discourse. In contemporary popular culture, Guerrero has become a construct, that is, an interplay between fact and fiction, in which history and art mix to make meaning for a nation hungry for a sense of its own beginnings. These constructs attempt to fill the gaps that have been left in the "official story." Guerrero as an emblem or icon balances fact and fiction so that now, centuries later, he fulfills a social function. His refusal to return to his compatriots and his founding of a family in the New World form the nucleus of the icon. Because information about Guerrero is scarce, inconclusive, and secondhand, the process to reelaborate and re-create him as a national myth continues.

If he was reviled by the chroniclers, Guerrero has enjoyed a vindication of sorts, since he has become an exemplar who fills the need to connect the colonizers from Europe and the indigenous of the Americas in a domestic context. As a symbol of resistance he continues to inspire Mexican artists and writers of fiction today, having become a cultural hero in the imagination of the modern inhabitants not only in Yucatan, but all of Mexico.

Bibliography

Adorno, Rolena. 1996. "La estatua de Gonzalo Guerrero en Akumal: Iconos culturales y la reactualización del pasado colonial." *Revista Iberoamericana* 62, no. 166–67: 905–23.

Aguirre, Eugenio. *Gonzalo Guerrero: novela histórica.* Mexico: UNAM, 1980.

Aguirre Rosas, Mario. 1975. *Gonzalo de Guerrero: Padre del mestizaje iberomexicano.* Prólogo de Alfonso Taracena. Mexico: Editorial Jus.

Calatayud, Miguel. 1992. *Conquistadores en Yucatán: La desaparición de Gonzalo Guerrero.* Barcelona: Planeta-Agostini, Socieded Estatal Quinto Centenario.

Chamberlain, Robert. 1966. *The Conquest and Colonization of Yucatan, 1517–1550.* New York: Octagon Books.

Landa, Diego de. 1975. *Account of the Affairs of Yucatan.* Edited and translated by A. R. Pagden. Chicago: Philip O'Hara.

San Buenavantura, Fray Joseph de. 1994. *Historias de la conquista del Mayab, 1511–1697.* Edited by Gabriela Soliś Robleada and Pedro Bracamonte y Sosa. Merida: Universidad Autónoma de Yucatán.

Scholes, France V. and Ralph L. Roys. 1968. *The Maya-Chontal Indians of Acalan-Tixchel.* Norman: University of Oklahoma Press.

Villa Roiz, Carlos. 1995. *Gonzalo Guerrero: Memoria olvidada, trauma de México.* Mexico: Plaza y Valdés.

Naked in the Wilderness: The Transculturation of Cabeza de Vaca in Abel Posse's *El largo atardecer del caminante*

KIMBERLE S. LÓPEZ

ARGENTINE NOVELIST ABEL POSSE'S *El largo atardecer del caminante* (1992) is a historical fiction recounted in the first person by a narrator who represents the explorer Álvar Núñez Cabeza de Vaca writing his memoirs upon returning to Spain after failed expeditions to both North and South America. This fictionalized narrator, like the historical Cabeza de Vaca as he represents himself in his chronicle *Naufragios* (1542), is, although in theory a conquistador, in practice a man who stands out as being more open to contact and exchange with other cultures than the rest of the conquistadors who left written records. Four hundred and fifty years later, Posse's historical fiction *El largo atardecer del caminante* further highlights this aspect of Cabeza de Vaca's uniqueness and offers several explanations for his openness to cultural exchange. Some of these, such as his experiences wandering naked and hungry in the wilderness and his general maladaptation within the enterprise of the conquest, are suggested in Cabeza de Vaca's own chronicle. Additional explanations, such as Cabeza de Vaca's rejection of the Spanish identity forced upon him by virtue of his noble birth, are literary elaborations. In the chronicle *Naufragios* and the historical fiction *El largo atardecer del caminante,* the figure of Álvar Núñez Cabeza de Vaca stands out as unique among the conquistadors for his willingness to participate in the process of transculturation between Old and New Worlds, which will ultimately result in the formation of distinct Spanish American identities.

The term "transculturation," coined in 1940 by Fernando Ortiz in reaction to the sociological concept of acculturation, was elaborated in reference to literature by Angel Rama in his *Transculturación narrativa en América Latina,* and was further developed in reference to ethnography by Mary Louise Pratt, in her *Imperial Eyes.* In the colonial and postcolonial situations, transculturation refers to the existence of a multidirectional exchange of cultural artifacts, practices, and discursive modes between colonizer and colonized, albeit from unequal positions (Pratt 1992, 4–7). In the present analysis of the historical Cabeza de Vaca's *Naufragios* and Posse's historical fiction *El largo atardecer del caminante,* the explorer's nakedness will be demonstrated to symbolize Cabeza de Vaca's willingness to participate in the incipient process of transculturation in the Americas.

As the tradition of reconquest, inquisition, and expulsion of the Jews and Moors reveals, late-fifteenth-century Spain was not receptive to the idea of cultural diversity. The discovery and colonization of the Americas, however, prompted European society to confront heterogeneity in new ways and to see itself as part of a larger universe, no longer as the center of the known world. Although Catholic Spain had already encountered the religious difference of Moors and Jews, its means of dealing with these other cultures generally involved assimilation or expulsion. Upon their contact with the New World, the explorers and conquerors were compelled to invent original ways of confronting diversity. Naturally, the Old World did not become "old" until it compared itself to the newly discovered Americas; 1492 and the ensuing years marked, as much as the discovery of an "Other," a self-discovery of Europe as part of a universe larger and more heterogeneous than previously thought. Europe had long been aware of other cultures, but America was something new: an Other against which to construct a more modern identity. This encounter forced a reevaluation of the coexistence of culturally diverse groups, compelling the Old World to reinvent itself within a more heterogeneous context. In the original chronicle *Naufragios,* the question of the explorer's transculturation can be attributed to his sense of marginality and nonconformity within the project of the conquest, and to his lack of the external accoutrements of the conquistador, which force him to adapt to indigenous cultures. His repeated references to his nakedness have been interpreted by scholars as an implicit reference to his lack of cultural baggage; in *El largo atardecer del caminante,* Cabeza de Vaca's nakedness in the wilderness is explicitly linked to his nonconformity to the ideological project of conquest. The historical Cabeza de Vaca's self-representation as naked and hungry in the wilderness is an element that Posse develops in his historical fiction, elaborating that Cabeza de Vaca experiences his noble Spanish lineage as a cumbersome identity that he needs to shed in order to participate in the incipient process of cultural exchange between Old and New Worlds.

I. Transculturation in the Historical Cabeza de Vaca's Chronicle *Naufragios*

Álvar Núñez Cabeza de Vaca is known to history as the explorer who was shipwrecked and wandered throughout what is now the southwestern United States for nearly a decade in the early sixteenth century. Published in 1542, and revised for a second edition in 1555, Cabeza de Vaca's *relación* of his adventures in North America from 1527 through 1536, after the shipwreck of Pánfilo de Narváez's expedition to Florida, is best known by the title *Naufragios.*[1] After returning to Spain in 1537, and after writing his *relación* as part of an effort to secure another royal appointment from the emperor Charles V, Cabeza de Vaca set out toward South America in 1540, to assume his post as governor of the Río de la Plata region, a commission from which he returned in chains.[2]

Although he arrives in the Americas in the guise of conquistador, Álvar Núñez Cabeza de Vaca narrates from a perspective of marginality in his *Naufragios;* this apparent contradiction is due to the fact that he formed part of Pánfilo Narváez's failed expedition to Florida, which resulted in shipwreck and slavery for Cabeza de Vaca. In order to approach the question of transculturation in *Naufragios,* we must examine Cabeza de Vaca's marginalized position within the hierarchy of conquest and within the first indigenous societies he encounters. Although he begins as an outsider and a slave among the Amerindians, he soon rises to the position of intertribal merchant and ultimately traveling shaman; and, as he transforms his status, he also becomes partially transculturated, to the degree that when he rejoins Hispanic society at the end of his narrative his cultural identification with the Spaniards has become tenuous.

Álvar Núñez Cabeza de Vaca was born in Jerez de la Frontera around 1490; a member of the nobility, he was appointed as "treasurer and constable major" [*tesorero y alguacil mayor*] of the 1527 Narváez expedition to Florida. Unlike most of the members of the journey, Cabeza de Vaca had noble blood on both sides of his family (Lafaye 1970, 76–77). Nevertheless, he sees himself as less powerful than the captains on the voyage and for this reason as marginal to the burgeoning enterprise of Spanish imperialism. Cabeza de Vaca's identification with the Amerindians and his openness to cultural exchange is due at least in part to this sense of marginality within the project of the conquest, which in *Naufragios* is explained in the political terms of his antagonism toward Narváez. According to *Naufragios,* the only firsthand description of the events by a survivor of the expedition, Cabeza de Vaca urged Narváez not to separate a land party from the ships on the Florida coast. Disregarding these pleas, Narváez makes a series of decisions including a cowardly call of "every man for himself," ultimately resulting in his own death and that of all his men except a handful of shipwreck victims, only four of whom eventually make their way back to the Spanish settlements of New Spain: Andrés Dorantes, Alonso del Castillo, the Moorish slave Estebanico, and Álvar Núñez Cabeza de Vaca.

In order to legitimize his own discourse, Cabeza de Vaca uses a strategy that Beatriz Pastor terms the "discourse of defeat," in which the failure of the mission becomes the point of departure for a consciousness-raising that ultimately leads to the questioning of the enterprise of the conquest and an identification with the critical discourse of resistance (Pastor 1988, 236). Through this discursive feat, Cabeza de Vaca is able to turn the material failure of the mission into a positive sign; this is necessary since the expedition, being a failure, could not "speak for itself." It is also an integral part of Cabeza de Vaca's self-fashioning: he represents his suffering as his service to the crown and on that basis requests, and is granted, a new expedition to South America.

After the shipwreck of the Narváez expedition, Cabeza de Vaca comes into contact with different indigenous tribes, in relation to whom he is at first a servant of many masters, and only later a master of his own fate. Living among different tribes, Cabeza de Vaca gradually ascends from the status of slave to that of merchant, and finally becomes a traveling healer who combines European Christian rites with indigenous customs to perform miraculous cures. As slave, and even later as syncretic shaman, Cabeza de Vaca is a half-outsider within these native societies. Sylvia Molloy notes that the Amerindians always recognize his difference by placing him in extreme positions, either in a state of submission or in a space of privilege (Molloy 1987, 439).

When Cabeza de Vaca rejoins Hispanic society at the end of his decade-long journey, it is clear that he has been transformed by his contact with the North American natives to the extent that his reassimilation into the Spanish community can no longer be taken for granted. His main concern is to shield the Amerindians from the Spanish invaders, who threaten to kill or enslave the wanderers' indigenous companions. Throughout his journey Cabeza de Vaca has maintained his cultural difference from the native Americans, but at the same time he has identified with them. Now that he is in a position to resume the authority of a conquistador, he realizes that he can no longer identify wholeheartedly with the Spaniards, nor with the goals of the conquest. Beatriz Pastor perceives Cabeza de Vaca's transculturation as a form of resistance to the developing patterns of colonization: she describes the discourse of *Naufragios* as displaying a critical consciousness that questions the dominant model of the conquest and subverts it by representing solidarity, communication, and understanding with the indigenous Other (Pastor 1988, 225–36).

Against the background of Spain's efforts to seal itself off from ethnic diversity through reconquest and expulsion, Cabeza de Vaca appears unique in his openness to cultural exchange. David Bost notes that *Naufragios* was an anomaly in its time, since Cabeza de Vaca's "extended, intimate experiences among various American tribes gave him profound insight into the devastating impact of the conquest on the New World" (Bost 1995, 43). Silvia Spitta observes that Cabeza de Vaca's narrative is one of the earliest examples of Spanish American transculturation, and that it is singular for this reason (Spitta 1995, 29–30). Juan Bruce-Novoa goes so far as to claim that Cabeza de Vaca's *Naufragios* could be counted as the first Chicano narrative, due to the extent of the explorer's transculturation. Because he is in unknown territory and among people of a culture new to him, Cabeza de Vaca has the space to create himself, and he does this through his adventures and later through his reconstruction of these in *Naufragios.* Lucía Invernizzi Santa Cruz refers to Cabeza de Vaca as "this new man, forged in the struggle against adversity and by contact with and assimilation by—even if only partial—the indigenous world" (Invernizzi 1987, 15). This new man, created through contact with a heterogeneous world, finds that America provides him with the opportunity for transculturation that life in the peninsula denied him.

By far the most salient aspect of Cabeza de Vaca's transcultural experience elaborated in Posse's historical novel is the theme of the would-be conquistador as naked in the wilderness, a portrayal that has ample support within the historical Cabeza de Vaca's own chronicle, in which textual references to nakedness abound. There are two such references within Cabeza de Vaca's brief prologue, in which he describes himself as having "wandered lost and naked through many and very strange lands" (Núñez Cabeza de Vaca 1993, 4) and begs the emperor to accept his *relación* "as a mark of service, for it is the only thing that a man who left those lands naked could bring out with him" (Núñez Cabeza de Vaca 1993, 4).[3] Cabeza de Vaca describes several shipwrecks, during the course of which the group of Spaniards increasingly becomes smaller; after the final shipwreck, the group is left with no material evidence of their status as conquerors. Those who did not drown in this final shipwreck "were naked as the day we were born and had lost all that we had with us, which though it was not worth much, was everything to us at that time" (Núñez Cabeza de Vaca 1993, 41). The Amerindians who had brought them food the previous day initially do not recognize the Spaniards in this naked state:

> when they saw us in such different circumstances as at first, and in such a strange condition, they were so frightened that they turned back. . . . When the Indians saw the disaster that had come upon us and the disaster we were in, with so much ill luck and misery, they sat down among us and, with the great grief and pity they felt on seeing us in such a desperate plight, all of them began to weep loudly, and so sincerely that they could be heard a long way off, and this lasted more than half an hour. (Núñez Cabeza de Vaca 1993, 42)

After the final shipwreck, Cabeza de Vaca continues to underscore the theme of nakedness in the wilderness: "The time that I spent in this land was almost six years, alone among them and as naked as they" (53); "I had no other protection against the cold, being naked as the day I was born" (69); "I have already mentioned how we were naked everywhere in this country, and as we were not used to it, we shed our skin like snakes twice a year" (75).

When the group of shipwreck survivors is reunited with Spanish society at the end of Cabeza de Vaca's narrative, they are given clothing: "We reached Mexico City on a Sunday . . . where we were very well treated by the viceroy and by the Marqués del Valle and received with much pleasure, and they gave us clothing and offered us everything they had" (120). The wanderers accept the gifts, but clearly have become unaccustomed to the accoutrements of civilization: "And when we reached Compostela the governor received us very well and gave us clothing from his own supplies, which I could not wear for many days, nor could we sleep except on the floor" (120). Cabeza de Vaca explains that when they first reencountered the Spaniards, the Amerindians who accompany them refuse to believe that Cabeza de Vaca and his companions are like the other Christians, since "we cured the sick and they killed the healthy; . . . we had come naked and barefoot and they well dressed and on horses and with lances; . . . we did not covet anything, rather we returned everything that they gave us and were left with nothing, and the only aim of the others was to steal everything they found" (114). Here Cabeza de Vaca's nakedness clearly sets him apart from the Spaniards and distances him ideologically from the enterprise of the conquest, which is represented as pure marauding.

Sylvia Molloy and Beatriz Pastor both see Cabeza de Vaca's self-proclaimed nakedness in the wilderness as both a literal lack of clothing and a figurative absence of cultural and ideological baggage.[4] This absence is seen as an opportunity for self-creation: "Thus naked, the 'I' would be a sort of divested space (Spain has been left behind) that would begin to fill with the unknown—America—until culminating in a new being, a new identity" (Molloy 1987, 432). Although he is an educated Spaniard and not a tabula rasa, Cabeza de Vaca is open to experience, and creates himself in the space of the unknown, drawing upon the concepts of identity and alterity. This hybrid person, this "new man" created in the conflict of cultures in the newly discovered Americas, although still a Spaniard, has become someone different who can no longer adhere unquestioningly to the ideology of the conquest. Cabeza de Vaca's nakedness represents this hybridity: "The nakedness has integrated the 'I' into a system; it has declassified it from another, turning it into an incongruent hybrid—*Indianned* but not Indian; Spanish-speaking but not Spanish" (Molloy 1987, 447). His nakedness represents the shedding of his identity as a Spanish conquistador and metaphorically opens up a space for him to question the goals of the conquest: "This nakedness expresses the ultimate form of disowning in regards to the cultural and ideological context in which the figure of the conqueror and his project were defined" (Molloy 1987, 224).

The most exceptional aspect of *Naufragios* is the development of a critical consciousness that is capable of imagining the possibility of an encounter of cultures in America distinct from the colonial pattern that was already being established. In this context, Pastor refers to "the process of progressive development of a critical conscience from which a distinct perception of the American reality will be formulated, and of the possible terms for a relationship between the Spanish and that reality" (Pastor 1988, 223). This ability to imagine new and different cultural relations is part and parcel of the incipient process of transculturation. Thus *Naufragios* exemplifies how, even before the conquest is fully underway, a Spanish American identity is beginning to emerge through early cultural exchange in the Americas, a theme that is developed in the text of Abel Posse's historical fiction, *El largo atardecer del caminante,* through the imagery of Cabeza de Vaca as naked in the wilderness.

II. Nakedness and Transculturation in Abel Posse's *El largo atardecer del caminante*

Of Abel Posse's three novels on the conquest, *El largo atardecer del caminante* is the most recent and consequently has received the least critical attention to date. *El largo atardecer* is the long-awaited third novel of Posse's promised trilogy: the first novel, *Daimón,* on renegade conquistador Lope de Aguirre, was published in 1978, and the second, focussed on Columbus, *Los perros del paraíso,* appeared first in 1983.[5] By the time the trilogy was completed in 1992 with *El largo atardecer del caminante,* nearly a decade had passed since *Los perros del paraíso* and both of the previous historical novels had been reprinted several times and had appeared in English translation.[6] Over the last several years, dozens of critical articles have appeared on Posse's trilogy, principally on *Daimón* and *Los perros del paraíso.*[7]

In Abel Posse's *El largo atardecer del caminante,* the fictionalized narrator representing Álvar Núñez Cabeza de Vaca is a sexagenarian living in Seville[8] after his adventures in the Americas, which concluded with a prolonged trial following his return in chains after serving briefly as governor of the Río de la Plata region. In Seville, the narrator frequents a library to look at maps; there he meets the *conversa* Lucía de Aranha, who gives him a ream of paper on which he writes the memoirs of his voyages to North and South America. In the novel, his New World adventures are recounted as flashbacks intermingled with his current experiences in Seville. In North America, the fictionalized Cabeza de Vaca marries and has a family, in contrast to the real Cabeza de Vaca, who in *Naufragios* makes no reference to having engaged in sexual relations during nearly a decade living among the Amerindians. In order to reunite with the Spaniards, he leaves behind his indigenous wife Amaría, who dies after Hernando de Soto conquers the territory where she lives; their daughter Nube becomes a *guerrillera* in the indigenous resistance against the conquest; and their son Amadís arrives in Seville with a group of Amerindians on display in cages, and dies soon thereafter in spite of Cabeza de Vaca's efforts to secure his release and provide him with medical attention. This arrival of his *mestizo* son in Spain serves as a point of intersection between the narrator's New and Old World experiences.

In a brief prologue preceding the first-person narration, Posse describes Cabeza de Vaca as a wanderer who stood apart from the typical conquistador because of his nakedness in the wilderness; within the context of the novel, Cabeza de Vaca's status as hungry and naked is directly associated with his willingness to adapt to his surroundings. He is described in transcultural terms as "on foot, naked as an Indian" [*a pie, desnudo como un indio*] (Posse 1992, 11). In this prologue, Posse offers as evidence of Cabeza de Vaca's transculturation the fact that upon reuniting with the Spaniards after a decade of traversing North America, "he realized that he still had the foot of an Indian; boots no longer fit him" [*se dio cuenta que ya tenía pie de indio: no le entraban las*] (11).

The novel per se begins with a declaration of Cabeza de Vaca's cultural identity: "I am a Spaniard, I am Andalusian, from Extremadura. In any case, a man from deep Spain. From a house with more lineage and pride than wealth" [*Soy español, soy andaluz, soy extremeño. En todo caso, hombre de la España profunda. De una casa con más linaje y orgullo que riquezas*] (16). The reference to lineage alludes specifically to the honors his grandfathers received for military service. His paternal grandfather, Pedro de Vera, was eminent for his role in the conquest of the Canary Islands,[9] and a maternal ancestor was granted the name Cabeza de Vaca as an honor for his service to the crown. It is notable that the historical Cabeza de Vaca signs his chronicle with this maternal surname, which in the context of Posse's novel corresponds to the mother's high position in the balance of household power in the narrator's boyhood home in Jerez. In *El largo atardecer del caminante,* flashbacks reveal that as a young boy, the future conquistador was pressured by his mother to identify with his grandfather who conquered the Canary Islands and to live up to his noble surnames, which his father failed to do. The fictionalized Cabeza de Vaca resents the pressure of "This surname, that my mother made me live since childhood as a heroic destiny that had to be fulfilled. . . . (Nothing more negative for a man than having to live committed to achieving a destiny imposed or imagined by others)" [*Ese apellido, que mi madre me hizo vivir desde la infancia como un destino heroico que debía ser cumplido. . . . (Nada más negativo para un hombre que tener que vivir empeñado en alcanzar un destino impuesto o imaginado por otros)*] (16). Precisely because his mother forces him to identify with traditional Spanish values, the narrator of *El largo atardecer* experiences the desire to associate with other cultures, since he feels the weight of his lineage bearing down on him as a cumbersome identity.

Cabeza de Vaca's nakedness in the wilderness comes to symbolize the desire to abandon the burden of the conquistador and adopt a transcultural identity: "We were as Indians among Indians; such our poverty, or lack of imperiousness and power. Curious destiny: having arrived with the will and investiture of the conqueror and immediately having fallen to a position inferior and more arduous than that of the last vanquished" [*Éramos como indios entre los indios; tal nuestra pobreza, nuestra falta de imperio y poder. Curioso destino: haber llegado con voluntad e investidura de conquistador y enseguida haber caído en una posición inferior y más penosa que la del último conquistado*] (74). Like the historical Cabeza de Vaca, Posse's fictionalized narrator is touched by the humanity of the Amerindians who rescue the castaways and weep heartily for their loss, demonstrating more Christianity than the Christian conquistadors would have done if the situation had been reversed. Because they are naked, the shipwrecked Spaniards are the ones who must adapt to the native culture: "We, the lords of the world, naked and without armor or sword, had to learn from the savages to gather nonpoisonous fish and roots" [*Nosotros, los dominadores del mundo desnudos y sin coraza ni espada, debíamos aprender de los salvajes a coger peces y raíces no venenosas*] (75).

Living among the Amerindians, *El largo atardecer*'s narrator admits that he has resigned himself to his circumstances and has experienced the desire to abandon his Spanish identity altogether: "I yielded to that dark temptation that I never confessed, but rather I hid carefully: to accept my situation, stripping myself of everything that could be synthesized by the word Spain. It was the temptation as if to flee from myself" [*Cedía yo a esa oscura tentación que nunca confesé, que más bien oculté cuidadosamente: aceptar mi situación, despojarme de todo lo que podría sintetizar con la palabra España. Era la tentación como de huir de mí mismo*] (83). Here the narrator describes a desire for the unknown, for the Other: "It wasn't a new world. It was an other world" [*No era un nuevo mundo. Era otro mundo*] (83). The verb "to strip" [*despojar*] is especially suggestive of shedding his identity in order to transform himself into a transcultural being and to recognize that he is the stranger in this strange land (Posse 1992, 83). His situation is the opposite of that of the conquistador, "My life backwards, always backwards: I was Moctezuma, I was the Indian" [*Mi vida al revés, siempre al revés: yo era Moctezuma, yo era el indio*] (84). Here the fictionalized Cabeza de Vaca's transculturation has progressed to the stage of a complete identification with the Other.

One of the ways in which this fictionalized Cabeza de Vaca rebels against his burdensome noble heritage and participates in the incipient process of transculturation is by taking an indigenous wife, Amaría, the niece of Dulján,[10] the chief of the tribe with whom he spends six years. The fictionalized explorer accepts Dulján's offer of his niece's hand knowing that it means the loss of part of his Spanish identity: "I accepted although I knew that it meant a true marriage and the betrayal of my faith" [*Acepté aunque aquello significaba un verdadero matrimonio y la traición de mi fe*] (95). He later refers to this marriage alternately as "concubinage" [*amancebamiento*] (96) or "marriage" [*casamiento*] (99), indicating some ambivalence about his relationship with a woman who is not Spanish, not Christian, and not even "civilized." The narrator recognizes his own hypocrisy in having silenced the sexual aspect of his adventures when he wrote the official *relación* of his journey, and admits that he is not like the Spaniards who boast of their sexual conquests with vanquished races, but more like the hypocritical northern conquerors: "They tell me that the perfidious Britains and the Dutch hold it as the worst shame to confess their loves with Indians and other native women. . . . In this bad sense I have been more British than good Spaniard, that is, Christian" [*Me dicen que los pérfidos britanos y los holandeses tienen como la peor vergüenza confesar sus amores con indias y otras nativas. . . . En este mal sentido he sido más británico que buen español, esto es, cristiano*] (99).

When he bids farewell to the indigenous wife with whom he has lived for six years, the narrator is exhilarated by the prospect of heading out naked in the wilderness, without the ideological baggage of the conquistador, with only "the will to confront alone and without Spain or Christ or anyone, the open spaces of this new and virgin world" [*La voluntad de enfrentar solo y sin España ni Cristo ni nadie, los espacios abiertos de ese mundo nuevo y virgen*] (140). He persuades his two Spanish companions, Dorantes and Castillo, to leave behind their knives, leather garments, scapulars, and Bible, since the chief Dulján advises them to "present ourselves to the successive villages of the path of the corn, naked of everything, unarmed and without the authority of feeling we are the arm of God" [*presentarnos a los sucesivos pueblos del rumbo del maíz, desnudos de todo, desarmados y sin la prepotencia de sentirse el brazo de Dios*] (142). He convinces his companions to forge forth as new men in a new land without the external trappings of the conquistadors, since to take them "would be like entering into America carrying all Spain in tow" [*Sería como entrar en América con toda España encima*] (141). Avoiding all reference to Castilian culture, which could be dangerous considering that they were advancing toward tribes who were aware of the violence of the Spanish conquest, the wanderers affirm that "Our greatest weapon . . . was our nakedness" [*Nuestra arma mayor . . . era nuestra desnudez*] (144).

In flashbacks throughout the novel, the narrator reconstructs his adventures in the New World, emphasizing his nakedness in the wilderness as a lack of both the external trappings and cultural baggage of the conquistador. Clothing for this fictionalized Cabeza de Vaca represents the false masks and posturing of "civilized" society: "Clothing: vestments, investitures, impostures. . . . Only eight years have I spent naked, without them. . . . Eight years as returned to myself, out of clothing" [*Trajes: vestiduras/investiduras/imposturas. . . . Sólo ocho años he pasado desnudo, sin ellos. . . . Ocho años como devuelto a mí mismo, fuera de los trajes*] (24). During his wanderings, he not only sheds his clothing, he sheds his skin as well—reminiscent of the historical Cabeza de Vaca's declaration that "we shed our skin like snakes twice a year" (Posse 1992, 75), Posse's narrator refers to leaving shed skins along the wayside as symbolic of shedding and abandoning a series of identities (24).

So contradictory is the position of the wanderers that, in order to reencounter Spanish culture, they must walk in the opposite direction of Spain: "I did not propose to them to go in the direction of Cuba and Spain but rather toward the west, counter-Spainwise, as it were" [*No les propuse ir en dirección a Cuba y España sino hacia el Poniente, a contra-España, digamos*] (128). Earlier, the narrator had referred to his temptation to walk westward rather than toward Spain: "A secret voice tempted me to keep walking behind the sun, in the direction opposite to that of my world" [*Una secreta voz me tentaba para seguir andando detrás del sol, en dirección opuesta a la de mi mundo*] (79). This notion of walking away from Spain can be seen as a metaphorical representation of Cabeza de Vaca's desire to abandon his Spanish identity in favor of transculturation, yet ironically his westward journey leads him back to Spanish society.

Posse's Cabeza de Vaca underscores not only his status as naked, but also as barefoot. Like his skin, which he sheds periodically, his feet become so hardened and used to walking—"savage feet" [*pies salvajes*]—that by the end of his adventures he cannot conform to wearing boots (44). The narrator explicitly associates his barefoot state with his adaptation to the indigenous mode of life resulting in a transcultural identity maladapted to the career of conquistador. When he is reunited with the Spaniards at the end of his journey, his unease in wearing boots is directly linked to his altered identity: "I had lost the habit of being a Spanish soldier (perhaps even of being Spanish) and I wobbled a little as if I were entering on stilts the room where they were honoring me" [*Yo ya había perdido la costumbre de ser soldado español (tal vez, incluso, de ser español) y me bamboleaba un poco como si entrase en zancos en el salón donde se me homenajeaba*] (45). In addition to lacking boots and clothing, another essential part of the conquistador's gear that Cabeza de Vaca lacks is a horse: "I was the naked conqueror, the pedestrian" [*Fui el conquistador desnudo, el peatón*] (63). When he narrates the scene of the final shipwreck, he registers the meaning of his nakedness as a loss of the external trappings of the conquistador, and also of his Spanish identity: "I had lost vestments and investiture. The sea had swallowed the sword and the cross. . . . This was the true shipwreck: naked and without Spain" [*Había perdido vestiduras e investiduras. El mar se había tragado la espada y la cruz. . . . Ése fue el verdadero naufragio: desnudo y sin España*] (65).

The narrator conflates the act of writing with the act of wandering, and in one passage he refers to the process of writing his memoirs in terms of "An exaltation like that of the morning when we decided to leave this 'civilization' of adventurers and tyrants and we set out naked, toward the desert, toward the open space" [*Una exaltación como la de aquella mañana cuando decidimos dejar esta "civilización" de aventureros y tiranos y nos lanzamos desnudos, hacia el desierto, hacia el espacio abierto*] (38). Significantly, in the above passage the fictionalized Cabeza de Vaca portrays himself and his companions more as voluntary deserters to the imperial cause than as shipwreck victims naked by necessity. Thus, more explicitly than in Cabeza de Vaca's original chronicle, Posse's fictionalized narrator defines himself as a dissenter within the ranks of the conquistadors.

His nakedness, his status as the barefoot conquistador, symbolizes the fictionalized Cabeza de Vaca's nonconformity within the enterprise of the conquest. When he meets Hernán Cortés back in Spain, the conqueror of Mexico is surprised to find Cabeza de Vaca "less Indian, less naked" [*menos indio, menos desnudo*] (152). The narrator describes himself as unique among the conquistadors for having been an "Indian among the Indians," a conquistador who tried to be different, but failed. He even attempts to convince Cortés that the entire enterprise of the conquest was a failure, since it only succeeded in adding territories to a weak, decadent empire (154). It is during his conversation with Cortés that Cabeza de Vaca begins to perceive that his maladaptation to the goals of the conquest was a direct result of his desire to escape the cumbersome identity imposed by his noble Spanish lineage: "While Cortés spoke, I felt that I had never believed in that future. I was born with my future set, given my lineage. I did nothing but try to unburden myself of it by searching more for adventure than conquest and power. I was a pedestrian, a wanderer . . . [I]n my deepest self I had never fulfilled the goals of the Empire" *[Mientras Cortés hablaba, sentí que yo nunca había creído en ese futuro. Nací con el futuro puesto, dada mi estirpe. No hice otra cosa sino tratar de desembarazarme de él buscando más la aventura que la conquista y el poder. Fui un peatón, un caminante. . . . [E]n lo profundo de mí nunca había cumplido con los propósitos del Imperio]* (152). Thus Posse's Cabeza de Vaca is the pedestrian conquistador who is not in accord with the goals and means of the conquest. In *El largo atardecer,* Cabeza de Vaca's dissidence within the enterprise of the conquest is represented by the slogan, "Only faith cures, only goodness conquers" [*Sólo la fe cura, sólo la bondad conquista*] (154).[11] Ultimately, for Posse's Cabeza de Vaca the conquest resulted not in the discovery of another world, but rather in Spain's self-discovery: "We have discovered nothing in the Indies. What we have discovered is Spain. A sick

Spain" [*No hemos descubierto nada en las Indias. Lo que hemos descubierto es España. Esta España enferma*] (163).

During his wanderings in North America, Cabeza de Vaca glimpses the possibility of a new order based on individual worth rather than on the yoke of lineage (164–65). In this world, he becomes a new man by giving himself over to the process of transculturation through which he gives birth to a new self; after participating in a ritual involving a hallucinogen, the narrator exclaims, "I gave birth to myself from my own body" [*Me parí desde mi propio cuerpo*] (172). When he and his companions are reunited with the Christians at the end of their travels, the narrator underscores again that the Spaniards did not recognize him as one of their own, because of his nakedness: "I, naked, with a loincloth" [*Yo, desnudo, con un taparrabos*] (175); "they didn't respect my rank because I was naked and gone savage" [*no respetaban mi jerarquía por estar yo desnudo y asalvajado*] (176). By this point in the narration, Cabeza de Vaca's nakedness has clearly become established as an emblem of the desire to shed his burdensome identity as a Spanish conquistador of noble lineage in favor of a transcultural identity.

Just as shedding his clothing represents shedding the ideology of the conquest, putting on clothing represents putting that ideology back on as well: "I went back to being treated as an accomplice and protagonist of our Spain: they gave me clothes" [*Volví a ser tratado como cómplice y protagonista de nuestra España: me dieron ropa*] (176). The narrator elaborates on his difficulty adjusting to Spanish clothing, boots, and even sleeping in a bed. Although he has returned to the external trappings of Spanish civilization, his inner self has been permanently altered through the process of transculturation: "I was once again Don Álvar Núñez Cabeza de Vaca, gentleman of Jerez. But I was an Other, no matter how much I pretended. I was now, and forever, an Other" [*Era otra vez don Alvar Núñez Cabeza de Vaca, el señor de Xerés. Pero era otro, por más que yo simulase. Era ya, para siempre, un otro*] (177). He describes himself as a failed conquistador, who neither took possession of territories, renamed lands, nor reduced natives to service to the crown: a "conquered conqueror" [*conquistador conquistado*] (177). Now neither Spaniard nor Amerindian, Cabeza de Vaca is a transculturated entity, simply an Other: "Neither rebellious enough to deny the god of his childhood, nor submissive enough to enslave and kill in the name of a king. An eccentric. An Other" [*Ni tan rebelde como para negar al dios de su infancia, ni tan sumiso como para esclavizar y matar en nombre de un Rey. Un excéntrico. Un otro*] (177–78). In order to receive another commission and continue to protect the Amerindians from the cruelty of the conquest, he must pretend to be a Spaniard, to go along with the project of imperialism, but he knows that he is just acting, since his pre-shipwreck Spanish identity no longer exists (179).

In his South American commission, as in his North American shipwreck,

Cabeza de Vaca's transculturated identity continues to make it impossible for him to implement the ideology of conquest: "I was not a man faithful to the Empire. I was an 'Other' " [*Yo no era un hombre fiel al Imperio. Yo era un "otro"*] (216). His first act as governor upon disembarking on South American soil is to order the Spaniards to bathe naked. Having bathed, their bodies are "purified, redeemed from a very sick Spain, from a very sick culture" [*purificados, redimidos de una España, de una cultura, muy enfermas*] (219). Only now, having purified their naked bodies of the decadence of Spain, can the soldiers go forward on Cabeza de Vaca's mission, which is not a conquest but an anticonquest. Because his mission does not fit in with the goals of the other conquistadors in South America, he is arrested and returned to the Iberian peninsula in chains. After prolonged imprisonment, trial, and sentencing, Cabeza de Vaca is stripped of his titles, truly a "naked discoverer" [*descubridor desnudo*] (234).

In Seville after the failure of his governorship in the Río de la Plata, the narrator continues to express a distinct sense of not fitting into Spanish culture. When he is obliged to attend an auto-da-fé, he is appalled by the brutality of the Inquisition, and rejects the worldview it represents, "No. Nothing ties me any longer to the city of my childhood (which is the same, but I changed)" [*No. Nada me une ya a mi pueblo ni a la ciudad de mi infancia (que es la misma, pero yo cambié)*] (117). He ends up walking away from the auto-da-fé, concluding, "No. Already I am definitively another . . . I am another. I am he who saw too much" [*No. Ya soy definitivamente otro . . . Soy otro. Soy él que vio demasiado*] (117). The theme of nakedness as freedom from ideological baggage is reiterated here, since after abandoning the scene of the auto-da-fé, Cabeza de Vaca goes home and changes his clothes: "I shed my ceremonial clothing and dressed as a beggar . . . I rushed into the street . . . My clothing transformed me into an unpretentious old vagabond" [*me despojé de mi traje de ceremonias y vestido como un pordiosero . . . me lancé a la calle. . . . Mi indumentaria me transformaba en un viejo vagabundo sin pretensiones*] (118). Here in Seville, as in the Americas, lack of clothing is associated with freedom from the oppressive constraints of Cabeza de Vaca's Spanish heritage.

Published in the year of the quintcentennial of Columbus's first voyage and exactly four hundred and fifty years after the publication of Cabeza de Vaca's *Naufragios,* Abel Posse's historical novel *El largo atardecer del caminante* elaborates upon many of the themes suggested in *Naufragios,* making explicit an ideological position of dissidence only hinted at in the original chronicle. In both the chronicle and the novel, Cabeza de Vaca's nakedness in the wilderness and his openness to transculturation are underscored. In *Naufragios,* this can be attributed to Cabeza de Vaca's marginality within the enterprise of the conquest and his lack of the external trappings of the conquistador during his wanderings in North America. *El largo atardecer del caminante* explicitly attributes his transculturation to an internal sense of nonconformity with the goals of the conquest due to a desire to shed his burdensome noble Spanish identity. In Posse's novel, then, Cabeza de Vaca's "nakedness in the wilderness" is explicitly identified as a symbol of his disposition toward transculturation and his rejection of the ideological and cultural baggage of the conquistador.

Notes

1. Textual references to *Naufragios* here are from the translation *Castaways,* edited by Enrique Pupo-Walker and translated by Frances M. López-Morillas.

2. The reasons given for his arrest vary; some scholars attribute his imprisonment primarily to his unpopular defense of the Amerindians (Todorov 1987, 197). The most extensive original source on the issue, the *Comentarios* written by Cabeza de Vaca's own amanuensis and apologist, Pedro Hernández, does not suggest such a univocal perspective, but rather points to a variety of political conflicts between Cabeza de Vaca and the other conquistadors.

3. In a footnote to his edition of *Naufragios,* Juan Francisco Maura notes that Cabeza de Vaca continually represents himself as naked, in spite of the fact that he is repeatedly offered gifts of furs (Núñez Cabeza de Vaca 1989, 182n).

4. Tzvetan Todorov observes in reference to the first mention of the Amerindians in a European document, Columbus's diary, that "the first characteristic of these people to strike Columbus is the absence of clothes—which in their turn symbolize culture" (Todorov 1987, 34).

5. *El largo atardecer* is the only novel of the trilogy that has not yet appeared in English translation. For this reason, the textual translations here are mine.

6. Before *El largo atardecer* appeared, Posse had announced that the third novel would be entitled *Los heraldos negros* and would deal with early Jesuit missions (García Pinto 1989, 499).

7. Seymour Menton, Donald Shaw, Raymond Souza, Elzbieta Sklodowska, David Bost, and Juan José Barrientos are among the scholars who have published critical articles and book chapters on the first two novels of Posse's trilogy. Of these, only Menton's book and Bost's article refer to *El largo atardecer del caminante;* Bost's article specifically develops the relationship between *Naufragios* and *El largo atardecer.*

8. Little is known about the historical Cabeza de Vaca after his return to Spain. He was imprisoned, stripped of his titles, and permanently banned from returning to the Río de la Plata. He is believed to have died poverty-stricken in the late 1550s, most likely in Valladolid, not in Seville as portrayed in Posse's novel (Pupo-Walker 1993, xxv; Howard 1997, 190).

9. Ninety years before Columbus's first voyage, the conquest of the Canary Islands marked the beginning of the westward movement of Spanish imperialism; as Posse's narrator claims, his grandfather set the pace for a series of conquistadors who would establish Spain as the empire whose sun never set (Posse 1992, 18).

10. The name Dulján can be seen as a tribute to the only Amerindian referred to by a proper name in the text of *Naufragios,* Dulchanchellín (Núñez Cabeza de Vaca 1993, 19).

11. The narrator's slogan echoes the historical Cabeza de Vaca's plea to the emperor to promote pacific evangelization of the Amerindians: "if they are to be brought to be Christians and into obedience of Your Imperial Majesty, they must be

led by good treatment, and . . . this is a very sure way, and no other will suffice" (Núñez Cabeza de Vaca 1993, 108). Cabeza de Vaca's attitude toward the Amerindians has been likened to that of Bartolomé de las Casas (Todorov 1987, 197); Rolena Adorno observes that "His advocacy of humane treatment for these peoples makes him a Lascasian by experience rather than reading" (Adorno 1991, 186).

Bibliography

Adorno, Rolena. 1991. "The Negotiation of Fear in Cabeza de Vaca's *Naufragios.*" *Representations* 33: 163-99.

Barrientos, Juan José. 1986. "América, ese paraíso perdido." *Omnia* 2, no. 3:69-75.

Bost, David H. 1995. "Reassessing the Past: Abel Posse and the New Historical Novel." In *La Chispa '95: Selected Proceedings,* edited by Claire J. Paolini, 39-47. New Orleans: Tulane University Press.

Bruce-Novoa, Juan. 1993. "Shipwrecked in the Sea of Signification: Cabeza de Vaca's *Relación* and Chicano Literature." In *Reconstructing a Chicano/a Literary Heritage,* ed. María Herrera-Sobek, 3-23. Tucson: University of Arizona Press.

García Pinto, Magdalena. 1989. "Entrevista con Abel Posse." *Revista Iberoamericana* 55: 493-505.

Howard, David A. 1997. *Conquistador in Chains: Cabeza de Vaca and the Indians of the Americas.* Tuscaloosa: University of Alabama Press.

Invernizzi Santa Cruz, Lucía. 1987. "Naufragios e Infortunios: Discurso que transforma fracasos en triunfos." *Revista chilena de literatura* 29 (April): 7-22.

Lafaye, Jacques. 1970. *Los conquistadores.* Translated by Elsa Cecilia Frost. Mexico City: Siglo Veintiuno.

Menton, Seymour. 1993. *Latin America's New Historical Novel.* Austin: University of Texas Press.

Molloy, Sylvia. 1987. "Alteridad y reconocimiento en los *Naufragios* de Alvar Núñez Cabeza de Vaca." *Nueva revista de filología hispánica* 35, 2: 425-49.

Núñez Cabeza de Vaca, Álvar. 1989. *Naufragios.* Edited by Juan Francisco Maura. Madrid: Cátedra.

———. 1993. *Castaways.* Edited by Enrique Pupo-Walker. Translated by Frances M. López-Morillas. Berkeley: University of California Press.

Ortiz, Fernando. 1940. *Contrapunteo cubano del tabaco y el azúcar.* Havana: J. Montero.

Pastor, Beatriz. 1988. *Discursos narrativos de la conquista: Mitificación y emergencia.* Hanover: Ediciones del Norte.

Posse, Abel. 1992. *El largo atardecer del caminante.* Buenos Aires: Emecé.

Pratt, Mary Louise. 1992. *Imperial Eyes: Travel Writing and Transculturation.* London: Routledge.

Pupo-Walker, Enrique. 1993. Introduction to *Castaways,* by Alvar Núñez Cabeza de Vaca. Edited by Enrique Pupo-Walker. Translated by Frances M. López-Morillas. Berkeley: University of California Press.

Rama, Angel. 1982. *Transculturación narrativa en América Latina.* Mexico City: Siglo Veintiuno.

Shaw, Donald. 1993. "Columbus and the Discovery in Carpentier and Posse." *Romance Quarterly* 40, 3: 181-89.

Sklodowska, Elzbieta. 1991. *La parodia en la nueva novela hispanoamericana.* Amsterdam: Benjamins.

Souza, Raymond D. 1992. "Columbus in the Novel of the Americas: Alejo Carpentier, Abel Posse, and Stephen Marlowe." In *The Novel in the Americas,* edited by Raymond Leslie Williams, 40-55. Niwot: University Press of Colorado.

Spitta, Silvia. 1995. *Between Two Waters: Narratives of Transculturation in Latin America.* Houston: Rice University Press.

Todorov, Tzvetan. 1987. *The Conquest of America.* Translated by Richard Howard. New York: Harper and Row.

Part Five
The Reinvention of the Past through Apocryphal Chronicles

Penetrating Texts: Testimonial Pseudo-Chronicle in *La noche oscura del Niño Avilés* by Edgardo Rodríguez Juliá Seen from Sigüenza y Góngora's *Infortunios de Alonso Ramírez*

ERIK CAMAYD-FREIXAS

I. Penetrating Texts

LATIN AMERICAN FICTION'S REAPPROPRIATION OF EUROPEAN TESTIMONIAL chronicles entails a process of authority construction that is both textual and historical, since it was already at work in certain narrative texts of the colonial period. Significantly, an inversion of power relations between colonizer and colonized will be seen to underlie that process. Thus, in the realm of mimicry as a discursive strategy for symbolic production and self-representation, the aesthetic and the ideological are conjoined, together with questions of identity.

The pretense of historical verity suggested by the mimicry of nonfictional discursive forms (and taken only half seriously in the interest of ludic plausibility) was already present in Sigüenza's protomodern 1690 account of Puerto Rican pauper Alonso Ramírez's toils around the world.[1] The *Infortunios* is a fictional retelling of the chronicles of the Indies, an inverted epic, now from the perspective of a Creole boy—a reluctant discoverer, a Puerto Rican Magellan who circumnavigates the globe as the captive and lackey of pirates: "And whilst from deeds which only subsisted in the fancy of those who feigned them, maxims and aphorisms . . . amid the delectable . . . are oft deduced, that shall not be what I should here attempt but to solicit tears which, though subsequent to my toils, shall at least render tolerable their memory" [*Y aunque de sucesos que sólo subsistieron en la idea de quien los finge, se suelen deducir máximas y aforismos . . . entre lo deleitable . . . , no será esto lo que yo aquí intente sino solicitar lágrimas que, aunque posteriores a mis trabajos, harán por lo menos tolerable su memoria*] (Sigüenza 1983, 9). In his twisted statement of purpose, there is no affirmation of truth but also no admission of falsehood. A duplicity of voices suggests that the autobiographical narration is "true" for the character, if "false" for the author. What we have here is, rather, a penetration of the text, in a dual sense: both a discursive entry of ludic plausibility into the text, and of the text into the reader. The abduction/seduction of authority is accomplished at the end of the book when Alonso Ramírez turns his account over to Sigüenza himself for redaction and publication.

Three hundred years later, another Puerto Rican chronicler, Edgardo Rodríguez Juliá, would recapture that mannerist handshake between author and character (reminiscent also of Mateo Alemán, Cervantes, Velázquez, Unamuno), in his search for the deformed (and handless) body of Child Avilés, mythical founder, in 1797, of the fictional city of New Venice—that angelical and demonic microcosm of San Juan—and the subject of a strangely fascinating portrait by the Puerto Rican Velázquez, José Campeche. The author's presence inside his own text is now accomplished by a penetrating "Prologue" à la Borges, cast like an essay in historical archaeology, complete with footnotes and a critique of source documents.

> That city of legends and canals is absent from our main collections of historical documents. But its fame was the scandal and marvel of that colonial society from two centuries ago; the image reaches us of a precinct apparently repressed by the collective memory. Hidden by oblivion, the accursed city is reborn before us. . . . González Campos's chronicle belongs to a collection of documents uncovered by the archivist Don José Pedreira Murillo in 1913. . . . Some historians grant no historical value at all to the documents of the Pedreira collection. It is, according to them, an 'apocryphal history' constructed around the visionary landscapes of the masterful painter.
>
> [*Aquella ciudad de leyendas y canales está ausente de nuestras principales colecciones de documentos históricos. Pero su fama fue escándalo y maravilla de aquella sociedad colonial de hace dos siglos; a nosostros llega la imagen de un recinto al parecer reprimido por la memoria colectiva. Oculta por el olvido, renace ante nosotros la ciudad maldita. . . . La crónica de González Campos pertenece a una colección de documentos descubierta por el archivero Don José Pedreira Murillo en el 1913. . . . Algunos historiadores no le conceden valor histórico alguno a los documentos de la colección Pedreira. Se trata, según ellos, de una "historia apócrifa" compuesta en torno a los paisajes visionarios del genial pintor.*] (Rodríguez Juliá 1984, ix–xi)

As in Sigüenza, there is no affirmation of truth nor admission of falsehood, only ludic plausibility, underscored by the fact that the last sentence applies self-reflexively to Rodríguez Juliá's novel, itself an "apocryphal history" constructed around two portraits by José Campeche (those of Child Avilés and Bishop Trespalacios) as well as a supposed series of visionary landscapes of New Venice belonging to the brush of one Silvestre Andino, Campeche's nephew and apprentice. Yet, rather than the pious rococo of the Campeche school, these landscapes (and the novel itself) resemble in style and subject matter the demonic baroque visions of Bosch's *Garden of Earthly Delights* and Quevedo's *Dreams.*

The function of prologue in testimonial pseudo-chronicles is, of course, to claim not so much absolute truth as historical plausibility. In Sigüenza's *Infortunios* this is accomplished immediately by the autobiographical framework of Alonso Ramírez's first-person narrative. Yet, in the censor's note that precedes the work and approves it for publication by virtue of its religious piety and exemplariness, the toils of the "subject" of the story are equated with those of the "author" (*laboriosas fatigas del autor*), equating the writing itself with the laborious journey it relates. A similar identification is intended in Rodríguez Juliá's prologue: its statement that "the accursed city is reborn before us" refers to the finding of the chronicles whose excerpts make up the body of the novel. Ultimately, the "city" *is* the novel, and the writing is the founding. Sigüenza's censor, Chaplain Ayerra, lends further credence to the story by calling Alonso Ramírez "my compatriot"—although he might have only met him on paper through his reading of the book. Rodríguez Juliá's prologue, in turn, is signed by a historian who adamantly defends the authenticity of the documents, a certain Professor Alejandro Cadalso, on "9 October 1946"—the novelist's date of birth, the historian Cadalso being one of the author's personae.

Such insistent claims to authenticity make testimonial pseudo-chronicles engage in considerable metanarrative (stories and reflections that justify the narrative and, at the same time, define its parameters). It might be pertinent at this point to recollect that useful distinction drawn by the Russian formalists between *sjuzet* and *fabula* (the complete story with all the facts, details, and events as it would have happened in real life versus those fragments that the author chooses to tell us). The same distinction may apply to metanarrative: obtaining, as it were, a meta-*sjuzet* and a meta-*fabula.* The latter, those fragments of justification that the author chooses to share, serves to establish historical plausibility; but if the whole metastory of justification were told, the plausibility of the main story would fall apart. Conversely, in withholding metafictional evidence, a complicity with the reader is built up and eventually taken for granted as a fait accompli. At that point, the author playfully stretches this pact of believability as though testing its limits, and may even transgress them, partly in jest and exaggeration. The result is what I have called ludic plausibility.

In Sigüenza's *Infortunios* the meta-*fabula* is not fully accomplished until the end of the novel, when Alonso Ramírez returns to Mexico from his voyage of captivity to tell his story and seal the metafictional pact. The elements of authenticity are not only whether Alonso truly existed but whether he actually traveled the globe and whether the events of the journey really occurred as he relates them.[2] Finally, there is the issue of whether the chronicler Sigüenza edited, modified, or embellished his testimony, turning fact into fiction. While Alonso's existence is assumed from the beginning and the sincerity of his account "protested" throughout the text, there are intimations at the end that he may have had motives to concoct, if not exaggerate, the story of his toils. In the telling, Alonso seeks not only pity but material favors from the colonial authorities—a common scheme among chroniclers of the Indies, notorious, for example, in Bernal Díaz, and not entirely alien to Sigüenza.[3] He even claims he visited Viceroy Gaspar de Sandoval who, compelled by the story, referred him finally to Sigüenza, who "gave it form" [*formó esta Relación*] and who pleaded with the viceroy to recognize Alonso. It was ordered as a result that Alonso be given a temporary naval post until he got settled, and that he be awarded the contents of the ship he had heroically taken from pirates and brought back to Mexico (and which he had been initially accused of stealing).[4] A complete meta-*sjuzet,* however, would include such details as the fact that Sigüenza (or the viceroy, for that matter) never bothered to corroborate the story with the other survivors of the journey, whom Alonso allegedly disbanded in Merida (Sigüenza 1983, 73) after they had made declarations to local authorities more interested in confiscating the ship's booty than in ascertaining truth. The meta-*fabula* only tells us in passing that Sigüenza was "ill" when he received Alonso's story (Sigüenza 1983, 75), thereby excusing him from further investigation. As to Sigüenza's embellishment of the testimony, one can cite the erudite author's balanced Gracianesque prose, inconceivable in his illiterate subject; the adaptation of the narrative to certain generic canons of the time ("gave it form"), particularly chronicle and picaresque; and the reversal of the picaresque scheme, which turns Alonso from a potential Lazarillo into a biblical Job, thereby fulfilling the ideal of moral edification in fiction, which so pleased the censor. Then there are the complex navigational courses didactically (and almost boastfully) plotted across the Pacific and the Atlantic, befitting a royal cosmographer, mathematician, and cartographer such as was Sigüenza's true occupation. In short, the author is stretching the meta-fictional pact.[5] Curiously, Viceroy Sandoval, to whom Sigüenza dedicates the book, appears at the end of Alonso's account addressed only as "Your Excellency" [*Su Excelencia*] (cf. Lazarillo's *Vuestra Merced*). We can only know his identity from the book's dedication (a metanarrative return to the beginning after the trip around the world). *Su Excelencia* is here the ultimate reader, arbiter, and judge of the (meta)story, the authority behind the text, to whom any readerly doubts are tacitly referred: if he accepts the story, so must the reader. In his dedication, Sigüenza praises Sandoval and entreats him to accept the book as he had accepted Alonso's oral account. Yet, he is also reporting back to Sandoval, who had accepted Alonso's story on the sole basis of his own compassion, but had referred it to Sigüenza precisely, by all appearances, for expert verification. Sigüenza's report on Alonso's story (and innocence) is positive: he offers Sandoval the written account "trusting of course, in what concerns me, upon the highest judgment he knows how to make to my astonishment of the world's hydrography and geography" [*confiado desde luego, por lo que me toca, . . . en la crisis altísima que sabe hacer con espanto mío de la hidrografía y geografía del mundo*] (Sigüenza 1983, 4). That is, Sigüenza defends the story on the basis of its greatest implausibility: the display of technical and scientific knowledge that was quite certainly his own addition. The argument, like the journey, is perfectly circular: the unbelievable becomes the very basis of belief.[6]

The judicial, legalizing character of colonial chronicles and picaresque testimony, aptly studied by González Echevarría in *Myth and Archive,* is also at work here.[7] Sigüenza's narrative can be read as a judicial record (*acta*), expert witness testimony, and summary report to the viceroy and captain general, whose end result is Alonso Ramírez's acquittal. Yet, in testimonial pseudo-chronicle what is actually being judged is not the character's actions but the metanarrative of historical plausibility. That is, what is sought is not judicial but historical legitimacy, acquittal of the story (not the character) by the reader (not a judge, even though a judge may be the story's implied reader). In short, the burden of proof is on the telling (meta-*fabula*), not the deeds (*sjuzet*).

This is perhaps most salient in Rodríguez Juliá's prologue, where the judge is the historian Cadalso examining the documentary evidence for the authenticity of the New Venice chronicles (and of the novel, composed entirely of quotations from those chronicles, with brief editorial introductions and transitions). Historical plausibility is easily established in testimonial pseudo-chronicles by the presence of historical characters such as Sandoval, Sigüenza himself, and many others who appear in *Infortunios.* Such presence should be considered part of the metanarrative. The same is achieved in *La noche oscura* and its prologue by the presence of painters José Campeche (1751–1809) and Luis Paret y Alcázar (1746–1799), Admiral Nelson (1758–1805), Bishop Trespalacios (d. 1799), Governor Ramón de Castro (as of 1795), and Child Avilés himself (b. 1806). All other characters, their chronicles, testimonies, and bibliography, are fictional, including Bishop Larra, maroon rebels Obatal and Mitume, The Renegade, chronicler Gracián, as well as the evidential sources in the prologue, archivist Pedreira, and painter-leper Silvestre Andino.[8] An uninformed reader, however, would be readily convinced by the documentary evidence in favor of the existence of the maroon city and the historical plausibility of the text. Yet, even the seemingly rigorous footnotes point to fictional sources[9]—a deliberate use of apocrypha reminiscent of Antonio de Guevara or Jorge Luis Borges. The result is the penetration of fiction into the metafictional narrative of legitimation. What starts as a historical essay becomes fictional narrative; but since *La noche oscura* is composed of the defended chronicles, the whole novel becomes an extended (if increasingly extravagant) metanarrative. Indeed, the prologue's metafictional plot is more complex than the novel's as a whole.[10] After such defense of its historical plausibility, the novel begins by quoting different "chroniclers" while invoking the authority of their trade: "Severino Pedrosa, first chronicler of the Town Hall, tells us in his *True account of the very famous rescue of the Child Avilés*" (Rodríguez Juliá 1984, 6). Later such introductions are reduced to "in the words of . . ." or "let us listen to the voice of . . ."; and finally the chroniclers are simply identified in chapter titles, while editorial introductions are suppressed. As events become more and more preposterous, the metafictional pact is transgressed and historical plausibility, having served its purpose as instrument of seduction and penetration of the text, becomes ludic plausibility. The chroniclers' authority no longer needs to be asserted, because the reader has become a full accomplice in the truthful hoax of fiction.

It is not surprising that *La noche oscura*'s first critics were historians who reacted to its blatant anachronisms and falsifications, complaining that this was not a historical novel (González 1986, 583). In fact, the infamous prologue is not only a parody of historical method but a vitriolic invective against official historiography (the meta*fabula* of history) and its repression of (*sjuzet*) the *historical unconscious*. The meta-fictional plot is nothing other than the story of a Church-State conspiracy (with participation of the timorous Creole bourgeoisie dependent on colonial power) to cover up the people's true *history of desire* represented in that "most accursed lacustrine city."

> The fact is that New Venice also disappeared from the collective memory of the people, forever banished now into oblivion, its memory turned into a nightmare of history, its brief abode in time erased from books and songs. New Venice thus became the dark reverse of our peaceful and respectable colonial history.
>
> [*Lo cierto es que Nueva Venecia también desapareció de la memoria colectiva del pueblo, ya para siempre desterrada al olvido, convertido su recuerdo en pesadilla de la historia, borrada de libros y canciones su breve posadura en el tiempo. Nueva Venecia se convertía así en oscuro reverso de nuestra pacífica y respetable historia colonial.*] (Rodríguez Juliá 1984, xiii)

Rodríguez Juliá posits the ultimate justification of fiction: the purpose of this novel-city is the liberation of our repressed historical unconscious, to tell not the history of deeds but of desires undone. In a perceptive study, Antonio Benítez Rojo detects the novel's desire to become history. Then, in the most sober prose of Fray Iñigo Abbad's *Historia geográfica, civil y natural de la isla de San Juan Bautista de Puerto Rico* (1782), the novel's enlightened reverse and historical counterpart, Benítez Rojo exposes a penchant for narrative, a thirst for the imaginary, and the desire to become fiction. He concludes that history and novel want to trade places, and calls Child Avilés "the libido of history." But for Rodríguez Juliá, as we shall see, the novel is also the *history of libido.*

II. The Body Politic

The picaresque framework (or its modification) is an often-noted aspect of *Infortunios.*[11] Also well recognized is its contribution to the formation of a *criollo* discourse at the origins of the Latin American novel.[12] Yet, the modern significance of Sigüenza's baroque text is that it lays bare the generic affinity and plasticity that extend among the European chronicle, the picaresque, the travelogue, and the *criollo* modern novel: *pseudo*crónica, *anti*crónica, *ana*crónica. Particularly, Sigüenza's fusion of chronicle and picaresque, or more precisely his reconversion of the former into the latter, yields an unexpected product, a generic particle that is historically and politically charged: antichronicle. There is an interesting process at work in historical narratology, largely unexplored by colonial studies: the passage from chronicle to picaresque and its implications. The sixteenth-century "chronicles of Indies," written by Europeans to legitimize the colonial enterprise, and also known appropriately as "the chronicles of the Conquest," belonged to a period of discovery, epic voyages, and wars, whose glory the American *Criollo* never shared. It was an exclusively European dream. However, by 1595, even Francis Drake had circumnavigated the globe. So when that age of heroic *epos* that gave us *La Araucana* was over, and the Europeans got down to the business of everyday life, which in America meant administering the colonies and populating the land, the dreams of glory gave way to the harsher realities of economic survival and social mobility in a caste society. The latter was a defining reality for the *Criollo,* and its appropriate form of expression, far from the epic, soon became the picaresque. By 1598, the poetry of Mateo Rosas de Oquendo was depicting the picaresque tenor of city life in Lima, Peru. But it was with the baroque concept of *desengaño* ("unmasking, undeceiving, disillusionment"—all at once), that the colonial picaresque reached its maturity. Quevedo had united *desengaño* and picaresque; Caviedes's *Diente del Parnaso* (1689) and Terralla Landa's *Lima por dentro y fuera* (1792) applied them in America. In Spain, Mateo Alemán's *Guzmán de Alfarache* (1604) and Vélez de Guevara's *El diablo cojuelo* (1641; see note 14) had already proclaimed America the new land of the rogue, pointing out satirically that Spaniards who went there "left their conscience in Seville." After all, it had always been "disillusion" [*desengaño*] that turned epic (the *ethos* of conquest) into picaresque (the *ethos* of colonial life).

Picaresque became the narrative, from *Infortunios* to *Concolorcorvo* to *Periquillo sarniento.* Modern novelists from Carpentier to Fuentes want to seek the origin of the Latin American novel in the chronicles, and yet, their own chronicles, from *El arpa y la sombra* to *Terra Nostra,* are suffused with picaresque.

Through the tropes of *desengaño,* the American picaresque exposed the false heroism of the conquest and the colonial enterprise. That "Imperial Gaze" which Mary Pratt has described in the European chronicles and travelogues had to be replaced with a subaltern gaze issuing from the bottom up. That is exactly the orientation of Alonso Ramírez's journey, an inverted voyage of world discovery issuing from America instead of Europe. The result is an antichronicle precisely in the measure that the picaresque is an antiepic—indeed a parody of the epic whose Homeric and Vergilian tradition had reached America by way of Tasso and Ariosto, in the ethos of Ercilla, Oña, and the chronicles of Indies. Censor Ayerra recognized as much in the hyperbolic comparison he makes of his "compatriot" Alonso Ramírez:

> The subject of this narration can very well feel satisfied that his misfortunes are twice fortunate today: once, because of having been already gloriously suffered, which is what the muse of Mantua [Vergil] praised through the words of Aeneas in like occasion before his Troyan comrades . . . and further because he had by stroke of luck the pen of this Homer [Sigüenza] . . . who with the orderliness of his discourses bestowed a soul [Aristotelean *form*] upon the embryo of confused untowardness of so many happenings and in the entwined labyrinth of such roundabouts found the thread of gold to crown himself with praises.
>
> [*Puede el sujeto de esta narración quedar muy desvanecido de que sus infortunios son hoy dos veces dichosos: una, por ya gloriosamente padecidos, que es lo que encareció la musa de Mantua [Vergil] en boca de Eneas en ocasión semejante a sus compañeros Troyanos . . . y otra porque le cupo en suerte la pluma de este Homero . . . que al embrión de la funestidad confusa de tanto suceso dio alma con lo aliñado de sus discursos y al laberinto enmarañado de tales rodeos halló el hilo de oro para coronarse de aplausos.* (Sigüenza 1983, 6)[13]]

Rodríguez Juliá will also make a parody of epic—"The rubicund Apollo was already fainting in his latest glimmer when . . . desirous to contemplate the crested locks of Neptune . . ." [*Ya desfallecía el rubicundo Apolo en sus últimos destellos cuando . . . deseoso de contemplar los encrespados rizos de Neptuno . . .*] (Rodríguez Juliá 1984, 78)—and particularly of Vergil's Aeneas in the face of battle—"With a slow pace, under ominous clouds and high thunderbolts, the infamous battle approached, too earthly a pain which sorrowed my conscience to the point of yearning for death" [*Con paso lento, bajo nubarrones y altos relámpagos, se acercó la batalla infame, dolor demasiado terreno que apenó mi conciencia hasta anhelar la muerte*] (Rodríguez Juliá 1984, 232). He often compares his New Venice to Troy and Tenochtitlan.

Yet the "soul" or "golden thread" that the ecclesiastical censor finds in Sigüenza's narrative is precisely the author's reconversion of the picaresque into the parable of Job (*Para eternizar Job lo que refería deseaba quien lo escribiera . . . cuanto él había sabido tolerar*). Sigüenza's narrative will ultimately be a "pious picaresque" [*picaresca a lo divino*]—another of his many bids for readmission into the Jesuit order from which he had been expelled in 1667? Of the three parts of Alonso's voyage—the journey of fortune (Lazarillo, Guzmán de Alfarache), the trials of captivity (Job), and the tribulations of the shipwreck (Jonas, Aeneas)—only the first is truly picaresque and it ends at the Philippines, which is also the end of the more "realistic" and historically plausible part of the story. The rest is at the very least Sigüenza's adaptation. However, in this latter inversion there is a double unmasking: after the false heroism of the chronicles, the false roguery of the *Criollo.* Alonso Ramírez triumphs over his fate because of the values of honesty and meekness instilled in him as a child by his Puerto Rican mother, whose last name he chooses over the patronymic of his Andalusian father. His toils as a captive of pirates is but a parallel intensification, a hyperbolic mirror of his travails as a *Criollo* in the colonial situation before and after his departure. In short, Sigüenza's inversions ultimately construct the *Criollo* as the everyday hero of the colonial enterprise.

Criollo reconversion of European imperial discourse into testimonial pseudo-chronicle always produces new versions of history and inversions of ideology. Sigüenza's rewriting of the heroic chronicles of the conquistadors, from Columbus to Cortés, becomes again a barefoot epic as the meek plebeian pauper Alonso Ramírez, the emblematic *Criollo,* stoically endures, with truer heroism, all the toils and tribulations of colonial life, without ever turning evil. Rodríguez Juliá's Child Avilés, in turn, becomes a degraded Columbus, trading the three mighty caravels for thirteen canoes (*chalupas*) and the Ocean Sea for the muddy marshes (*caños*) of inner San Juan Bay in his founding expedition of a parallel city, New Venice, "crossroads of Sodom and the New Jerusalem." The self-proclaimed *Christo ferens* (who would die of syphilis in Valladolid) has become the deformed armless torso of Child Avilés, the antimessiah, a close cousin of García Márquez's "Pigtail" in another chronicle subverted by the coils of history, if not the tropics of discourse.

However, if Alonso Ramírez is the emblematic *Criollo,* who is this deformed child, born without arms, with tiny legs the very image of atrophy, attached to an otherwise normal torso and head, except for that ageless, anguished gaze in two eyes that look astray from the bottom of Campeche's portrait? This little-devil-in-a-bottle, cousin of José Donoso's *imbunche* in *The Obscene Bird of Night,* is the very emblem of psychic repression.[14] Rodríguez

Juliá makes this reading of the portrait in his *Campeche, o los diablejos de la melancolía* (1986):

> According to the legend at the foot [of the painting], this child from Coamo was born on 2 July 1806. He was brought by his parents to San Juan, where he received the sacrament of confirmation on 6 April 1808. It was then that Bishop Arizmendi commanded this portrait from Campeche. What could have been the bishop's motivation? Dávila tells us: "In America and Spain these gestures of scientific curiosity were common on the part of bishops in the course of their pastoral visits, during the second half of the eighteenth century." . . . If that was the initial intention, Campeche soon surpasses it, turning the portrait into a metaphor of suffering. . . . And this suffering is related to the people: the painter's gaze—accustomed to capturing the personality and function of the Creole elite and the colonial administrative caste—rests here upon the deformed, upon a child of the people. . . . Avilés is bound within his own body, his hands tied by organic deformity. . . . An uncertainty becomes apparent regarding the child's age. It suddenly strikes us that we are really before the pitiful condition of a young man shrouded by the body of an infant. The head has nothing to do with the body. It has aged in that atrocious pain, in that rabid suffering . . . In that distance between the right eye and the left lie obedience and rebelliousness, salvation and damnation, sanctity and our sinful pride.
>
> [*Según la leyenda en la parte inferior, este niño de Coamo nació el 2 de julio de 1806. Fue traído por sus padres a San Juan, donde recibió el Sacramento de la Confirmación el 6 de abril de 1808. Entonces fue que el Obispo Arizmendi le ordenó a Campeche este retrato. ¿Cuál sería la motivación del Obispo? Dávila nos señala: "En América y España son corrientes estos gestos de curiosidad científica de parte de los obispos en el curso de las visitas pastorales, durante la segunda mitad del siglo dieciocho." . . . Si esa fue la intención inicial, Campeche la rebasa prontamente, convirtiendo el retrato en una metáfora del sufrimiento. . . . Y este sufrimiento está relacionado con el pueblo: la mirada del pintor—acostumbrada a captar la personalidad y función de la élite criolla y la casta administrativa colonial,—se posa aquí en lo disforme, en un hijo del pueblo. . . . El Avilés está atado dentro de su cuerpo, maniatado por la deformidad orgánica. . . . Se revela una incertidumbre en lo tocante a la edad del niño. De repente nos parece que en realidad estamos ante la condición lastimera de un joven amortajado en el cuerpo de un infante. La cabeza nada tiene que ver con el cuerpo. Ha envejecido en ese dolor atroz, en ese rabioso sufrimiento. . . . En esa distancia entre el ojo derecho y el izquierdo residen la obediencia y la rebeldía, la salvación y la maldición, la santidad y nuestra soberbia.*] (Rodríguez Juliá 1986, 117–123)[15]

According to the author, Child Avilés represents "the people" and, at the same time, Campeche's own opportunity for subversion. José Campeche was the son of a former slave indebted for the purchase of his freedom and an immigrant woman from the Canary Islands. The mulatto, trained by Luis

Paret y Alcázar, chamber painter of Charles III, became the artistic property of the Church and the political elite, never free to paint his own people. Rodríguez Juliá's inversion of history (*oscuro reverso*) will begin as the unleashing of Campeche's repressed desire and become the liberation of "the people's" historical libido.

The novel begins as a quotation from Campeche's fictional *Diary* accompanying Avilés in his founding expedition, because the text is first the liminal reading of the painter's emblematics that Rodríguez Juliá considers a "pictorial writing" in search of a liberating voice (Rodríguez Juliá 1986, 24). The year is 1797. Immediately, the novel goes back to the night of 9 October (the novelist's birthday), 1772, to relate the rescue of a shipwreck whose sole survivor is the newborn Avilés, floating like a Moses inside a basket. At shore, the crowd turns to carnival with improvised music, dancing, fritter sales and all, as will be the case whenever Caribbean people gather around an event. The anachronism (Avilés was born in 1806) is supported by his aged appearance in Campeche's rendition, but it also serves to suggest the emblematic agelessness of this "child of the people." Rodríguez Juliá chooses the late-eighteenth-century setting because it is the foundational moment of Puerto Rico's (official) historical identity. Up to that point, San Juan had been little more than a military prison settlement, with fewer than three hundred houses organized around El Morro garrison. Yet the island's population soared to 45,000 in 1765, and to 155,000 by 1800 (Blanco 1970, 43–44). After a sleep of three centuries, interrupted only by Drake's and Cumberland's sackings (1595, 1598), the island capital enters into the annals of modernity, with the Royal Order of Free Trade with the Antilles (1765); its first administrative code (Muesas's *Directorio General,* 1770); its first official painter (Campeche, 1772); its first official survey (Miyares, 1779); its first official history (Iñigo Abbad, 1782); consolidation of Church power (Trespalacios, 1784–89); and the scientific expedition of French naturalists Ledru and Baudin to record the flora, fauna, and customs (1798). Given the English takeover of Havana in 1764, these also became the years of timely expansion of fortifications around El Morro (1766–95)—which features prominently in the novel as Obatal's castle—for which hundreds of convicts and slaves were imported. Instead of the founding of New Venice, 1797 is the year of the English attack under Harvey and Abercromby, who landed with sixty-five vessels and eight thousand men at Cangrejos (the same spot of Avilés's shipwreck and symbolic birth) for an unsuccessful siege of the city. Campeche, who participated in the defense, had issued from his studio dozens of copies of the Flemish *Virgin of Bethlehem:* the citizens will credit the painting with saving the city. Later that year a royal decree confers the title of "Most Noble and Loyal City of San Juan Bautista de Puerto Rico." Just across the Mona Channel, however, the neighboring island of Saint Domingue had seen a slave uprising (1791) that led to the independence of black Haiti (1804). Like the fortification of El Morro in response to the English threat, the black threat spurred the fearful repression and official "whitening" of Puerto Rico, which lies at the foundation of the colonial State like an original sin buried deep in the national conscience, and which Child Avilés's epiphany—as the catalyst of collective catharsis—has come to redeem.

The novel sets out to penetrate officialdom and tell the "dark reverse" of the foundational deeds, the history of repressed desire. Rodríguez Juliá's unmasking links Quevedo's *desengaño* in *"El mundo por de dentro"* ["The World from Within"] with Lacanian psychoanalysis to uncover the history of libido, *la historia por de dentro.*[16] The "Child of the People" will not be the protagonist but rather the object of desire. He will be carried off the beach by the diabolical Bishop Larra and placed inside The Ear, a labyrinthine annex of the Episcopal Palace designed to amplify the child's wailing, where sadistic nuns drive spikes into his flesh—a mortification that recalls the toils of Alonso Ramírez. Avilés's demonic reputation grows together with the power of Larra, who has created his own demons in order to exorcize them publicly. He pays Juan Pires, a Sephardic actor, to play the role of exorcist, but, believing his own sermons, the Jew turns into a prophet who hails Avilés as the second Messiah and founds the heterodox sect of "the Avilesians" before burning at the stake. Determined to enforce a Catholic restoration, Bishop Trespalacios's fleet bombards Larra's city from the sea. The battle of the bishops (the colonial civil and military apparatus is conspicuously absent) represents the *bellum intestinum* inside Hispanic Catholicism's own repressive tradition. The whole novel becomes an epic battle against the demons, inspired by Fernando Ortiz's *Historia de una pelea cubana contra los demonios* (1959)—ostensibly its main intertextual source.[17] Inspired by the battle, Larra's elite black guards rebel, led by Obatal who brings his black hordes from the east to overthrow Larra, establishing a neo-African kingdom from the tower of El Morro fortress, while the white Avilesians retreat to Cataño on the west side of the bay. Obatal takes Child Avilés as a talisman of power, but unlike Larra, he gags the infant into silence. Soon there is dissent among the black leaders, and Mitume establishes an opposing faction on the eastern shores. Machiavellian Bishop Trespalacios, the indirect instigator, still waits at sea. The Renegade, a *criollo* sympathizer (Obatal's envoy, Mitume's comrade, and Trespalacios's spy), leaves a series of chronicles in which he becomes protagonist. Obatal sends him on a peacemaking mission with his beloved African Queen through the wondrous land of Yyaloide in search of Mitume's camp, which he finds decimated by a hurricane and tidal wave. The parties must regroup and wage war in the mangroves by boat, with the Avilesians participating in some skirmishes. The battle, modeled after Bernal Díaz's description of the conquest of Tenochtitlan, will be lacustrine: the divided blacks will be Aztecs and Tlaxcaltecs; the Avilesians, men of Narváez; The Renegade, La Malinche; and Trespalacios, Cortés. Trespalacios and his chronicler Gracián will watch this Ethiopian epic from within a "spying machine" fashioned in the form of a hollow giraffe (the novel's Trojan horse), which, of course, goes unnoticed by the Africans. The rebel Mitume emerges with a precarious victory, but now the fat bishop from Campeche's portrait, who ate his way through the novel in compensation for celibacy, will make his move into power while his chronicler Gracián dominates the narrative. Trespalacios reestablishes order with the banishment of the black devils, the exorcism of Avilés, the cleansing (*despojo*) of the city, and the founding of the State. On Christmas Day, 1773, he baptizes Avilés, and the Avilesians return to a Christian San Juan. The Bishop's "secret diary" will tell of his dreams of constructing the City of God, the New Jerusalem; of his never-ending battles against the demons, instigators of Arcadia and Utopia; and of his prophetic nightmares of a lacustrine city on stilts above the mangroves, reflecting its vain nature on the water, as the space for endless hope and unfulfilled desire.

Aníbal González has called the novel an "allegory of Puerto Rican culture," noting that its various utopias (Obatal's African kingdom, Trespalacios's City of God, Pepe Díaz's *Arcadia jíbara,* and Avilés's New Venice) correspond to the 1930s interpretations of national culture: Antonio S. Pedreira, *Insularismo* (1934), Tomás Blanco, *Prontuario histórico* (1935), and Luis Palés Matos, *Tuntún de pasa y grifería* (1937). The correspondence is not exact, and his notion of "culture" is rather narrow. Moreover, Rubén Ríos Ávila and Jean Franco rule out the role of allegory, the latter preferring "pastiche." But González is on to something, whether we call it "allegory of culture" or, more appropriately, with Campeche, emblematics of power. Rubén Ríos Ávila, in his excellent study, suggests that the author goes back to the eignteenth century in search of a national ethos and, like González, he places the novel's true referentiality in the twentieth century. These interpretations are all consistent with the view of Avilés as emblem of "the people." Benítez Rojo and Duchesne see the model for New Venice in the *palenque* or Maroon community, a space of freedom stolen away from the space of repression, a haven of hope for the runaway slave. They with Guillermo Baralt's *Esclavos rebeldes,* point out that despite some revolts, the *palenque,* so common in Brazil and the Caribbean, is conspicuously absent from Puerto Rican history, remaining a place of desire, a could-have-been, much like Avilés's mythical city. Yet this was already suggested by Obatal's African kingdom more than by New Venice, whose founding is only prophesied but never actually reached. On the other hand, it is worth noting that the novel presents a racially unmixed society where the mulatto (Campeche's breed) is another conspicuous absence, and that the foundational possibility of miscegenation —represented in The Renegade and the African Queen—is deliberately thwarted. Moreover, the above-mentioned utopias and interpretations of culture—except for New Venice—correspond to ethnic myths and aspirations that are exclusively Hispanic, *Criollo, or* black. Contrary to Tomás Blanco's portrayal of racial harmony in the colonial period, Rodríguez Juliá refers us to a modern Puerto Rican society whose organic appearance comes apart at the seams.[18] The very word "mulatto" (*hybrid,* from the Greek for *mule*), so common in Cuba, is rarely used in Puerto Rico, where even *negro* has been replaced by the euphemisms *moreno* and *trigueño,* while mulattoes are simply considered white—a sociolinguistic analogue of the "whitening" of the national consciousness. *Nueva Venecia* is, in turn, the space of racial entropy, that "never land" of harmonious hybridity and permissive heterogeneity: "My novels suffer the disquiet, the anxiety of a society in the making, that is yet to define itself. Our best cities are the utopian; the others are crossroads of the ceaseless parades and pilgrimages of colonialism, exile, and emigration" [*Mis novelas padecen el trasiego, la inquietud de una sociedad a medio hacer, que está por definirse. Nuestras mejores ciudades son las utópicas; las otras son encrucijadas de las incesantes comparsas y peregrinaciones del colonialismo, del exilio y la emigración*] (Rodríguez Juliá 1985, 10).

Ríos Ávila perceives Rodríguez Juliá himself as an author "still in the making" like his infant Avilés, pointing out that in his first novel, *La renuncia del héroe Baltasar* (1974), his various chroniclers have composite, coded names that refer to other authors as intertextual coordinates where his own authorial identity is disseminated. The same can be said about *La noche oscura,* which provides in its prologue the context for its own reading. Here, however, the authors alluded to are subverted, exposed, as it were, from their libido, their "demons" liberated: such being the mechanism by which Rodríguez Juliá encodes his "dark reversal" of history. The Alejandro Cadalso who signs the prologue would be Alejandro Tapia, Campeche's first biographer (1855), who gives us a harmonious reading of the mulatto painter, which the novel sets out to subvert. The archivist Pedreira would be the dark reversal of the Hispanophile author of *Insularismo,* while Julián Flores, presumed to be The Renegade, would be Juan Flores, author of *Insularismo e ideología burguesa en Antonio S. Pedreira* (1979). Pedreira defined the national character by its timid isolation (the opposite of Alonso Ramírez's globalizing enterprise), an *insularity* that bred *docility* (the opposite of Child Avilés). *Insularismo* and its complementary essay, René Marqués's *El puertorriqueño dócil,* ruminate old versions of docility from Iñigo Abbad's "tropical laziness" to Manuel Zeno Gandía's "pathological abulia" in la charca: *crónicas de un mundo enfermo* (1894). Rodríguez Juliá parodies these conceptions in Trespalacios's battle against Diablo Cojuelo, the demon of laziness (cf. Abbad 1970 181–88; Rodríguez Juliá 387). Tomás Castelló Pérez Moris, who impeaches the authenticity of the New Venice chronicles, would be a composite of *criollo* historians Tomás Blanco, aforementioned, and José Pérez Moris (1840–1881), chronicler of the Lares nationalist insurrection (1868). The other archivist, who "risks his salvation" to save the chronicles for posterity and whom skeptics regard as the true inventor of New Venice, Don Ramón García *Quevedo,* is none other than the Spanish baroque master of *desengaño,* author of *The Pigsties of Pluto.* Trespalacios's chronicler Gracián is the verbose libido of the ultra-succinct Baltasar Gracián (whose work *El criticón,* incidentally, was the stylistic model for Sigüenza's *Infortunios*), but he could just as easily be the dark reverse of enlightened historian Fray Iñigo Abbad who, in 1772, was himself the secretary and confessor of the bishop of San Juan.

And what about that chronicler-protagonist nicknamed "The Renegade?" In his social chronicle about the funeral of Luis Muñoz Marín, *Las tribulaciones de Jonás* (1981), Rodríguez Juliá refers to the ex-governor as *El Renegado.* It is not difficult to see why. Muñoz was a young nationalist leader who, as governor, found political accommodation with the United States. A "would be" writer himself, Muñoz became "the architect" of the modern commonwealth by translating "dependent-subaltern-colony" as "Free Associated State." Antonio Benítez Rojo has found another close cousin of Child Avilés in Julio Cortázar's *axolotl:* that repressed *other,* tired of being a deformed child of fiction, waits patiently from within his portrait-cage for his faithful visitor, his counterpart, the normal child of history he always wanted to be, who one day will set him free and take his rightful place on *that* side of the looking glass. In *The Cage of Melancholy,* Roger Bartra notes that the amphibian *axolotl,* a lacustrine creature indigenous only to Lake Xochimilco in old Tenochtitlan and perfectly incapable of reproducing in any other habitat, is biologically the larval stage of the salamander, which reaches adulthood without developing, ages, grows, and yet refuses to ever let go of its peculiar and perpetual embryonic state. He holds it as a symbol of the Mexican *polis.* That, too, is Child Avilés, a yearning young man buried inside the body of a tadpole. The fiction of the *muñocista* commonwealth, that perpetual embryonic state of the nation, condemns him to endless atrophy and melancholy. The child of the people, that *puer aeternus,* has now become the larval stage of the body politic.

III. The City as Palimpsest

The novel's simulacrum of return (in order to construct a present, twentieth-century referentiality) is an aspect of testimonial pseudo-chronicle that naturally differs from Sigüenza's prototype. Rodríguez Juliá's present referentiality is signaled by ellipse and anachronism. To begin with, New Venice, though prophesied, never appears in the novel, and yet, *La noche oscura del Niño Avilés,* as it turns out, is only a subtitle, "Part I" of the novel's true identity as *Crónica de Nueva Venecia*—the city itself being the whole point of the story. For years critics awaited the rest of the trilogy, which Rodríguez Juliá would never deliver. Skeptics rumored that the author, disenchanted with the result, had abandoned the enterprise. Believers came to realize that New Venice was indeed unfathomable, that fixing it in time and space would forever destroy its utopian character. Eventually, Rodríguez Juliá confessed that in youthful enthusiasm he had indeed written an unpublishable 1,500–page novel in which Avilés was raised and educated by Trespalacios: *La noche oscura* was the final compromise (see his Gracianesque essay "At the Middle of the Road"). What we have is that signature of the baroque that Severo Sarduy referred to as an apotheosis of the ellipse: New Venice will never arrive because it already exists.

Present referentiality enables a final, third-level penetration into another buried text: Rodríguez Juliá's San Juan, the city as palimpsest; an archaeological dig into the five centuries of history that overlay its landscape, of successive generations that expired, leaving faint characters upon the topography; an incursion into the chronotopian reconstruction of its ever-incomplete urban renewal. The salient difference with Sigüenza's *Odyssey* is that his boy Alonso Ramírez leaves Puerto Rico to sail the world in the space of a few years, while in his *Iliad,* Rodríguez Juliá becomes a pilgrim at home, traveling through layers of time around a single spot, but with no less a picaresque élan. Sigüenza is obsessed with hydrography, not geography; so he will tell us little about the places he visits. When he arrives at the eastern city of Batavia in Java, a boiling emporium of world trade like today's Hong Kong, he wraps it up in a phrase, with typical Gracianesque succinctness: "But in saying that there the Universe is condensed I say it all" [*Pero con decir estar allí compendiado el Universo lo digo todo*] (Sigüenza 1983, 20). When we return, we feel we have seen nothing of the world except the inside of Sigüenza's ship, a vessel of words, the discourse of pseudo-chronicle and travelogue, which is the whole point of the story. Rodríguez Juliá, however, is obsessed with historical topography, so he will give us in his *laudes civitatum* an endless physical and moral description of the city, exploding with the eye of a miniaturist the microcosm of Nueva Venecia, that liminal San Juan, the *multus in parvo,* the Universe summarized. *His* "chronicler Gracián" has a different baroque style, imbued with the piercing satirical overwroughtness of Quevedo, Lezama, and Cabrera Infante.

Real or imaginary, Rodríguez Juliá's Nueva Venecia is the libidinal archaeology of modern metropolitan San Juan, an incisive commentary on the city's contradictory fusion of discipline and desire, of Catholic repression and sexual liberation. The times superimposed, in the writing of old Nueva Venecia and the modern San Juan reading, are a function of the mixed deployment of the archaic language of chronicle and the modern language of the Puerto Rican streets—the latter responding to the contemporary literary project of "writing in Puerto Rican" propelled by Luis Rafael Sánchez's *Macho Camacho's Beat.* The numerous insertions of modern slang words (*incordio, galán, molleto, compio*), popular songs lyrics (*pare, cochero, cachito pa huelê*), and the language of the drug culture (*perico, date un pase, les voló los sesos, los arrebataba*) serve as anachronistic markers of present referentiality. Moreover, the discourse of the old chronicles is in fact formally married to the neopicaresque genre of *crónicas de sociedad* amply cultivated by Rodríguez Juliá, as a neorealist, quasi-journalistic, but carnivalesque portrayal of modern urban Puerto Rican pop culture. Such mixture of old and new histories, cultured and popular forms, reflects the generic plasticity between testimonial pseudo-chronicle in *La noche oscura,* and the smaller "social chronicles" that surround it in the author's production.[19] The common thread running through Sigüenza's Gracianesque travelogue, picaresque and Quevedesque satire, and Rodríguez Juliá's modern chronicles of pop culture is the baroque ideal of *desengaño*—the penetration of appearances and public facades, the unmasking of official society. Sigüenza's succinct portrayal of Puerto Rico in 1690 is limited to that gist of *desengaño:* the Rich Port's very name is a fraud; the rivers had run out of the few gold pebbles they once had, together with the Indians who worked them; hurricanes had decimated the cocoa trees that constituted the island's main crop; and the "riches" of its name became the "poverty" of its inhabitants (Sigüenza 1983, 10).

A central marker in the novel's uchronian geography is the transposition of modern Piñones to the eighteenth century. Piñones is a lower-class, black, beachfront village adjacent to Boca de Cangrejos, where Avilés was rescued from the shipwreck. Modernly, Piñones is famous as a sex haven, with its secluded shacks and *cabarets* (dark dancing bars with juke box and pool table), where city folk can go for an escapade without being seen by the prudish society of parochial gossipmongers, for whom frequenting the place is already proof of guilt. During Avilés's rescue, a search party finds a couple in the bushes making love, "[N]ot at all a rare occurrence in Piñones, a quite notorious place indeed, as a hideaway for illicit love affairs" [*suceso nada raro en Piñones, lugar a la verdad que muy notorio por ser escondite de ilícitos amores*] (Rodríguez Juliá 1984, 8). Piñones is the hidden San Juan, Asmodeo's kingdom, a lascivious space cast outside the city limits, but it is also the bridge between San Juan and Loiza Aldea, the most culturally pure neo-African community left in Puerto Rico. Significantly, Obatal's African kingdom in El Morro was fed by a "supply line" from Piñones that Trespalacios bombarded, a libidinal chord the bishop had to sever in order to found the State (see note 17).

However, to fully understand Child Avilés's New Venice, one must arrive at the San Juan of Rodríguez Juliá's youth (which was also my own). The novel's mythical city was located in a stretch of marshlands southeast of Old

San Juan, passing the row of brothels that once flanked the bay's port and fed on the cruise ships' mariners and tourists, as well as on the city's youth—for generations of whom, the pier-side brothels were a rite of passage into adulthood. Converging behind Trastalleres and Miraflores, the marshlands (now partly filled by a new expressway) extended from the inner bay to the modern Plaza de Las Américas shopping mall, along the famous Caño Martín Peña. Significantly, what was most recently located in that infectious network of mangrove canals was San Juan's most notorious slum, El Fanguito (The Little Mud Hole), a squatter community of zinc-roofed wooden shacks on stilts over the fetid water, for those passengers of René Marqués's *The Oxcart* who could not afford dry land. Out of sight for decades, the vast slum became visible in all its squalor from the new, adjacent Las Américas Expressway. Painted red or blue during elections, with the banners of either political party raised high on bamboo poles, reading "Bread, Land, Liberty," the hundreds of shacks became a visual Gallup Poll and often accurate predictor of electoral results. However, the picturesque slum, romantically depicted as a "watercolor of poverty" [*acuarela de pobreza*] in hundreds of stories, paintings, poems, and popular songs, became a central embarrassment for the tourism-driven city, and a negation of the progressivist enterprise proclaimed by the *muñocista* U.S. Commonwealth.

Rodríguez Juliá's prologue claims that the mangrove-ridden ruins of New Venice were further decimated by the Yankee bombings of the 1898 occupation, but this is only a symbolic theory, for why bombard an empty marshland? (El Fanguito was not yet there). The fact is that Rodríguez Juliá, like the rest of us, witnessed the "cleansing" of the city slums and brothels by the newly empowered annexationist party (under the aegis of cement magnate turned governor Luis A. Ferré) during the 1970s and 1980s—a process that mirrors the "exorcism" of the accursed mythical city at the end of the novel. Many Fanguito residents, who refused to leave, were forcibly relocated to housing projects or ferried across the bay to Cataño (like the Avilesians), where they could enjoy the breeze of progress by breathing sulfur dioxide from the local CORCO oil refinery. El Fanguito was leveled by bulldozers, and the squalor driven underground. Ironically, as part of the city's embellishment in preparation for the grand 1992 quincentennial celebration of Columbus, the Caño Martín Peña—where Child Avilés presumably sailed his thirteen canoes during his founding expedition—was modernized with a shuttle boat service to Old San Juan ferrying thousands of spectators to the fairgrounds of El Morro fortress, to watch once again the mighty tall ships parade across the bay.

Whether the infamous lacustrine city of Nueva Venecia was ever real or only chimerical is of course no longer the question. The New Jerusalem hides Sodom underground. Rodríguez Juliá shows that in the dark nights of Child Avilés, Nueva Venecia must exist, still today, under the cobblestones, the asphalt, the concrete, for what it really is: the liminal, libidinal San Juan. Its new symptom appearing in the early eighties as the city's AIDS epidemic bore sad testimony to this fact. *La noche oscura del Niño Avilés* was a second reminder of Nueva Venecia's existence, for now the novel itself *is* the lettered city.

NOTES

1. The work's full title is: *Infortunios que Alonso Ramírez, natural de la ciudad de San Juan de Puerto Rico padeció, así en poder de ingleses piratas que lo apresaron en las islas Filipinas como navegando por sí sólo, y sin derrota, hasta varar en la costa de Yucatán, consiguiendo por este medio dar vuelta al mundo* (*Misfortunes that Alonso Ramirez, born in the City of San Juan of Puerto Rico Suffered, as Much at the Mercy of English Pirates Who Captured Him at the Philippine Isles as Sailing by Himself, and without Course, 'til Running Aground at the Coast of Yucatan, Succeeding in this Fashion to go around the World*). All translations and emphases are mine.

2. Most critics agree upon Alonso Ramírez's existence, although there is no other record of him outside of Sigüenza's "novelized biography." It is deemed unlikely that he should be fictional given the book's dedication to the viceroy of New Spain, who is said to have referred the case originally to Sigüenza and perhaps even commissioned the account. Yet belief is not unanimous: the pretense of being a commissioned scribe of another's "true account" was a literary device in vogue (Pérez Blanco 1982). Some events reported in the Philippines are verifiable and perhaps too recent to have reached Mexico by means other than a recent visitor (Cummins 1984). But at best, this only places Alonso as far as the Philippines. Pirates Donkin and Bell, said to have captured Alonso, have left no trace in the voluminous historical records of the time, and the description of places beyond the Philippines (and until the return to Yucatan), when at all provided, are too schematic to have any credible weight. J. Arrom, who emphasizes the book's irony and literariness, admits that Alonso was probably a real person, but then again, he reminds us, so were Hamlet and El Caballero de Olmedo. Beyond the Philippines, the story is full of inconsistencies and lacunae: "If it had been true that Alonso received from the pirates the bare minimum not to die of hunger, how was he able to buy his black slave 'negrillo Pedro'? How did they allow such luxury to an impecunious prisoner? What arrangement did he make with the pirates so that these, with their ships replete with riches, instead of continuing to England to enjoy them, turned their bows to Brazil, in order to leave him and his on American waters? What fairy intervened to have his comrades disappear from the narrative, one by one, until he alone was left to tell the story? How much did he add and how much did he keep to make his adventures appear more pathetic?" (Arrom 1987, 44–45).

3. "Your Excellency . . . Sent me (or by the affection with which you look at it or perhaps because being ill the news of my many ills would take your mind from it), to go visit Don Carlos de Sigüenza y Góngora, cosmographer and professor of mathematics of our lord the King at the Mexican Academy, and Chaplain major of the Love of God Royal Hospital in Mexico City (titles like these which sound like much but are not worth much . . .) [*Su Excelencia . . . Mandóme (o por el afecto con que lo mira o quizá porque estando enfermo divirtiere sus males con la noticia que yo le daría de los muchos míos), fuese a visitar a don Carlos de Sigüenza y Góngora, cosmógrafo y catedrático de matemáticas del Rey nuestro señor en la Academia mexicana, y capellán mayor del hospital Real del Amor de*

Dios de la ciudad de México (títulos son éstos que suenan mucho y valen muy poco . . .)] (Sigüenza 1983, 75). For a discussion of *Infortunios* as a rewriting of Bernal Díaz's chronicle of the conquest of Mexico, see Kathleen Ross 1995, 1993.

4. The ship's booty is the story's greatest inconsistency. In chapter 4, Alonso claims that the pirates set them free in an empty frigate (*Desembarazada la fragata que me daban, de cuanto había en ella, y cambiado a las suyas*). Two chapters later, upon their shipwreck in Yucatan, he gives us an inventory of his later claim: nine canons, over 2,000 rounds, tons of lead, tin, iron, and copper bars; many Chinese porcelain jars, seven elephant tusks, etc.

5. The frequent invocations to the Virgin of Guadalupe almost certainly belong to Sigüenza, who was one of the initiators of *guadalupanismo* in Mexico. So is the miraculous downpour of rain upon the men dying of thirst in Yucatan, which Cummins calls "a hagiographical cliché" (Cummins 1984, 301).

6. It is entirely possible that Sigüenza fed back to Sandoval exactly what he wanted to read, particularly if the work was in fact commissioned. The viceroy was known for his compassion, described as "the relief of the poor" [*el alivio de los pobres*], and accustomed to "hearing generally everyone in his supreme kindness and receptivity without failing to console the most miserable and ill" [*oir generalmente a todos en suma benignidad y agasajo, sin dejar de consolar el más miserable e infirmo*] (L. Hanke, *Guía de fuentes virreinales,* 1:174–76, quoted in Cummins 1984, 302 no. 17).

7. For a detailed interpretation of the *Infortunios* as a legal text, see Invernizzi 1986.

8. I have not been able to establish the existence of Silvestre Andino Campeche, who could nevertheless be the son of José Campeche's real-life brother-in-law and music teacher, Domingo de Andino.

9. "José Pedreira Murillo, *Historia de un descubrimiento,* Editorial Antillana, San Juan, 1915, Pág. 9" and "Tomás Castelló Pérez Moris, *Historia de un embeleco,* Editorial La Milagrosa, San Juan, 1920, Pág. 1" (Rodríguez Juliá 1984, xi–xii).

10. Child Avilés founds New Venice in 1797, and in 1799 it is destroyed by English pirates paid by Governor Castro and commanded by one Samuel Wright. In 1820, all the documents and chronicles pertaining to the libertine city are burned in a bonfire. Only the paintings of Silvestre Andino are spared and buried in an archive, including a triptych, not unlike Bosch's, that depicted in "visionary landscapes" the beehive-shaped towers of New Venice. Archivist Pedreira discovers some New Venice chronicles in 1913, including one by a certain González Campos, who quotes the historical Admiral Nelson's apocryphal book *Great Naval Occasions of the Middle Seas,* where Nelson quotes his supposed friend Samuel Wright, who narrates his attack on the infernal city and describes its towers as "portentous beehives." Pedreira remembers Andino's triptych at the San Juan Municipal Archive and publishes his findings in 1915. Castelló Pérez Moris attacks their authenticity in 1920, and calls the whole thing "a hoax engrossed in the feverish minds of Freemasons and Bolsheviks" (Rodríguez Juliá 1984, xi). In an article of 1932, Gustavo Castro defends the collection, narrating how Pedreira found the documents in a ruined beehive-tower hidden in the mangroves, where he was led by a limping neighbor known only as "Pedro el Cojo" (see "Diablo Cojuelo" in notes 14 & 17), and then found the chronicle that recounts Avilés's death in the remains of the (real) towers of Isle of Goats at the mouth of San Juan Bay, bombarded during the Yankee invasion of 1898. In a letter of 1820 found with the documents, García Quevedo, secretary of the Episcopal Archive, explains how he saved and hid the extant chronicles: "Even at the risk of my eternal salvation, it is sweet to maintain that idea . . . where Avilés founded that magnificent vision that was the lacustrine city" (Rodríguez Juliá 1984, xv). That

statement led to conjectures that the city had only existed as a vision in the apocryphal documents written by Avilés himself, by García Quevedo, or even by Pedreira. "Others assigned it a greater historical reality, affirming that it was a swindler friend of the libertine Luis Paret Alcázar [chamber painter of Charles III sentenced to banishment in Puerto Rico, 1775–78, and teacher of José Campeche]" (Rodríguez Juliá 1984, xvi). In 1946, Alejandro Cadalso writes the prologue, where he draws the history of the case; and in 1984 the first part of the collected Chronicles of New Venice is published as *La noche oscura del niño Avilés.*

11. See Casas 1977, Castagnino 1971, Chang 1982, Forne t1995, González 1986, Johnson 1981, Ross 1995, 1993, and Sacido 1989.

12. See Arrom 1987, López 1996, and Moraña 1990.

13. Censor Ayerra, Puerto Rican poet and chaplain of the convent of Jesús María in Mexico, with which Sigüenza had close ties since his writing of *Parayso Occidental,* was a longtime friend who knew what the author was up to and whose ultimate contribution to the work may never be known.

14. Luis Vélez de Guevara's *El diablo cojuelo* (1641) is a main source for Julia's Child Avilés. This deformed "little limping devil" is a messenger demon of Spanish folklore (*el diablo cojuelo es buen mensajero*), which Vélez presents *trapped inside a bottle,* like the genie of *Arabian Nights.* A student, Don Cleofás, will open the bottle and let him out. As repayment, the limping devil takes him on a tour of *desengaño,* unmasking the pretenses of Spanish society. Child Avilés is that messenger demon bottled-up in Campeche's unconscious, which Rodríguez Juliá's writing lets out. Archivist Pedreira, like Don Cleofás, freed the devil when he uncovered the manuscripts. Finally, the act of reading, of opening the book like a Pandora's box, unleashes the textual pandemonium of the novel and liberates the bottled up demons of the historical libido. See also note 17.

15. The portrait's legend reads: "Juan Pantaleón legitimate son of Luis de Avilés and Martina de Luna Alvarado. Farmers residing in the village of Coamo in the Island of S. J. Bautista de P. R. Born July 2nd, 1806, and brought to this Capital by his parents, he was conferred the Sacrament of Confirmation on April 6, 1808, by the most Illustrious Bishop Diocno D. D. Juan Alexo de Arismendi by whose order this copy was made, taken after the natural." The author's reference is to Dávila 1971, 43.

16. Rodríguez Juliá's enterprise expands the counterpoint of two predecessors. In the prologue to his fictionalized history of the Haitian uprising, *El reino de este mundo* (1949), Alejo Carpentier warns that "the story about to be read has been established upon an extremely rigorous documentation which not only respects the historical truth of the events, the names of (even secondary) characters, places, and even streets, but hides, under its apparent timelessness, a detailed correspondence of dates and chronologies." Meanwhile, in the prologue to his rewriting of Fray Servando, *El mundo alucinante* (1969), Reinaldo Arenas proposes to tell the story "as it was, as it might have been, and as I would have liked it had been." "These novels are not historical. They are utopian foundations that disguise their textuality as historicism" (Rodríguez Juliá 1985, 10).

17. Like Rodríguez Juliá, Fernando Ortiz sets out to tell an unknown and forgotten story, not registered by official historiography, about a seventeenth-century battle against the demons waged during the founding of the Cuban town of San Juan de los Remedios (Ortiz 1975, 29). According to archival documents of ecclesiastical provinces, over 800,000 demons were exorcized from a population of less than 700, mostly from negroes, although even some priests had been possessed. A notarial certificate of 1682 records a sworn statement taken from Lucifer himself (who had invaded, with thirty-five legions of demons, the body of an old black woman); it

stated that the demons had come because of the sins of those possessed and of their *Parents,* and that the town would literally sink (Ortiz 1975, 597–98). The anthropologist Ortiz traces the roots of European demonology, its arrival in America, and its use against Afro-Cuban culture. All the demons in Rodríguez Juliá's novel are taken directly from Ortiz, who in turn quotes Vélez de Guevara's *El diablo cojuelo* to recount the names and attributes of demons in medieval Spanish folklore (Ortiz 1975, 104). The most important of these are: *Asmodeo,* prince of lechery; and *Renfás* or *"Diablo Cojuelo,"* the limping devil himself, known as the master of laziness (cf. Rodríguez Juliá's chapters 44–47). One unleashes the other. Vélez, for example, presents the *Cojuelo* as the inspirer of all the lascivious dances brought from Africa to the New World and finally to Spain. Ortiz finds its counterpart in the Yoruba one-legged deity *Obatalá.*

18. Tomás Blanco's *Prontuario histórico* holds that by 1770, public schools were officially promoted and encouraged to admit all remitted children whether white, mulatto, or free black—"this being worthy of emphasis, since it denotes the early harmony (*temprana convivencia*) among the races" (Blanco 1970, 60). Given that the size of the mountainous island did not provide for large plantations, the number of slaves, according to Blanco, never surpassed 13 percent of the total population, compared to Haiti's 90 percent , Jamaica's 81 percent, Brazil's 51 percent, and Cuba's 36 percent (Blanco 1970, 77–78). This would of course explain the absence of *palenques* in Puerto Rican history. The "dark reverse" of Tomás Blanco would show, however, that the sharp population increase after the mid-eighteenth century obeyed a policy of "whitening" that by 1834, had *reduced* the proportion of blacks to 46 percent, almost one third of whom remained slaves.

19. *Las tribulaciones de Jonás* (1981), *El entierro de Cortijo* (1983), *Una noche con Iris Chacón* (1986), *El cruce de la Bahía de Guánica* (1989).

Bibliography

Abbad y Lasierra, Fray Agustín Iñigo. [1788] 1970. *Historia geográfica, civil y natural de la isla de San Juan Bautista de Puerto Rico.* San Juan: Editorial de la Universidad de Puerto Rico.

Arrom, José Juan. 1987. "Carlos de Sigüenza y Góngora. Relectura criolla de *Infortunios de Alonso Ramírez.*" *Thesaurus* 42: 23–46.

Baralt, Guillermo A. 1985. *Esclavos rebeldes. Conspiraciones y sublevaciones de esclavos en Puerto Rico (1795–1873).* Río Piedras: Ediciones Huracán.

Bartra, Roger. 1992. *The Cage of Melancholy: Identity and Metamorphosis in the Mexican Character.* New Brunswick: Rutgers University Press.

Benítez Rojo, Antonio. 1989. "*Niño Avilés,* o la libido de la historia." In *La isla que se repite: El Caribe y la perspectiva posmoderna,* 277–304. Hanover: Ediciones del Norte.

Blanco, Tomás. [1935] 1970. *Prontuario histórico de Puerto Rico.* San Juan: Instituto de Cultura Puertorriqueña.

Casas de Faunce, María. 1977. *La novela picaresca latinoamericana.* Madrid: Cupsa.

Castagnino, Raúl H. 1971. "Carlos de Sigüenza y Góngora o la picaresca a la inversa." *Razón y Fábula* 25: 27–34.

Chang Rodríguez, Raquel. 1982. "La transgresión de la picaresca en los *Infortunios de Alonso Ramírez.*" In *Violencia y subversión en la prosa colonial hispanoamericana,* 85–108. Madrid: José Porrúa Turanzas.

Cummins, J. S. 1984. "*Infortunios de Alonso Ramírez:* 'A Just History of Fact'?" *Bulletin of Hispanic Studies* 61: 295–303.

Dávila, Arturo V. 1971. *José Campeche, 1751–1809*. San Juan: Instituto de Cultura Puertorriqueña.

Díaz del Castillo, Bernal. 1968. *Historia verdadera de la conquista de la Nueva España*. Madrid: Espasa-Calpe.

Duchesne, Juan Ramón. 1985. "Una lectura en *La noche oscura del Niño Avilés.*" *Cuadernos Americanos* 259, no. 2: 219–24.

Flores, Juan. 1979. *Insularismo e ideología burguesa en Antonio S. Pedreira*. Havana: Casa de las Américas.

Fornet, Jorge. 1995. "Ironía y cuestionamiento ideológico en *Infortunios de Alonso Ramírez.*" *Cuadernos Americanos* 9, no. 1: 200–11.

Franco, Jean. 1989. "The Nation as Imagined Community." In *The New Historicism*, edited by H. Aram Veeser, 204–12. New York: Routledge.

González, Aníbal. 1983. "*Los Infortunios de Alonso Ramírez:* Picaresca e historia." *Hispanic Review* 51: 189–204.

———. 1986. "Una alegoría de la cultura puertorriqueña: *La noche oscura del Niño Avilés,* de Edgardo Rodríguez Juliá." *Revista Iberoamericana* 52, no. 135–36: 583–90.

González Echevarría, Roberto. 1990. *Myth and Archive: A Theory of Latin American Narrative*. Cambridge: Cambridge University Press.

González Stephan, Beatriz. 1987. "Narrativa de la estabilización colonial." *Ideologies and Literatures* 1, no. 1: 7–52.

Gracián, Baltasar. [1651]. 1996. *El criticón* Madrid: Cátedra.

Invernizzi Santa Cruz, Lucia. 1986. "Naufragios e infortunios: Discurso que transforma fracasos en triunfos." *Dispositio* 40: 99–111.

Johnson, Julie Greer. 1981. "Picaresque Elements in Carlos de Sigüenza y Góngora's *Los Infortunios de Alonso Ramírez.*" *Hispania* 64: 60–7.

López, Kimberle S. 1996. "Identity and Alterity in the Emergence of a Creole Discourse: Sigüenza y Góngora's *Infortunios de Alonso Ramírez.*" *Colonial Latin American Review* 5, no. 2: 253–76.

Marqués, René. 1977. *El puertorriqueño dócil y otros ensayos*. San Juan: Editorial Antillana.

Moraña, Mabel. 1990. "Máscara autobiográfica y conciencia criolla en *Infortunios de Alonso Romírez.*" *Dispositio* 15: 10–17.

Ortiz, Fernando. [1959] 1975. *Historia de una pelea cubana contra los demonios*. Havana: Instituto Cubano del Libro.

Palés Matos, Luis. 1937. *Tuntún de passa y griteía*. San Juan: Biblioteca de Autores Puertoriqueños.

Pedreira, Antonio S. [1934] 1970. *Insularismo. Obras* In *de Antonio S. Pedreira*. San Juan: Instituto de Cultura Puertorriqueña.

Pérez Blanco, Lucrecio. 1982. "Novela ilustrada y desmitificación de América." *Cuadernos Americanos* 244, no. 5: 176–95.

Pratt, Mary Louise. 1992. *Imperial Eyes: Travel Writing and Transculturation*. London: Routledge.

Ríos Ávila, Rubén. 1993. "La invención de un autor: Escritura y poder en Edgardo Rodríguez Juliá." *Revista Iberoamericana* 59, nos. 162–63: 203–19.

Rodríguez Juliá, Edgardo. 1984. *La noche oscura del Niño Avilés*. San Juan: Editorial de la Universidad de Puerto Rico.

———. 1985. "Tradición y utopía en el barroco caribeño." *Caribán: Revista de Literatura* 2: 8–10.

———. 1986. *Campeche o los diablejos de la melancolía.* San Juan: Instituto de Cultura Puertorriqueña.

———. 1987. "At the Middle of the Road." In *Images and Identities: The Puerto Rican in Two World Contexts,* edited by Asela Rodríguez de Laguna. New Brunswick: Transaction Books.

Ross, Kathleen. 1993. *The Baroque Narrative of Carlos de Sigüenza y Góngora: A New World Paradise.* New York: Cambridge University Press.

———. "Cuestiones de género en *Infortunios de Alonso Ramírez.*" *Revista Iberoamericana* 61.172–3:591–603.

———. Sacido Romero, Alberto. 1989. "La ambigüedad genérica de los *Infortunios de Alonso Ramírez* como producto de la dialéctica entre discurso oral y discurso escrito." *Bulletin Hispanique* 94: 1–21.

Sigüenza y Góngora, Carlos de. 1983. *Infortunios de Alonso Ramírez.* In *Obras históricas.* Mexico: Porrúa.

Vélez de Guevara, Luis. [1641] 1968. *El diablo cojuelo.* Madrid: Ediciones Alcalá.

Zeno Gandía, Manuel. [1894] 1995. *La Charca: Crónicas de un mundo enfermo.* Río Piedras, Puerto Rico: Editorial Edil.

Ana Lydia Vega's *Falsas crónicas del Sur*: Reconstruction and Revision of Puerto Rico's Past

MARY ANN GOSSER-ESQUILÍN

ENRIQUE PUPO-WALKER ARGUES THAT FOR MANY READERS, THE WORD *CRÓnica* "refers us . . . to an archaic legacy characterized by dogmatic stolidness, that is to say, to texts in which the discourse seems to lack an individual writer and which are organized in the manner of monovalent inventories, coded in primary chronologies" (Pupo-Walker 1985, 92). He hastens to add that texts grouped under the banner of chronicles are multiple and varied, yet modern in how they question the nature of historical discourse. In *La Florida* (1605) and the *Comentarios reales* (1609) of the Inca Garcilaso de la Vega (1536–1616), son of an Inca princess and a Spaniard, Pupo-Walker explores how his *cronista*'s writings seek to establish a correlation between the process of describing the history of the Indies, while creating a suitable discourse to capture the process. Fascination with these colonial texts, which transcend the purely historical and exploit the literary, becomes evident in other contemporary Latin American critics as well. Roberto González Echevarría, for example, takes a close look at the *Historia verdadera de la conquista de la Nueva España* (1568) by Bernal Díaz del Castillo (1496–1584). Bernal describes his *historia* as a *relación,* a word or concept that González Echevarría convincingly maintains ought to be understood as a legal report. He insists that

> if history concerned itself with the culminating moments, with the political and military movements that stand out the most, then the *relación* of events, given its legal character, narrates incidents of daily life; it does not presume to reflect a transcendental truth that it extracts from the events narrated, but rather is part of those events, of the very reality it recounts, and thusly derives its anthropological and historical value. . . . That which is isolated legal formula in every point of the historical poetics becomes a detailed story of a life in its specific, individual, and social occurrence, as well as of the problems this presents in being narrated. . . . History leads to poetics; *relación* leads to literature. (González Echevarría 1983, 23)

These critics' conclusions vis-à-vis colonial texts could be summarized as follows: be they *crónicas* or *relaciones,* the works represent the rhetorical and legal product of Europe's humanism, nonetheless facing the new and wondrous reality of the Americas, and eventually, given the crossroads, become the literary base of much of contemporary Latin America's fictional production, as examples from Ana Lydia Vega's stories will illustrate.

European humanism owes much to the Italian Renaissance, in particular to Pico Della Mirandola and Marsilio Ficino and their belief in human freedom. According to Pupo-Walker, the *cronistas* from Spain were decidedly inspired by Petrarch, Leonardo Bruni, Lorenzo Valla, and Guicciardini (1982b, 80). Humanist subjects such as rhetoric, history, poetry, and philosophy, among others, become obligatory areas of study. Any humanistic endeavor was expected to better the world. The human being becomes the focus and center of the universe, displacing the theocentrism of the Middle Ages. In Spain, as Kathleen Ross asserts, the situation is unique because religious rigidity turns Spain into a closed country in terms of tolerance, and the Inquisition will reign supreme (Ross 1996, 106–9). A logical question then arises: how can one describe and pretend to better a world one does not know? For some chroniclers, the enterprise simply called for the imposition of European models of rhetoric and historiography. In the case of Garcilaso de la Vega, an educated writer and a *mestizo,* writing history, or just *comentarios* (as he calls them), is marked not only by Neoplatonic ideals but also by a consciousness of (and a commitment to incorporate in his work) the Incas' conception of the cosmos and the role their society plays within universal history. As an educated chronicler of the New World born there, he was caught between the European Middle Ages, the Renaissance, the effects of the Counter-Reformation, and the glorious past of the Incas: how could he represent or account for all these currents? Because much of the official conquest was sanctioned by the Spanish crown, deeply involved in counter-Reformation activities, any humanistic inclination had to be veiled. Meanwhile, the New World's reality needed to be reported and this necessitated writers. At the onset, these were official court historians. Eventually, the unofficial ones added their voices. These new discourses displayed more latitude in the presentation of the facts (and oftentimes fables) because their rhetorical structure was humanistic, and to avoid censure, there were plenty of opportunities to allude to the religious aspect of the colonization and justify it in terms of Christianization. The heroes of the Conquest were featured as epic heroes, but always in the name of the crown or the Catholic Church—usually not for their own sake, at least rhetorically; indeed, Bernal is criticized because : as a mere soldier of Cortés he dared to extol the role he played in so many battles. As did other chroniclers, Fray Bartolomé de Las Casas demythifies many of the so-called heroes in his *Brevísima relación de la destrucción de las Indias* (1552), because they act selfishly and not really in the name of the crown. This polarity in the presentation of motives finds its way into the unofficial accounts.

Christopher Columbus's *First Letter from the New World* (14 March 1493) certainly demonstrates this and opens the way for the history of the New World to be invented as the conquest advances. He presents himself in terms of an epic hero: he forbids the bartering of trinkets for gold, seeking to demonstrate his loftier moral standards; he emphasizes the fact that the "Indians" traveling with him entertain the idea that he has descended from heaven, so he acquires a divine dimension; and, not the least among his heroic feats, he has taken possession of all those islands in the name of the invincible king, hence playing a crucial part in the founding of a new kingdom—a trait common to all epic heroes as they endure endless struggles to partake in the forming of a nation. The text, wrought with a carefully crafted rhetorical apparatus, fascinates us to this day because Columbus not only writes about the exploits of a hero of epic proportions, but moreover they are his own, and he presents them in such a way that no other character shares center stage in this public letter. This trait also characterizes the texts of Garcilaso and Bernal, partial witnesses to the history they are recounting. More cunningly, to enhance his story Garcilaso exploits the classical myths of men with tails or human monsters who feed on human flesh. These are the intercalated or interrupting stories that Pupo-Walker remarks in the Inca's texts. These are the vestiges of the Middle Ages set against the backdrop of an individual—a humanistic trait—who recognizes the importance of the Church in the venture and reminds the Spanish crown that these people could be easily converted to Christianity. This letter foreshadows what is to come in subsequent *historias,* all or most claiming to be "natural" in the tradition of Pliny, indicating a place for the historian within this venerable classic tradition, or "true" (*verdaderas*) in regards to humanist ideals.

The chroniclers we are interested in, Bernal Díaz del Castillo and Garcilaso de la Vega, question the veracity of the history written by people who were either not there to witness the events or could not understand the languages. Bernal is alluding to Francisco López de Gómara's *Historia de las Indias y la conquista de México* (1552), which exalts Hernán Cortés and his heroic conquest of Mexico based on interviews done with him and some others. As for Garcilaso, he is referring to the official historical works on Peru by Pedro Cieza de León and José de Acosta. Pupo-Walker summarizes the enterprise against which Bernal and Garcilaso are reacting when he explains that:

> In this way, in the first decades of the sixteenth century, in the minds of many Europeans America was represented as a vast, imaginary space, verified and yet undiscovered; it was a reality observed at the same time

with exceptional rigor but also with surprise and fascination. Some saw what there was in those lands, and others freely contemplated that which they hoped to find. However, above the news and the legendary transpositions, America increasingly was seen as the fulfilment of a great dream that for centuries Western culture had cherished. (Pupo-Walker 1982b, 47–48)

Precisely because of the juxtaposed rhetorical currents and the conflation of visions of the role of the New World, combined with the fact that one is a soldier in Cortés's army and the other is "born in the city of Cuzco" [*natural de la ciudad del Cuzco*], the relationship of these two writers to their texts and the way in which they attempt to describe a space that they know firsthand and is being reconstructed is, to say the least, ambivalent. Moreover, considering the marginalized position they seem to occupy, yet knowing that their place in the writing of the history of the New World is vital, these writers in their works create a tension comparable to the one found in Ana Lydia Vega's texts in the twentieth century. These voices coming from the margins of "traditional" European history were forging rhetorical paths for writers like Vega to adopt. Like them, she will make the position of the marginal (a woman writer from Puerto Rico) work in her favor as the vehicle through which unrecorded history can be best presented. She therefore shares much with these two *cronistas,* more than with so many other writers who were either well educated or were Spaniards. The history of Puerto Rico has been recorded by many "official" historians, and it has been awaiting the advent of today's writers to be rerecorded by a variety of unofficial voices. In his text, Bernal expresses resentment, jealousy, and even despair whenever he interrupts his *historia,* realizing he faces the paradigms of quite an extraordinary rhetorical apparatus, mastered and manipulated by other historians. Pupo-Walker argues that the Inca Garcilaso de la Vega, fully aware of the European rhetorical principles involved, sought to reveal the subtle correspondences between the historical process being described and the natural birth and development of a creative (read imaginative/literary) style used to describe that process. The Inca strives to elaborate a discourse, which implicitly supposes another reality—in this case the New World reality.

Much has been written on the irruption of the imaginary in historical texts of the colonial period to translate or to try to explain New World reality to European readers. The repercussions of such attempts find their way into texts as diverse as Montaigne's 1592 *Essais* ("Des cannibales" and "Des coches"), Shakespeare's *The Tempest* (1611), and even Voltaire's eponymous character Candide (in 1759), who goes to the New World and stumbles into the legendary Eldorado. Thanks to chroniclers such as Bernal and the Inca Garcilaso, the echoes of that incipient American reality become popularized and assimilated into European discourses. These texts were long neglected (at least by Hispanic scholars), yet their relevance to literary production in Latin America today cannot be underestimated. Pupo-Walker asserts that the chroniclers of the New World began to subvert the traditional European rhetorical apparatus for the presentation of history by converting the inventory-type of history into a truly narrative discourse, that is, one in which an anecdotal insertion would be as important and revealing of the event at hand as "objectively" listed facts. The inserted story complements the historical testimony (Pupo-Walker 1982a, 154). From Borges to García Márquez, in most of today's Latin American writers one is able to recognize the debt they owe to these original experiments with rhetorical devices by writers of the *crónica* and the *relación*. In countries where censure exists and "official" histories present a unilateral view of the events, literary fiction remains the medium within which other perspectives of a historical event may be presented.

The most revealing and shared rhetorical strategy of Bernal, Garcilaso, and Vega is to be found in the preliminary and closing sections of their texts, in other words the story framing the history or in Vega's case the history framing the story. Starting chronologically with Bernal's text, the reader is immediately confronted with his disavowal of authority, for he says he cannot compete with the great Roman historians, the models he is supposed to imitate. The entire passage merits quoting in full because in one paragraph, Bernal not only summarizes a lengthy project but he delineates how he envisions the project will unravel. He even provides an excuse: he is no Latin rhetorician, so he will *not* write a preamble or a prologue. He will just state the unadorned facts, because for him this is not merely a rhetorical project, but the story of an individual expressing himself in his own environment. Moreover, he is a witness to the events, and his age ought to confer upon him authority and dignity. He bequeaths the text to his descendants who, in a larger context, are also children of all those he met and fought against in the New World. We are Bernal's heirs. In the "Nota preliminar," Bernal is clear as to how he sees himself and the role his text will play:

> I have observed that the most celebrated chroniclers, before they begin to write their histories, first set forth a Prologue and Preface with the argument expressed in loft rhetoric in order to give lustre and repute to their statements, so that the studious readers who peruse them may partake of their melody and flavour. But I, being no Latin scholar, dare not venture on such a preamble or prologue, for in order properly to extol the adventures which we met with and the heroic deeds we accomplished during the Conquest of New Spain and its provinces in the company of that valiant and enterprising Captain, Don Hernando Cortés (who later on, on account of his heroic deeds, was made Marqués del Valle) there would be needed an eloquence and rhetoric far beyond my powers. That which I have myself seen and the fighting I have gone through, with the help of

> God, I will describe quite simply, as a fair eye witness without twisting events one way or another. I am now an old man, over eighty-four years of age, and I have lost my sight and hearing; and, as luck would have it, I have gained nothing of value to leave to my children and descendants but this my true story, and they will presently find out what a wonderful story it is. (Díaz del Castillo 1956, xxxiii)

The first requirement is the need of readers. In Bernal's case, these are those "curious readers" who have to be induced to read texts by the author's astute use of a rhetorical melody. The only way he can lure readers is by asserting his authority: he was there, he heard and saw what was happening, he will the tell the truth plainly. His old age ought to confirm the veracity of his history, for he claims he has no more to gain from the telling of his true history. He then inscribes his text within the legal tradition by emphasizing it is a true and noteworthy *relación;* this *historia* is the telling of the facts as seen by the one and only man who would be able and capable of telling it. The narrative is framed by a preliminary excuse that clarifies that there is no prologue, that is, no introduction because truth needs no ornaments. Later in the passage, he states that he will satisfy the readers' curiosity and will inform them of where he is from, when he left, who he fought with, and what his present condition is. The objective listing of facts should speak for itself, reintroducing the text into the historical domain of corroboratory facts.

Bernal's *Historia* details the conquest of Mexico, the trials and tribulations of Cortés's men, the various betrayals, the role of Doña Marina/Malinche, the Spaniards' greed, the violence, and the assimilation/acculturation of other Spaniards living among the natives. The text is very thorough. He does enumerate and present facts of this New World, yet, as Hayden White suggests, he emplots history. That is, he borrows from the fictional narrative genre the structures that will enhance the telling of the story. The sections dedicated to Montezuma and the splendors of his kingdom are perfect examples of this technique, which Hayden White has termed emplotment (1973, 7). The magnificence of the Aztec civilization is presented as a compilation of details. Nevertheless, two traits place this text into a narrative mode. Bernal peppers the text with "Indian" words he needs to describe utensils, food, architecture, cities, and other things previously unknown to the Europeans that are now part of the Spanish language. Language, a new kind of language, describing a new world, is at the base of this twice-told tale, one that needed to be told twice because López de Gómara had told it incompletely. In addition to this new lexicon, Bernal, as the first-person narrator, censures other parts of the text in order to build up the readers' suspense, to avoid moments too horrific or repetitive, or, most importantly, to interrupt what many would consider a tangential, insignificant passage in the *relación*. Selection of facts serves the edifying humanist purpose of bettering humankind:

> I say that there would be so much to write about, each thing by itself, that I should not know where to begin, but we stood astonished at the excellent arrangements and the great abundance of provisions that he had in all, but I must add what I had forgotten, for it is as well to go back and relate it, and that is, that while Montezuma was at table eating, as I have described, there were waiting on him two graceful women to bring him tortillas, kneaded with eggs and other sustaining ingredients, and these tortillas were very white, and they were brought on plates covered with clean napkins, and they also brought him another kind of bread, like long balls kneaded with other kinds of sustaining food, and *pan pachol,* for so they call it in this country, which is a sort of wafer. There were also placed on the table three tubes much painted and gilded, which held *liquidambar* mixed with certain herbs which they call *tabaco,* and when he had finished eating, after they had danced before him and sung and the table was removed, he inhaled the smoke from one of those tubes, but he took very little of it and with that he fell asleep. (Díaz del Castillo 1956, 211)

This selection serves as a microcosm of the macrocosm that is the entire *relación*. Note the intercalation of the description of Montezuma's dinner and postprandial activities that Bernal deems worthy of inclusion. The details, two women, very white tortillas, appear as a straightforward description and form the core of the juxtaposition of Montezuma and Cortés: two formidable men facing each other. When the time comes for the battles against the Aztecs and other groups, the readers should remember this grandeur, and Cortés and his men, logically and dialectically, will have to be considered highly in light of the enormity of the opponent. When Bernal considers that enough has been said, as a first-person plural narrator, he interrupts the narration and decides to return to the *relación,* as if the preceding passage were not really a part of it. In reality, passages similar to the one quoted abound in Bernal's *Historia* and probably play a great role as to why we read him today. Another important aspect of his text is that he gives credit to and names as many participants as he can remember, giving history a more humanist turn: history is not just about great men, but about the everyday occurrences of people in their daily activities.

As for the closing of his text, he mentions that as he was cleaning up his copy, two *licenciados* wanted to read his *relación*. He acquiesces because "it seemed to me that some little knowledge always sticks from wise gentlemen to an illiterate like myself" [*pareciome que de varones sabios siempre se pega algo de su ciencia a los idiotas sin letras como yo soy*] (Díaz del Castillo 1956, 614), reiterating his lack of rhetorical training. Ironically, one of the *licenciados* comments that Bernal had used many beautifully rhetorical strategies; that his recollection of details was extraordinary; that, however, he should have quoted more witnesses because he (although he was there) cannot serve as a witness to himself; and that he should not have praised himself so much. Of course, they are judging him by the standards set by the official court *cronistas* of the era. They failed to see Bernal's innovations, astuteness, or ingenuity. Bernal defends himself, quotes others who have exalted his merits, and goes on to list the battles he was in and the governors of Nueva España, and, lest he is accused of being guilty of what he accuses others of, he resists the temptation to "put by memory the entry of Francisco Vázquez Coronado from Mexico into the cities they say are of Cibola; because I did not go with him, I have nothing to say about it: the soldiers who went on that trip would know better how to tell the story" [*poner por memoria la entrada que fue desde Méjico Francisco Vázquez Coronado a las ciudades que dicen de Cibola; porque yo no fui con él, no tengo que hablar en ello: los soldados que fueron aquel viaje lo sabrán mejor relatar*] (Díaz del Castillo 1955, 635). And so, at the age of eighty-four as he states at the beginning, he concludes this "*relación de la historia*" (Díaz del Castillo 1955, 25).

As for Garcilaso, what are some of the lessons that Vega as a modern chronicler could learn? Once again, the inaugural and closing sections framing the *comentarios* contain the essence of the project. As with Bernal, there is a need to invoke past historians' efforts because one has to demonstrate that one knows and seemingly respects the tradition from which one will eventually deviate. He adds that his intention is not to correct but to add to the written material. Garcilaso's text opens seeking the protection of Princess Doña Catalina de Portugal, with the following words:

> The common custom of ancient and modern writers, who always strive to dedicate their works, fruits of their creativity, to generous monarchs and powerful kings and princes, so that with their support and protection they may live more favored by the virtues and freer of the defamation of slanderers, inspired me, Most Serene Princess, in imitation of their custom, to dedicate these COMMENTARIES to Your Highness.
>
> [*La común costumbre de los antiguos y modernos escritores, que siempre se esfuerzan a dedicar sus obras, primicias de sus ingenios, a generosos monarcas y poderosos Reyes y Príncipes, para que con el amparo y protección de ellos vivan más favorecidos de los virtuosos y más libres de las calumnias de los maldicientes, me dio ánimo, Serenísima Princesa, a que yo, imitando el ejemplo de ellos, me atreviese a dedicar estos COMENTARIOS a Vuestra Alteza*] (G. de la Vega 1990, 3)

With great humility, Garcilaso abides by rhetorical tradition, invoking a royal lady's protection so that the text may not be attacked. He then proceeds to address the reader in a *Proemio al lector,* fully integrating himself in the classical tradition—contrary to Bernal, who established that he did not have enough learning to write such a prologue. Yet from the first sentence, it is clear that Garcilaso's strict and restricting affiliation to an expected model will end there. He immediately makes clear what is at stake for him and whose rhetorical and historical methods he will confront:

> Although there have been curious Spaniards who have written of the republics of the New World, such as that of Mexico and that of Peru and those of other kingdoms of those people, it has not been the full tale that they could give, which I have noted particularly in the things that I have seen written of Peru, of which, having been born in the city of Cuzco, which was another Rome in that empire, I have much wider and clearer news than that which until now the writers have given.
>
> [*Aunque ha habido españoles curiosos que han escrito las repúblicas del Nuevo Mundo, como la de México y la del Perú y las de otros reinos de aquella gentilidad, no ha sido con la relación entera que de ellos se pudiera dar, que lo he notado particularmente en las cosas que del Perú he visto escritas, de las cuales, como natural de la ciudad del Cuzco, que fue otra Roma en aquel Imperio, tengo más larga y clara noticia que la que hasta ahora los escritores han dado.*] (G. de la Vega 1990, 4)

A totalizing *relación* on Peru, a legally binding text purporting to tell the truth, has not been offered to the reader, so how can anyone proclaim he is telling the whole story? He loses credibility. Garcilaso adds that not only is he a native of Cuzco, but he knows his classics to the point of establishing a comparison between it and Rome. His aim is not to contradict Spanish historians, but to "serve them as comment and gloss and as interpreter of the many Indian terms" [*servirles de comento y glosa y de intérprete en muchos vocablos indios*] (G. de la Vega 1990, 4). Hence the title of his work: *Comentarios,* for according to him he will just comment, add a few things, and address the language of the natives. Like Bernal, he will veer from places or people he does not know, and as far as the ancient history of the Incas, he has access to it though the testimony of his mother's elders who, when pressed by him, will describe the past as it was in turn described to them orally by their elders. The crux of the matter for Garcilaso resides in the use of language, be it for the oral transmission of history or be it, in a truly humanistic vein, to better the understanding of the Incas: if one has access to their words one cna understand their looking at and understanding the cosmos. In perhaps one of the most famous chapters of the first book of the *Comentarios,* "The Author's Protest about the History" [*Protestación del autor sobre la historia*], he reiterates and further explains the purpose and method he had stated in the prologue. The chapter ends with an apparent apology and an appeal to the reader: "I beg that the discreet reader receive my spirit, which is to give him pleasure and contentment, even though the efforts and the ability of an Indian born among Indians and raised among arms and horses cannot reach that point" [*Al discreto lector suplico reciba a mi ánimo, que es de darle gusto y contento, aunque las fuerzas ni la habilidad de un indio nacido entre los indios y criado entre armas y caballos no puedan llegar allá*] (G. de la Vega 1990, 36). Much like Bernal, he disclaims any talents because he is not a Spaniard, and he would not be valued to the same extent the official Spanish historians were. Much like Bernal, it is an eyewitness's account, describing events and in search of Inca testimonies, not a panegyric dedicated to an individual hero. On the contrary, it chronicles all of the great Inca monarchs while detailing foods, rituals, changes, and transformations. To his credit, he not only alludes to the Inca words and terms, he establishes the coinage of new Spanish words generated in the New World to describe the racial and ethnic changes taking place. He especially defines the words that describe people of mixed origins, such as: *criolla/o, negra/o* or *guinea/o, mulata/o, mestiza/o, cuatralbas/os, tresalbas/os.* He proclaims to be proud of being a *mestizo,* although he immediately clarifies that for many in the Indies, because of inveterate racism, it is considered pejorative.

Garcilaso prefers to insist on the advantage of his double perspective. Being of mixed blood, bilingual, and bicultural, he convinces his reader, in spite of all the disclaimers, that he is the one called to document the glorious regal past of the Incas and then proceed to tell the history of Peru—to describe in European terms the irruption of his nation into the modern era. Ross establishes that his work seeks "to negotiate his own harmonious balance among two cultures . . . [and presents] the futility and frustration of a desire for justice between colonizer and colonized that, ultimately, was impossible" (Ross 1996, 138). Ana Lydia Vega shares this distress at the seeming impossibility of recording the fact of being a woman, a writer, and a Puerto Rican, subject to the colonial rule of the United States. What differentiates her from Bernal and Garcilaso is her sardonic use of humor in her writing.

From the sixteenth- and seventeenth-century chroniclers, we move to Ana Lydia Vega (b. 1946), one of Puerto Rico's leading short story writers. She is not just a fiction writer, but also a university professor, an advocate for human rights, a commentator on the political situation of Puerto Rico within its Caribbean setting, and a woman interested in the *Histoire/histoires.* In her interviews, she emphasizes her fascination with the history of the Caribbean, which includes nineteenth-century pro-independence movements, turn-of-the-century events, and contemporary politics. Her work includes a collection of short stories published jointly with Carmen Lugo Filippi, titled *Vírgenes y mártires* (1981) and two other short story collections, *Encancaranublado y otros cuentos de naufragio* (1982) and *Pasión de historia y otras historias de pasión* (1987). She also edited a book of essays, *El tramo ancla: Ensayos puertorriqueños de hoy* (1988). The collection that interests us, *Falsas crónicas del Sur* (1991), resumes her interest in history, although this time forewarning of what lies ahead. These are not just chronicles, but "false chronicles," and they deal with the south of Puerto Rico, a neglected literary space in Puerto Rican fiction.[1]

By choosing the term *crónicas* in the title of the collection, Vega inscribes herself into the tradition of colonial literature. Vega chooses to write these stories from the privileged narratological stance of the "genre" of the *crónica,* with its promised objectivity, its rhetorical tendency for the use (abuse) of legal language, and the insertion of fiction into the historical discourse. If the Old World *crónica,* at the threshold of a new era, represents the most appropriate method for sixteenth- and seventeenth-century chroniclers to tell of the New World's reality, then representing the status quo of the Commonwealth lived by Puerto Ricans (the only such political situation in the world) requires a rhetorical construct capable of undertaking the depiction of that most unusual and unique reality. Aware of the fact that alluding to the *crónicas* suggests the ingrained need to justify the use of total authorial control to write history, Vega adds the word "false," hence undermining the authoritarian discourse passed on to her by her literary fathers. Vega's leap into "false" chronicles is a subversion of those original models, which, in the case of Bernal and the Inca, have been proven to be subversions of Europe's standard rhetorical guidelines inherited from the Renaissance. The ridiculousness of the political limbo in which the island stands today calls for the re-creation of models that had made an effort at combining the Old World rhetoric and the representation of New World experiences. Vega takes on the Herculean task of rewriting long-forgotten, almost legendary events of Puerto Rican history. If in the standard view the recording of events is to be found in newspaper articles, chronicles, and other archival documents, then the versions to be found in the oral folklore (the *petites histoires*) are not legitimate because they are unrecorded, and because they have no proper authority to support them. They are the product of a collective memory and not of an individual author. As reversions (and not simply revisions) they are then false, because, as Vega clearly states in the preliminary words to her text, "Chronicle of the Falsification,"

> My interest in this fascinating region [coastal villages in the south of Puerto Rico] was born many years ago from the stories I used to hear from the mouth of my maternal family, originally from Arroyo. With my antenna always up to catch a good narrative project, I soon dedicated myself more consciously to interviewing whichever southerner had the dubious luck of crossing my path. The obsessions and preferences of these stories orientated to some extent my thematic selection. Then I immersed myself in the dense universe of public libraries and private archives to confirm the shifting multiplicity of the "facts" and the disconcerting ambiguity of the perspectives. Upon the ever-changing versions of events lived or heard, I constructed what I now submit to your imagination. (A. L. Vega 1991, 1)

Indeed, the chronicles are called false because they try to accommodate the disconcerting ambiguousness of oral retelling/recounting, as opposed to the typical monoglossic, authoritative discourse of a historian, especially the Puerto Rican ones. As a false or counterfeiting chronicler, Vega utilizes written texts as her last resort. Intentionally, she incorporates information from the yellow, sensationalist press to add further "unreliability," yet perhaps more readability, to her texts.

By ascribing the notion of "false" to the use of the imaginary capability of a fiction writer, as opposed to the "objective" responsibility of a historian, she adds another "counterfeiting" dimension to her *crónicas.* Her comments reinforce this quest for a polyvalent value of the "false": "I have here a false, satiric *crónica* that revolves around the little literary world from the beginning of the century (1913 to be exact). In the center of the plot, the visit of the famous Peruvian poet José Santos Chocano to the now-defunct Bernardini Theater as well as the surprising and dramatic event that finished the evening. . . . The protagonist is only a figment of my fevered fantasy" (A.L. Vega 1991, 86). One sees the dichotomy at work: on the one hand, exact dates, places, and a known author; on the other, the false satirical chronicle, its surprising ending, and a character she has imagined. Her text forces its readers to keep in mind the arbitrariness of such concepts as truth, reality, objectivity, fiction, and the imaginary, especially in the so-called *crónicas.*

Vega maintains some of Bernal's and Garcilaso's rhetorical devices, with added variants. She incorporates others to complete her false chronicles. The collection has a framing narrative, the aforementioned "Chronicle of the Falsification," a text that serves as a false prologue because it is a chronicle all by itself, and, like her predecessors', her project is clearly delineated. Unlike her predecessors, she does not apologize but rather boldly proclaims the multiplicity of sources. Nor does she claim to have been a witness to the events; she has gone to people who were there. Contrary to a López de Gómara though, her aim is not to praise the well-known figures, but rather those that had fallen through the cracks of the officially recorded history, people who, like the people in Bernal, have also played a role in the creation of the legends of an entire nation. Each of the eight stories has a framing introduction (deepening the falsification process). She, however, acting as a supposedly nonmanipulating editor, tells her readers that if they come from that part of the country, they can happily do away with these informative preambles, and that, of course, they will enter into a direct dialogue with the text (A. L. Vega 1991, 1). As a twentieth-century short story teller, she does not want to be credited with a historical *récit.* The project is narrative, the themes are guided by her own interests: the voices of women, including that of a young girl, and the perspectives of the marginalized in general.

Examining some of these pre-texts or mini-prologues, one sees Vega's ludic seriousness when dealing with folkloric facts or with racism and political massacres. The first *crónica,* a novella entitled "Miss Florence's Chest: Fragments of a Romantic Novella" [*El baúl de Miss Florence: fragmentos para un novelón romántico*], is indeed made up of fragments supposedly written by Miss Florence, an English nanny who came to Puerto Rico to take care of Samuel Morse's grandson. From the prologue to this story, we learn the following: that Morse had indeed a daughter, Susan Walker Lind, née Morse, who married a slave owner, Edward Lind, and lived in Puerto Rico in the nineteenth century (A. L. Vega 1991, 2). Morse did visit them in December 1858, and set up a telegraph line between the son-in-law's hacienda and his warehouse. As with the rest of the *crónicas,* the story emanates from a true, verifiable, historical fact. What Vega does is imagine possible characters or enhance their voices and enable them to offer us the perspective of a participant, but one who has not been privileged or selected by the historians.

To complicate matters in this story, as the title indicates, it is made up of fragments, adding to the multiplicity of voices. The story is framed by a third-person omniscient narrator who observes Miss Florence. For most of the first part, the perspective shifts, and we read Miss Florence's journal entries as she is rereading them many years later in New York. These comprise the romantic style of the author-character who loves to read George Sand's works. Before moving into the second part, however, there are also a few letters written to Miss Florence by her pupil Charlie, and which we surmise are inside her journal too.

In the second part, Miss Florence starts another journal upon returning to Puerto Rico several decades later. The presence of the narrator is more marked because of the temporal proximity of the character to the actions being presented. After learning of the tragic lives of the Lind family, the third part, consisting of two short paragraphs, presents Miss Florence burning up all the souvenirs of that time she spent in Puerto Rico.

Like the unofficial *cronistas,* Vega tries to multiply the "I"s and therefore the perspectives, because the themes discussed in this novella require as many representative views as possible. At the outset of the story, slavery is very much alive in Puerto Rico; discrimination and abuses based on race and gender differences are rampant. The two epigraphs, both in English, summarize the concerns of the text. Vega has written them in English not so much for an alienating effect as for their shock value. She has a quote from Morse, whom everyone remembers not for his proslavery concerns but for the telegraph, in which he states: "Slavery per se in not a sin. It is a social condition ordained from the beginning of time for the wisest purposes, benevolent and disciplinary, by Divine Wisdom" (A. L. Vega 1991, 4). And through a quote from his daughter, Vega establishes the plight of women in general. Because she is the daughter of Samuel Morse—rich, beautiful, educated—she ought to have been happy, but her husband, abusing his position as both the master of his wife and of his slaves, openly and defiantly has affairs with slave women, has them live in the house and impregnates them. Susan writes to a friend, and Vega quotes: "Folks here pity my loneliness but I continue to exist" (A. L. Vega 1991, 4). She does exist, but upon reading the text, we realize that she has very little control over her household, her body, or her destiny. So onto the denunciation of slavery, Vega grafts the less-addressed issues of abuse of slave women and of white women: slaves of social constraints, prisoners of a society not willing to allow them to decide anything for themselves.

The young character offers hope. But he is crushed by the authority of his father, who does not want him to study art and does not want him to marry a mulatta because that is not acceptable. To have them as sexual objects is acceptable, to make them respectable is not. So Charlie commits suicide, and slowly the Lind family disintegrates. His blood lives in Andrés, the bastard son he had. Ironically, his name survives in the slaves who outlived him and who adopted his last name when they were registered to a new owner.

The actions described in the closing section of the novella are significant in so far as the evidence and memories of Miss Florence's life in Puerto Rico are carefully destroyed but not forgotten, for they are registered in the story itself. Because the story is told from the perspective of a British nanny, it conveys a cold, detached, perhaps more objective perspective to be contrasted to the heated and passionate action it presents. After all, the subjects of slavery, adultery, rape, and sexual abuses are explosive, especially in the period right before emancipation in 1873 and right after it, which are the periods covered by the story.

In another story, "A Sunday for Lilliane" [*Un domingo de Lilliane*], the focus is on the Ponce Massacre of Nationalists on 21 March 1937. Once again the characters are based on historical facts and figures, enhanced by Vega through poetic license. Vega, like Bernal, multiplies the perspectives of the voices telling the story: "In order to tell this story, I listened to voices for a long time. Even the infamous General Blanton Winship, mastermind of the crime, demanded from hell equal time to give his version of the facts. By means of and thanks to authorial authority *autoridad autoril,* no point of view seemed to me as seductive as that of little Lilliane, who—paradoxically—was not present" (A. L. Vega 1991, 106). Unlike Bernal and Garcilaso, she is interested in emphasizing the voice of a young girl who was not there but whose narrative, focused on the outing to the grandparents' country house and the interested yet detached recording of unusual details that day, serves to heighten the tension, because the reader knows about the massacre, just not how Vega will describe it. Most of the story, like Miss Florence's novella, consists of alternating fragments. The first and then alternating "odd" segments are told by Lilliane. The "even" fragments are told from a third-person perspective alternating between Angel, an onlooker who is riding his bicycle back from the beach after collecting seashells and is curious to see what this meeting is all about, and Carlos, the *Imparcial* reporter who wants to find the perfect spot from which to get that front-page news photograph of the event. The order of the fragments is respected until the shootout when, to heighten the chaos and emphasize the trap that the police had set, the Carlos and Angel fragments are reversed and follow each other; they are not separated by a Lilliane one. One shoots the photo before ducking, the other is shot before he could duck the bullets. The text immediately shifts to Lilliane's perspective, announcing that "the black car with a cop at the wheel and police insignia on the back bumper entered through the gate like an ominous, big black beetle" (A. L. Vega 1991, 120). It comes to fetch Lilliane's father, el Fiscal ("Prosecuting Attorney"), whose fragment (told by the third-person narrator) closes the text. The innocent mediating perspective of the child disappears once it becomes obvious that believing in a democratic system that allows for freedom of expression is naive. The Prosecuting Attorney has to recognize and record officially that this event was an "attempt" against the security of the state as per the colonel's report. History, as Bernal and Garcilaso knew, is written by the victors. Vega exhumes this dark moment in Puerto Rican history, one many would rather forget because of the ambivalence many experience vis-à-vis the relationship to the United States. Should one pretend it was an attempt, a terrorist-type of attack; or should it be viewed as a demonstration others claim was peaceful, led by unarmed people who were set up? Much in line with Garcilaso, she is attempting the arousal of a collective consciousness that would rather forget. She is stirring Puerto Ricans' memories and forcing all of us to deal with the somber moments of our past. And, just like him, she is vying for her place within this Puerto Rican space of letters.

Because she is not a witness to any of the events, she relies on the transmission of what others have seen and heard throughout the years. She follows the *cronistas*' example (of entering themselves into the *crónicas* as characters in order to distort them) by writing an "I" as a protagonist into the closing and final framing story of the collection. In this story, this female "I" is riding in a hired car with several other people. The driver asks his passengers for stories, otherwise he will fall asleep. Some of the stories are shorter versions of the ones the book contains, others are new stories. The "I" is the only who will not tell stories. "I" does not want to participate in the storytelling act. "I" is the one who hides her profession (writer) from the others. The collection ends with the following phrases: "I did not want to break the magic of the moment. My head was full of words, and I was anxious to sit at my desk and uncover the typewriter" (A. L. Vega 1991, 188). "I" seeks to remain a "collector" or "reporter" of words, but note that it is a magical moment (where the imagination takes hold).[2]

Similar basic elements are there, but "I," unlike the chroniclers, does not claim to be the sole authority on the subject (in this case Puerto Rican history). Quite the contrary, "I" is a vehicle for the recording of histories. Does this position give the "I" more objective distancing from the text? Not really. "I" may have diffused the traditional setup of the author(ity), first by granting liberty to the reader (if you are from the south, do not read the prefatory remarks at the beginning of each *crónica*), and then by silencing her voice when others are producing their stories.

The "I" stays out of the discussion, smiling. With an extraordinary tour de force, she has pretended to insert this "real" story into the fictional collection, contrary to the inserted fiction into the history practiced by the chroniclers. Needless to say, it is another rhetorical device, but coming, as she states in the story, from someone who is not from the south of Puerto Rico, "I's" writing brings all the readers as writers into the text. Her list of readerse is not exclusionary. More importantly, she hints at looking at the Puerto Rican situation from a humorous and inclusive perspective, which possibly may save Puerto Ricans as a people, because to deal with that fragile falsehood that is the Commonwealth is as tricky as trying to write false chronicles. This dual status of a free and associated state creates some unlikely situations, which in the text are suggested by the following incident: a young man listening to rap music on his Walkman tries to seduce "I" as soon as they get out of the car in Río Piedras because he interprets her smiles and silences as being in complicity with and responding to his winks. He, like many, misreads her silences, which were a mere shield necessary to protect what "I" sees as her integrity as a writer.

Vega takes her métier as a twentieth-century Puerto Rican woman writer seriously. Her style is marked by the use of colloquial language and elements of popular culture; nonetheless, her avowed goal is to bring to light events from the past that could enlighten her contemporary readers, such as the tensions between women and men and how they react to sexual exploitation, racial and social discrimination, and the role of the United States as a neoimperialist power in Puerto Rican affairs. Vega goes back to the models of sixteenth- and seventeenth-century chronicles that sought to represent the New World and turns her own work into false chronicles in order to heighten the elusive quality of today's so-called New World order. Europe no longer controls the Caribbean; the United States does. Ana Lydia Vega's shifting literary paradigms illustrate this change in political paradigms.

NOTES

1. Other contemporary Puerto Rican authors, such as Rosario Ferré, write extensively on the Southern city that Ponce, the second largest city in Puerto Rico. However, Ponce, known as the *Ciudad Señorial,* is not the only city which interests Vega.

She aims to unearth the untold history of the popular classes and not exclusively of the sugar barons.

2. In Spanish, she does not need to write the subject pronoun "yo." The verb ending will indicate the grammatical person. The character is effectively erased from the page, adding to the ambivalence of the position of this seemingly unauthoritative chronicler.

Bibliography

Columbus, Christopher. 1978. *Four Voyages to the New World: Letters and Selected Documents.* Edited and translated by R. H. Major. Gloucester, Mass.: Corinth.

Díaz del Castillo, Bernal. 1955. *Historia verdadera de la conquista de la Nueva España.* Edited by Carlos Pereyra. Madrid: Espasa-Calpe.

———. 1956. *The Discovery and Conquest of Mexico, 1517–1521.* Edited and traslated by A. P. Maudslay. New York: Farrar, Straus and Cudahy.

González Echevarría, Roberto. 1983. "Humanismo, retórica y las crónicas de la conquista." In *Isla a su vuelo fugitiva: Ensayos críticos sobre literatura hispanoamericana,* 9–25. Madrid: Porrúa Turanzas.

Pupo-Walker, Enrique. 1982a. "La ficción intercalada: Su relevancia en el discurso de la historia." In *Historia, creación y profecía en los textos del Inca Garcilaso de la Vega,* 149–93. Madrid: Porrúa Turanzas.

———. 1982b. *La vocación literaria del pensamiento histórico en América: Desarrollo de la prosa de ficción: Siglos XVI, XVII, XVIII y XIX.* Madrid: Editorial Gredos.

———. 1985. "*La Florida,* del Inca Garcilaso: Notas sobre la problematización del discurso histórico en los siglos XVI y XVII." *Cuadernos Hispanoamericanos* 417: 91–111.

Ross, Kathleen. 1996. "Historians of the Conquest and Colonization of the New World: 1550–1620." In *The Cambridge History of Latin American Literature: Discovery to Modernism,* edited by Roberto González Echevarría and Enrique Pupo-Walker, 101–42. Vol. 1. Cambridge: Cambridge University Press.

Vega, Ana Lydia. 1991. *Falsas crónicas del Sur.* Río Piedras: Editorial de la Universidad de Puerto Rico.

Vega, Garcilaso de la (the Inca). 1990. *Comentarios reales.* Edited by. José de la Riva-Agüero. Mexico, D. F.: Porrúa.

White, Hayden. 1973. *Metahistory: The Historical Imagination in Nineteenth-Century Europe.* Baltimore & London: The Johns Hopkins University Press.

Cervantes in America: Between New World Chronicle and Chivalric Romance

LUIS CORREA-DÍAZ

Escucha, divino Rolando del sueño,/ A un enamorado de tu Clavileño

[Listen, divine Roland of the dream, / To a lover of your Clavileño]

—Rubén Darío

La Mancha, en verdad, adquirió todo su sentido en las Américas

[La Mancha, in truth, acquired all of its meaning in the Americas]

—Carlos Fuentes

IN A LECTURE READ 17 MARCH 1911 IN THE HISPANIC AMERICAN CULTURAL Center and later published in *Estudios Cervantinos* in 1947, the great Cervantes scholar Francisco Rodríguez Marín speaks of how, by 1607, Don Quixote de la Mancha had already arrived (as a literary character) in the New World, represented there by a certain Luis de Córdoba in some carnivalesque festivities in Peru. As is well known, Miguel de Cervantes Saavedra, who had a rather unlucky life–like "a rosary of misfortunes" (Maeztu 1972, 37)—hoped to go to America in search of the economic security and status denied to him in Spain. Cervantes's wanderlust was not indulged by the powers of the day, however. Thus the arrival Rodríguez Marín about talks can be seen as a kind of symbolic arrival, like the arrival of the novel itself, an event to which he refers in another lecture on 10 March of the same year, titled "El *Quijote* en América." Don Francisco concludes heuristically in the first of these lectures that "Don Quixote, in person, took real and corporal possession of [the American continent], in the name of Miguel de Cervantes and the beautiful language of Castile" (Rodríguez Marín 1947, 109).

The list of Latin American authors who have concerned themselves with *Don Quixote* and with Cervantes by writing something about either or perhaps incorporating one of their many features into their own works, is extensive, dating from certain New World chronicles, and continuing/ proliferating up to this century, a phenomenon that Julio Ortega has pointed out in his *La Cervantiada* (1992). In this list we find Rubén Darío, Jorge Luis Borges, Juan José Arreola, Marco Denevi, Pedro Lastra, Eduardo Galeano, and Angélica Muñiz-Huberman, all of whom have written noteworthy passages. This influence/intertextuality even shows up in the "plurigeneric" writings of Subcommander Marcos of the Zapatista Liberation Army (EZLN, Chiapas, Mexico), who has become "a figure of Mexican letters," as Juan Pellicer points out in a recent article titled "La gravedad y la gracia: El discurso del Subcomandante Marcos" (1996). This revolutionary (and *indigenista*) hero has turned to combining weapons and letters, an idea that was very dear to Cervantes and that constituted a "curious discourse" of Don Quixote in the thirty-eighth chapter of part one of his novel. In fact, Pellicer observes that "the spirit of Cervantes's work will be a constant presence in the writings of Marcos," a visionary who makes no small use of *Don Quixote* as a model of allegorical and satirical writing that permits him to fight with words as well as with other weapons, without language losing its aesthetic value within that effort.

Nevertheless, none of these authors has dared to imagine in writing the arrival of Cervantes (Don Quixote)[1] in the New World, not even Eduardo Galeano, who published a pair of short texts touching on the matter in *Los nacimientos,* the first volume of his *Memorias del fuego* (1990), titled "En un lugar de la cárcel" and "Cervantes." In the first, Miguel de Cervantes, after hearing that his request for a position in the West Indies had been denied, "alone in his cell . . . he begins to relate the misfortunes of a wandering poet, *knight of the sheathed sword, ancient shield, skinny nag, and running greyhound*" (Galeano 1990, 188). The Uruguayan writer imagines and narrates this Seville episode (1597) so as to show how Cervantes wrote his immortal work from prison, thus joining other critics and writers who believe it was this providential event that produced the *Quixote.*[2] In the second text, Galeano creates a dialogue between Don Quixote and Sancho at Cervantes's deathbed (Madrid, 1616). In this conversation, responding to Sancho Panza's question of what they will do after the death of their "father," Don Quixote urges his companion to embark on a new (and last?) voyage: "We will go where he wanted to and could not." "To right the wrongs on the coasts of Cartagena, in ravines of La Paz, and the forests of Socunusco." This quixotic proposal, which tries to do away with Sancho's laziness and doubts, is expressed by the *hidalgo* himself: "*¡Pues allá iremos, a lavar la honra de quien libres nos parió en la cárcel!*" And the story ends when Don Quixote asks his squire for his sword, in order to set out on the adventure (Galeano 1990, 213). Galeano thus comes very close to telling the tale of Don Quixote's (Cervantes's)[3] appearance in America.

It was Pedro Gómez Valderrama (1923–1992), however, a Colombian writer and diplomat contemporary with Alvaro Mutis and Gabriel García Márquez,[4] who brought the author of the *Quixote* to the New World in a short story written in 1970, entitled "En un lugar de las Indias," published for the first time in an offprint of the magazine *Eco* (3–4) in 1972.[5] This story, along with the novel *La otra raya del tigre* (1976/77) and the short story "Tierra . . . !" (1959/60), is among Gómez Valderrama's most widely read texts. Not only did the author himself select it on various occasions as representative of his work, but many other readers also included it in anthologies, and it was twice translated into German as part of selections of Columbian and Caribbean short stories.[6]

As the intertextual twist of the title suggests, the author indulges the first phrase with which Cervantes initiates the adventures of the Man of La Mancha to recount the *famosa historia* of what I have allowed myself to call here a *Quijote indiano/caribeño.*[7] In the story, Don Miguel [de Cervantes y Saavedra] is the character, the knight-errant, and Don Alonso [Quijano] becomes the writer-historian who chronicles his adventures in America, thus converting the imaginary *hidalgo* to a kind of New World chronicler (*cronista de Indias*) and Cervantes in his own character through the words of Don Pedro [Gómez Valderrama], although this time in an overseas setting. This highly original tale, in which Gómez Valderrama invents some historic events and inverts literary facts, is possible thanks to a metafictional strategy that the author employs throughout his work and that he called "historical conjecture," that is, the imaginative literary development of hypotheses based in the shadows of history.[8]

Gómez Valderrama's hybrid writing, consisting of short stories that are also historical essays, acts by uncovering the hidden aspects of some facts and by playing with others, thus bringing to light the political-erotic forces motivate the characters, including the Colombian author himself, given that this kind of apocryphal biographical novelization of Cervantes and of Don Quixote is also a self-portrayal, and given that the contemporization of a *Quijote indiano/caribeño* allows the author to explore in his text the possibilities and consequences—both literary and historic—of a quixotic sally in the Indies, a *quijotería indiana,* as an element of our American identity. Jorge Mañach has reflected on this in the chapter "El quijotismo y América" in his *Examen del quijotismo* (1950), where he says that "the conquest of America was a 'knightly enterprise.' The deeds and gestures of the conquistadors weave a kind of barbarous, yet at the same time magnificient, Quixotism" (Mañach 1950, 153–54), which forms part of our history and psychology. Mañach continues by tracing the pros and cons of this phenomenon (which includes characteristics of Sancho Panza as well) up to the middle of this century, suggesting a kind of transcendence of this duality by concluding that "our America does not want to die of tradition [like Don Quixote] nor let itself be reduced to the province [like Sancho]" (Mañach 1950, 162). This conclusion implies a profound recognition of the fact that, as Mañach himself points out, we all carry within us "a small Quixote." And if we carry him in our history and our behavior, then he is also present in our literature.

Milan Kundera, in "The Depreciated Legacy of Cervantes," the first part of his *The Art of the Novel* (1988), assigns to the Spanish author, along with the French philosopher René Descartes, a fundamental role in the development of the novel, because "with Cervantes and his contemporaries, it inquires into the nature of adventure" (Kundera 1988, 5). This adventure is none other than that of the modern era: "the world as ambiguity," the world of relative, contradictory truths, and the nostalgia for a "single, divine Truth." According to Kundera, the novel as a genre is daughter and mother, "the image and model of that world" (Kundera 1988, 6). Gómez Valderrama voiced a similar opinion in one of his essays: "All of this is in the Quixote [the novel as a prototype with all its protocols], which contains astonishing technical surprises, such as how the novel itself is mentioned within the novel, the author and his plagiarists are discussed, and incidental stories are lived that nevertheless form part of the immense tableau—the tableau of *maese* Pedro—which constitutes a good part of the great novels not only of Spain but also of the world" (Gómez Valderrama 1988a, 131).[9]

Almost four centuries later, and with the "terminal paradoxes of the Modern Era" in full force, as Kundera would say,[10] we find ourselves with a minimalist text, aesthetically speaking, that takes us in a straight line back to the Cervantine hero. In Gómez Valderrama's minimalist novel (his short story[11]), in order to continue the game already established in the *Quixote,* the historical author of the seventeenth-century text is incorporated as the character, and the imaginary character is made to live in history, in this case in the story of a text, as its author. Don Alonso [Quijano] is portrayed as the author of a chivalric romance written in the style of a New World chronicle, given the temporal and geographic context in which the story is played out, although this narrator himself is presented in a fragmentary manner, since his narration is offered within the contemporary frame of a metaliterary and historiographic reflection on the part of an extradiegetic narrator (Genette 1980, 280) who introduces the story and periodically comments on it, without the reader knowing for certain whether he is presenting it as a fact or inventing it as a tale.

Thus Pedro Gómez Valderrama grapples with, both theoretically and creatively, the always unsettling problem of our cultural *mestizaje,* as he had done earlier in the story "Tierra . . . !" by concentrating on the biological aspect of this (dis)encounter, of this invention of the New World by/for the Europeans. He takes up the theme of the New World chronicle as the starting point of all reflections concerning the origin and evolution of narratives (historical and/or literary) that refer to our never-resolved (Latin) American[12] identity, not discounting its quixotic nature shaped by the notion of a chivalric utopia, given that this was one of the two frames of the chronicles that we have inherited, the other being the anti-utopian picaresque.[13] With the tale "En un lugar de las Indias," the author became part of the risky adventure—somewhat criminal if one remembers the plagiarsm/conspiracy of Alonso Fernández de Avellaneda[14]—of having written an apocryphal *Don Quixote,* although in this case his less sinister intentions exempt him from a fixed interpretation of the *famoso español* (whether the author or his character, because in any case they are the same thing), because for him the entire novel becomes finally a *teoría de Dulcinea,* to employ the expression Juan José Arreola used to title one of his *(micro)cuentos* (Arreola 1962, 19). This is a theory of Dulcinea and nothing more, so as not to diverge here and declare unexpectedly that it is a treatise of courtly love in every sense of the word,[15] given that she, "the most beloved woman of all time?" (Costa Vieira 1995, 19), is spoken of in every line, although sometimes in silence, and seemingly as if it were another subject that the writer as well as his alter ego were discussing. Pedro Gómez Valderrama uncovers, through his own reading of the text, the theory of an overseas Dulcinea—tropical and Caribbean—who plays at the same time the roles of enchanting and enchanted lady for a certain Don Miguel, a kind of phantasmagorical *Quijote indiano.*

The historical and literary conjecture in this tale, the imagining of a possible adventure in the heroic and exemplary life of Cervantes—so described by Astrana Marín—is constructed on the base of a real and documented fact: in May of 1590, at the age of forty-three and fifteen years prior to the appearance of part one of *El Ingenioso Hidalgo Don Quijote de la Mancha* (1605), by means of a letter directed to the "Presidente del Consejo de Indias," Cervantes solicited in one of his most desperate moments[16] "an overseas destination," which was "natural refuge for a Spaniard ruined in his homeland" (Díaz-Plaja 1974, 84). Then Don Alonso, the intradiegetic narrator, cites the letter in its entirety as the documentary complement to his narration, specifying that it is no less than the "true text" [*texto verdadero*] (Gómez Valderrama 1996, 93). Nevertheless, at the end of the letter one finds an endnote that shows its source: "1. Citada por Sebastián Juan Arbó. *Cervantes,* Ediciones del Zodiaco, Barcelona 1945: Páginas 370 y 371" (Gómez Valderrama 1996, 94). This notice directs our attention back (or forward) to Don Pedro as the narrator, since it must be he who provides us with a bibliographic detail after 1945. It evidently cannot be Don Alonso, who could have had access to the text in manuscript form, even as a copy, but not as a book, given his temporal relationship with the protagonist: in the context of the story, Cervantes is still far from becoming one of the most notable, if not the greatest literary subjects ever, in terms of the volume of material related to his life and work.

In the "authentic text" of this letter, Don Miguel speaks in the third person, if one takes into account his presence in the story of Don Pedro and in the documentation of Don Alonso (Gómez Valderrama 1996, 93–94), reviewing in minute detail the list of services he (and his brother) have provided to the Spanish crown, noting that "in all this time no consideration has been given" as is warranted:

> He humbly requests and pleads that, as soon as possible, Your Grace may bestow upon him one of the three or four positions in the Indies which are currently vacant: the Accounting Office of the New Reign of Granada, or the Governorship of Soconusco in Guatemala, or Accountant of the galleys in Cartagena, or Magistrate in the city of La Paz . . . , because it is his wish to continue always in the service of Your Grace and live out his life like so many of his ancestors have done, and in which case he would be mercifully honored. (Gómez Valderrama 1996, 94)

It is with Cervantes's petition for a post in the Indies, one of many similar requests made in Spain and elsewhere at that time, that Gómez Valderrama performs his "historical conjecture" in a multiform literary tale (short story, essay, chivalric romance, and New World chronicle, all in miniature).

Thus, the Colombian author brings the Spaniard to America in 1590, and with him his quixotic heart. Gómez Valderrama is the one who conjures (hypothesizes), and Don Alonso the one who recounts that Cervantes's petition, contrary to the facts documented thus far, was in fact approved: "Doctor Núnez Marqueño, the Council's scribe, put this note on the letter: 'The petitioner goes as accountant of the galleys in Cartagena of the Indies'" (Gómez Valderrama 1996, 94).[17] Thus begins the chivalric romance of Don Alonso, Cervantes's hypothetical and redemptive overseas adventure. But the unusual thing here is not only the inventive modification of history, but also the steps to which (in its various meanings, including the dramatic one), this conjecture is carried to extremes, affecting what we know both of the fictional world of Don Quixote and of his civil personality, Alonso Quijano. The extradiegetic narrator recounts, in the paragraph that follows the one just cited—although it could as well be Don Alonso (the intradiegetic narrator) who narrates, since there is no textual clarity here but rather a very ludic ambiguity—that "On the same day that Don Miguel was given the poistion, one Núnez Marqueño put out another request, from one Alonso Quijano, the same nobleman who is trying to describe the tribulations of Don Miguel in America. The note read: 'Look here where consideration may be found'" (Gómez Valderrama 1996, 94). Alonso Quijano receives in this version of the (hi)story, whether it be the one which we read in the novel, in the tale of Don Pedro as narrator, or of Gómez Valderrama as author, the response that was in fact given to the other, real character: to Cervantes himself.[18] With this passage the Colombian writer affirms one of his greatest convictions: the inevitable and necessary indistinction, in general terms, between life and art; and in more specific terms, such as historiographic or literary, between biography and the novel.[19] It is a minimalist novel that sinks its roots in a particular history of which its chivalric referent, real and fictitious, is only one part, and in a specific biography, which the novel transforms into a kind of historical autobiography, and which in this case also acquires all the features of a true hagiography, of a *Vita,* given that, as Borges says, "For us Don Quixote is not only a beloved friend but also a saint" (Borges 1982, 206). For if "*Don Quijote* is the history of Cervantes and of Spain" (Díaz-Plaja 1974, 94), then Cervantes through his novel has written his own (tragicomic)[20] hagiography as well as that of his people. He has of course written the hagiography of Europe and Western civilization as well, whose sin it was (and not virtue, as was believed) to have "opted for a decidedly antierotic society" (Argullol and Trías 1992, 99).[21] In "En un lugar de las Indias," Don Alonso remains in Spain, at some unspecified and uncelebrated *lugar de La Mancha,* writing the adventures (the "tribulations") of his hero, Don Miguel, who has received one of the overseas posts that both have solicited separately, and for which the latter sets off, the opportunity serving as his foray into the world as a knight (and conquistador/accountant). And this "place" [*lugar*] is none other than Cartagena de Indias, whose name and legendary fame Gómez Valderrama does hope to recall and perpetuate through his literary/historic narrative genius.

Given these interpretative coordinates in relation to the role of antieroticism as an essential failure that is lamented not without humor and purifying self-irony[22] in the histories of Don Quixote, Cervantes, Spain, and Europe, it is no coincidence that within this escape of Don Miguel [de Cervantes] and of Don Quixote from his Western, European world, the reason for which was a precarious economic situation (*un motivo indiano*), as has already been noted, there also existed a trip in search of love, a destination that for Don Quixote has no other name than Dulcinea. In this voyage we can see right from the very start, with Don Miguel's arrival in the New World (Cartagena), the thwarting of the myth of Dulcinea in its global dimension. For this knight-errant, the mythic figure of Dulcinea is equivalent to America, an America that seems maliciously enchanted by its inhabitants, who have changed her original being and have transformed her into an ugly copy of themselves (as her new gods):

> Don Miguel [notes Don Alonso] thinks that perhaps it would have been better to have arrived a century earlier, with Columbus himself, in order to see how these lands really were before the arrival of the Spanish, before they took their gold and their women, and created them as a semblance of Spain with its narrow, twisted streets designed so that the winter wind would not blow through you, here where the only winter is a warm rain that makes your clothes stick to your skin. (Gómez Valderrama 1996, 96)

After a short while, Don Miguel enters into a state of irreversible melancholy from which even his mulatta servant Piedad, "a real female" [*una real hembra*] and a Dulcinea in flesh and bone, cannot save him, although it is with her that he ends his erotic pilgrimage and with her he spends his most orgasmic and intense days. From the first night until the end of his life, Piedad remains his faithful companion.[23] It is in this way that the *indianización* (and *caribeñización*) of Don Miguel occur, like the law of *mestizaje:* he in fact enters the world of the Other only through (prohibited, illicit) copulation with that Other. Piedad rises up as a demoniacal figure, like the devil him/herself, and Don Miguel becomes someone who has dangerously broken his ties with society. Don Miguel moves from pleasure to the first serious symptoms of his (quixotic) illness, which occur at the same time as others that come from a real disease (*el tabardillo*). This happens while the city and its people, including "the religious sentinels of the Inquisition" provoked by his sinful and illegal conduct, "were interested in the case, without being able to do anything aside from contributing with their quota of gossip about the definitive clarification of the problem" (Gómez Valderrama 1996, 97). Notices of the (scandalous) fact reaches Spain but "they keep accumulating on the secretaries' desks" and remains there without being processed (Gómez Valderrama 1996, 97).

In the risky experiment of literary imagining that constitutes "En un lugar de las Indias," Gómez Valderrama assesses and reorganizes certain facts that history recognizes as true, and introduces, in the production of a "possible history," a conjecture: the approval of Cervantes's petition for an overseas post, and the consequent (Colombian)[24] trip of the character to the New World, where he is awaited by a Dulcinea that is America and also another, a concrete and sensual woman, the mulatta Piedad. Both together represent an (erotic) adventure of greater transcendence than any he has ever undertaken, although with the first of these Americas he remained disillusioned from the very first encounter in his utopian quest. Don Miguel becomes sick—although he has always been sick; he has a mor(t)al wound and there is nothing or no one in the world that can save him, not even his *real hembra,* the mulatta Dulcinea. Don Miguel suffers from melancholy, from black humor, and such suffering is equal to saying that the real Cervantes suffers from quixotism, this being nothing other than the feverish activity (*locura*) of a being who prefers passivity (*cordura*) (Arias de la Canal 1986 ix–xii).[25] This Don Quixote leaves for the (New) World to later return from it vanquished, back to his melancholy (loneliness), back to his Old World.[26] This Cervantes is disenchanted with America, because it is made "in the image and likeness of Spain" (Gómez Valderrama 1996, 96), just as the historic Cervantes was disenchanted with his own society and time. An inconsolable melancholy mercilessly consumes Don Miguel, in whose sad heart was born Don Quixote, a hypostatic figure in which creator (life) and creature (fiction) are united.[27] This lamentable/lamented (experimental) observation is without doubt the "most tragic passage" in Gómez Valderrama's tale, and the conclusive element in his theory of Don Quixote. This is why Don Pedro says, involving himself in the story, that "the most tragic passage in Don Alonso's story is the moment where Don Miguel, weakened by illness, lacking the will to respond, not wanting to return to the mother country, consumed by alcohol and the wicked sensuality of the mulatta, is indifferent to the point that nothing matters anymore" (Gómez Valderrama 1996, 97). Nothing matters to him to the point that, shortly before dying of melancholy, he declares to his doctor[28] that what he has done "with the big package of his literary work," the body of his literary production of which perhaps only "some sonnet" remains, has been to give it to Piedad "to light the fire" (Gómez Valderrama 1996, 97). Cervantes's impulse here implies the destruction not only of his written work up to that point, but also of the future *Don Quixote.* It is significant that the agent of this act of destruction is the (faithful) mulatta Piedad—that is, the Dulcinea of the tale. Don Miguel gives himself up to his own auto-da-fé, and it is Dulcinea who carries out the delicate and quasi-confessional task of purification. Through the words of Don Alonso Quijano, Cervantes spiritually aborts his other self, *Don Quixote,* though this action does not liberate him (them) from his (their) sickness (quixotism), nor from death.

So we arrive at the moment for which—paraphrasing the astute words of Borges in his "Análisis del último capítulo del *Quijote*" (Borges 1982, 203–13)—Gómez Valderrama's entire story has been written: the death of Don Miguel, this *Quijote indiano/caribeño.* The last lines of Don Alonso's narrative in "En un lugar de las Indias" are: "the melancholic end is approaching now, where the man dissolves in the tropics" (Gómez Valderrama 1996, 97). According to Don Alonso (the intradiegetic narrator, writer of chivalric romance, and New World chronicler), the protagonist, consumed by melancholy, simply disappears, and the hero and his people die a common death after all. This dissolution can be interpreted in symbolic terms related to the phenomenon of *mestizaje,* this being one ending, the novelistic one (and keeping in mind here the chronicle as well). But Don Pedro (the extradiegetic narrator, historian, and man of letters) immediately intervenes, entertaining himself by commenting on what he believes were the circumstances behind this ending: "It appears that Don Alonso dedicated long hours to the few sentences that form the description of this part. The end, we would say, is just a few shallow waves in the blue Caribbean sea" (Gómez Valderrama 1996, 97–98). Suddenly, in the midst of what would seem to be confidence in his source, Don Pedro exclaims, "But that is not the end" (Gómez Valderrama 1996, 97–98). He goes even further into the matter to reveal the truth, a truth that is opposed to fiction—apocryphal, of course, in literary and historiographic terms—and that is based on a revelation that occurs almost four centuries after the facts, on the same afternoon (in 1970) in which he rereads and comments on those historical events. Very sure of himself, Don Pedro says, "I will find the true ending this afternoon, and it is a noble scene on an afternoon in La Mancha, in the serenity of the abolished austerity where Don Miguel de Cervantes visits Don Alonso Quijano, author of the narration, and Don Alonso reads to him his story of that overseas adventure" (Gómez Valderrama 1996, 98). Nevertheless, this second and "true" ending remains quite fictitious, although much less so. The fictitious character Don Quixote has disappeared in this ending, leaving face to face only the author and his model, Don Alonso, who has taken up the quill *motu proprio* in order to write, to narrate the (supposed) "tribulations of Don Miguel in America." Don Alonso, another Cervantine alter ego, recounts these events to Cervantes, and one can deduce, then, that the latter found the initial inspiration for his great work, both in topographical and sociological terms, in his own country.[29]

Don Pedro adds one more paragraph: "Don Miguel de Cervantes is silent, looking out the window at the brown soil of La Mancha, meditating for a long while on all that would have happened if he really had gone to Cartagena in the Indies, in the New Kingdom of Granada" (Gómez Valderrama 1996, 98). These lines, which seem to belong to the second ending, in reality contain yet a third ending no less "true" (or fictitious, at the same time) as the previous one. Don Pedro, or more likely the (real) author of "En un lugar de las Indias," correcting the tendency to imagine on the part of the extradiegetic narrator who plays the role of historian, proposes this alternative ending, which, according to the internal logic of the short story (essay), is essential. With this finishing touch, Don Alonso Quijano is made to disappear (and in this way dies symbolically), and his historicity, however certain it may be, is never able to supercede his fictitious literary condition. Only Cervantes, in whom live and die the other two characters, remains as a historical character, *meditando* (imagining and speculating) on a New World destiny that history seems to have denied him. With this ending we see that the Colombian writer, in the style of Alonso Quijano's renunciation in the closing moments of *Don Quixote,* takes the fundamental step of undoing his own conjecture, so that everything returns to normal, the normal state of an old, tired man—the Spaniard (then and there) and the Colombian (here and now)—who sits close to the window (un)writing a novel (a short story/essay) that is nothing less than his own errant autobiography, and at the same time an erotic chronicle of the Indies then and now. Still, for as long as Gómez Valderrama's felicitous historical conjecture lasts, it brings Cervantes and his just heart to those of us in America for the first time. It brings him here to the New World, to us who still suffer from "false paladins" which carry our communities down decidedly unerotic paths, and for whom Rubén Darío wrote a famous "Letanía" in 1905, where he asks of "Our Lord Don Quijote" that he pray for us:

> Pray for us, lord of the disenchanted,
> that by power you give us new spirit and bright dreams,
> crowned by a golden helmet of illusion,
> who no one has been able to conquer!
> due to the shield on your arm, which is all fantasy,
> and your lance always ready, which is all heart.
>
> [*Ora por nosotros, señor de los tristes,*
> *que de fuerza alientas y de ensueños vistes,*
> *coronado de áureo yelmo de ilusión,*
> *¡que nadie ha podido vencer todavía,*
> *por la adarga al brazo, toda fantasía,*
> *y la lanza en ristre, toda corazón.*] (Darío 1977, 296)

It is this heart marked by idealism and the search for justice that is repeated in the Latin American revolutionary struggles of the last half-century, despite ideological and generational differences. From a vantage point at the end of the century, in the the midst of the postrevolutionary moment, and from the perspective of a subject who cannot help but view these moments with nostalgia, these revolutions have been marked by agonizing processes that suggest culminations instead of beginnings, and that have carried us back to the origins of our history as a *mestizo* continent.

Translated by Marilyn Miller

Notes

1. I follow what Ramiro de Maeztu says in this regard: "Cervantes is explained by Don Quixote and the *Quixote* by Cervantes" (Maeztu 1972, 48).

2. See, for example, José Toribio Medina in his *Estudios Cervantinos* (1958), where he supports his thesis citing the fervent commentary of Antonio Batres Jáuregui in *El Castellano en América:* "What a fortunate failure, that one produced by Núñez Morquecho's pen, upon which the existence of the most creative work in the world depended!" (Medina 1958, 537). Fernando Díaz-Plaja in his *Cervantes* (1974) offers a less determinist opinion: "Honorably, I believe that the *Quixote* would have been born exactly the same, because [Cervantes] already carried it inside of himself" (Díaz-Plaja 1974, 86).

3. I reiterate from a different angle what I have already noted in terms of the relationship between author and character with another assertion of Maeztu: "in the *Quixote* one cannot conceive of even the possibility that the hero and the fable could be foreign to the writer" (Maeztu 1972, 33).

4. For more of a context (both in terms of Colombia and Latin America) and additional bio/bibliographic information, see Jorge Eliécer Ruiz's "Prólogo," "Cro-

nología," and "Bibliografía" in *Más arriba del reino* and Alonzo Aristizábal's *Pedro Gómez Valderrama*. Literary works of Gómez Valderrama include: *Norma para lo efímero* (poems, 1943), *Biografía de la campana* (poem, 1946), *Muestras del diablo* (chronicles and tales, 1958), *El retablo de maese Pedro* (short stories, 1967), *La procesión de los ardientes* (short stories and a novella, 1973), *Invenciones y artificios* (tales, 1975), *La otra raya del tigre* (novel, 1977), *Más arriba del reino* (anthology, 1977), *La nave de los locos* (narratives, 1984), and *Cuentos completos* (1996).

5. The story was later included in the collection *La procesión de los ardientes* (1973), in the critical edition and anthology *Más arriba del reino* (1977), the bio/bibliographic/anthological text *Pedro Gómez Valderrama* by Alonso Aristizábal (1992), and finally in *Cuentos completos* (1996. My citations come from this last publication, since this edition is identical to earlier, less accessible versions.

6. Beneath the suggestive titles "Die Wahreitsprobe des Gran Man" and "Die Westindischen Abenteur des fahrenden Ritters Dos Miguel" ("The Adventures of a Grand Man" and "The Adventures of the Errant Knight Don Miguel of the West Indies," respectively). See the "Bibliografía" section of Eliécer Ruiz (367–68).

7. *Indiano* is a term that in this case refers to a Spaniard who visits America and returns to Spain, usually used in the context of the conquest and early colonial period. There is no suitable equivalent term in English.

8. Gómez Valderrama explains this strategy in a lecture titled "Confesión personal": "the origin of the choice of historical conjecture as a fundamental theme of my narratives" is found in the fact that "history is full of misteries" and that the explanations that are formed in regard to specific facts and characters are never completely satisfactory (and sometimes hardly at all). Thus, due to the fact that "history is temptation" for literature, the response of the literary text is to try to "fill these gaps" and "illuminate these shadows," since these are the given functions of fiction (Gómez Valderrama 1988a, 29–35).

9. The Cervantine novel is so protean that, as Alvaro Pineda Botero has said, "metafiction, self-consciousness, *mise en abyme,* deconstruction, dissemination, and generally many concepts and experiments that are found in the postmodern novel and contemporary philosophy were already fully developed in the *Quixote*" (Pineda Botero 1995, 72). Furthermore, he adds, although without the clamor of the postmodern present, "The Quixote thus includes its anti-book: history and fiction, truth and verisimilitude, art and reality, literary work and literary criticism, the concept and the practice: the theory and the antidote for it" (Pineda Botero 1995, 72).

10. One of these paradoxes is that the novel has become its own most merciless parody (a fact already present in the *Quixote*), which for some has signified the death of the novel as a genre and as a model of the world, an idea that Kundera fervently rejects (13).

11. The author in question always wrote, as Aristizábal points out, "with the clear intent to make the short story into a synthesis of history" (Aristizábal 1992, 23). See Gaston Bachelard's ideas on the theme of the written *miniature* in *The Poetics of Space,* particularly his notion that "The miniature is one of the refuges of greatness" (Bachelard 1969, 155).

12. We should keep in mind here the words of Carlos Rangel regarding this polemic of naming that appear in the section of his book *Del buen salvaje al buen revolucionario* titled "Española y no latina" (1976, 19–21).

13. Utopia, nonexistent but imagined, and like Gómez Valderrama has said in "Academia y memoria," a place that exists nowhere except in language (Gómez Valderrama 1988b, 50), literature (and politics) having been charged with propagating it as an object and symptom of desire. For a consideration of the effects of the

arrival of Utopia in the new continent, see his essay *La utopía en el descubrimiento de América* (1988).

14. Whose spurious Quixote could never be more than a poor or unfortunate copy of the original text, which is light years away from the dark and inquisitorial intentions we find in his version. Arias de la Canal says of it, "In all, the book has only one objective: to baptize Don Quixote, to bring him into the church, to hang a rosary on him, to make him hear mass, and to substitute Dulcinea with the patroness of its order" (Arias de la Canal 1986, 177-178).

15. "Don Quijote is the prototype of love, in its highest expression of cosmic love, for all ages" if one looks beyond the circumstances of his epoch, if he is viewed for a moment not just from a historical perspective (Maeztu 1972, 69).

16. "[H]is situation already had reached such a precarious extreme that, after having thought about the most useless enterprises, he found himself at the verge of living off of public charity" (Gómez Valderrama 1996, 93). Thus Don Alonso summarizes the desperation of his character, something which historians and biographers would comment on at length throughout the centuries.

17. "When Don Miguel finally received the Council of the Indies' response to his petition for an overseas post . . . , he found himself at the verge of living off of public charity" (Gómez Valderrama 1996, 93).

18. Gómez Valderrama adds another layer to the familiar idea that the writer creates his or her characters and unreal worlds in order to live out in them, hypostatically, the adventures real life does not offer him/her: here he causes a character to return the favor to the writer, by exchanging roles and erasing the ontological boundary that separates them.

19. We know, nonetheless, that the creation of Alonso Quijano, like that of the rest of the characters, did not occur ex nihilo, but rather was based on certain observations and encounters of the author with real-life characters (Díaz-Plaja 1974, 94).

20. See Ortega y Gasset's comments regarding tragic and comic elements in relation to the novel in general and to *Don Quixote.*

21. The eroticism of a civilization would be found, according to these philosophers, in its openness to alterity. *Argullol* recalls what Hölderin said in this regard: "a civilization only reached its full potential if it was able to put itself in contradiction, to become 'foreign' to its own identity in order to make itself fertile with its otherness" (Argullol and Trias 1992, 99).

22. "The most genial work of peninsular literature is molded by a bitterness that only serves to alleviate or to sharpen the humor, sometimes sweet and resigned, sometimes sarcastic, that appears on its pages" (Díaz-Plaja 1974, 94). This bitterness and melancholy originated in the erotic failure (vital and social) of a man on whom Fortune did not smile in any field, except in the literary one when it was already too late.

23. "That night, as if it were of the devil, was stormy, with lightening bolts and flashes crisscrossing the sky, as if so that Don Miguel would not forget" (Gómez Valderrama 1996, 96).

24. Don Alonso says, "The route remains the same one of Don Cristóbal [Columbus]" (Gómez Valderrama 1996, 95).

25. The theme of *locura/cordura* in the novel and in the Cervantine character has been studied extensively. One should point out here, for a better understanding of the text, that Don Quixote demonstrates his good sense on innumerable occasions by wanting to commit "craziness" [*locuras*], thus revealing that he always "proceeds from reason" (Riquer 1970, 89). Melancholy appears here as a sad lucidity in which

the protagonist is acutely conscious that this desire to "go crazy" [*hacer locuras*] forms part of an idealistic protocol pertinent only to a bygone era.

26. For José Ortega y Gasset, "Cervantes composed the critique of pure effort in his Quixote." Pure effort (that of a "hero of little intelligence," of a "man of heart"), which, according to the philosopher, leads only to melancholy, or rather, to "nowhere." Note that "From Chapter LVIII until the end of the novel everything is bitterness." He later cites a passage of *Don Quixote* that here has much to do with Gómez Valderrama's tale: "'Melancholy spills out from my heart,' says the poet. 'I was so sad that I did not eat,' he adds, 'I was full of sadness and melancholy.' . . . 'Let me die,' he says to Sancho, 'at the hands of my thoughts, by the force of my misfortunes'" (Ortega y Gasset 1987, 360).

27. "I do not understand how one can read the *Quixote* without becoming saturated with the melancholy that a man and a people feel upon becoming disillusioned with their ideal; and if one adds that Cervantes suffered from it at the time of writing, and that Spain, just as its poet, needed to laugh at itself so as not to burst into tears; what blindness has this been that we have refused to see in Cervantes's work the voice of a fatigued race that retreats to rest after completing its work in the world?" (Maeztu 1972, 22). If one follows the account of the Colombian writer, this disenchantment occurs after witnessing and lamenting Spain's activity in the New World.

28. He confesses to a doctor because he is very ill, but also because he has been prohibited from receiving "spiritual assistance, because priests cannot enter a house stained by sin" (Gómez Valderrama 1996, 97): sin that is nothing other than erotic contentment behind the public's back.

29. "[*Don Quixote*] is a short novel that has grown as it developed. The idea first has a distant origin that we already know. Two relatives of his wife, a poor and proud nobleman and the priest who believed in the books of chivalry, have fused into a guy named like the authentic one—maybe Quijada, maybe Quijano—and will end up being called Don Quixote. The town where he was born is Esquivias, but the clues were already too clear to complete it with these details. It would be *In a Place in La Mancha Whose Name I Don't Want to Remember* [*En un lugar de la Mancha de cuyo nombre no quiero acordarme*]" (Díaz-Plaja 1974, 94).

Bibliography

Arbó, Sebastián Juan. 1945. *Cervantes.* Barcelona: Ediciones del Zodiaco.

Argullol, Rafael, and Eugenio Trías. 1992. *El cansancio de occidente.* Barcelona: Ediciones Destinos.

Arias de la Canal, Fredo. 1986. *Intento de psicoanálisis de Cervantes.* In *El Quijote de Benjumea,* by Nicolás Díaz de Benjumea Barcelona: Ediciones Rondas.

Aristizábal, Alonso. 1992. *Pedro Gómez Valderrama.* Bogotá: Procultura.

Arreola, Juan José. 1962. *Confabulario total.* Mexico: Fondo de Cultura Económica.

Astrana Marín, Luis. 1948–1958. *Vida ejemplar y heroica de Miguel de Cervantes Saavedra.* 7 vols. Madrid: Instituto Editorial Reus.

Bachelard, Gaston. 1969. *The Poetics of Space.* Translated by Maria Jolas. Boston: Beacon Press.

Borges, Jorge Luis. 1982. *Páginas de Jorge Luis Borges seleccionadas por el autor.* Edited by Alicia Jurado. Buenos Aires: Celtia.

Cervantes y Saavedra, Miguel de. 1983. *El ingenioso hidalgo Don Quijote de La Mancha.* Madrid: Espasa-Calpe.

Costa Vieira, Maria Augusta da. 1995. "Os amores de dom Quixote pela inigualável Dulcinéia, ou, Dulcinéia: A mulher mais amada de todos os tempos?" *Revista da Biblioteca Mário de Andrade* (São Paulo) 53: 19–23.

Darío, Rubén. 1977. *Poesías.* Prólogo de Angel Rama. Caracas: Biblioteca Ayacucho.

Díaz-Plaja, Fernando. 1974. *Cervantes.* Barcelona: Plaza and Janés.

Fuentes, Carlos. 1992. *El espejo enterrado.* Mexico: Fondo de Cultura Económica.

Galeano, Eduardo. 1990. *Memorias del fuego. Vol. 1, Los nacimiento.* Montevideo: Ediciones del Chanchito.

Genette, Gérard. 1980. *Narrative Discourse: An Essay in Method.* Translated by Jane E. Lewin. Ithaca: Cornell University Press.

Gómez Valderrama, Pedro. 1973. *La procesión de los ardientes.* Bogtá: n.p.

———. 1977. *Más arriba del reino. La otra raya del tigre.* Ed. Jorge Eliécer Ruiz. Caracas: Biblioteca Ayacucho.

———. 1988a. *La leyenda es la poesía de la historia. (Ensayos y conferencias).* Caracas: Academia Nacional de la Historia.

———. 1988b. *La utopía en el descubrimiento de América. Utopia in the Discovery of America.* Colombia: Dirección de Relaciones Públicas (Flota Mercante Grancolombiana).

———. 1996. *Cuentos Completos.* Bogotá: Alfaguara.

Kundera, Milan. 1988. *The Art of the Novel.* Translated by Linda Asher. New York: Grove Press.

Maeztu, Ramiro de. 1972. *Don Quijote, don Juan y la Celestina: Ensayos en simpatía.* Madrid: Espasa-Calpe.

Mañach, Jorge. 1950. *Examen del quijotismo.* Buenos Aires: Editorial Sudamericana.

Medina, José Toribio. 1958. *Estudios cervantinos.* Santiago, Chile: Fondo Historiográfico y Bibliográfico José Toribio Medina.

Montero Reguera, José. 1994. "Mujer, erotismo y sexualidad en el *Quijote.*" *Anales Cervantinos* 32: 97–116.

Ortega, Julio, ed. 1992. *La Cervantiada.* Mexico: UNAM, El Colegio de México.

Ortega y Gasset, José. 1981. *Meditaciones del Quijote.* Edited by María Garagorri. Madrid: Alianza Editorial.

———. 1987. *Meditaciones sobre la literatura y el arte (La manera española de ver las cosas).* Edited by E. Inman Fox. Madrid: Clásicos Castalia.

Pellicer, Juan. 1996. "La gravedad y la gracia: El discurso del Subcomandante Marcos." *Revista Iberoamericana* 62, no. 174: 199–208.

Pineda Botero, Alvaro. 1995. *Escrituras andantes. Textos críticos de literatura española.* Medellín: Colección Autores Antioqueños.

Rangel, Carlos. 1976. *Del buen salvaje al buen revolucionario.* Barcelona: Monte Avila.

Riquer, Martín de. 1970. *Aproximaciones al Quijote.* Navarra: Salvat Editores.

Rodríguez Marín, Francisco. 1947. "El Quijote en América." In *Estudios Cervantinos.*

Part Six
The "Discoverers" Rediscovered

The Americanization of Christopher Columbus in the Works of William Carlos Williams and Alejo Carpentier

MOLLY METHERD

CHRISTOPHER COLUMBUS HAS BEEN, FROM THE OUTSET, A CONSTRUCTED icon. He positioned himself in his own writings as an bold adventurer and a keen negotiator, while the Spanish crown characterized him first during his lifetime as a fortuitous accident and then later as an icon of Spain's imperialist power. For centuries scholars have returned to the vast Columbian archive in search of the elusive details to support or deny these various claims. Early royal historians like Gonzalo Fernández de Oviedo read Columbus as the intrepid sailor, guided by geographical knowledge and navigational expertise, and subsequent revisionists have portrayed Columbus in roles ranging from evangelist to pirate. These elaborate, and at times far-fetched, images were largely European attempts to negotiate and renegotiate the cultural legitimacy of the Columbus icon and Spain's historical authority as colonizer of the New World.

More recently, scholars, particularly in the United States and Latin America, have re-constructed Columbus as an icon of European hegemony and exploitation in the New World. This essay explores two American literary responses to the Columbian documents[1] and appropriations of the Columbian icon. The U.S. writer William Carlos Williams and the Cuban author Alejo Carpentier appropriate Columbus from his European origins, incorporating passages from the Columbian documents directly into their own texts. In so doing, they edit and reframe the texts, and refashion Columbus as a New World narrator.

Although both twentieth-century authors use the archive's complicated and mediated nature to revise the import of Christopher Columbus from Old World discoverer to New World narrator, they do so with different objectives in mind. Williams reads Columbus from a North American perspective as an icon of the exploited individual, while Carpentier characterizes Columbus from a Caribbean perspective as an icon of Spanish oppression.

I. The Mediated Documents: Columbus's Revisions

The archival documentation of Christopher Columbus's life and voyages has a complex history of transcription, manipulation, and appropriation.[2] This history of revision begins with Columbus himself, for Columbus read and mediated his own texts. He carefully narrated the events of his journeys and altered these events according to his intended audience and his own political needs. The document known as the "Letter to Santángel" announcing the discovery exemplifies this process.

There are three versions of this letter in the Columbian archive: a sixteenth-century copy dated 4 March to Ferdinand and Isabella and two very similar letters both dated 15 February and addressed to Luis de Santángel and to Rafaél Sánchez. The 4 March letter includes technical details of the ships and of navigation and contractual details of Columbus's rights and titles. It also petitions for favors from Ferdinand and Isabella and complains about certain crew members. Although the 4 March letter is dated later, the 15 February letter appears to be a stylized version of the 4 March letter to the Spanish crown. The 15 February letter summarizes certain passages, intensifies others, and omits any potentially negative or politically threatening details included in the letter to the Spanish sovereigns. For example, this later letter to Ferdinand and Isabella announces that "in seven years from today I will be able to pay Your Highnesses for five thousand cavalry and fifty thousand foot soldiers for the war and a conquest of Jerusalem for which purpose this enterprise was undertaken" (Zamora 1993, 19). The 4 March letter's highly charged statement linking the discovery of the New World to Spain's intent to conquer Jerusalem does not appear in the 15 February letter.

To be sure, it is impossible to tell if Columbus wrote the 15 February version or if it was an adaptation censored by the court for public release, but clearly the personal and political references have been edited out to create a public document, an official announcement of the discovery. It is this stylized and sanitized 15 February letter that has been translated into three languages and published throughout Europe. And, for almost five hundred years, it was this Santángel version of the letter that redefined the discovery from an "enterprise marked by significant national and private interests to a heroic, selfless mission on behalf of Christendom" (Zamora 1993, 19).

This letter is just one instance of the many versions of Columbus's own writings that abound in the Columbian archive. Since many of these inconsistencies in the Columbian documents can be traced to Columbus himself, later readers of the documents, and particularly American readers such as Williams and Carpentier, focus on the implications of these disparities in their characterizations of Columbus.

II. Initial Rewritings: Editorial Revisions

The complex manipulations of the Columbian documents begin during Columbus's lifetime. The admiral's original log, known as the *Diario,* and the court transcription of this document have been lost. Until 1825, two narratives of Fernando Columbus and of Bartolomé de Las Casas were the only known versions of Columbus's journal.[3]

In this year, Martín Fernández de Navarrete published a transcription of the *Diario* in a collection of writings by Spanish explorers. Although this text is in the original diary form, the document is not an exact copy of Columbus's *Diario,* but rather a sixteenth-century revision of the original text.

This version of the *Diario* was transcribed by Bartolomé de Las Casas, probably in preparation for writing his *Historia de las Indias.* In this edition of the *Diario,* Las Casas made over a thousand revisions in the margins and in the text itself.[4] One of his most overt editorial changes was to introduce a third-person narrative voice. This third-person subject summarizes and paraphrases some sections of Columbus's *Diario* and introduces other passages as first person quotations. Consequently, this editorial presence makes selective decisions about the importance of each entry and alters the rhetorical organization of the original work.[5]

Navarrete, the editor who found and first published Las Casas's version of the *Diario,* omits all of Las Casas's marginalia. He publishes the primary text of the *Diario* as revised by Las Casas as if it were a manuscript of Columbus's journal. In Navarrete's publication, there is no mention of Las Casas and no explanation for the third-person narrative voice in a personal log. By suppressing any mention of Las Casas, Navarrete initiated his own editorial fictions, and most of the subsequent Spanish editions and all of the English translations of the *Diario* follow his lead in erasing any mention of Las Casas from the text (Zamora 1993, 69). This revised *Diario,* then, is the document that is quoted as empirical evidence in countless academic studies and that was certainly consulted by Williams[6] and most likely by Carpentier in the writing of their own texts.

The Navarrete/Las Casas revisions represent just one link in a chain of compounding and confounding revisions.[7] In fact, the Columbian archive has undergone four centuries of editing and revision. Whether compelled by politics, propaganda, or accident, Columbus, or perhaps one of his contemporaries, writes differing versions of the letter announcing the discovery. The original manuscripts of the *Diario* are lost and then rewritten in narrative form by Fernando Columbus and Las Casas. Over a century later, Navarrete finds an annotated edition of the *Diario* and publishes it without acknowledging the Lascasian revisions. Navarrete's revisions are then reedited by modern publishers and presented not as revisions but as Columbus's actual documents. So, what is often published as the original *Diario* of the discovery of the Americas, then, is actually a revision itself.

The contradictory nature of the Columbian documents invites not only historical but also literary revisions of both the events of the discovery and the figure of Columbus. Authors from Washington Irving to Carlos Fuentes to Salman Rushdie have taken advantage of these nebulous Columbian texts to create Columbus as an icon for their respective cultural contexts. It is not surprising, then, that William Carlos Williams and Alejo Carpentier choose to retell the history of the discovery and to reevaluate the American present through the American past.

Nonetheless, Williams and Carpentier, reading and writing in different languages and in different decades, both engage the Columbian archives in much the same way. Both authors place long passages of these Columbian documents directly into their own texts, creating a pastiche of their own writing and the *Diario.* In so doing, they resurrect the Columbian documents and the figure of Columbus from their European origins and recast each as the source for their own American texts. Through this process of rereading, the discovery of America becomes an American discovery.

III. Columbus as American Narrator

Williams and Carpentier both inscribe Columbus as an American narrator and read the Columbian documents as a literary production. They reestablish Columbus as the first-person narrator by erasing Las Casas's third-person narrative voice. With this gesture, they function as Columbus's voice and narrative agency.

In *In the American Grain* (1925), each of the twenty-one chapters is dedicated to a figure in New World history, and chapter two, "The Discovery of the Indies," is dedicated to Columbus. Williams begins "The Discovery of the Indies" with the fourth voyage, when Columbus is aged and defeated, and organizes the chapter so that the discovery appears last. This atemporal organization creates a dramatic ending and contrasts Columbus's later rhetoric of despair to the earlier voice filled with wonder and hope. As the chapter moves forward into the past, the narrative relies more heavily on the documents, and the narrative voice takes less precedence, until the moment of the discovery when Columbus speaks from excerpts of the *Diario* with no editorial interruptions.

Part two of Carpentier's novel *The Harp and the Shadow* (1979) is structured in much the same way as Williams's text, although stylistically the two are very different. Columbus, old and humbled, lies on his death bed awaiting his confessor and recounts his own version of the discovery. He reexamines the drafts of his journals and letters, turning "the yellowed pages, with their faint, lingering smell of saltpeter" (Carpentier 1990, 94), reviewing his life and reflecting on his choices and his mistakes. Carpentier's Columbus literally rereads the documents to reconstruct the discovery.

So, in both *In the American Grain* and *The Harp and the Shadow,* Columbus is portrayed at the end of his life as a very different character from the reckless and infatuated Columbus of 12 October 1492. In both books, Columbus, enfeebled and humbled, retells the story of his voyages and his discovery, creating a single narrative out of his experiences. To do this, the aged Columbus narrator must refer to his own archive in order to tell his story. Consequently, the Columbus narrator in both of these texts mirrors Williams's and Carpentier's own process of reading the *Diario* and re-narrating the document in *In the American Grain* and *The Harp and the Shadow.*[8]

Both American authors also choose passages from the *Diario* that manifest Columbus's own fictions and his labor of writing. These labors include how to write of the New World for an Old World audience and how to express New World realities in an Old World language. In so doing, they identify Columbus's narrative obstacles as the seeds of all New World writing. Columbus, burdened with the task of describing the unknown, is thus repositioned as the first Western narrator of the New World.

They both choose an instance in the *Diario* where Columbus is caught between the institutional constraints of contemporary European knowledge and his personal desires to encounter and to represent a New World. In the *Diario* entry of 9 September,[9] Columbus tells of lying to his crew about the miles they have traveled, or double reckoning, so that the crew will not become discouraged and want to turn back. In this entry he literally reads the distance traveled and re-narrates this distance to mollify his crew. He resolves this conflict through his own fictions: "This day the Admiral made 19 leagues, and he arranged to reckon less than the number run, because if the voyage was of long duration, the people would not be so terrified and disheartened. In the night he made 120 miles, at the rate of 12 miles an hour, which are 30 leagues" (Olson and Bourne 1906, 94).

Similarly, in *In the American Grain,* Williams's Columbus writes that: "Sunday we made nineteen leagues, and I decided to reckon less than the number run, for should the voyage prove of long duration, the people would not be so terrified and disheartened. This day we lost sight of land, and many fearful of not seeing it again sighed and shed tears" (Williams 1956, 17). Williams includes not only this incident of Columbus reading himself and narrating a particular version of the events to his crew, he also adds a second sentence that suggests Columbus is the fearless and resourceful leader of the frightened and fainthearted crew.

In *The Harp and the Shadow,* Carpentier also reemplots this event of Columbus reading himself. However, Carpentier takes the *Diario* text and expands it:

> I knew that if the voyage took much longer than I had projected—which could easily happen—the men, aware that with each passing day they were farther from the continent they had left behind, unable to see land ahead (and they were all anxious to see it, since the crown had offered a reward of ten thousand to the man who gave the first alert), would be easy prey to discouragement, disobedience, and the desire to turn back. . . . So I resorted to a lie, a deception, the constant fiction I had promulgated since Sunday, the ninth of September . . . which was to record fewer leagues than we had actually traveled, so that the crew would not be shocked or alarmed if the voyage went on too long. (Carpentier 1990, 72–73)

While Williams reads this invention as an imaginative narration to protect his crew, Carpentier reads this same account as an uneasy attempt to pacify a potential mutiny. Yet both twentieth-century authors pick out this instance from the *Diario* where Columbus reads himself and narrates his own fictions. They embrace Columbus's own fiction of double reckoning that, much like the multiple versions of the letter announcing the discovery, reveals a concerted attempt to fashion realities for a particular audience. In these two American texts, Columbus becomes an author of a self-conscious New World fiction.

This action of reading and narrating mirrors both Columbus narrators in *In the American Grain* and *The Harp and the Shadow* who, at the end of life, review and narrate their own *Diario.* These mirror images of Columbus reading himself in the *Diario* and in the American texts also reflect the figures of Williams and Carpentier rereading the Columbian documents and writing their own texts. Through this mirroring process, this *mise-en-abîme,* Williams and Carpentier identify their own positions as American narrators with the figure of Columbus.

Columbus's *Diario* also presents a persistent theme in American literature as a whole, that is, "how to write in a European language about realities never seen in Europe before" (González Echevarría 1990, 26). Both Williams and Carpentier incorporate passages from the *Diario* in which Columbus's repetitions suggest his difficulty narrating the landscape and reality of a New World. The prose of *In the American Grain* typically omits the long descriptions and repetitions of the *Diario.* Yet Williams does not edit Columbus's labored attempts to describe the landscape.[10] For example, Williams's chapter reads:

> I saw many trees very unlike those of our country. Branches growing in different ways and all from one trunk; one twig is one form and another is

> a different shape and so unlike that it is the greatest wonder in the world to see the diversity; thus one branch has leaves like those of a cane, and others like those of a mastic tree; and on a single tree there are five different kinds. The fish so unlike ours that it is wonderful. Some are the shape of dories and of the finest colors, so bright that there is not a man who would not be astounded, and would not take great delight in seeing them. (Williams 1956, 26)

Williams, here, embraces both Columbus's wonder at the New World and his poetic potential. When these elaborate and somewhat awkward descriptions of the trees and fish are juxtaposed with other shortened excerpts and concise narrative language, they reveal, in Columbus's voice, some of the difficulties Columbus has in describing the New World.

In *The Harp and the Shadow,* Columbus also elaborates on cultural translation as an articulatory problem. He writes, "those trees, all tangled together, their forms new to me: that one, whose leaves are gray in back and green in front, which, when they fall and dry, curl up on themselves like hands around a rope; that other, reddish, whose trunk grows by shedding transparent skins like moulting snakes . . . all new, unique, pleasing despite their difference, but so far nothing very useful" (Carpentier 1990, 86–87). Yet in *The Harp and the Shadow,* Columbus is not nearly so subtle about the challenge of finding language with which to express the unfamiliar:

> I had to describe that new land. But when I tried to do so, I was halted by the perplexity of one who tries to name things totally different from what is known—things that must have names, since things that have no names cannot be imagined, but whose names I did not know, and I was not another Adam, chosen by Christ to name the things of the world. I could make up words, certainly; but the words would *not reveal the thing,* if the thing were not already known. (Carpentier 1990, 87)

This difficulty in finding the appropriate words to describe something new is an issue for most New World writers who must describe American realities in a European language. Williams and Carpentier, in their efforts to invoke the voices of these writers, face different challenges. Williams, writing in the U.S. in the 1920s, and Carpentier, writing his first novels in Cuba in the 1940s, both seek a unique American expression but are also constrained by European standards and expectations of literary production. U.S. literature in the first decades of this century was relegated to the periphery of the British literary canon. And while Williams's contemporaries, Pound and Eliot, leave the U.S. to find "culture" in Europe, Williams stays in the U.S. to write *In the American Grain,* the premise for which is that Americans must throw off European models and ground themselves in the American landscape and embrace an American past. Likewise, Latin American literature in the forties and fifties was still marginalized to European literary production. While Carpentier did go to Europe, spending much of his career in France, his literary works all deal with questions of Latin American, and particularly Caribbean, history and identity, and this Old World/ New World relationship is a frequent subject of his essays and interviews.

Both authors believe that American writers must not abandon European models, but must work from them to create a unique American expression. In this sense, Williams and Carpentier read the narrative and language of the *Diario* as also reworking conventional European models. Columbus's role as narrator, forced to adapt his imaginative potential, subject matter, and language to appeal to a European audience, reflects Williams's and Carpentier's own concerns and constraints as American narrators. By the same token, Columbus's action in both the *Diario* and the twentieth century texts of rereading and renarrating mirrors Williams's and Carpentier's own process of reading and writing.

IV. The Discoverer Discovered

Although both Williams and Carpentier reread and reinscribe the Columbus icon from its European origins to an American context, these revisions are far from a unified American expression. These two twentieth-century works say very different things about Columbus and the discovery. Williams reads Columbus from a North American perspective as an icon of the exploited individual, while Carpentier characterizes Columbus from a Caribbean perspective as a icon of Spanish oppression. These distinct characterizations reflect their cultural positions as North American and Cuban authors and are created via their distinct aesthetic ideologies.

Williams, writing in 1925, anticipates the American historiography that emerges from the 30s on and that reevaluates Columbus's discovery as the root of European colonialism in the New World. In *In the American Grain,* Williams distinguishes Columbus's first voyage from both his and other Europeans' later exploits in the Americas. Columbus undertakes a "miraculous first voyage. For it is as the achievement of a flower, pure, white, waxlike and fragrant, that Columbus's infatuated course must be depicted, especially when compared with the acrid and poisonous apple which was later by him to be proved" (Williams 1956, 7). Williams, then, writing from his cultural position as a U.S. author in the 1920s, portrays Columbus within the U.S. trope of a frontier man, a defiant individual acting against all odds.

In Williams's novel, Columbus's imagination and the "streamlike human purity of purpose" (Williams 1956, 11) that characterize his first voyage end with this first voyage. Thereafter, he becomes America's first victim—a sacrifice to forces beyond his control. Nature, the Spanish crown, fortune: all overwhelm his initiatives. He becomes a "straw in the play of elemental giants" (Williams 1956, 10). This early Columbus figure is also in sharp contrast to other Europeans who travel to the New World and who are the subject of subsequent chapters of *In the American Grain:* Hernán Cortés, Ponce de León, and Hernando De Soto and the English pilgrims. Unlike the bold and imaginative Columbus of the first voyage, these figures are followers not leaders, they all move "in the force of the pack" (Williams 1956, 27).

Carpentier, on the other hand, characterizes Columbus as a chameleon, willing to be any color, to play any part, to fulfill any expectation as long as it furthers his purpose. His Columbus is not an intrepid explorer of new worlds, but a pawn in the European quest for gold and the power it conveys. He is an "actor," a "protagonist of fiction," an "impresario of spectacles," and a "promoter of a sacred representation" (Carpentier 1990, 122). Ultimately, he is a minor character in an international drama, a minor magician in a game of greater illusions than he could ever conjure, and the prize: the New World. Narrating from his death bed, Carpentier's Columbus realizes that after all his attempts to invent himself, he has been, from the moment he reached the New World, constructed by others. Consequently, he is the "Discoverer-discovered . . . the Conqueror-conquered" (Carpentier 1990, 125). He admits that: "It is those lands that have formed me, sculpted my shape . . . it is those lands that confer on me, in my own eyes, an epic stature that everyone denies me . . . bound to me in an exploit full of marvels worthy of a chivalric song—but a chivalric song erased, before being written, by the themes of the new romances that people want to hear now" (Carpentier 1990, 125).

This reading reflects Columbian historiography of the 1950s and 1960s by scholars like Edmundo O'Gorman, who investigates the very notion of discovery and Carl Sauer, who argues that the explorations and the subsequent initiation of the slave trade were driven by Columbus's obsessive search for gold.

Williams and Carpentier, thus, characterize Columbus very differently, and yet, they fashion their distinct characterizations from the same entries in the *Diario.* A comparative reading of the Columbian document and the two twentieth-century texts reveals that often Williams chooses to use one part of a sentence and Carpentier borrows the other, almost as if they divide up the journal between them. They examine each word and each phrase to find some ambiguity in the text or some gap between their own perceptions of America and Columbus's writings that can be deleted (Williams) or expanded (Carpentier) into their own rewriting of the event. These choices are governed not only by the authors' cultural positions, but also by their literary aesthetic.

Williams's concise poetic style and economy of language is evident in his early prose work *In the American Grain.* In "The Discovery of the Indies" chapter, he carefully pares down Columbus's phrases to reemplot the discovery and the character of Columbus. In Williams's reading, what he leaves out becomes as important as what he adds. Carpentier's style, on the other hand, is baroque and expansive. Although he also chooses certain phrases and omits others from the journal, Carpentier merely utilizes Columbus's words as a point of departure for his own exaggerated style.

The stylistic differences between the two authors are evident in the extrapolation of Columbus's journal entry of 12 October, the date of landing in the New World. On the morning of the twelfth the *Diario* states that:

> The Admiral went on shore in the armed boat, and Martin Alonso Pinzón and Vicente Yañez, his brother, who was captain of the Niña. The Admiral took the royal standard, and the captains went with two banners of the green cross, which the Admiral took in all the ships as a sign, with an F and a Y and a crown over each letter, one on one side of the cross and the other on the other. (Olson and Bourne 1906, 110)

Williams, who reads Columbus, at this point, not as an agent in the imperialist expansion, but as a brave adventurer and an American hero, only writes in *In the American Grain,* "Presently we went to shore in the armed boat and took the royal standard, and Martin Alonzo and Vincent Yañez his brother captain of the Niña" (Williams 1956, 25). Williams does not change any of the explicit facts, he includes the armed boat, the royal standard, and the characters; however, he excludes the description of the banners. That exclusion can be understood on aesthetic grounds: the detailed description would slow down the speed of the narrative and is in contrast to his style of paring down images. Throughout the work he cuts back Columbus's longer descriptions and repetitions. Arguably, however, Williams also alters Columbus's language in his description of the arrival of the Europeans to downplay the antagonistic nature of this first expedition.

Carpentier seems to do the exact opposite with the 12 October journal entry. He grasps the short description of the banner, that Williams leaves out, as an example of the ostentatious and somewhat comical arrival of the crew in the New World and elaborates and embellishes from there. In *The Harp and the Shadow,* Columbus's entry reads:

> I have dressed in my finest garments, as all the Spaniards aboard the ships are doing. From the great shield, I have taken the royal banner, mounting it on a lance, and I have done the same for the banners of the green cross that my two captains will carry . . . which ostentatiously display, beneath their corresponding crowns of embroidered silk, the initials F and Y—the later especially pleasing to me, since, together with the five letters that complete the name Ysabel, it becomes for me the almost present image of the person to whom I owe my election and investiture. (Carpentier 1990, 79)

By embellishing the sentence describing the banners, linking them to Columbus's vanity, his affinity for spectacle, and his love for Queen Isabella, Carpentier emplots Columbus and his crew as conquerors, rather than as explorers. Thus, Williams and Carpentier use two sentences from the Columbian archive to create two different narratives of the arrival of the Spaniards in the New World.

Williams and Carpentier also read Columbus's meeting with the Taínos very differently, and these distinct readings engender different characterizations of Columbus. Williams chooses all the positive comments about the indigenous peoples from the journal, while Carpentier chooses all the negative. The *Diario* entry reads:

> That we might form a great friendship, for I knew that they were a people who could be more easily freed and converted to our holy faith by love than force, I gave to some of them red caps, and glass beads to put round their necks, and many other things of little value, which gave them great pleasure, and made them so much our friends that it was a marvel to see. They afterwards came to the ship's boats where we were, swimming and bringing us parrots, cotton threads in skeins, darts, and many other things; and we exchanged them for other things that we gave them, such as glass beads and small bells. In fine, they took all, and gave what they had with good will. (Olson and Bourne 1906, 110–11)

This entry describes the indigenous people swimming to the boat as "a marvel to see." Both Williams and Carpentier take advantage of the ambiguity of the term "marvel" to rewrite Columbus's encounter with the Taínos.[11]

Williams's reading of the term marvel is consistent with the approach just explicated. Marvel is an expression of curiosity and wonder. Again, Williams pares down the *Diario* entry, taking only the phrases that anticipate a positive relationship forming between the two cultures and that describe the indigenous peoples favorably. In *In the American Grain,* Columbus writes:

> I gave to them some red caps and glass beads to put round their necks, and many other things of little value. They came to the ship's boats afterward, where we were, swimming and bringing us parrots, cotton threads in skeins, darts—what they had, with good will. (Williams 1956, 25)

In Williams's version, it appears that Columbus gave the indigenous group the caps and beads in a gesture of good will and friendship, with no intention of colonizing or converting them. The Taínos swim to the boats to welcome the Spaniards with their gifts in return. Williams picks up the expression "good will" and the action of them swimming to the ship from the Columbian document to portray this idyllic scene. He omits mention of conversion present in the source material.

Where Williams reads this marvel positively, as a wonder, a reward for Columbus's curiosity and desire to find something new, Carpentier reads "marvel" cynically. In *The Harp and the Shadow,* Columbus marvels at the ignorance of these people, and the ease with which they are manipulated.

> They exchanged everything for some things that weren't worth a fig, which we had brought along onshore in anticipation of possible trade: small glass beads, hawk's bells—hawk's bells that they especially liked to hold to their ears to hear them better—rings of brass, along with the many colored caps I had bought in the markets of Seville. . . . In exchange for these trifles, they gave us their parrots and cotton. (Carpentier 1990, 82–83)

Here, there is no mention of either the Taínos's good will or of their swimming to the ship. Instead, the inhabitants are childish and gullible, easy targets for Columbus's ambition. Columbus originally offers them caps and beads to gain their friendship in order to create obedient servants and coerce them into telling him the location of the gold.

Williams's Columbus also appears to be much more an ethnographer than a conqueror. The Columbus of *In the American Grain* writes that the people he encountered were "[a]s naked as their mothers bore them, and so the women, though I did not see more than one young girl. All I saw were youths, well made, with very handsome bodies and very good countenances" (Williams 1956, 25). In Williams's text, this first simile appears as a comparison of the indigenous peoples to the purity and naturalness of an infant at birth. Although Columbus seems to mainly praise the Taínos in this passage, the actual judgment is apparent in Williams's own choice of language. The only way the reader can know this is by returning to read the Columbian document. The *Diario* says: "It appeared to me to be a race of people very poor in everything. They go as naked as when their mothers bore them, and so do the women, although I did not see more than one young girl. All I saw were youths, none more than thirty years of age. They are very well made, with very handsome bodies, and very good countenances" (Olson and Bourne 1906, 111). Williams leaves out the first derogatory sentence, and only includes the positive descriptions of the handsome bodies and good countenances.

Carpentier works from the very sentence in the *Diario* that Williams omits. He focuses his interpretation on the relationship of the first two sentences in the above passage from the *Diario,* that the island's inhabitants "appeared to be a race of people poor in everything. They go as naked as when their mothers bore them." In *The Harp and the Shadow,* Columbus writes that the indigenous people are: "naked, with barely even a handkerchief to cover their shame. . . . I felt that they must be miserable people, very miserable, tremendously miserable, since they went naked—or nearly so—as the day they were born, even a young woman whose exposed breasts were studied by my men, who wanted to touch them, with a lust that raised my fury." (Carpentier 1990, 82). Carpentier's Columbus associates nakedness with poverty and, in this revision, misery. This Columbus also picks up the reference to the single woman in the *Diario* and links this woman to the lust of the crew. He later tells his crew, "We didn't come here to fuck but to find gold" (Carpentier 1990, 85). Columbus clearly judges the New World inhabitants according to European values. In this way, these two authors read one simile in the *Diario* according to two very different Western value systems and include this same simile to create very different characterizations of Columbus.

Thus these mediated readings of the *Diario* result in different emplotments of the moment of discovery, and these emplotments are, in turn, framed within each author's aesthetic philosophy. Williams pares down the descriptions in the *Diario,* focusing not on Columbus's reflections, but on his language and his actions. This reduction reflects Williams's philosophy of "no ideas but in things." Carpentier, on the other hand, uses the language and events of the *Diario* as a framework for his narrative but elaborates and embellishes on the Columbian text in order to explore the gaps between Columbus's language and his actions. This elaborating corresponds to Carpentier's baroque stylistics. When reading these two revisions together with the Columbian text, it becomes evident that Williams and Carpentier are not only exposing the myth of discovery but also the ways in which historical knowledge has been and can be created through language. Consequently, in these two twentieth century accounts of the discovery, the language itself becomes an event.

V. Conclusion

Both Williams and Carpentier, then, return to the Columbian documents to appropriate the figure of Columbus from his European origins and position him as the founder of an American literary tradition. Consequently, they subordinate questions of Columbus's Genovese roots and his Spanish legal ties in order to locate Columbus as the first New World narrator. They both inscribe and identify with Columbus as an American narrator, a writer of fictions who has the difficult task of describing a new reality to a European audience.

This role of American narrator, however, means different things for each of these American authors. Their characterizations of Columbus reflect both the contemporary historiography and their different cultural and aesthetic positions as U.S. and Cuban authors. Williams views Columbus as a bold but fallible individual, weakened by his own ambition and ultimately destroyed by the savage forces of nature and of European imperialism. Carpentier, on the other hand, portrays Columbus as a master of illusions, complicit with the European imperialist project, but ultimately outdone by connivers more conniving than he. They interrogate the European reading of the Columbus figure as valiant explorer in order to refashion him into two distinct American icons, each of which conveys a Columbus who speaks to and inhabits different American cultures.

Notes

I would like to thank César Salgado, Brian Bremen, and Janet Swaffar for their invaluable suggestions on an earlier draft of this paper.

1. The present documents that comprise the Columbian archive have been altered and edited by so many different hands that it is almost impossible to credit Columbus as the original author. To limit confusion this study will follow Zamora and refer to the documents as "Columbian texts" rather than attributing them directly to Columbus.

2. For a detailed account of the European transcriptions of the Columbian documents, see Zamora 1993 or Varela 1992.

3. There are two narrative accounts of Columbus's first voyage that were composed from the copy of the original *Diario.* These narrative accounts are direct mediations of the original text. Fernando Columbus, the admiral's son, wrote an account of his father's life, which was only published posthumously in an Italian translation in Venice in 1571. This document was written while the Columbus family was petitioning the Spanish court for the return of expropriated titles and land. Consequently, many scholars believe that Fernando Columbus recorded Columbus's successes in this document not only as a familial record but also to influence the outcome of these trials.

In 1564 Fray Bartolomé de las Casas completed *Historia de las Indias,* his account of the discovery and colonization of the Americas from 1492 to 1520. Las Casas worked from the *Diario* to write the narrative account of the discovery in the *Historia de las Indias,* a vehement critique of the Spanish government's policies toward the indigenous inhabitants. Las Casas, then, is not an objective transcriber of the *Diario.*

4. For a more detailed analysis of the Lascasian editorialization of the *Diario,* see Zamora 1993, Hanke 1953, or Varela 1982. For a bilingual publication of the *Diario* complete with Las Casas's notes, see Dunn and Kelley 1989.

5. In *Reading Columbus,* Zamora points out how Las Casas's editorial revisions reflect his own political reading of the discovery and colonization of the Americas. She finds that Columbus speaks in the first person when he idealizes the "Indians" or the landscape and when he speaks of evangelization.

6. Williams did his research for *In the American Grain* in the New York Public Library. For more information about Williams's sources for *In the American Grain,* see Conrad 1990.

7. For a more detailed explication, see Swift 1995.

8. Roberto González Echevarría also finds that Carpentier identifies with the figure of Columbus.

9. As the *Diario* is a translation of a version of a transcription by Las Casas, it is difficult to know to whom to attribute the quoted passages. These English translations are taken from *The Northman Columbus and Cabot: Original Narratives of Early*

American History. Although there are more recent and perhaps more accurate translations, this is the version that Williams consulted to write his chapter. Because I am quoting in English it seemed appropriate to work from this text. Henceforth all quotes from this volume will be cited with the names of the editors, Olson and Bourne.

10. The *Diario* reads: "I saw many trees very unlike those of our country. Many of them have their branches growing in different ways and all from one trunk, and one twig is one form, and another in a different shape, and so unlike that it is the greatest wonder in the world to see the great diversity; thus one branch has leaves like those of a cane, and others like those of a mastick tree: and on a single tree there are five or six different kinds" (Olson and Bourne 1906, 119).

11. Stephen Greenblatt reads Columbus's early uses of the marvelous as an agent of appropriation in *Marvelous Possessions: The Wonder of the New World.*

Bibliography

Carpentier, Alejo. 1983. *El arpa y la sombra.* In *Obras completas de Alejo Carpentier.* Vol. 4. Mexico: Siglo XXI.

———. [1979] *The Harp and the Shadow.* Translated by Thomas Christensen and Carol Christensen. San Francisco: Mercury House.

Conrad, Bryce. 1990. *Refiguring America: A Study of William Carlos Williams' "In the American Grain."* Chicago: University of Illinois Press.

Dunn, Oliver, and James E. Kelley, Jr., eds. 1989. *The "Diario" of Christopher Columbus's First Voyage to America, 1492–1493.* Norman: University of Oklahoma Press.

Fernández de Navarrete, Martín. 1945. *Colección de los Viajes y Descubrimientos que hicieron por mar los españoles desde fines del siglo XV.* Buenos Aires: Editorial Guaranía.

González Echevarría, Roberto. 1990. *Alejo Carpentier. The Pilgrim at Home.* Austin: University of Texas Press.

Greenblatt, Stephen. 1991. *Marvelous Possessions: The Wonder of the New World.* Chicago: University of Chicago Press.

Hanke, Lewis. 1953. *Bartolomé de Las Casas and the Spanish Empire in America: Four Centuries of Misunderstanding. American Philosophical Society* 97, no. 1 (February).

Las Casas, Bartolomé de. 1985. *Historia de las Indias.* 3 vols. Hollywood, Fla.: Ediciones del Continente.

O'Gorman, Edmundo. 1958. *La invención de América: El universalismo de la cultura del Occidente.* México: Fondo de Cultrua Económica.

Olson, Julius E., and Edward Gaylord Bourne, eds. 1906. *The Northmen Columbus and Cabot 985–1503: Original Narratives of Early American History.* New York: Charles Scribner's Sons.

Sauer, Carl Ortwin. 1966. *The Early Spanish Main.* Berkeley: University of California Press.

Swift, Molly. 1995. "Visions and Revisions: The Americanization of Christopher Columbus in the Works of Bartolomé de las Casas, William Carlos Williams, and Alejo Carpentier." Ph.D. diss., University of Texas at Austin.

Varela, Consuelo. 1992. *Cristóbol Colón: Retrato de un hombre.* Madrid: Alianza Editorial.

———, ed. 1982. *Cristóbal Colón. Textos y documentos completos.* Madrid: Alianza Editorial.

Williams, William Carlos. [1925] 1956. *In the American Grain.* New York: New Directions.

Zamora, Margarita. 1993. *Reading Columbus.* Berkeley: University of California Press.

"This Miraculous Lie": Lope de Aguirre and the Search for El Dorado in the Latin American Historical Novel

BART L. LEWIS

FUNDAMENTAL TO AN UNDERSTANDING OF LATIN AMERICAN NOVELISTS' current interest in Lope de Aguirre's sixteenth-century search for El Dorado is the recognition that Aguirre sought the gold of power, not that encrusted on the eternal lord of an enchanted lake. Working maniacally to steer his expedition *away* from any route that might promise a way to El Dorado, Lope's voyage to political supremacy would have taken him to the mouth of the Amazon, back to the Spanish Main, then overland to Peru, there to overthrow the viceroy and establish a free government of the first Spanish-Americans, the conquistadors who had given their own sweat and toil in these inhospitable lands. But he ended up beheaded and quartered on the high plains of Venezuela by the very men whom he had so hypnotically led to that point. No Spanish colonial adventure has been so well documented, or is so replete with novelistic elements, as the 1559 El Dorado-bound expedition of the heroic and enamored Pedro de Ursúa, accompanied by his field commander Lope de Aguirre. My essay proposes a contrastive analysis of the archive and of the novels of Ursúa's search for El Dorado, one that puts the historical record of the expedition, amply supplied by both eyewitness chroniclers and others writing after the event, alongside various novelized accounts of this doomed quest, with the intent of understanding how art transforms the historical theme, and why these novelists have undertaken such a transformation. The chief elements of contrast between these two written documents—archive and novel—are point of view, circumstances, and motivation of composition, depiction of the tyrannical figure himself, form and structure of the narration, and the author's intent in choosing this theme.

Three generations of chroniclers tell the bloody tale of Ursúa's, then Lope de Aguirre's, search for El Dorado. At the conclusion of the disastrous expedition in 1561, the first to write were Gonzalo de Zúñiga, Francisco Vázquez, and Pedrerías de Almesto, all soldiers under Aguirre. The second generation is represented by Toribio de Ortiguera who, relying on eyewitness accounts, wrote his chronicle between 1581 and 1585. Inaugurating a third epoch in chronicling Aguirre's momentous defeat is Fray Pedro de Simón, who wrote his account in 1621. In contrast to these chronicle accounts are the Latin American historical novels that relate the episode: Arturo Uslar Pietri's *El camino de El Dorado* (Venezuela, 1947), Abel Posse's *Daimón* (Argentina, 1978), *Lope de Aguirre, príncipe de la libertad* (1979) by the Venezuelan Miguel Otero Silva, Jorge Ernesto Funes's *Una lanza por Lope de Aguirre* (Argentina, 1984), and *Crónica de blasfemos* (1986) by Peru's Félix Álvarez Sáenz.[1] The archive, the chronicle, the official story: here are the facts that make known this colonial episode, and that give the figure of Lope de Aguirre to history. The first chroniclers sought to exculpate themselves and cast the blame for the expedition's failure fully on Lope, but by the time of Fray Pedro Simón's seventeenth-century account, stylized novelistic elements have become prominent. Recent research that finds artistic prose among historical accounts of the colonial period, despite and ultimately because of Spanish bans on the novel in the American colonies, leads us directly to Latin America's twentieth-century explosion of historical fiction. With treatments varying from traditional *criollista* techniques to postmodern historiographic metafiction, the Latin American novel of El Dorado, written by his artistic descendants, finds the voice of Lope de Aguirre himself, silenced by the historical record, and gives it discourse, reflection, and resonance.

Circumstances had infused Ursúa's 1559 expedition with a cynical spirit from the start, and Lope de Aguirre was its primary purveyor, a restless soul ripe for the writing of history as the acts of "audacious" (Vargas Llosa 1997, 425) individuals, and eminently suitable for the character studies of literature. Between 1492 and 1589, states Beatriz Pastor Bodmer, the colonial chronicle had moved "from fantasy to reality, from complicity to rejection, from mythification to criticism" (Pastor Bodmer 1992, 1). So it was that the questing expeditions of the north immediately following discovery, such as that of Hernán Cortés, had gradually given way to the defiant cry in the south that no golden man or golden city existed. Orellana's discovery of the Amazon, a gratuitous step on the path of his search for El Dorado, was perhaps a final goodness to come from this burst of expeditions in the second and third decades of the sixteenth century, a time that saw the passing of the legend into its "complete form" with its Spanish name, *el dorado,* as "the golden *man*" (Silverberg 1996, 123).[2]

When Charles V's New Laws of 1542, which had prohibited further exploration and conquest, were rescinded in 1559, Peru's viceroy, the Marquis de Cañete, eager to rid his realm of malcontents and failed fortune seekers, authorized a new search for the land of gold and cinnamon. Aguirre's rise to power over the slain bodies of the expedition's first, then second, commanders both gives history the natural unfolding of his dramatic life story ("he led an episode that had major political and ideological significance" [Pastor Bodmer 1992, 194]), and invests it with artful potential ("From a literary perspective, his significance comes . . . from a series of elements that tie his perception and representation of the realities of the conquest to certain aspects of baroque thinking and aesthetics" [Pastor Bodmer 1992, 194]. Lope's presence in Latin American colonial history has warranted a literary cycle that has not yet ended (Carrillo Espejo 1989, 279). The Latin American case of fiction versus fact in the colonial period, novel versus historical chronicle in its modern-day incarnation, is fittingly sui generis, leading the novelist-critic Mario Vargas Llosa to declare that the colonial chronicle is a "literature that is totalizing, in the sense that it is a literature that embraces not only objective reality but also subjective reality in a new synthesis" (Vargas Llosa 1997, 433). But he grants the novelist a mystic vision by allowing that "the difference, of course, is that the chronicles accomplished that synthesis out of ignorance and naiveté and that modern writers have accomplished it through sophistication" (Vargas Llosa 1997, 433). By common critical consent, the contemporary Latin American novel, experimental and highly regarded, in attempting to find a history for its people that was denied them by colonial Spanish overlords, gains knowledge of itself when it recognizes its founding texts: the chronicles of the Indies (Fuentes 1990, 47). In either case, fact or fiction, we must confront the question of intentionality: both chronicler and novelist are motivated, privately stirred, to produce their works. Yet as the historical moment of Aguirre's adventure dissolves into a remote past, fresh, sublime intentions arise—dramatic possibilities capture the artist's, not the royal subject's, attention.

However, determining intentionality is a crowning, and elusive, task, and the contrastive characteristics leading to it are more conclusively shown. The colonial chronicle responded to conventions of its time, "translat[ing] history into stories to shape historical facts, in the process relying on the techniques of literature [and] the ancient concept of history [as] a subgenre of fiction" (Murray 1994, 11). We see these conventions at work in the first-generation chronicle, yet an initial contrast with the modern historical novel emerges in point of view. Francisco Vázquez relates an artful tale principally in the third person, with suitable indignation directed throughout at "the tyrant," intruding with a first-person commentary only to record the physical progress of the journey ("when we arrived at this town, two guides fled from us" [Vázquez 1989, 103]. The final pages of the chronicle accuse and condemn, and the self-exoneration of this soldier "who never [wished] to deny his king and lord, nor his fatherland . . . worthy of being credited as a good and hoest man" (Vazquez 1989, 170) concludes the account.

Fray Pedro Simón's *historial* of Aguirre's many treacheries, understood both as "record" and "case history," was written fifty years after the events occurred, and displays a greater number of elements common to narrative fiction. It is as if chronological remove invests the tale with the remoteness necessary for historical fiction, in the view of Feuchtwanger and others, and Lope's evil can threaten only characters living in memory and imagination. By the second generation of reporting, Lope had already become a literary figure, thanks to his inclusion in Juan de Castellanos's *Elegias de varones ilustres de Indias* (1589). (Extremely put, three centuries later, in Clement Markham's 1861 account of Ursúa's expedition, the first in English, Aguirre had become "fitter for the pages of King Arthur's romance" [Smith 1990, 91]). Simón, while again mixing first- and third-'person point of view, adds suspense, lacking in the dutiful and adorned (yet flat) first-generation chronicles. Simón's first-person plural is not the "we" of the participant, but rather the reader's collusive "we." He pauses for moralizing, so appropriate to the nineteenth-century novel, and opens certain sections with a prosy settling-in to hear the next atrocities.

The variation in point of view presented by the novels of El Dorado reminds us that literature wants to get at the story in ways that make us marvel at presentation and not feel glutted on content. Master of traditional fiction Uslar Pietri narrates the Ursúa expedition with the grave third-person voice of self-conscious history; his ornate prose clanks the way Aguirre's armor surely did, swooshes like vines along the Amazon being pushed away by a sword. Abel Posse's postmodern rendering of the adventure is in the third person as well, but the narrator is history's antagonist, filling in unimaginable gaps and taking Lope into an eternal future. With Miguel Otero Silva's mixed-genre account, point of view darts in all three directions: Aguirre is examined by the judges of history, a judge of morality and conscience, and himself. Jorge Ernesto Funes's *Una lanza por Lope de Aguirre* is a dialogue between a *cronista* and Aguirre, and Lope sets the record straight with a first-person account of his deeds. Félix Álvarez Sáenz's *Crónica de blasfemos* is told in the first person by Estebanillo, a fictitious scribe who allows Lope once again to move famously against the backdrop of his age, while understanding intimately his nature and his fearful respect for words, allowing him this sympathetic portrayal as a final atonement for his murderous deeds.

Point of view in the chronicle determines its structure—a tale with a message—while the full freedom of literature finds for narratorial perspective a place within the greater, and transcendent, consideration of art, the work's form. Strictly purposeful, the colonial chronicle exhibits literary elements, to be sure, but "writing was [in the Renaissance] an activity that took place within a grid of strict rules and formulae which comprised what could loosely be called rhetoric" (González Echevarría 1990, 44). Yet contemporary attempts to redefine literary types are just that, modern perspectives on the ageless enterprise of art. As Seymour Menton has noted, "the various definitions of the word 'chronicle,' plus the use by postmodern literary critics of the umbrella term 'historical discourse' to cover a variety of literary genres, reflect the blurring of lines between literary genres that is typical of the postmodern period" (Menton 1993, 31). But the denials and justifications of these chroniclers, ornamented as they are by rhetorical devices and imitative of the model of humanist historiography (Murray 1994, 9–10), pointedly seek the understanding and forgiveness of a monarch. The accounts are straighforward, chronological renderings of the event, carefully placing this expedition within the grand colonial scheme: "At this time, Pedro de Orsúa [sic] had arrived from Panama, coming by order of the aforementioned viceroy," avers Gonzalo de Zúñiga (Carrillo Espejo 1989, 284), for example.

The novelists of El Dorado need nothing more than an absorbing subject who will offer up his demons, and Aguirre, the self-styled "wrath of God," has those to spare. The early chroniclers, all employing some variant of the epithet "cruel tyrant," had taken up his story and unleashed it into a continent's popular culture. As Latin America attempts to establish its true identity in the twentieth century, "not . . . a social and classist identity, but rather one that is national and legitimate" (Jitrik 1986, 17), this early *caudillo,* widely recognizable, engages novelists for both his political and personal struggles. He is the "gap at the core of the Archive," as González Echevarría says, to which "archival fictions return . . . because it is the very source of fiction" (González Echevarría 1990, 186). The variation in form found in the five novels of El Dorado speaks impressively for the creativity that fiction brings to historical subjects, "the reinterpretation of a rhetoric or of certain rules of practice" (Jitrik 1986, 22).

Let it be said as well that to understand the form of these novels, ranging in composition date from 1947 to 1986, is to trace the development of Latin American fiction from *criollista* days to the full burst of the Boom and beyond. The novels that strain to rescue Aguirre from the opprobrium of history all employ modernist/postmodernist techniques, unlike Uslar Pietri's merely novelized account of the expedition. Abel Posse's *Daimón* (1978) is an absurdist narrative of a Lope who lives far beyond the sixteenth century, illustrating Seymour Menton's view of the new Latin American historical novel as the "conscious distortion of history through omissions, exaggerations, and anachronisms" (Menton 1993, 23). Linda Hutcheon labels such parodic narratives "historiographic metafiction," in which "the process of narrativization has come to be seen as a central form of human comprehension, of imposition of meaning and formal coherence on the chaos of events" (Hutcheon 1988, 121). The form is fanciful—Aguirre frolics at one point with the Queen of the Amazons, Cuñan—but, like *Una lanza por Lope de Aguirre,* the intent of the novel is to establish a dialogue between Lope and the voice of history: in Posse's case, the supposed chronicler of the journey Blas Gutiérrez, in Funes's novel an unnamed, archetypal *cronista.* Otero Silva's *Lope de Aguirre, Príncipe de la libertad* also takes full advantage of art's originality by including dramatized episodes, complete with musical accompaniment, and a final stream of consciousness section, in which a narrative "you" condemns Lope after death in an unpunctuated sending off into hell, while a first-person Lope moans a final lament for his murdered daughter. *Crónica de blasfemos,* perhaps the best of the lot, cares more for a metaphysical understanding of this man so vilified in life and death. True to its modernist composition, the novel allows Estebanillo, the chronicler, to continue narrating even after Lope beheads him, uniting forever the legend and those who would perpetuate it: "now my head hangs from your sword. We will be one: Lope and I" (Álvarez Sáenz 1986, 240).

A final contrastive point in this study of narratives concerns circumstances of composition, the depiction of Lope himself, and each author's intent in writing Lope's story, all matters hinted at earlier, but holding perhaps a tentative final answer in discerning meaningful differences between chronicle and novel. Like all colonial chronicles, first-generation El Dorado accounts were written "on the run," with a pressing story to tell. The novel of Aguirre, written more than four centuries after the events described, gives off no such urgency, other than that shared by all modern Latin American novelists from García Márquez to Tomás Eloy Martínez to speculate on their continent's true history and identity.

As for the figure of Lope that arises from narratives based on his life, the sharpest contrast comes into focus. The chronicles of all three generations present the same picture of Lope: physical characteristics, unfolding of the expedition, behavior of the other soldiers, Lope's letters to his superiors, direct quotations spoken at critical moments. With certain exceptions, the novelists include these same well-reported features, but they do so in order to refute, ridicule, expand, stylize, or transform them: "to develop [historical situations] by means of fiction is to question them at the same time that they are integrated into the imagination as a force that operates in two ways: on the one hand, it allows one to approach [the objective of seeking identity] and, on the other, it provides the formal path to reach [the objective]" (Jitrik 1986, 16). Lope de Aguirre was a conquistador who aroused strong interest in all those around him, those engaged in Spain's conquering mission in the New World, and was chronicled by soldier, priest, historian, and poet in his own time. Bartolomé de las Casas took on the cause of justice for Spain's New World subjects, Bernardino de Sahagún sought to preserve a record of indigenous culture, and Lope's chroniclers meant to hold before King Philip II their scorn for this vicious mutineer. Contemporary Latin

American novelists intend to reinterpret their history by inserting subjects as diverse as the Empress Carlota, the Liberator Simón Bolívar, and the rebel Lope de Aguirre into their countries' discourses of culture and art, attempting always to understand a continent muted by the dominating voices of others.

Notes

1. The largest audience worldwide was probably reached by Werner Herzog's filmic reworking of the tale, *Aguirre; or, the Wrath of God* (1972; *Aguirre, der Zorn Gottes*).
2. *El dorado* may also be read as "the golden *one*."

Bibliography

Álvarez Sáenz, Félix. 1986. *Crónica de blasfemos.* Lima: Editorial Hipatia.

Carrillo Espejo, Francisco. 1989. *Cronistas de las guerras civiles, así como del levantamiento de Manco-Inca y el de Don Lope de Aguirre llamado "la ira de Dios."* Lima: Editorial Horizonte.

Feuchtwanger, Lion. 1963. *The House of Desdemona: Or, the Laurels and Limitations of Historical Fiction.* Detroit: Wayne State University Press.

Fuentes, Carlos. 1990. *Valiente mundo nuevo: Épica, utopía y mito en la novela hispanoamericana.* Mexico: Fondo de Cultura Económica.

González Echevarría, Roberto. 1990. *Myth and Archive: A Theory of Latin American Narrative.* Cambridge: Cambridge University Press.

Hutcheon, Linda. 1988. *A Poetics of Postmodernism: History, Theory, Fiction.* New York: Routledge.

Jitrik, Noé. 1986. "De la historia a la escritura: predominios disimetrías, acuerdos en la novela histórica latinoamericana." In *The Historical Novel in Latin America,* edited by Daniel Balderston, 13–29. Gaithersburg, Md.: Ediciones Hispamérica.

Menton, Seymour. 1993. *Latin America's New Historical Novel.* Austin: University of Texas Press.

Murray, James C. 1994. *Spanish Chronicles of the Indies.* New York: Twayne Publishers.

Pastor Bodmer, Beatriz. 1992. *The Armature of Conquest: Spanish Accounts of the Discovery of America, 1492–1589.* Translated by Lydia Longstreth Hunt. Stanford: Stanford University Press.

Silverberg, Robert. 1996. *The Golden Dream: Seekers of El Dorado.* Athens: Ohio University Press.

Smith, Anthony. 1990. *Explorers of the Amazon.* London: Viking.

Vargas Llosa, Mario. 1997. "Novels Disguised as History." Translated by Myron I. Lichtblau. In *Latin American Essays,* edited by Ilan Stavans, 422–34. New York: Oxford University Press.

Vazquez, Francisco. 1989. *El Dorado: Cronica de la expedicion de Pedro de Ursúa y Lope de Aguirre.* Edited by Javier Ortiz de la Tabla. Madrid: Alianza Editorial.

Part Seven
Parody and the Carnivalization of History

A Fool's Point of View: Parody, Laughter, and the History of the Discovery in *Maluco: La novela de los descubridores* by Napoleón Baccino Ponce de León

MAGDALENA PERKOWSKA-ALVAREZ

> Do you never doubt, Guzmán? Does a Devil never approach you and say, that wasn't how it was, it was not only that way, it could have happened that way but also in a thousand different ways, depending upon who is telling it, depending on who saw it and how he chanced to see it; imagine for an instant, Guzmán what would happen if everyone offered their multiple and contradictory versions of what had happened, and even what had not happened; everyone, I tell you, Lords as well as serfs, the sane and mad, the devout and the heretical, then what would happen, Guzmán?
>
> —Carlos Fuentes, *Terra nostra*

IN THE ESSAY "NIETZSCHE, GENEALOGY, HISTORY," MICHEL FOUCAULT PROposes the idea of knowledge as perspective (Foucault 1984, 90). Given that all power rests upon knowledge, there exists a significant link between power and the locus of enunciation, that is, the social place where the reconstruction of the past originates.[1] Foucault suggests that traditional history establishes a very particular perspective between the historian and the object of his discourse: the perspective of frogs (Foucault 1984, 89). It registers "the noblest periods, the highest forms, the most abstract ideas, the purest individualities" (Foucault 1984, 89), contemplating them from an admiring distance.[2]

This kind of historical perspective is useful to power because through the conversion of the past into a monument, the historian institutionalizes an official version (said to be objective, accurate, and true), one that is supposed to be universal and, therefore, controlled and controlling. To lose control over the perspective means thus to put power at risk. This explains the fear of alternative versions—unknown, unforeseeable, and contradictory—that Carlos Fuentes attributes in his novel *Terra nostra* to King Philip II (epigraph).

In this essay, I propose to examine the restaging of history through laughter in *Five Black Ships: A Novel of the Discoverers* [*Maluco: La novela de los descubridores*] by Napoleón Baccino Ponce de León (Uruguay 1989). The novel rewrites Magellan's circumnavigation of the globe (1519–1522)—one of the most outstanding exploits of the age of discovery—from the perspective of the fleet's buffoon, Juanillo Ponce. The buffoon represents the most disadvantaged classes of Spanish society, those who are subaltern and insignificant; he embodies marginalization condemned to silence. Although Juanillo is a fictional character, he represents a collective historical *personage* that existed but didn't manage to transcend. Through him the novel inscribes into historical space the seafaring community, those men who joined expeditions of discovery as anonymous participants: "Two hundred and more men just like your Highness, not so much *regal* as *real.* Thirsty, hungry, with all their weariness, their dreams, their fears. . . . Pleased to enjoy a good wine, a good woman, a sunny morning or a plateful of food, spiced or not. Fathers, sons, husbands, lovers, solitary bachelors. . . . Seamen, captains, caulkers, boatswains, gunners, coopers, cabin boys, pages and all the rest" (Baccino 1994, 50; emphasis added).

The beginning of the Spanish quotation reads "no tan Reales ni menos reales." In Spanish, *real* means both "royal" and "real." Baccino Ponce de León plays with this double meaning, suggesting that in traditional historiography only those who are "royal' (*Real* with a capital "R," and in the broad sense of the term designating members of high classes) are also "real" because they enter history through writing. For being real only with a lowercase "r," the subaltern classes are situated outside the space where history is made. Their force is apparent through labor, monuments, and accomplishments requiring team effort, but they leave no trace with words. By giving voice to Juanillo, Baccino Ponce de León displaces the focus of dominant versions toward an alternative reality and inscribes the experiences of those who were omitted from the official records.

I. Rewriting History from the Margins

To rewrite history from the margins and to inscribe in its space those who traditionally have been relegated to the sociopolitical and cultural periphery is a complex process. It both challenges official versions and affirms history as a system of legitimization, because those who don't have history need it in order to exist historically. Given that any attack on history would be also a self-annihilation, rewriting from the oppositional stand of the margin has to be an act of negotiation, a play of acceptance and negation, which seeks to recover the past while reformulating at the same time the very discourse constructing it: "The social articulation of difference, from the minority perspective, is a complex on-going negotiation that seeks to authorize cultural hybridities that emerge in moments of historical transformation" (Bhabha 1994, 2).

In *Maluco,* parody is the principal strategy of this challenge to the history that belongs to "the men of deeds and power" (Nietzsche 1983, 67). Linda Hutcheon defines parody as repetition with a difference (Hutcheon 1985, 32). The parodying act involves norms and conventions that become destabilized from within the discourse: "Parody seems to offer a perspective on the present and the past which allows an artist to speak *to* a discourse from *within* (Hutcheon 1988, 35). For this reason, its ideological implications are contradictory: it is both a respectful homage and an irreverent gesture (Hutcheon 1985, 33). This ideological ambivalence makes parody one of the most efficient strategies for rewriting history from the margins: it both installs an accepted convention or version of the past and subverts it.

Baccino's novel is a parodic rewriting of chronicles and accounts of discovery, a perfect example of parody as "repetition with a difference."[3] Walter Mignolo affirms that the accounts of the conquest were written to inform the crown of the advances of the Spanish venture on new lands (1982). The discourse of chronicles, diaries, records, and histories is determined by their principal addressee, the king, who embodies the empire and its power: the chronicle is for him. These accounts present the voyages of discovery from an official perspective that commemorates the historical importance of the events and, frequently, monumentalizes the past, describing its highest achievements and greatest individualities, considered to be elevated enough to figure in history.[4] In *Maluco,* the narrator resorts to the official versions of the chronicles of discovery and repeats their objective of informing the king about the fate of the expedition, but he also constantly redefines their discourse, their way of producing history from shreds left by the past. By adopting a different perspective—the shortened vision characteristic of "effective history" (Foucault 1984, 89)—the novel parodies this centripetal version of History, written from and toward the center of power, and inscribes the standpoint of an anonymous and (in)significant participant, who devaluates what history values and enhances its untold and unofficial aspects. But the buffoon rewrites history without destroying it, because the annihilation of historicity would make impossible any inscription of new agencies.

Hutcheon explains that the differentiated and differentiating repetition of parody is carried out by means of a critical distance, which frequently expresses itself through irony (Hutcheon 1985, 32). In her most recent study on irony as a rhetorical trope and a way of seeing the world, Hutcheon remarks that irony—with its emphasis on the context, perspective, and the instability of meaning—embodies the actual (postmodern) condition of knowledge (Hutcheon 1994, 31). However, its destabilizing potential, which deconstructs and decenters dominant discourses, proves to be particularly useful as a political strategy: "[T]he last few decades have seen many claims made for irony as a most appropriate mode not only for those in political opposition but, more generally, for those with the 'divided allegiance' . . . that comes from their difference from the dominant norms of race, ethnicity, gender or sexual choice" (Hutcheon 1994, 31).

Irony is a critical strategy that recodifies and repositions the meanings at the foundation of the social construction of reality. Its main mechanisms—double optics, humor, stress on context and perspective—destabilize and subvert; through them, any assumption of a univocal truth or authoritarian and dogmatic representation of the past is deprived of the reassuring stability of universals and, therefore, undermined. The unsteadiness of irony permeates *Maluco,* legitimizing a new discursive space: a contested space of history written by a buffoon, history as buffoonery.

Central to this parodic restaging is the narrator and protagonist of the novel, who writes a personal account of the expedition, totally dominated by his perspective and voice. His story is an example of an account overtly controlled by the narrator, identified by Hutcheon as one of the narrative modes privileged by historiographic metafiction (Hutcheon 1988, 117). The narrative "I" signals a personal, autobiographical discourse (although, in *Maluco,* its is a fictional autobiography). This inscription of subjectivity into history challenges the principle of the third-person impersonal account that, according to Emile Benveniste, characterizes and determines historical discourse: "We shall define historical narration as the mode of utterance that excludes every autobiographical linguistic form. The historian will never say *je* or *tu* or *maintenant,* because he will never make use of the formal apparatus of discourse, which resides primarily in the relationship of the persons *je* : *tu.* Hence we shall find only the forms of the third person in a historical narrative strictly followed" (Benveniste 1971, 206–7).[5]

The third-person voice "feigns to make the world speak itself" (White 1987, 2); it masks the presence of a speaking subject and insinuates that the events tell themselves (Benveniste 1971, 207). This dissimulation seeks to produce the effect of history being an objective, neutral, transparent, and impersonal representation of reality, devoid of passions, preferences, subjective evaluations, and discursive distortions. The subjectivity of the first-person narrative signals an agent behind any utterance and reveals that the objectivity of historical discourse is only an illusion or a mask: every enunciation is determined by an "I" who selects, analyzes, organizes, and interprets the facts and data, constructing a textual reality. In *Maluco,* the first-person representation localizes the perspective shaping the enunciation in the subjectivity of the narrator and protagonist of the novel:

> For them [our chroniclers] it's as simple as cooking a stew, once they have prepared its four or five ingredients. But what do they know, Sire, of how each of us really *felt* as we lived through the four or five historic events they base their accounts on? I would say that *the truth lies in the feelings which those of us who took part in the expedition experienced,* and which no one else can know, not even your Majesty. Nor can you find this truth anywhere else: it is useless to search for it in archives or libraries; nothing of it is there. (Baccino 1994, 64; emphasis added)

An important issue here is that Juanillo's subjective point of view on history is determined by his social status, which is marginal, and by the position and function he has in the world reconstructed in his story.

II. Dialogical Gaze

From the standpoint of traditional historiography, Juanillo does not belong to History. Son of a prostitute, he is ignorant of the identity of his father and is, therefore, a being without origin and without filiation. He is also very poor: Juanillo considers himself "less than a hen" (Baccino 1994, 163) and remembers having seen his little sister die from hunger and exposure. His own life is constantly at risk from these threats and he enlists in the expedition to Maluco to escape them. However, it is not only that Juanillo belongs to the bottom of the socioeconomic hierarchy; his marginalization is intensified by his physical appearance and his religious status. He is both a deformed dwarf and a convert from Judaism, associated thus with groups that attract suspicion and disdain by the traditional Christian society of Spain (*cristianos viejos*).

Juanillo's social otherness determines his vision of history, which is displaced with respect to the dominant view, peripheral with regard to the center. This dislocation is articulated in two different ways. First, as a "banal subject" (Balandier 1983, 8) submerged in ordinary life, Juanillo stresses everyday experiences. He substitutes microhistorical space for the macrohistorical visions of learned historians, observes with a magnifying glass the reality surrounding him, recovers details discarded by history as insignificant, and privileges lived experiences over institutionalized knowledge. The second displacement is directly linked to the first one. George Balandier observes that an everyday life perspective is always transgressive: "Daily life can become the territory where the individual, and the small groups with which he associates, stage their debate or confrontation with global society. It is in this way that the old expression daily struggle makes sense. Daily life appears . . . as the means of *dissidence* . . . or as the creative *alternative* to experimental enclaves within the very heart of great society. On a higher level, it sets up a place for *resistance* . . . because it creates obstacles for totalitarian behavior; conditioning and domination of power stopping partially at its borders" (Balandier 1983, 12).

The otherness embodied by Juanillo activates an alternative optics, another way of seeing and perceiving reality. The novel illustrates symbolically the social place where Juanillo's perspective originates, as well as his own consciousness of how important this displacement is, in a scene depicting the trial of traitorous captains, which Juanillo witnesses hidden under a table:

> Tell me, O August Majesty, have you ever been under a table observing the feet of those present while you follow their conversation? No? Well then, more's the pity, because it is no good thing for a prince to see the world only from his throne. . . . Underneath a table you see things differently. You can see how nervous some feet are, the way a leg moves here, a pair of knees bobs up and down there, or spot a hand's furtive gesture. You can judge the sound of words without the risk of being taken in by the speakers's face, and you will learn much more about men and the affairs of state than from all speeches, all the scandals you see or hear from high on your platform of purple velvet. Take the word of someone who has spied on life from every corner; what little knowledge I have has always been through a keyhole, concealed behind a chair, or underneath a table. (Baccino 1994, 135)

Two perspectives challenge each other in this quotation: the dominant and the marginal. The buffoon's displaced gaze discovers things veiled to the dominant perspective and defamiliarizes what the latter perceives as familiar and conventional. In another place, Baccino uses the metaphor of the forest to describe the narrator's positionality: "I understand nothing of these great things: great ambitions, great dreams, great loves. None of that is for the likes of me, who cannot see the forest for the trees" (Baccino 1994, 117). In *Maluco,* the narrator's position at the bottom, literally and symbolically at the feet of his superiors gives origin to his peripheral perspective, which participates in what Homi Bhabha calls the "restaging" of the past (Bhabha 1994, 2): he reinvents received and accepted traditions by rewriting history in terms alien to illustrious projects.

However, Juanillo's optics on history is not only displaced but also actively displaces itself. Its mobility stems from the ambivalence of a buffoon's position. On the one hand, as one of the seafaring rabble, he belongs to the social margin; on the other, he has access to the space, both public and private, restricted to those in power. His profession, as well as his apparent naivete, ignorance, and lack of worldly experiences, free him from distrust or suspicion: "[A] jester is like a hired friend. People can console and unburden themselves knowing there won't be any consequences, because nobody takes a fool serious, do they? They can tell us things they wouldn't tell their closer friends, and treat us in a way they wouldn't dare treat their worst enemies" (Baccino 1994, 228).

The buffoon's position may be compared with that of a rogue, adventurer, parvenu, servant, prostitute, or courtesan, characters studied by Bakhtin in *The Dialogic Imagination.* Bakhtin points out that the position of such characters is very well suited to uncover all layers and levels of human life and behavior; with regard to private life, all of them occupy the "third-person" position of external observer (1981, 126). They do not share directly the private space of the others (who are, in most cases, members of the well-to-do classes), nor do they occupy in it any definite fixed place. Despite these apparent limitations, their position is very convenient for spying and eavesdropping (Bakhtin 1981, 124–27). For novelists, the use of this "included outsider" is a means of textual subversion, allowing for a recodification of the discourse of power through the perspective of the powerless.

Among ordinary crew members, Juanillo is the only one allowed to enter Magellan's cabin, wander around the ship, listen to conversations between both captains and ordinary sailors. He moves freely between the two spaces of historical reality—the public and the private of the famous navigator, the heroic and the humble of the expedition—without being firmly identified with any of them. Homi Bhabha would describe Juanillo as "a subject that inhabits the rim of an 'in-between' reality" for whom the "private and public, past and present, the psyche and the social develop an interstitial intimacy. It is an intimacy that questions binary divisions through which such spheres of social experience are often spatially opposed" (1990, 13). Juanillo's interstitial position indelibly marks his account. His marginality and transitoriness between several social spaces produce a dialogical perspective that defies the monumental and monological vision of official accounts, and reorganizes historical space. The buffoon's gaze moves between the public and the private, the grandiose and the ordinary, the significant and the trivial, the positive and the negative, the central and the peripheral, between transcendent projects and personal experiences. He acts as a translator of these spaces, who rearticulates them in his own discourse, creating a hybrid and dialogical reality: "now . . . in my old age . . . I made up my mind that before I died I would acquaint your Majesty with the many *wonders and hardships* we saw and suffered throughout that journey, the *great amount of pain and hunger* we had to endure, as well as *the myriad marvels and joys* we experienced" (Baccino 1994, 4; emphasis added).

This quote reveals one of the fundamental strategies used by the narrator in *Maluco:* each element of what used to be presented as a dichotomy shares something of its opposite and is rearticulated through contact with its signifying zone. "Hardships," "sufferings" and "hunger" are juxtaposed with "wonders," "marvels" and "joys," modifying each other, creating new (or different) shadows, erasing fixed oppositions and/or definite boundaries.

According to official chronicles, the principal achievement of Magellan's expedition was the discovery of the strait, which opened to the Spanish crown the route to the spice islands. In his chronicle, Juanillo reports this event without playing down its importance but, at the same time, he expands on it with other descriptions of elements that he, as an anonymous participant and discoverer, considers outstanding:

> There, at the farthest reaches of the ship, hidden by the hull's bulge from the boatswain's eyes, I was able to discover many aspects of our adventure that have escaped the other royal chroniclers, who have arrogantly disregarded the explorer's true task. Take the different kinds of seaweed, for example. Some of them were like lettuces but of a deeper green, dark and soft like moss . . . , like scraps of leather sticky to the touch; still others resembled deer antlers, or fragments of red coral, or oak leaves in autumn, or the down of women's pubises, or angels, roses, feathers. (Baccino 1994, 84)

The reader discovers on the pages of Juanillo's story meticulous descriptions of the jungle, the coast seen from the ships skirting it, land and marine animals and plants, colors of the bottom of the sea, fishes, bird nests, and the tumultuous currents of the river that years later would be called *de la Plata*. He connects events and details considered noteworthy by historiographical tradition with those that would be dismissed as insignificant. He places them at the same level—that of the discovered reality—to rearticulate each other in the buffoon's account. This blurring of boundaries between the important and the petty produces what Carmen Bustillo calls "the revitalizing drive of images" (Bustillo 1994, 301): glorious reality is pushed into the background and devaluated, while the trivial one is revaluated through the acquisition of new meanings and nuances.

This re-imag(in)ing also affects the vision of historical figures, especially that of Magellan. The legendary head of the expedition that achieved the impossible is demystified and humanized in the buffoon's account. The paragraphs elaborating upon the Portuguese sailor clearly establish how wandering between several spaces opens to Juanillo perspectives veiled to those who have never crossed the borders of their own social and cultural space. When Juanillo temporarily forgets his double status and thinks of himself as a simple member of the crew, he perceives the public image of Magellan, the man-god, chosen by destiny to carry out extraordinary deeds and exploits: "At their head, proud against the white sky, came Don Fernando, a truly godlike figure. His clashing armor, the green velvet cape around his shoulders, the mighty haunches of his steed, all gave him an inhuman, supernatural air" (Baccino 1994, 16).

Throughout his account, Juanillo observes that Magellan always wears his armor for fear of treason. This pragmatic behavior is also symbolic. The armor hides from view what is the most vulnerable and human in the captain: his body. Covered by shining metal, Magellan is no longer a mortal, perishable being, exposed to pain, fatigue, and sickness; in other words, he is dehumanized. In armor, his figure grows larger and nobler, his presence becomes imposing, and in the sailors' eyes, he must be like a god who holds the reins of their lives.[6]

Nevertheless, as buffoon, Juanillo also has access to the hero's private space, and during their encounters in the captain's cabin he witnesses a metamorphosis that transforms the god into a man: "I remained silent. . . . I knew that sooner or later he would crawl out of his suit of armor like a caterpillar out of its chrysalis, and turn into a gaudy butterfly as he fluttered among his memories and my inventions. It had happened before when the two of us were alone in his cabin" (Baccino 1994, 109).

The armor, in its literal and figurative meaning, conceals a human being like all others, with desires, dreams, fears, joys, and sufferings. Juanillo, who knows the complexity of Magellan's public and private space, notices that his master's identity is a gray zone of unanswered questions, where nothing is fixed or coherent. "Which of the two are you really?" (Baccino 1994, 117) he asks, confused, without finding a satisfactory answer. The text underlines this indeterminacy with a blank space following Juanillo's question. Human beings, great and small, are blank spaces where circumstances print different signs—at times contradictory and irreconcilable.

The displacement of the perspective also activates a dialogue between history as a transcendent project and history as a personal experience. The narrator draws attention to this dichotomy, comparing his own account with the one proposed by official chronicles. In the latter, the chroniclers highlight the event, the deed, emphasizing as well the straightforward rapport of cause and effect. By contrast, Juanillo is attracted by interstices, "in-between" spaces, by what happens *between* the cause and the effect, and, above all, by the numerous bifurcations of reality. For instance, making reference to the stillness that immobilized the fleet in the Pacific for three months, the narrator complains that royal chroniclers "deal with this part of the journey, which is taking [me] so many pages, in a couple of paragraphs" (Baccino 1994, 221), and asks ironically: "Wouldn't it have been enough simply to say that we were becalmed for several months, that our food ran out completely and we all nearly starved, then take up the story again from the point when the winds returned and we continued on with our journey? Why all this beating around the bush?" (Baccino 1994, 221–22).

For Juanillo, this *detour* is crucial, because he perceives the crossing of the Pacific in two dimensions that complement each other: the (historical) deed and the (personal) experience. This is why he insists on experience:

hunger, illnesses, fears, strategies of survival, the relentless calm of the water shining like a mirror, and the smell of putrefaction and death. In his account, all these details recontextualize and play ironically with the meaning of the word *deed.*

On the discursive level, this problematization of the binary opposition *history (deed) / (hi)story (experience)* is clearly articulated by the narrator's preference for the present tense. It signals a difference in respect to the historiographic convention privileging the past tense as the mode of enunciation: "The historical utterance admits of three tenses: the aorist (= the simple past, or past definite), the imperfect (which also includes the form in *-rait* called the conditional), and the pluperfect. Secondarily, and in a limited way, there is a periphrastic substitute for the future, which we shall call the *prospective. The present is excluded*" (Benveniste 1971, 239; emphasis added).

The past tense connotes wholeness, semantic stability, and a conclusive and immutable reality; it conceals gaps and dispels doubts; it presents events as unequivocal and irrefutable facts.[7] Conversely, the verb in the present tense does not impose limits (Barthes calls it a "word without limits"); it opens the world to new insights and transformations, establishing a semantically unstable universe, a transitory reality that is in the process of becoming, without beginning or end. The use of the present tense in *Maluco* reevaluates history in terms of immediacy; events and experiences are inconclusive and open-ended, and their ultimate meaning always eludes its participants.

In order to stress the immediacy of experience articulated through the present tense as the time of narration, Baccino Ponce de León also exploits the narrative tempo that establishes the link between the time of the experience (the time as perceived by the characters; the time of the recounted events) and the time of narration, which is that of the enunciation.[8] Occasionally, the action slows down, becomes lethargic; at other moments, it accelerates vertiginously. This play with temporal dynamics is best illustrated in the description of the long crossing of the Pacific. The fleet is trapped for three months in the calm waters of the ocean; for three long months nothing happens. The narrator reconstructs this situation through long sentences, accumulation of descriptive adjectives and, above all, repetitions. For instance, the phrase "It is that we talked a lot" [*Es que hablábamos mucho*] appears time and again throughout chapter seven. By contrast, when after three months the winds pick up, the narration accelerates, the phrasing becomes brief and quick, and is dominated by nouns and verbs: "His Majesty opens his eyes. . . . What his Highness sees is something else. He sees the *Trinidad,* busy as a smashed anthill. Rearing like a colt. Sails suddenly bloom from every mast. Sails whose shapes had almost been forgotten" (Baccino 1994, 245).[9] The narrative tempo varies throughout the novel, because not all moments of the venture are experienced in the same way. The reconstruction of Magellan's voyage of discovery in experiential terms contests the conventions of the historical chronicle, which places an emphasis on "the thrill of action" (Baccino 1994, 202).

As a narrator, Juanillo is very much aware that through the imposition of narrative norms that make transparent what in reality is opaque and blurred, every act of writing betrays and impoverishes experience. Moreover, he knows that the story also betrays the act of writing, eliminating the narrator's world, the context of enunciation that surrounds and conditions him:

> [W]hat do you know of the real story behind that page? How do you know whether, just as Don Fernando was about to . . . the chronicler perhaps had to break off because he was told his mother had died, or because he was shivering with cold . . . ? That is why, your Highness, I am often disgusted by the flow of my narrative. I am ashamed to think that the peace and protection its continuity offers you is achieved by my hiding my wounds, disappearing behind the mask of words, the faces of my characters, the invented pains of those phantasmagoric creatures who steal through these pages which either delight or bore you. (Baccino 1994, 223)

In order to incorporate experience into the writing of history, to write it as history or (his)story, Juanillo subverts the temporal axes of his account, inscribing in it the moment of enunciation: his old age and fatigue, as well as his disillusionment with history, which forgets Juanillo as soon as he is no longer needed. In this way, the novel combines two histories and two experiences: the expedition to Maluco and the enterprise of recounting it.

III. History and Humor

Further reexamination of the chronicles' discourse is due to the narrator's positionality and his function in the world he describes. Juanillo was hired as a buffoon and a buffoon is one who laughs and makes others laugh. As a narrator of a historical account, Juanillo laughs and makes us laugh at history. One of the principal strategies of the reevaluation of historical discourses in his story is the laughter that originates in the displaced social perspective. As Bakhtin states in *Rabelais and His World,* history, as well as other socially and politically significant discourses, cannot be comical: "Laughter is not a universal, philosophical form. It can refer only to individual and individually typical phenomena of social life. That which is important and essential cannot be comical. Neither can history and persons representing it—kings, generals, heroes—be shown in a comic aspect. The sphere of the comic is narrow and specific (private and social voices); the essential truth about the world and about man cannot be told in the language of laughter" (Bakhtin 1984, 67).

More than just a tone, seriousness is a perspective on the world. Solemnity eliminates ambivalence and stabilizes meaning, reducing semantic ambivalence to a single, stable, and closed meaning. According to Bakhtin, a serious word is unequivocal, it doesn't produce truths but *the* truth, protecting therefore established order and dominant ideology, blocking change and renovation (Bakhtin 1984, 67–81). This is why official discourses, originating in and oriented toward power, privilege genres from which laughter has been banned. Historiography and all its subgenres belong to this "serious" category.

Fear of laughter comes from its "therapeutic power," which liberates, heals, and regenerates (Bakhtin 1984, 67, 70). Valuing a particular point of view, comicality destabilizes fixed meanings; it changes the relationship between the subject, its discourse, and its object, causing a reorganization of perspectives. To permeate history with laughter is thus a way of subverting the official or traditional (in the sense given by Hobsbawm in 1983, 12) version of the past. Through its "therapeutic power," laughter defamiliarizes what convention presents as normal and familiar. In other words, laughter *alters* reality, opening the discourse to otherness. These characteristics make laughter and comicality the essential elements of the parodic rewriting of the official history of the discovery in *Maluco.*[10]

Juanillo's story is marked by irony, jokes, mockery, and sarcasm that challenge the meaning of both the events described and the Western values and concepts in which they are grounded, such as King, Empire, Civilization, Culture, God. The protagonist perceives these concepts with a naiveté that is only apparent. Beneath the mask of a fool lies a shrewdness that constantly undermines the ideological and cultural presumptions of the West. For example, the buffoon's common sense easily recognizes the meaninglessness and arrogance of the dominant (European) theories of world geography, in particular, Columbus's idea of earthly paradise. Juanillo exposes the absurdity of the admiral's theory by contrasting it with his own knowledge of reality and, above all, with his critical judgment sharpened through immersion in daily life:

> [T]he great Admiral Colón had a different theory about Paradise. . . . [A]ccording to that illustrious explorer, the world is shaped like a woman's breast, with the nipple pointing upward, closest to the sky. Which is why, that fearless sailor wrote, "ships rise gently toward the sky, and we enjoy a feeling of gentle temperance," with the result that he imagined Paradise to be on that "sweet nipple." What I cannot tell you is whether the great Admiral meant his mother's breast or mine. I think it must have been his mother's, because if Paradise were part of my

> mother's scrawny teat, it would have little bounty to offer. (Baccino 1994, 77)

This fragment suggests a parallel between Juanillo's discourse and the way in which Sancho Panza recodifies Don Quixote's chivalric universe. Both Columbus and Don Quixote create a vision of the world based on a cultural (religious or literary) ideal. The displaced gaze—prosaic, popular, trivial, and naive—of *low* characters such as Juanillo and Sancho Panza *translates* this vision, activates a reevaluation of perspectives. The above quote (indeed, the entire novel) illustrates "the process through which the low troubles the high" (Stallybrass and White 1986, 3), creating a comical and therefore more flexible vision of the world.

The buffoon's laughter also reexamines the discovery as a political and cultural project. The dominant discourse, what Michel de Certeau calls "conquering writing" (Certeau 1975, 3), constructed an essentialized and simplified vision of the reality and inhabitants of the American continent. Special significance was given to indigenous customs—the practices of the body, such as nakedness, sexuality, or anthropophagy—and to the "primitive" nature of the indigenous peoples' souls. Emphasis on these aspects represented America as a "deformed or monstrous creature" (O'Gorman 1972, 134) to be civilized by means of domination. The Christianizing and civilizing mission that constituted the ideological basis of the conquest is constantly challenged in *Maluco.* Combining wits with his experience as a convert, Juanillo undermines this colonizing project. His chronicle derides the objectives, methods, and results of the colonizers' missionary endeavors:

> [O]n more than one occasion I heard Sánchez de la Reina's reedy voice, together with the booming tones of Chaplain Balderrama, outlining the principles of our Christian faith to an invisible congregation. . . . Both of them mentioned Sodom and Gomorrah, the seven plagues of Egypt, and many other disasters illustrating how God behaves toward anyone who rebels against His command. So convincing were they that as I lay on my trestle in the shadow of the ship's hull I began to work even harder, lest any slackness on my part should draw down God's wrath on my head. If their sermons were in fact directed at the women who were supposedly hidden in the hold, those unfortunate creatures must have been delighted by the plain, straightforward way in which the priests explained such things as the Holy Trinity, Reincarnation, the Ascension and other similar trifles. They also warned them about Hell, doubtless showing them pictures like the ones I was shown when I was converted. I can see the images to this day. (Baccino 1994, 86–87)

The buffoon doesn't limit himself to verbal irony. With an irreverent gesture he parodies the Spanish custom of baptizing and giving Christian names to every human being and land encountered. Juanillo emulates the conventional solemnity of the act, but recontextualizes it radically, because his "neophytes" are not humans but animals:

> That afternoon, in a simple but moving ceremony, I baptized my monkeys with Christian names. It was shortly before the angelus, and I was back on board the Trinidad, I took advantage of the chaplain's absence to borrow his habit. I donned the amice, the alb, and even put on the spare chasuble he kept in a trunk, then went out onto the gangway to offer the sacrament to my animals. . . . I had two crows . . . whom I decided to name Fonseca and Cristobão. I called a pair of buzzards I had brought with me the Hapsburgs. . . . I also had a talkative, hysterical parakeet which I christened Juanita la Loca, and an elegant yellow and blue parrot I called Isabelita. (Baccino 1994, 89)

Naming reconstructs reality; the discoverers and colonizers were well aware of it when they appropriated lands through naming. Juanillo imitates these acts, deforming them through mockery. Bakhtin observes that laughter defamiliarizes by making contiguous what normally is not associated together and by distancing realities that used to be perceived as related (Bakhtin 1981, 237). Baptism administrated to animals produces a hybrid world where distant realities—exotic animals and distinguished figures from Spanish history—coexist. The effect of this defamiliarization is double: on one hand, it degrades the image of the dominant class; on the other, it exposes and ridicules the Western practice of appropriation through naming.

The idea of discovery itself changes when it is presented from the perspective of this buffoon-discoverer. For him, it is not an illustrious project or a heroic deed: at times, Juanillo even doubts the political and missionary aims of the expedition. He portrays it as a culinary enterprise; they left Spain to find and supply spices that would enhance the flavors on the imperial table: "who were we with our ridiculous dreams and childish fears but puppets on invisible strings, governed by the whims of a few crazy men seeking to please their rich masters so that these latter could have pepper on their tables to add savor to their meat, and cloves and cinnamon to spice their wine" (Baccino 1994, 15).

It is also noteworthy that Juanillo constantly insists upon the expedition being an act of madness. The very title of the novel is a wordplay on the Spanish name of Magellan's destination—Islas Molucas—and its fictional name—Maluco—which in Portuguese (Magellan's native language) means *crazy* or *mad*. The narrator underscores his perception of the expedition, resorting to these last two words and their derivatives for its description. Every person involved in the enterprise was infected by a collective madness:

> We were mad, yes, just as Ruy Faleiro and our Captain General, Don Fernando, had always been, just as you youself were, your Imperial Maj-

esty, and the high officials at the Colonies' Office, and Bishop Fonseca, and Don Cristobão de Haro, who financed the expedition. Mad like the women who sewed the sails with loving fingers, the smiths who forged the bronze of all our fittings, the carpenters who shaped our masts while neighbors looked on in awe and children frolicked around them. (Baccino 1994, 11)

The members of the crew were "wandering madmen," "crazed ants," or "little madmen." Sometimes they behaved as "a handful of madwomen very excited by something" (Baccino 1994, 187); at other times, "boredom and madness crowded round [them] like a pack of hounds" (Baccino 1994, 150). In Juanillo's story the expedition is presented as "a fateful voyage round the entire world" (Baccino 1994, 4), "a mad project" elaborated by a man who went insane (Baccino 1994, 25). The strait now is named after Magellan is described as "an absurd sight" that "seems to have been created by the imagination of a crazy god" (Baccino 1994, 192, 193).

An intertextual reference to *Don Quixote* intensifies this encoding of the enterprise in terms of madness. For reasons of chronological verisimilitude, in *Maluco* there are no direct allusions to Cervantes's novel, published many years after Magellan's voyage. Nevertheless, Juanillo mentions a boy whose name was Alonso Quijana and who lived in the parish of the fleet priest, Sánchez Reina (Baccino 1994, 102). Other intertextual links between the two novels also deserve the readers' attention: like Don Quixote, Magellan almost never takes off his armor; and like Don Quixote, who promises Sancho a county for his services, Magellan promises Juanillo the title of the Count of Maluco (Baccino 1994, 51). This intertextuality underscores the novel's parodic restaging of Magellan's voyage as a quixotic enterprise. By rewriting the expedition as an act of madness, Baccino Ponce de León demythifies and desublimates the events of discovery. At the same time, he questions the rationality of history, which no longer is to be perceived as a conscious project but as an irrational force that sweeps away all human beings without any preference for their social condition. It should also be noticed that through this intertextual reference to *Don Quixote* (as well as to other major works of Spanish literature, for example, *The Poem of the Cid*, [Baccino 1994, 25–27], the narrator draws a parallel in his text between literature and history, and thus blurs the division between the two: Juanillo inserts a fictive character into the course of history, and by doing so, he also inserts history into his own fiction.

The buffoon's laughter does not spare anyone, not even the addressee of his story, King Carlos V. The entire chronicle is a long epistle addressed to the king, but Juanillo interrupts its flow frequently to interpellate the aging monarch through temerarious and irreverent digressions, characteristic of the carnivalesque spirit defined by Bakhtin as "[a] temporary liberation from the prevailing truth and from the established order; . . . the suspension of all hierarchical rank, privileges, norms, and prohibitions; . . . the true feast of time, the feast of becoming, change and renewal . . . hostile to all that was immortalized and completed" (Bakhtin 1984, 10).

The principal feature of carnival in Juanillo's apostrophes is the grotesque, which degrades and materializes, destroying the aura surrounding the king. For Stallybrass and White, grotesque realism represents "transcodings and displacements effected between the high/low image of the physical body and other social domains" (Stallybrass and White 1986, 9) and results in an inversion of the hierarchies: popular culture rewrites high culture, producing an inverted perspective (Stallybrass and White 1986, 4). One of the most important emblems of high culture is what Stallybrass and White designate, following Bakhtin's terminology, as the *classical body:* an aesthetic form inherent in high official culture, universal and transcendent; elevated, static, and monumental; closed and distanced from the social milieu. The disrespectful creativity of carnival rewrites this classical body, merging its features with those of a *grotesque body* that is multiple, protuberant, decentered, impure, and never closed off from social-cultural reality.

This reevaluation of high culture through the prism of low culture is a salient characteristic of Baccino's rewriting of the age of discovery in *Maluco.* In his digressions, Juanillo is curious about whether the royal body of Carlos V is like that of the common people, namely, if it is a physiological body:

> I have even wondered whether kings do in fact shit—if you, in all your majesty, go and squat over a bucket and strain like the rest of us, if you take off your layers of ermine, silks and velvets with your own hands or whether a pageboy has that task and the added honor of wiping the royal ass. Is there a special place reserved for these functions among all the gold and perfumes of your palaces? I am truly confused about this, because it seems to me that with all you swallow, guzzle, gnaw and consume—and always the best and largest portions—it would make no sense for you to do only the eating and the rest of us to do all the shitting. (Baccino 1994, 107)

> [Y]ou were born in pomp and splendor, and I would wager that you did not even come into the world all sticky and dirty as we mere mortals did, but were spotless and proud even then. And that you did not wail when air of this world first entered your lungs but instead gave your first order. (Baccino 1994, 174)

The juxtaposition of royal space—pristine, pure, noble, and static—with the physiological functions of the body undoes the binary structure that used to fix, in social terms, the high and the low, the official and the popular, and produces a hybrid reality, heterogeneous and unstable.

Language is one of the buffoon's principal means of creating this dislocated reality. Bakhtin observes that one of the most important sources of laughter in Rabelais's work is the unofficial side of speech: indecencies, words concerning drinking, sex, defecation, and other physiological functions of the body, but also the language used by the underworld of cities and villages. Rabelais used the unofficial speech to create a specific point of view on the world and a linguistic system that differed considerably from the official one (Bakhtin 1984, 238). Not surprisingly then, indecencies, jokes, puns, sayings, and erotic stories are a source of laughter and a strategy of displacement in *Maluco.* For instance, his apostrophes to the king, as well as the totality of the narrative, are replete with indecent, obscene, and crude language; his jokes almost always reveal a double entendre with strong sexual connotations. Important here is that the narrator applies this unofficial speech to the dominant space that used to distance itself from the reality designated by this very language: body, popular culture, and everyday life. A combination of words like *to shit, ass, buttocks,* and *tit,* with others such as *king, empire, captain, prince, order,* and *palace,* results in a transgressive incongruence that impregnates the discourse to undermine any system of fixed meaning. Colloquialisms with which Juanillo permeates his account materialize that which does not seem to have or be a body, and challenge ideological constructions created by the dominant classes as the principal mechanism of control over discourse.

Royal space, which may be interpreted as a dematerialized reality, is one of these constructions. In *Bodies That Matter,* Judith Butler speaks of the "figuration of masculine reason as disembodied body" (Butler 1993, 49). The author suggests that as an embodiment of instrumental reason (and therefore of power), man is represented as a figure without a body: without childhood, without the necessity to eat, defecate, live, and die. By contrast, women, children, slaves, and other subaltern subjects used to "perform the bodily functions" (Butler 1993, 49). This strategy symbolizes the opposition between the rationality of power (center) and the materiality of the margins. The dematerialization of the spaces of power is a means of their sublimation, which, according to Stallybrass and White, is "the main mechanism whereby a group or class or individual bids for symbolic superiority over others; sublimation is inseparable from strategies of cultural domination" (Stallybrass and White 1986, 197). By merging the sublime with the grotesque and by rewriting the monarch in physiological terms, Juanillo rematerializes royal space and troubles the abstract and symbolic image of power.

However, this reinterpretation of royal space is also a reflection on decadence.[11] Juanillo's story depicts for the reader the monarch's degenerated and old body, a dying man, sleepy and drowsy, drooling, and suffering from all sorts of ailments: "Wrinkled, sallow skin. Toothless mouth. Twitching lips. A trail of spittle escaping from the right-hand corner of his mouth and dribbling into his white-flecked beard" (Baccino 1994, 284).

> He slowly crosses the room draped for mourning. . . . Until finally he reaches his seat. There he pauses once more. He climbs awkwardly into it, like a child, his twisted, rheumatic fingers clutching the black velvet curtain behind it. His cane falls from his grasp. He supports himself against the chair back, and finally manages to settle into it. Sitting on the pile of cushions under the black curtain, he looks like the portrait of a newborn baby. One of those frail princes whose life drains away in the cradle. (Baccino 1994, 244)

At times, Juanillo's laughter becomes cruel, because he feels very little compassion for his monarch, destroyed by blindness, gout, and a general weakening of the body; his enumeration of royal ailments reveals satisfaction or even morbid pleasure. María Eugenia Mudrovcic observes that the emphasis on the physical decline of national heroes "changes the relationship between body/idea institutionalized by dominant historical discourse" (Mudrovcic 1993, 454). In these contemporary reworkings, prominent figures from national pantheons no longer die for an *idea,* but they battle the corruption of their own *body.*

Thus, this physical "phantasmalization" is also symbolic. In *Maluco,* the decomposition not only rots the body of Carlos V but also invades royal space: his family, his palace, his court, and, finally, the whole empire. The moral and physical decline of the monarch equals the nation's decadence. Through an irreverent image of the dying emperor, the buffoon articulates his mocking attitude toward the country that hoped to be the standard-bearer of civilization. Both Carlos V and his metropolitan space are demythified. History (with a capital H) becomes vulnerable, stripped of the ethereal quality and heroic value that make it an instrument of power and domination.

The buffoon's laughter, at times light, at others sarcastic and accusing, is an irreverent gesture (a *jest-ure*) that undermines the rigid skeleton of historical discourse, a means of de- and re-codification of signs inscribed in history. Bakhtin shows that laughter introduces "a critique on the one-sided seriousness of the lofty word, the corrective of reality that is always richer, more fundamental and most importantly *too contradictory and heteroglot* to be fit into a high and straightforward genre" (Bakhtin 1981, 55). In *Maluco,* Juanillo's humor *corrects* official chronicles, creates new shades, destroys conventions that define what is significant or insignificant in History, and proposes a plural, inclusive, and more flexible vision of the past.

With good reason then, the fictional Philip II in Carlos Fuentes's *Terra nostra*—and probably the historical figure as well—so feared the "multiple and contradictory versions of what happened" (Fuentes 1976, 188). Juanillo's account in *Maluco* by Napoleón Baccino Ponce de León attacks the official version of the history of the "discovery," transforming it into a laughable space, a buffoonery. This strategy of degradation, as Stallybrass and White would suggest, humiliates and mortifies historical discourse, but at the same time, revives and renews it.

Notes

1. A similar complicity between the construction of reality through writing and dominant structures is the object of Angel Rama's reflections on the relationship between the *lettered city* and power in *La ciudad letrada.*

2. What Foucault refers to as the perspective of frogs is reminiscent of Walter Benjamin's notion of *aura,* which similarly implies distance and veneration.

3. Since the 1970s, the rewriting of the discovery has been a notable tendency of the Latin American historical novel. *Terra nostra* by Carlos Fuentes (1975), *El arpa y la sombra* by Alejo Carpentier (1979), *El mar de las lentejas* by Antonio Benítez Rojo (1979), *Lope de Aguirre, príncipe de la libertad* by Miguel Otero Silva (1979), *La crónica del descubrimiento* by Alejandro Paternain (1980), *El entenado* by Juan José Saer (1983), *Los perros del paraíso* by Abel Posse (1983), *1492. Vida y tiempos de Juan Cabezón de Castilla* by Homero Aridjis (1985), and *Vigilia del Almirante* by Augusto Roa Bastos (1992) are the best known examples of novels that rewrite historiographic texts of the conquest with a revisionist purpose.

4. There are, of course, exceptions. Besides Gómara's chronicle, recounting the deeds of a "valiente capitán" and written "en loa a las glorias de España" (Mignolo 1982, 81), there exist also the *Verdadera historia de los sucesos de la conquista de la Nueva España* by Bernal Díaz de Castillo, which, narrated from the point of view of an ordinary soldier, presents a different profile of the conquest of Mexico; the *Brevísima relación de la destrucción de las Indias* by Bartolomé de las Casas, who denounces the atrocities of the conquest; and *Comentarios reales* by Inca Garcilaso de la Vega, who portrays reality from a *mestizo* perspective, that is, decentered vis-à-vis the centralized Spanish version. The intertextual relationship of *Maluco* to Bernal Díaz del Castillo's account is quite striking. Both texts present a similar enunciative situation: the narrator is an old man who realizes the errors of an official chronicle and decides to tell what he regards as the true story.

5. Significantly, in the same work Benveniste defines the first-person pronoun as a verbal representation of a subjective person (*personne subjective*) and the *he/she* pronoun as a *no-person* (*non-personne*) sign (Benveniste 1971, 200—201). According to this reasoning, in the historical discourse, no-person is involved.

6. When, at some point, Magellan takes off his armor, Juanillo observes that he "was very small [pequeñito] without it" (Baccino 1994, 139).

7. On the distancing value of closure of the past tense in historical discourse, see Bakhtin 1981, Barthes 1972, *Le degré zéro de l'écriture,* and Ricoeur 1983.

8. See G. Genette 1972 and Ricoeur 1983.

9. The issue of expressive dynamism is discussed at length in C. Bousoño, *Teoría de la expresión poética.* Bousoño distinguishes between positive and negative dynamism: "a sentence has positive dynamism if the structure forces us to a rapid reading, and, on the other hand, it contains negative dynamism if its structure forces us into a slow reading" (Bousoño 1970, 337). Positive dynamism resides in verbs and nouns, which transport new notions. By contrast, negative dynamism relies on modifiers such as adjectives and adverbs. The dynamic value of repetition is always negative because it doesn't contribute anything new.

10. Parody is not necessarily comical, as Hutcheon and Morson observe (Hutcheon 1985, 32; Morson 1989, 69). For instance, *Castigo divino* by Sergio

Ramírez parodies conventions of both the historical and the detective novel but does not resort to humor as a strategy of recodification. On the other hand, it is notable that, in most cases, historical novels belong to the serious-genre category. There are comical scenes in many of them (i.e., *Santa Evita* by Tomás Eloy Martínez), but very few use humor as the principle of the construction of reality. In Latin America, along with *Maluco, Los relámpagos de agosto* by Jorge Ibargüengoitia (1963) uses devastating humor to caricaturize the Mexican Revolution. At the same time, it is interesting to observe that Umberto Eco's *The Name of the Rose* (1980), a novel that theorizes the subversive potential of laughter, remains serious throughout its five hundred pages. Eco's novel evidences a tension between the ideological proposal and the praxis of writing.

11. Many Latin American authors use the image of the body as a site for the revision of historical discourse. I list the following novels as examples: *El otoño del patriarca* and *El general en su laberinto* by Gabriel García Márquez, *Yo el supremo* by Augusto Roa Bastos, *Terra nostra* by Carlos Fuentes, *El mar de las lentejas* by Antonio Benítez Rojo, *La tragedia del generalísimo* by Denzil Romero, *Sota de bastos, caballo de espadas* by Héctor Tizón, *La novela de Perón* by Tomás Eloy Martínez, and *Noticias del imperio* by Fernando del Paso. All of them reexamine the dichotomy of *body/idea* signaled by Mudrovcic.

Bibliography

Aridjis, Homero. 1985. *1492: Vida y tiempos de Juan Cabezón de Castilla.* Mexico: Siglo XXI.

Baccino Ponce de León, Napoleón. 1990. *Maluco. La novela de los descubridores.* Barcelona: Seix Barral.

———. 1994. *Five Black Ships: A Novel of the Discoverers.* Translated by Nick Caistor. New York: Harcourt Brace & Co.

Bakhtin, Mikhail M. 1981. *The Dialogic Imagination: Four Essays.* Ed. Michael Holquist. Austin: University of Texas Press.

———. 1984. *Rabelais and His World.* Bloomington: Indiana University Press.

Balandier, George. 1983. "Essai d'identification du quotidien." *Cahiers Internationaux de Sociologie* 74: 5–12.

Barthes, Roland. 1972. *Le Degré zéro de l'écriture.* Paris: Seuil.

Bartolomé de las Casas. 1986. *Historia de las Indias.* Caracas: Biblioteca Ayacucho.

Benítez Rojo, Antonio. 1984. *El mar de las lentejas.* Barcelona: Plaza and Janes.

Benjamin, Walter. 1971. *Iluminaciones I.* Edited by Jesús Aguirre. Madrid: Taurus.

Benveniste, Émile. 1971. *Problems in General Linguistics.* Coral Gables: University of Miami Press.

Bhabha, Homi K. 1994. *The Location of Culture.* London: Routledge.

Bousoño, Carlos. *Teoría de la expresión poética.* Madrid: Gredos, 1970.

Bustillo, Carmen. 1994. "Personaje y tiempo en *La tragedia del generalísimo* de Denzil Romero." *Revista Iberoamericana* 166–67: 289–305.

Butler, Judith. 1993. *Bodies That Matter.* New York: Routledge.

Carpentier, Alejo. 1980. *El arpa y la sombra.* Mexico: Siglo Veintiuno Editores.

Certeau, Michel de. 1975. *L'Écriture de l'histoire.* Paris: Gallimard.

Del Paso, Fernando. 1987. *Noticias del imperio.* Madrid: Mondadori.

Foucault, Michel. 1984. "Nietzsche, Genealogy, History." In *The Foucault Reader,* edited by Paul Rabinow, 76–100. New York: Pantheon Books.

Fuentes, Carlos. 1975. *Terra nostra.* Barcelona: Seix Barral.

———. 1976. *Terra nostra.* Translated by Margaret Sayers Peden. Toronto: MacGraw-Hill Ryerson.

García Márquez, Gabriel. 1978. *El otoño del patriarca.* Bogotá: Editorial Oveja Negra.

———. 1989. *El general en su laberinto.* Bogotá: Editorial Oveja Negra.

Genette, Gérard. 1972. *Figures III.* Paris: Éditions du Seuil.

Hobsbawm, Eric. 1983. "Introduction: Inventing of Traditions." In *The Invention of Tradition,* edited by Eric Hobsbawm and Terence Ranger, 1–14. Cambridge: Cambridge University Press.

Hutcheon, Linda. 1985. *A Theory of Parody.* New York: Methuen.

———. 1988. *A Poetics of Postmodernism: History, Theory, Fiction.* New York: Routledge.

———. 1994. *Irony's Edge: The Theory and Politics of Irony.* London: Routledge.

Ibargüengoitia, Jorge. 1968. *Los relámpagos de agosto.* Mexico: J. Mortiz.

Martínez, Tomás Eloy. 1985. *La novela de Perón.* Madrid: Alianza Editorial.

———. 1995. *Santa Evita.* Barcelona: Seix Barral.

Mignolo, Walter. 1982. "Cartas, crónicas y relaciones del descubrimiento y la conquista." In *Historia de la literatura hispanoamericana: Época colonial,* ed.ited by Iñigo Madrigal, 57–116. Vol. 1. Madrid: Cátedra.

Morson, Gary Saul. 1989. "Parody, History and Metaparody." In *Rethinking Bakhtin: Extensions and Challenges,* edited by Gary Saul Morson and Caryl Emerson, 63–89. Evanston: Northwestern University Press.

Mudrovcic, María Eugenia. 1993. "En busca de dos décadas perdidas: La novela latinoamericana de los años 70 y 80." *Revista Iberoamericana* 164–165: 445–68.

Nietzsche, Friedrich. 1983. *Untimely Meditations.* Cambridge: Cambridge University Press.

O'Gorman, Edmundo. 1972. *The Invention of America.* Westport, Conn.: Greenwood Press.

Otero Silva, Miguel. 1985. *Lope de Aguirre, príncipe de la libertad.* Caracas: Biblioteca Ayacucho.

Paternain, Alejandro. 1980. *Crónica del descubrimiento.* Montevideo: Lectores de Banda Oriental.

Posse, Abel. 1987. *Los perros del paraíso.* Barcelona: Plaza y Janes.

Rama, Angel. 1984. *La ciudad letrada.* Hanover, N.H.: Ediciones del Norte.

Ramírez, Sergio. 1988. *Castigo divino.* Madrid: Mondadori.

Ricoeur, Paul. 1983. *Temps et récit.* 3 vols. Paris: Éditions du Seuil.

Roa Bastos, Augusto. 1974. *Yo el supremo.* Mexico: Siglo Veintiuno Editores.

———. 1992. *Vigilia del Almirante.* Madrid: Alfaguara.

Romero, Denzil. 1987. *La tragedia del generalísimo.* Caracas: Alfadil Ediciones.

Saer, Juan José. 1988. *El entenado.* Barcelona: Ediciones Destino.

Stallybrass, Peter, and Allon White. 1986. *The Politics and Poetics of Transgression.* Ithaca: Cornell University Press.

Tizón, Héctor. 1975. *Sota de bastos, caballo de espadas.* Buenos Aires: Crisis.

Vega, Garcilaso de la (the Inca). 1991. *Commentarios reales.* 2 vols. Caracas: Biblioteca Ayacucho.

White, Hayden. 1987. *The Content of the Form: Narrative Discourse and Historical Representation.* Baltimore and London: The Johns Hopkins University Press.

La isla amarilla: (Re)vision and Subversion of the Discovery

SUSAN P. BERARDINI

THOUGHTS OF DISCOVERY AND EXPLORATION EVOKE IMAGES OF WESTERN explorers in distant, exotic lands, where they encounter indigenous, "uncivilized" communities. As evidenced by history, such explorers have felt compelled to civilize the primitive groups found during their expeditions. This was usually accomplished by force and the imposition of Western culture, which was generally considered superior by the invading groups. But what if the roles were reversed? That is, what would transpire if the explorer was an indigenous individual who ventured to the civilized world? What would s/he report to her/his people upon returning from an expedition, and how would s/he share the experience? These are precisely some of the issues raised in Paloma Pedrero's 1995 play entitled *La isla amarilla,* which was first performed at the Carabanchel prison for men under the direction of Elena Cánovas, and was performed by female inmates for the first time at the Yeserías prison in Madrid.[1]

In *La isla amarilla* Pedrero focuses sharply on an analysis of not only Spanish, but also European—and, by extension, Western—collective identity, as the work constitutes a comic, modern (re)vision of the Europeans as a colonizing group. Pedrero was inspired for this play by the speeches of the Samoan chief Tuiavii of Tiavea, who traveled to Europe for the first time in the 1920s to explore and experience the "civilized" world. Tuiavii's speeches were published by the German anthropologist Eric Scheurmann, who invited the chief to travel with him to Europe, and Pedrero read them in the late 1970s. In his prologue to *La isla amarilla,* Robert Muro affirms that it is in these speeches, directed to his compatriots, that Tuiavii "husks that which his eyes and his heart have perceived during the months in which he lived with the white man (papalagi) in Europe back in the 1920s" (Muro 1995, 11).

In *La isla amarilla* Pedrero dramatizes the meeting of a Samoan tribe that is about to be invaded by the Europeans, whose principal interest lies in the abundance of gold that is found on the island.[2] In exchange for the treasure, the *papalagi* offer the Samoans their material goods, sophisticated culture, and advanced technology.[3] Kuavi, the tribal chief, and four compatriots have just returned from Europe, where they had their first encounter with the Western world. During their reunion with the tribe, the travelers perform a series of brief skits through which they inform the islanders about Western life with respect to exorbitant consumption, technological advances, housing, materialism, pastimes, work, the battle of the sexes, and other topics of interest. Based on these scenes, the tribe will decide if it is willing to share its land and treasures with the Europeans.

Pedrero offers her audience/readers a twice-told tale of the Old World–New World encounter in many ways, not only through her theatrical interpretation of Tuiavii's experiences and her parodic (re)vision of the discovery of a new world, but also, literally, through the use of the metadramatic play-within-the-play structure. According to Robert J. Nelson, drama-within-drama is "a formal imitation of an event through the dialogue and action of impersonated characters occurring within and not suspending the action of just such another imitation" (Nelson 1958, 7). Richard Hornby notes that this phenomenon occurs in two ways: "in one, the 'inset' type, the inner play is secondary, a performance set apart from the main action . . . ; in the other, the 'framed' type, the inner play is primary, with the outer play a framing device" (Hornby 1986, 33). The play-within-the-play structure results in a doubling that shatters the theatrical illusion (Hornby 1986, 35). Furthermore, it tends to distance the spectators, who often find themselves "excluded" from the show by some fictitious audience or simply by the exterior play that frames the inner performance.

Pedrero considers *La isla amarilla* "a curious experiment" (Harris 1993, 34). The work consists of a series of random metadramatic scenes whose brevity and rapid transition add a cinematographic effect to the play. These fragments are linked together by the narrations of Kuavi and form an inner, framed drama in which the change of scenes is signaled by variations of light. Although Pedrero includes in the dramatis personae more than forty-five different characters, the majority of them are metafictional figures that correspond to the framed drama and that, according to the author, may be interpreted by a minimum of seven actors. This suggests from the beginning the extensive role-playing that will dominate the play. In fact, all of the metadramatic scenes are performed for the tribe by the four young Samoans that accompanied Kuavi to Europe: Nei, Kalita, Asur and Nazin. While the presence of a fictitious public would normally distance the real audience from a metadramatic play, precisely the opposite occurs in *La isla amarilla,* as we become part of the tribe beginning with the initial stage direction: "The indigenous people—the public—anxiously await the arrival on the beach of Kuavi, the tribal chief" (Pedrero 1995, 31). At this point Pedrero immediately draws her public into the drama, because we are also awaiting the arrival of the chief and the beginning of the play(s). As Muro affirms: "The sensation, obviously intentional, that the work is presented to an indigenous community of which we are part—in the theater or reading the work—only serves to enrich the theatrical possibilities to entertain and to delight without the mind being on vacation" (Muro 1995, 17). By merging her spectators with the tribal audience, Pedrero manages to distance them from their world so they may contemplate and reevaluate their lives from a more objective point of view. Furthermore, themes are developed from a primitive and impartial perspective, and in this way Pedrero provides us with "a clean, polished mirror in which we may observe ourselves" (Muro 1995, 12).

In *La isla amarilla* Pedrero compares and contrasts two sharply different worlds: that of the Samoans and that of the *papalagi*. The Samoans exist in the exterior drama and, through the observations made by Kuavi regarding the Europeans, one may infer that the natives enjoy a tranquil life on their island, in harmony with nature. Their world is not contaminated by money, machines, or factories. In contrast, the framed drama constitutes a theatrical collage that offers a thorough sampling of modern, Western life. The Samoans observe various scenes that portray the *papalagi* in daily contexts, reflecting their behavior, rituals, priorities, and general living conditions. The cultural exposition begins with the lifestyle of the individual *palagi*, emphasizing the most basic elements: clothing and housing. It is through these seemingly mundane topics that Pedrero sets the humorous and impartial tone, along with the primitive perspective, for the entire play. In his commentary on Western fashion, for example, Kuavi notes that shoes are like "small canoes" made of thick animal skins, women wear a "transparent skin" on their legs, girdles are fastened with many little "shells" and seem to be some kind of punishment for women with insatiable appetites, and bras are worn because the *papalagi* do not like breasts in their natural state and try to maintain them constantly erect (Pedrero 1995, 33–35). Throughout the narration Kalita performs a rather clumsy striptease to exhibit each item, and she has particular difficulty with the girdle and high heels.

Kuavi's observations regarding Western fashion reveal a strong obsession with personal appearance, image, and the body, and these values are later reiterated in a humorous reenactment of the typical activities that take place in a beauty salon, where customers undergo their "torture session" (Pedrero 1995, 60). Screams and sighs accompany images of a bald man receiving a hair transplant, a woman undergoing treatment for severe acne (during which she also loses part of her nose!), and another client having her legs waxed. Such practices are typical of the "grooming rituals" that are carried out in Western societies which, according to Grant McCracken, "insure that special and perishable properties resident in certain clothes, certain hair styles, certain looks, are, as it were, 'coaxed' out of their resident goods and made to live, however briefly and precariously, in the individual consumer"

(McCracken 1990, 86). The absurdity of Western grooming rituals is underscored by the fact that the wealthier *papalagi* will go so far as to change their noses, eyes, and mouths, evidently a reference to the popularity of plastic surgery.

Kuavi's comments on European housing also reveal the primitive perspective and tone of wonder regarding his discoveries in the "new" world. He describes apartment buildings, for example, as "giant stone boxes" that are full of holes from top to bottom (Pedrero 1995, 40). With respect to the various rooms that comprise the *papalagi's* "huts," the chief expresses amazement regarding the bathroom. He is particularly intrigued by the "enormous receptacle" in which the *papalagi* wash themselves and remove the "sand" from their bodies, and, of course, the toilet, which is perceived as a "throne with a great hole in the middle" (Pedrero 1995, 43).

Following the initial scenes on fashion and housing, the Samoan travelers elaborate on the issue of Western materialism, a theme developed throughout *La isla amarilla* through a series of detailed sketches that illustrate the *papalagi's* obsession with consumer goods, money, and work. The concept of materialism is conveyed to the tribal audience in several stages, beginning with a very simplistic, show-and-tell format in which the explorers display a series of typical household items—a broom, a mop, a cup, a pan, a water glass, etc.—in order to communicate the idea of "things." The exhibition of these material objects, along with others, contributes to the cultural portrayal of the *papalagi* that is developed throughout the play. McCracken considers consumer goods the "locus of cultural meaning" (83) and notes the following: "Objects contribute thus to the construction of the culturally constituted world precisely because they are a vital, visible record of cultural meaning that is otherwise intangible" (74). Kuavi emphasizes that Europeans are obsessed with producing and possessing objects, both for personal enjoyment and out of the desire to improve nature. The resulting work ethic is evidently foreign to the Samoans: "thousands and thousands of hands do nothing more than produce 'things' from dawn to dusk. Their hands burn, their backs hunch, but still they jump for joy when they triumph in making a new 'thing' and everyone wants to have it" (Pedrero 1995, 36). With this remark, Kuavi also alludes to the insatiable desire of Westerners to possess material goods. McCracken attributes such materialism to the fact that consumer goods serve as a means of reestablishing cultural meaning: "The use of goods to recover displaced meaning is one of the engines of consumption in modern society. It helps perpetuate consumer appetite. It helps declare certain purchases obsolete . . . and demands the purchase of new goods" (McCracken 1990, 115).

Kuavi's exposé of Western materialism culminates in a series of sketches on money and work. The chief thoroughly elaborates on "money," which is unknown to the indigenous spectators and is perceived as "rough paper" [*papel tosco*] and "round metal" [*metal redondo*], and concludes that it is "the most valued, desired, and adored thing in the *papalagis'* world" (Pedrero 1995, 46). The Western world revolves around money and one must pay for everything, as illustrated by the entertaining reenactment of Asur's first encounter with a prostitute.

Kuavi's explanation of money includes various examples of the process by which most of the *papalagi* obtain it: that is, work. He cites examples both familiar to his audience, such as piloting a canoe, raising animals, and building boats, and unfamiliar examples such as the work of intellectuals. With this last example, Pedrero is undoubtedly teasing her academic public, as Kuavi states: "Yes, althoug it may seem incredible to you, there are many *papalagi* who charge rough paper for the mere act of thinking. And yet others who charge money to give their opinion about the thoughts of everyone else" (Pedrero 1995, 51).

Kuavi's summary of the *papalagi's* obsession with money and work climaxes in a parodic banking scene that highlights our ritualistic behavior with currency. Kuavi informs the tribe that in addition to work one can earn money through the funds that one already has in a bank. This phenomenon leads the chief to suspect witchcraft for lack of another way to explain how the "rough paper" generates itself. The mystery of financial interest is explained in the context of magic, which seems to be a familiar medium for the Samoan audience.[4] Kuavi's traveling companions perform a comical scene in which a client arrives at a bank with a box full of cash and offers it to the banker, who initiates a magic ceremony that includes the typical elements: ritualistic action, symbolic object (the money), and a chant. While he shakes the box and throws the bills into the air, the banker pronounces the following words: "The title holder has at his disposal three payment modalities with a referential percentage without value-added tax and a delayed payment system with ten percent interest and amortization based upon the balance produced by commissions and taxes with liquidation of the statement" (Pedrero 1995, 53). At the end of the ritual the banker emerges from his "ecstasy." With this scene Pedrero develops a caricature of banking activities through the exaggerated juxtaposition of financial jargon, which approximates a sorcerer's incantation, and the presentation of the banker as if he were a magician. Pedrero incorporates magic in this play in one of its oldest functions: the creation or transformation of something. The creation of money through magic adds a self-reflexive element to the scene, given that in various primitive communities money is or has been associated with sorcery. In "Les Origines de la notion de la monnaie," for example, Marcel Mauss notes that several indigenous languages use their "mana" word, which alludes both to social power and to magic, to also signify money.[5] In modern Western societies money maintains a mystical quality because it is intangible and extremely powerful. In the words of

William H. Desmonde, "to many of us, money is a mystery, a symbol handled mainly by the priests of high finance, and regarded by us with much of the same reverence and awe as the primitive feels toward the sacred relics providing magical potency in a tribal ritual. As if in a higher plane of reality, the symbol seems to operate in an incomprehensible, mystical way, understood and controllable only by the magic of brokers, accountants, lawyers, and financiers" (Desmonde 1962, 3–4). Albeit exaggerated, the banking ritual in *La isla amarilla* effectively reflects the modern attitudes toward money noted by Desmonde. The scene also suggests that ritual may serve as a point of encounter and understanding between different cultures.

One of the consequences of Western materialism that the Samoan travelers share with their audience is the commercialization and objectification of everything, including people. This tendency is illustrated through the reenactment of a game show in which the contestant plays from the comfort of her own home.[6] The situation challenges traditional theatrical boundaries because the viewer, represented by the woman at home, becomes a participant in the program. The physical barrier of the television screen is transcended when the contestant speaks directly to the game show host and when he hands her prizes through the screen. After winning a car and a luxury apartment, the woman has the opportunity to continue playing for the host himself, whose description not only provokes laughter but also reflects Western values and modern concerns: "First-class television announcer, blond, six feet tall, 180 pounds, well-educated, and with a certificate that he is free of AIDS and premature ejaculation" (Pedrero 1995, 63). Curiously, the quoted value of the grand prize is "all the gold in the world," which brings to mind the treasure of the Samoan tribe. When the contestant wins the game show host, they kiss and it becomes even more apparent that the screen no longer marks a limit. On the contrary, there is an explicit (con)fusion of "reality" and illusion. Through this scene, along with others that focus on cinema and theater, Pedrero establishes yet another level of performance through which she blurs the limits of "reality" and fiction, and once again disrupts the theatrical illusion.

Finally, Kuavi addresses the Western obsession with technology, which is one of the principal themes of *La isla amarilla.* In the words of Pedrero, this play is about "the irrational advance of science and technology, the destructiveness that can result from progress when the goal of making peaceful and happy societies is lost" (Harris 1993, 34). The consequences of modern technology, which is perceived by Kuavi as the *papalagi*'s attempt to improve nature, are introduced first through the chief's comments on European cities and his allusions to the problem of environmental pollution. Kuavi indicates that the sky in the new world is always full of smoke and ashes and that the contamination is even noticeable in the physical appearance of the *papalagi:* "the people have black soot in their eyes and hair, and sand in their teeth" (Pedrero 1995, 44). Technology is presented as an even greater threat when the chief describes, as an example of typical items found in a newspaper, the meeting of two tribal leaders to discuss arms reduction. The parallel between this example and the nuclear weapons crisis in the "civilized" world is quite evident, as one chief rejects the proposal of the other to destroy "half of the poisoned arrows, which could destroy the entire pig population" (Pedrero 1995, 73–74).

Pedrero then introduces two situations that further underscore the irrational advances of science and technology. In a scene that recalls the theater of the absurd, two scientists dissect a giant spider, and the procedure is carried out as if it were surgery. They anesthetize the arachnid, which is on an operating table, and when the "patient" loses its pulse they give it oxygen. Shortly afterward, the electroencephalogram goes flat and the researchers try, unsuccessfully, to revive the spider by cardiopulmonary resuscitation. Ironically, cardiac massage fails because the researchers have already extracted the heart from the spider as part of the dissection procedures.

In the following scene, Pedrero reiterates her perspective on technology through the irony of an image that contrasts with Kuavi's narration. During this sketch, Kuavi praises the "great knowledge" achieved by the *papalagi* through scientific research and how they have invented great machines to prolong life. While the chief elaborates on the Western advances in medicine, a decrepit old man full of tubes crosses the stage in a wheelchair, which forces one to question the value of such an extended life. Through these scenes, Pedrero satirizes the absurd extremes that we have reached in the fields of science and medicine. Pedrero feels that we are progressing blindly with technology:

> I always think that progress can take us in unexpected and fairly dangerous places because we progress in a compulsive manner and we are not stopping to measure, to reflect upon where the hell we're going with so much science and so much new technology. . . . I'm in favor of progress, but in another way, not this progress that I consider at the least rather one-eyed, if not blind. (Pedrero 1997)

While technology may indeed "improve nature" to a certain extent, Pedrero suggests that the parameters need to be modified and our perspective revised in order to avoid the dehumanizing and potentially destructive course we have set.

In addition to the multiple thematic development in *La isla amarilla,* Pedrero's reinvention of the Old World–New World encounter derives from her technical innovations. As noted earlier, this play has an overt metadramatic structure that facilitates the representation of slices of Western life. A closer look at the fragments that compose the framed drama, however, will reveal other unique aspects that contribute to the experimental nature of the work. The topics regarding the Occidental world are always initiated through the voice of Kuavi, whose narrations resemble monologues because he generally addresses his audience without speaking to the other characters on stage. Furthermore, the tribal leader never participates in the metadramatic performances of his traveling companions.

Pedrero experiments with various ways of generating a concept, and her scenes range from the most simple to a "sophisticated" level that approximates traditional theater. Pedrero reworks each idea through a series of brief sketches that feature generic characters and little or no dialogue. The minimalist attitude regarding dialogue reflects Pedrero's philosophy on theater: "I believe that the less the characters speak, the better it will be. What they do say should be substantial, free from empty words, because the theatrical writer has the advantage of counting on the bodies, the hearts, the minds, and the souls of something as alive as an actor" (Pedrero 1993, 113). In the absence of dialogue, Pedrero often employs pantomime in *La isla amarilla,* which gives the impression that she is exploring the limits of staging. One can observe this tendency, for example, in the episodes relating to the battle of the sexes. According to Kuavi, the gender conflict is an absurd consequence of the need or desire of women to work outside of the home. The chief relates this decision specifically to the economic need and desire for professional satisfaction, noting that the female *papalagi* are the people who least like their profession because they spend the day cleaning and organizing the "hut" without pay. Pedrero dramatizes the battle of the sexes through a series of seven metadramatic sketches performed through mime. Sounds and imaginary language are employed, and the absence of dialogue not only emphasizes the lack of communication between the sexes, but also establishes the universality of the topic.[7]

The sketches on the gender conflict are developed in a primitive context, given that the protagonists are cave couples. In comparison with the other scenes that form part of the framed drama, this series emphasizes Pedrero's interest in experimenting with new forms of theatrical expression, as each scene proposes a variation, and the likely consequences, with respect to the domestic and professional circumstances of the couple. Pedrero initiates the lively sequence on the troglodytic couple with a traditional situation: the housewife dedicates herself exclusively to her family and home. In the second sketch, the husband and wife both hunt bear and could be considered "professionals" from a modern prospective. The wife continues to shoulder the burden of domestic chores, however, and when the man returns to find her not at home, he becomes enraged.

In the following scenes the relationship of the couple deteriorates. Both spouses hunt bear, but now the element of rivalry is added. In the third fragment, for example, the woman kills a bear but the man is not as successful and becomes furious. Later, the competition is underscored between the man and woman when the two try to hunt the same bear. Each one claims it as his/her own, and the animal escapes as a result of the ensuing argument. The rivalry between the married couple intensifies in the fifth and sixth scenes, when both resort to violence to surpass the other. Pedrero concludes this series by concentrating on the result of the situations portrayed in the previous scenes: the man and woman now live separately in their own caves, each with his or her own bear.

The simplicity of the minidramas on the gender conflict exemplifies Pedrero's philosophy of theater, which she perceives as:

> the place of the essential, a character, another, an occurrence. Happening, that's what fills the theatrical area, a happening the more simple, the better, the more extraordinary, the better. The lives of all beings are filled with simple, extraordinary occurrences, situations, sensations, thoughts, conflicts, struggles, surrenderings, transformations. Perhaps writing theater consists of first becoming aware, and then condensing it, taking it to ground zero and gestating it so that one day it may shine like in this fragment of the universe that is the set. (Pedrero 1993, 113)

Pedrero reduces the sketches on the battle of the sexes, as well as other scenes, to the bare essentials—to ground zero—in order to demonstrate her theory. She eliminates dialogue and minimizes action. There is no stage scenery for the metadramatic fragments, although they are performed before the backdrop of the island images of the frame play, which include the beach, seagulls, and palm trees. The lack of scenery for the framed dramas maintains the focus on the essential elements of theater. Pedrero prefers to leave out "all these adornments" and feels that "it is better to adorn the theater with imagination than with money; besides being less expensive it's more authentic" (Pedrero 1988, 125).

According to Agustina Sangüesa, *La isla amarilla* constitutes "an inverse cultural-anthropological history" (Sangüesa 1989, 25). Paloma Pedrero inverts the tale of the "discovery"; the experience with an unknown civilization is narrated and dramatized from the indigenous point of view, are often supplemented with contemporary examples relevant to Pedrero's public. Pedrero's (re)vision of the "discovery" is also marked by modifications of the historical circumstances surrounding the exploration and invasions of Samoa. Throughout *La isla amarilla,* the gold motive is stressed with respect to European interest in the island, and there is a slight indication that it could very well be the Spaniards who are about to arrive. Interestingly enough, however, it was not the Spaniards, but the British and the Germans who represented Europe in Samoa, and the principal motives were the strategic location and agricultural resources of the islands. Historical references to Samoa fail to include gold among the islands' natural treasures, and the precious metal is never mentioned in the original speeches of

Tuiavii. Through these circumstantial alterations Pedrero's play becomes a more general, universal commentary on "discovery," "conquest," and the clash of cultures.

The role reversal of the explorer vs. the explored in *La isla amarilla* casts a new perspective on the Western world. Unlike Tuiavii, who was highly critical of the *papalagi,* Kuavi offers a more objective portrayal of the Europeans that allows his audience to draw its own conclusions regarding the Western way of life. Furthermore, the historical inversion and subversion offered by Pedrero are reinforced by the open ending of the drama. At the close of the play(s), Kuavi encourages his subjects to reflect on the cultural sketches they have just witnessed to determine if they will permit the Europeans to occupy their land and take possession of their gold. The Samoans will decide their future through a democratic process, and they have the opportunity to reject the pending invasion.

Finally, it is important to note that (meta)theater serves as the vehicle of communication, exploration, and discovery in *La isla amarilla* not only for the Samoans, but also for Pedrero's public. Through the framed drama the playwright provides us with a humorous, and sometimes cynical, vision of Western life, revealing our passions, customs, obsessions, idiosyncrasies, and general ways. This study has focused on just a few of the many cultural notions dramatized in the play. In addition to Western materialism, gender relations, and attitudes regarding work, fashion, and housing, Pedrero highlights the destructive nature of the technological "advances" that we "enjoy," leading us to reexamine our values and question whether we really do live in such a civilized society after all.

Notes

1. *La isla amarilla* was both premiered and published in 1995, however it was written in the early 1990s.

2. The island's names—"Isla amarilla" and "La isla del oro"—derive from this treasure.

3. The term *papalagi* refers to the Europeans and literally means "sky-bursters." As Malama Meleisea explains, "When Europeans first sailed close to the shores of the Polynesian islands of the central Pacific, the people termed them 'papalagi'—sky-bursters—because it was believed that they had come from outside the universe and burst through the domes of heaven" (Meleisea 1992, 20).

4. According to Sally F. Moore and Barbara G. Myerhoff, rituals in general serve to explain a phenomenon because they establish order: whenever items are ordered, connections are established or asserted and some systematic relationships are suggested. By definition, the connection provides an explanation, implies meaning and comprehensibility. Rituals always provide meaning in this way (Moore and Myerhoff 1977, 17).

5. Daniel Lawrence O'Keefe explains this tendency in *Stolen Lightning: The Social Theory of Magic:* Money is, precisely, the sacred good that will trade for all other sacred

objects, and some object to which the most universal mana ideas attached was picked as the universal standard of measure, which is perhaps why the mana word often became the word for money (O'Keefe 1982, 385).

6. The game show scene is one of many that represent Western pastimes. Others include scenes of bingo, a family at the park, patrons at a bar, people doing drugs, and spectators at both a theater and the movies.

7. Through the absence of language, the protagonists of these scenes fail to be identified with any particular ethnic group. Universality also results from the fact that the characters portrayed in the inner dramas generally lack psychological depth. They are merely generic figures that serve to demonstrate a situation.

Bibliography

Desmonde, William H. 1962. *Magic, Myth, and Money: The Origin of Money in Religious Ritual.* New York: Free.

Harris, Carolyn J. 1993. "Concha Romero y Paloma Pedrero hablan de sus obras." *Estreno* 19, no. 1: 29–35.

Hornby, Richard. 1986. *Drama, Metadrama, and Perception.* Lewisburg: Bucknell University Press.

Mauss, Marcel. 1968–69. "Les Origines de la notion de la monnaie." In *Oeuvres,* 2: 106–12. Paris: Editions de Minuit.

McCracken, Grant. 1990. *Culture & Consumption: New Approaches to the Symbolic Character of Consumer Goods and Activities.* Bloomington: Indiana University Press.

Meleisea, Malama. 1992. *Change and Adaptations in Western Samoa.* Christchurch, New Zealand: Macmillan Brown Centre for Pacific Studies.

Moore, Sally F., and Barbara G. Myerhoff. 1977. Introduction to *Secular Ritual,* edited by Sally F. Moore and Barbara G. Myerhoff, 3–24. Amsterdam: Van Gorcum.

Muro, Robert. 1995. Introduction to *La isla amarilla,* by Paloma Pedrero. Ciudad Real: Naque Editora.

Nelson, Robert J. 1958. *Play within a Play: The Dramatist's Conception of His Art: Shakespeare to Anouilh.* New Haven: Yale University Press.

O'Keefe, Daniel Lawrence. 1982. *Stolen Lightning: The Social Theory of Magic.* New York: Continuum.

Pedrero, Paloma. 1988. "Escribir algo vivo y sin miedo." *Primer acto* 222: 124–25.

———. 1993. "El escenario, territorio de las letras." *Primer acto* 251: 112–14.

———. 1995. *La isla amarilla.* Ciudad Real: Naque Editora.

———. 1997. Interview by author. New York, 2 October.

Sangüesa, Agustina. 1989. "El realismo marginal de un sueño." *El público* 66: 23–25.

Notes on Contributors

SUSAN P. BERARDINI is an assistant professor of Spanish at Pace University, and her research focuses on the theater of contemporary Spanish female playwrights. Her 1996 doctoral dissertation, entitled "El metateatro en las obras de Paloma Pedrero," examined the function of role-playing, ritual and intertextuality in the works of this Spanish dramatist. She has published on "El toreo como vía de la identidad en *Invierno de luna alegre*" in *De lo particular a lo universal: El teatro español del siglo XX y su contexto,* as well as "The Subversion of Ritual in the Theater of Paloma Pedrero" in a forthcoming anthology on anthropology and literature. She continues to research feminist issues, the search for identity, and the use of metatheater in Spanish theater by women, and has presented numerous conference papers on these topics.

ERIK CAMAYD-FREIXAS is an assistant professor of Latin American literature and interpretation at Florida International University. Specializing in both the literature and intellectual history of Latin America, he is the author of *Realismo mágico y primitivismo: Relecturas de Carpentier, Asturias, Rulfo y García Márquez* (University Press of America, 1998). His articles have appeared in *Revista de crítica literaria latinoamericana, Latin American Issues, Romance Languages Annual, Canadian Review of Comparative Literature, Romance Review,* and *Cuadernos del lazarillo,* among others. Additionally, he contributed seventeen articles on Latin American writers for *Benet's Readers' Encyclopedia.* His current projects include a discussion of Miguel Angel Asturias's *Hombres de maiz* as a surrealist reading of Mayan texts, as well as a socioanthropological look at a Puerto Rican urban religion, "The Cult of the Goddess Mita on the Eve of a New Millennium."

VICTORIA E. CAMPOS is an assistant professor of Spanish in the department of romance languages at Wake Forest University. She earned her Ph.D. at Princeton University in 1996 under the direction of Professor Rolena Adorno in the field of late-twentieth-century Mexican historical novels. She studied the genre in light of twentieth-century debates on the social function of history. Currently she is at work on the redefinition of *lo mexicano* in

Elena Poniatowska's *novela-testimonio,* "Hasta no verte Jesús mío," and is engaged in the study of the "feminization" of historical discourse in recent Mexican novels.

LUIS CORREA-DÍAZ is an assistant professor of Latin American studies and literature at the University of Georgia, Athens. His works in progress include a book-length project on the literary iconography of Ernesto Che Guevara, and articles on the revisitation of revolutionary and guerrilla poetry in Latin America. In 1996 he published *Lengua muerta: Poesía, post-literatura y erotismo en Enrique Lihn* (Providence: Ediciones INTI, 1996), which examines the relation among language, death and eroticism. His second book, entitled *Todas las muertes de Pinochet* is forthcoming in Ball State University Press. A book devoted to Colombian writer Pedro Gómez Valderrama (*El arto de la conjetura histórica*) will be published in Colombia. He has presented papers at Columbia University, Barnard College, ACLA, IILI, LASA, NEMLA, the Mid-American Conference on Hispanic Literature, the Cincinnati Foreign Language Conference, and the University of Oregon, and has participated in international conferences in France, Colombia, Venezuela, and Chile. His articles have appeared in *Hispanic Journal, Nueva Revista de Filología Hispánica, Revista Iberoamericana, Cuadernos Hispanoamericanos, Escritura,* and *Revista de Estudios Colombianos, Revista chilena de literatura.*

WA-KÍ FRASER DE ZAMBRANO is an instructor of Spanish language and literature at the University of Colorado, Denver. Her doctoral dissertation, "El discurso colonial/postcolonial y el erotismo en las novelas de dos escritoras: Reedición del encuentro, conquista y colonización de América" (1996), has proven to be fertile terrain for continued research and refinements. Interdisciplinary in nature, Dr. Zambrano's investigations scrutinize contemporary writings of women, retrieving from them codified references to fifteenth- and sixteenth-century sources, such as letters, histories, chronicles, and *relaciones,* as they pertain to Latin American and Peninsular literary traditions and to the intersections of current literary and cultural theory. A recent article, "Lo impenetrable: La ruta al Paraíso Terrenal," was published in *Monographic Review/Revista monográfica* 12 (Hispanic Travel Literature). She is currently researching eroticized terror and loathing as it relates to castration and "indianization" in women's texts.

MARY ANN GOSSER-ESQUILÍN is an associate professor of Latin American and comparative literature and the head of the Spanish program in the department of languages and linguistics at Florida Atlantic University. She has contributed to numerous anthologies on Latin American and Caribbean literature (*Hacia un nuevo canon literario* [1995]; *Latin American Writers on Gay and Lesbian Themes: A Bio-Critical Sourcebook* [1994]; *Critical Essays on the Literature of Spain and Spanish America,* [1991] and is currently working on a book on comparative Caribbean poetics. She has presented papers on similar topics at NEMLA, SAMLA, AATSP, the Conference of the International Society for the Study of European Ideas (Graz, Austria), the Caribbean Study Association Conference (Merida, Mexico), and the Congreso Internacional de la Asociación Internacional Asiática de Hispanistas (Tokyo, Japan), among others.

GLADYS M. ILARREGUI is an assistant professor of languages and cultural studies at Trinity College in Washington, D.C. Her current research deals with sixteenth-century documentation of women in post-conquest Florentine *Codex* (Mexico, ca. 1550), applying contemporary theoretical tools to the questions of gender, ethnography, and writing to a contact period. She has attended a Folger Seminar on anthropology (1993–1994), directed by Irene Silberblatt on the topics of Andean cosmology and ethnographic research. Some of her works have been presented in conferences in Venezuela, Mexico, France, and in LASA, MLA, SAMLA, MACLAS, and others in the States. She has published a book of poetry, *Oficios y personas* (1996) and received the García Lorca Prize in 1994 and the Plural Prize in Mexico in 1993.

SANTIAGO JUAN-NAVARRO is an assistant professor of Spanish at Florida International University. His book, *Archival Reflections: Postmodern Fiction of the Americas* (Bucknell University Press, 2000), centers on the study of fiction and history in the works of major contemporary Latin American and U.S. writers. Works in progress include a book on "Twentieth-Century Representations on the Myth of El Dorado," a collection of essays entitled "Between Apocalypse and Utopia: Toward a New Theory of Postmodernism in the Americas," and articles on contemporary reconstructions of the age of the discovery and conquest. He has previously presented papers and organized sessions at MLA, NEMLA, LASA, AATSP, the Kentucky Foreign Language Conference, the Louisiana Conference on Hispanic Literature, and international conferences in Mexico and Spain. His related articles have appeared in *Revista Iberoamericana, Revista canadiense de estudios hispánicos, Hispanic Journal, Hispanófila, Journal of Interdisciplinary Literary Studies,* and *Neohelicon.*

BART L. LEWIS is the J. William Fulbright professor of modern languages at Lyon College, Batesville, Arkansas. He has presented over forty conference papers and published more than twenty-five articles on Latin American literature in such journals as *Hispanic Review, Revista Iberoamericana, Revista interamericana de bibliografía, Hispania, Latin American Research Review, Hispanófila, Latin American Literary Review, Crítica hispánica, Romance Notes,* and *Chasqui.* He is a member of the editorial board of the *Cincinnati Romance*

Review and has been chair of the Mexican literature section in the American Association of Teachers of Spanish and Portuguese. His current projects are a book-length study of the contemporary Latin American historical novel of El Dorado, specifically the central figure in Spain's last full-scale effort to find the legendary gilded city, Lope de Aguirre, and a history of Latin American literary criticism.

KIMBERLE S. LÓPEZ is an associate professor of Latin American literature in the department of Spanish and Portuguese at the University of New Mexico. In 1994, she completed her Ph.D. at the University of California at Berkeley with a dissertation entitled, "New World Rogues: Transculturation and Identity in the Latin American Picaresque Novel." She has published articles on the Latin American Novel in *Colonial Latin American Review, Luso-Brazilian Review, Symposium, Letras Femeninas, Chasqui,* and *Revista de Crítica Literaria Latinoamericana.* The present article forms part of a larger research project, for which she has received grants from the National Endowment for the Humanities and from the Oregon Humanities Center. The latter investigates the representation of colonial desire in a corpus of recent Latin American historical fictions that rewrite the chronicles of the conquest and colonization of the Americas.

MOLLY METHERD is a Ph.D. candidate in comparative literature at the University of Texas at Austin. Her dissertation, "Within Two Worlds: A Case for Intra-American Literature," theorizes the emergence of a group of U.S. and Latin American texts written and marketed for hemispheric readership. She has presented research on the narrative and linguistic characteristics of cultural identity in works addressing hemispheric audiences at annual meetings of the ACLA, the conference "1898–1998: Nation, Culture, and Identity" at Florida International University, and the Modern Language Association.

ROSEANNA M. MUELLER is professor of Spanish and humanities coordinator at Columbia College Chicago. Her fields of specialization include sixteenth-century literature of Spain, Italy, and England; Italo-Hispanic relations, the Spanish chronicles of the conquest of the New World, and contemporary women's Latin American literature. She has contributed to *Canadian Review of Comparative Literature, Voices in Italian Americana, Hispania, Renaissance Quarterly, Cultures, Communities and the Arts, Foreign Language Accents,* and the essay collection *Latin America as Its Literature* (Griffin House Press, 1995), as well as the forthcoming *The Encyclopedia of Mexico: History, Society, and Culture* (Fitzroy Dearborn) and *The Feminist Encyclopedia of Spanish Literature* (Greenwood Press). Works in progress include a book-length project on Gonzalo Guerrero. She has previously presented related papers on Cabeza de Vaca,

La Malinche, Gonzalo Guerrero and Columbus at MMLA, NEMLA, AATSP, MACHL, ICTFL, AAIT, the Kentucky Foreign Language Conference, and at international conferences in Mexico, Canada, and the Netherlands.

MAGDALENA PERKOWSKA-ALVAREZ is an Assistant Professor in Latin American Literature at the Universiteit Leiden, The Netherlands. Her current research, "Hybrid Spaces: Latin American Historical Novel, 1985–1995," centers on the redefinition of historical space through incorporation into the historical fictions of spheres traditionally banned from history: marginality, anonymity, popular culture, madness, body, ghetto, laughter, and the private. Perkowska's related research revolves around the postmodern rewriting of the conventions of historical discourse and its implications for the interpretation of history. Her conference papers include presentations at MLA, LASA, IILI, SECOLAS, and ICLA. Her articles have appeared in *Explicación de textos literarios, Estudios, Cahiers du CRICCAL* and *Homenaje a Carlos Rojas.*

VIVIANA PLOTNIK is an assistant professor of Spanish at Oglethorpe University. Her 1993 doctoral dissertation, "La reescritura del descubrimiento de América en cuatro novelas hispanoamericanas contemporáneas," examines the fictionalization of history in Spanish American literature. Her current research ("Colonialismo y aculturación en Borges y Saer") centers on the perception of and the relationship to the cultural Other in travel literature. Her contributions include "Alegoría y proceso de reorganización nacional" (*Fascismo y experiencia literaria,* 1985), "Cuando el margen se traslada al centro: *El entenado* de Juan José Saer" (*Proyecciones sobre la novela,* Ediciones de Norte, 1997), and articles on Borges and Neruda. Her work on contemporary Latin American writers has been published by *The Institute of Ideologies and Literatures, Monographic Review,* and *Revista de estudios hispánicos.* She has lectured on similar topics at scholarly meetings around the United States and abroad.

TERRY SEYMOUR is a senior lecturer in Spanish at Yale University. Her main interest at present is the role of eroticism in twentieth-century historical narratives that deal thematically with the Spanish conquest. She has presented several papers on related subjects, including "History, Eroticism, and the Play of Language: Carlos Fuentes's *El naranjo*" and "The Reverse Conquest in 'Concierto Barroco.'" Her doctoral thesis for Columbia University, an examination of recent narrative reworkings of the conquest of Mexico, includes studies of Gonzalo Guerrero, "Fantasmas aztecas," and *El naranjo.*

EDUARDO SUBIRATS is one of Spain's most dynamic, prolific, and polemical intellectuals. A philosopher by training, Subirats earned his Ph.D. summa cum laude from the University of Barcelona. Before accepting his current position as professor of Spanish at New York University, he had been a professor of aesthetics at Barcelona's Escuela de Arquitectura, of philosophy at the UNED (Spain), professor of aesthetics and art history at the Universidade Estadual de Campinas, São Paulo (Brazil), and Professor of Romance Languages and Literatures at Princeton University. Subirat's essays of political and cultural criticism appear frequently in the major dailies and weeklies of Spain, Mexico, Argentina, Brazil. He is the author of over fifteen books, including *La ilustración insuficiente* (Taurus, 1981), *El alma y la muerte* (Anthropos, 1983), *La cultura como espectáculo* (FCE, 1988), *El continente vacio* (Muchnik, 1994), and *Linterna mágica. Vanguaridias, media y cutlura tardomoderna* (Siruela, 1997). His oeuvre crystallizes around certain episodes in Spain's thoroughly problematic relationship to modernity: Counter-Reformation and conquest, the Englightenment, nineteenth-century liberalism, and the early twentieth-century avant-garde movements. He held the King Juan Carlos I of Spain Chair (New York University, 1996–97).

THEODORE ROBERT YOUNG is an associate professor of Portuguese and Spanish at Florida International University. His first book, *O questionamento da história em O Tempo e o Vento,* was published in 1997 by FATES University Press in Brazil. In a book-length work in progress ("The Appropriation of Tupi-Guarani Language in Brazilian Letters"), he addresses socio-political as well as literary considerations of the incorporation of the Tupi-Guarani language into the works of the (Luso) Brazilian canon, ranging from sixteenth-century chronicles to twentieth-century novels. A second book-length work in progress ("Magic & Politics: Contemporary Brazilian Cinema") analyzes recent Brazilian films of the post-Cinema Novo era. His articles have appeared in *O amor das letras e das gentes,* as well as the journals *Luso-Brazilian Review, Hispanic American Historical Review, Signos, Crossroads/Encruzilhada, Mester,* and *Aleph.* His related conference papers include presentations at MLA, AATSP, LASA, Associação Internacional de Lusitanistas, the Carolina Conference on Romance Literatures, the UCLA Symposium on Portuguese Traditions, the Louisiana State University Symposium "Rediscovering America, 1492–1992," and the Cincinnati Conference on Romance Languages.

Index